Labour Market Policy and Unemployment

Labour Markets and Employment Policy

Series Editor: Günther Schmid

This volume is part of a series arising from an international research network on 'Social Integration Through Transitional Labour Markets' that was funded under the European Commission's Fourth Framework Programme of Targeted Socio-Economic Research (TSER) 1996–9. This project focused on the potential of a new regulatory idea – 'transitional labour markets' – for building institutional bridges which support individual transitions between various employment statuses (unpaid and voluntary civil work, part-time and full-time work, continuous education or training, dependent employment and self-employment). A basic premise of the series is that 'making transitions pay' enhances the employment intensity of growth and avoids the dilemma of growing segmentation of the labour market into 'insiders' and 'outsiders' thereby fostering social integration in a world of rapid structural change.

ALSO PUBLISHED IN THIS SERIES

Working-Time Changes: Social Integration Through Transitional Labour Markets
Edited by Jacqueline O'Reilly, Inmaculada Cebrián, and Michel Lallement

Education, Training and Employment Dynamics: Transitional Labour Markets in the European Union
Edited by Klaus Schömann and Philip J. O'Connell

The Dynamics of Full Employment: Social Integration through Transitional Labour Markets
Edited by Günther Schmid and Bernard Gazier

Labour Market Policy and Unemployment

Impact and Process Evaluations in Selected European Countries

Edited by
Jaap de Koning

Social Economic Research Institute (SEOR), Erasmus University, Rotterdam, The Netherlands

and

Hugh Mosley

Social Science Research Centre Berlin (WZB), Germany

LABOUR MARKETS AND EMPLOYMENT POLICY

Edward Elgar
Cheltenham, UK • Northampton, MA, USA

Published by
Edward Elgar Publishing Limited
Glensanda House
Montpellier Parade
Cheltenham
Glos GL50 1UA
UK

Edward Elgar Publishing, Inc.
136 West Street
Northampton
Massachusetts 01060
USA

A catalogue record for this book
is available from the British Library

Library of Congress Cataloguing in Publication Data
Labour market policy and unemployment : impact and process evaluations in selected European countries / edited by Jaap de Koning and Hugh Mosley.
p. cm.—(Labour markets and employment policy)
Includes bibliographical references and index.
1. Manpower policy—Europe. 2. Labor market—Europe. 3. Unemployment—Europe. I. Koning, J. de (Jaap) II. Mosley, Hugh. III. Series.

HD5764.A6 L273 2000
331.12'094—dc21 00–037606

ISBN 1 84064 279 3

Typeset by Manton Typesetters, Louth, Lincolnshire, UK.
Printed and bound in Great Britain by MPG Books Ltd, Bodmin, Cornwall.

Contents

Figures

Tables

Contributors

Dominique Anxo is Co-director of the Centre of European Labour Market Studies and Associate Professor at the Department of Economics, University of Göteborg, Sweden. His research interests fall broadly into the area of labour market policy. He has previously co-edited *Work Patterns and Capital Utilisation* (Kluwer Academic Publishers, 1995) and is presently editing a book on 'The Job Creation Potential of the Service Sector in Europe'.

Marike Arents is a Labour Economist who works as a Researcher in the Division of Labour and Education at the Netherlands Economic Institute in Rotterdam. She has carried out several Dutch and international studies in the field of active labour market policies and social security.

Lars Behrenz is a Lecturer at Växjö University, Sweden. His main fields of research are evaluation of labour market policy, efficiency analysis and employers' recruitment behaviour.

Stéphane Carcillo is a Lecturer at the University of Paris 1 – Panthéon-Sorbonne and a Research Fellow at the MATISSE – SET. He is specialized in labour market macroeconomics and his current research interest is the role of institutional systems of job and worker flows.

María A. Davia is Lecturer in Economics at the University of Castilla-La Mancha. Her previous research, mainly at the University of Alcalá, Madrid, has been linked to European projects, especially the TRANSLAM project in the fields of human capital, transitions between different working-time schedules, and active labour market policies. Her current research is on youth insertion in the labour market in a European context. She has been a Visiting Fellow at the WZB (Social Science Research Centre, Berlin) and at the European Work and Employment Research Centre at the UMIST (University of Manchester Institute of Technology).

Lennart Delander is a Senior Lecturer at Växjö University, Sweden. His principal research interests are in methodological issues related to the evaluation of labour market policy.

Christine Erhel is an Assistant Professor in Economics at the University of Paris. She has specialized in comparative research on European labour market policies and macroeconomic evaluation.

Carlos García-Serrano has a Ph.D in Economics from the University of Alcalá, Madrid, Spain. He was Visiting Researcher in the Institute for Employment Research at the University of Warwick and in the ESRC Research Centre on Micro-Social Change (currently Institute for Social and Economic Research) at the University of Essex, UK, during 1995 and 1996. He is currently Senior Lecturer in the Department of Economic Analysis at the University of Alcalá. His field of research is labour economics, having published research works in national and international journals and books on issues related to unemployment benefits and duration, labour and job mobility, educational mismatch, and poverty and social exclusion.

Virginia Hernanz is a Lecturer at the University of Alcalá and a Researcher at the FEDEA (Fundación de Estudios de Economía Aplicada). She has participated in different national and international research projects on transitions in the labour market, human capital, employment policies, and the youth labour market. She is currently working on segmentation in the Spanish labour market and the links between temporary jobs and segmentation. She has been a Visiting Fellow in the European Work and Employment Research Centre at the UMIST (University of Manchester Institute of Technology) and at the WZB.

Christoph Hilbert is a Research Fellow in the Labour Market and Employment Research Unit at the WZB. He is an economist and a graduate of the Humboldt University, Berlin. His research interests are in labour economics, especially labour market policy, training and compensation issues.

Jaap de Koning is Professor of Labour Market Policy at the Erasmus University, Rotterdam. He is also a Director at the Social Economic Research Institute (SEOR) at the same university. He was previously Director of the Labour and Education Division, and member of the management team of the Netherlands Economic Institute. He has been active in the field of evaluation of labour market policy for more than 10 years. He has also done extensive research in the closely related field of the economics of training.

Miguel A. Malo is Professor of Economics in the Department of Economics and Economic History at the University of Salamanca, Spain where he teaches macroeconomics and economic modelling. His main research interests are in redundancies and the determinants of severance pay, employment policies, gross labour market flows, educational mismatch, and the economic analysis of social exclusion. He has published a number of books and articles in specialized journals.

Hugh Mosley is a Senior Research Fellow in the Labour Market and Employment Research Unit at the WZB. He is a political scientist specializing in comparative research on labour market policies. His research has focused on implementation, working-time issues and labour market regulation.

Harald Niklasson is an Associate Professor at Växjö University, Sweden. He specializes in methods of labour market policy evaluation and has written about management by objectives in labour market policies.

Günther Schmid is Director of the Research Unit on Labour Market Policy and Employment at the WZB. He is also Professor of Political Economics at the Free University of Berlin. His main research is on equity and efficiency in labour market policy.

Holger Schütz is a Research Fellow at the WZB. His research areas include the modernization of public employment services, implementation and evaluation of active labour market policies, and benchmarking of labour market performance and policies.

Els Sol is Research Associate of the Hugo Sinzheimer Institute for Labour Law and Social Security, Faculty of Law, University of Amsterdam, the Netherlands.

Stefan Speckesser graduated in 1996 in Political Science from the Berlin Free University. After participating in the TRANSLAM project as a Research Fellow at the WZB, he now works as a teaching assistant in the Faculty of Economics at Mannheim University, Germany. He is currently writing his doctoral dissertation on microeconomic evaluation of labour market policy in Germany based on observational data.

Luis Toharia Cortés is Professor of Economics at the University of Alcalá, Spain. He has published on various aspects of the labour market in Spain, including the measurement of employment and unemployment, the causes and consequences of unemployment, the nature of employment growth and the rise of fixed-term and part-time employment, the cost of dismissals, the unemployment benefit system, and active labour market policies. He recently directed a study on the Spanish labour market for the European Commission (1997) and has acted on several occasions as expert and consultant for the Spanish government as well as for the European Commission.

Martijn van Velzen is a Labour Sociologist and a Researcher in the Hugo Sinzheimer Institute at the University of Amsterdam. He has written on industrial relations, particularly for the European Industrial Relations Observatory. As a visiting scholar in the Institute of Industrial Relations at the University of California at Berkeley, van Velzen is currently writing a dissertation on the regulation of training for temporary workers in the Netherlands and in the United States.

Foreword

Günther Schmid

The reasons to look for new institutional arrangements to cope with structural change are straightforward. Unemployment in most post-industrial societies has risen to levels unprecedented in postwar history. In countries that face this phenomenon, rising levels of unemployment have led to persistent long-term unemployment. The economic and social problems related to this development are clear: the longer the exclusion from gainful employment, the higher the risk of also being excluded from full participation in social and political life. This holds especially true for women and for young people with low skills. This threat to social integration may even undermine the trust in the basic institutions of our democratic societies. An *underlying assumption* of this series is that a return to full employment in the traditional sense is highly unlikely or only at unacceptable social costs. If some countries succeeded in recent years in reaching levels of unemployment similar to those of the 1960s, it was either at the cost of high income differentials and increasing numbers of working poor or many precarious employment relationships, especially for women, and more or less involuntary early retirement for a great many older workers. The objective of this project, therefore, is the search for alternatives to such ill-conceived responses to '*globalization*' and '*individualization*', which in different ways can generate forms of social exclusion.

It is not only structural unemployment that is of concern, although this is the most visible change. More importantly, the underlying forces of balancing supply and demand on the labour market seem to be quite different from in the past. The aim of our common effort was, therefore, also to understand these new dynamics and to ask which institutional arrangements would be able to prevent or to alleviate the high flows into unemployment and to mitigate the concomitant adverse selection mechanisms during the subsequent difficult processes of reintegration, which often result in the unemployed also becoming victims of social exclusion. Social exclusion is the counterpart of social integration which erodes the 'cement of societies'. Social integration in modern societies, thereby, means not just having a permanent job and being protected by social rights such as unemployment benefits. It also means having the prospect of evolutionary job careers, having access to the means of ensuring employability by lifelong learning, and being able to participate fully in all relevant areas of social life. The risk of unemployment is always a risk of reducing substantially the freedom of choice as well as the range of social participation for a significant minority of people concerned.

The project was subdivided into three modules around the following topics: social integration through working-time transitions (I), social integration through training and human capital investment (II), and social integration through active labour market policy (III); outside the formal contractual support, a fourth module was set up to work on a larger theoretical and empirical framework of employment systems (IV). The common underlying argument of the four modules is based on the *concept of transitional labour markets*. Transitional labour markets (TLM), as an *analytical concept*, refer to the observation that the borderlines between gainful employment and other productive activities are becoming increasingly blurred. The 'standard labour contract' is eroding but we do not know yet which new standards will develop. People transit more and more between different employment statuses, for instance between different working-time regimes, between unemployment and employment, between education or training and employment, between unpaid family work and gainful labour market work, and between work and retirement. Thus, as an analytical concept, TLM emphasizes the dynamics of labour markets, which means focusing the analysis on flows rather than purely on stocks, and applying methodologies that find out and explain patterns in the many transitions during the life cycles of individuals or groups in different societies.

Some of these transitions are critical in the sense that they may lead to downward spirals of job careers (*exclusionary transitions*), ending in recurrent unemployment or (finally) in long-term unemployment, poverty, discouraged inactivity or violent protest. We identified five major critical transitions during a life cycle: (1) The transition from school to work, (2) the transition from part-time to full-time work or *vice versa*, (3) the transition between family work and labour market work, (4) the transition between employment and unemployment, and (5) the transition to retirement. As a *normative concept*, TLM envisage new kinds of institutional arrangements to prevent those transitions from becoming gates to social exclusion and to transform them into gates for a wider range of opportunities of the employed (*maintenance transitions*) as well as for the inactive or unemployed people (*integrative transitions*). '*Making transitions pay*' requires institutions that realize in one way or the other the following principles: *work organizations* which enable people to combine wages or salaries with other income sources such as transfers, equity shares or savings; *entitlements or social rights* which allow choices to be made between different employment statuses according to shifting preferences and circumstances during the life cycle; *policy provi-*

sions which support multiple use of insurance funds, especially the use of income (unemployment) insurance for financing measures that enhance employability.

The following research institutions were involved in the joint venture to search for solutions to these problems: Economic and Social Research Institute (ESRI), Dublin; Hugo Sinzheimer Institute at the University of Amsterdam, Amsterdam; Economic Faculty of the Universidad de Alcalá de Henares, Madrid; Institute for Employment Studies (IES), University of Sussex, Brighton; Manchester School of Management (UMIST), Manchester; Netherlands Economic Institute (NEI), Rotterdam; Centre for European Labour Market Studies (CELMS), Göteborg, in co-operation with the University of Växjö; Modélisations Appliquées, Trajectoires Institutionelles et Stratégies Socio-Economiques (MATISSE, CNRS) Université de Paris 1; Sociological Faculty at Tilburg University, Tilburg; and as co-ordinating institution the Labour Market Policy and Employment Research Unit at the Social Science Research Centre Berlin (WZB).

Preface and acknowledgements

This book examines the effectiveness of active labour market policies (ALMP) and their contribution to the prevention of social exclusion. The evaluation studies reported in this volume focus on two aspects of ALMP that have been relatively neglected in previous research and merit special attention: 1) aggregate impact analysis and 2) process evaluation. The methodology for impact assessment is most developed for research designs using micro-data, but effects on the micro-level may be different from those on the macro-level, and it is the effects on macro-level that matter most. Furthermore, the potential effects of ALMP may be positive even though the actual effects are not. This is due to the fact that the impact of ALMP depends to a large extent on the way in which it is implemented.

In the vast literature on the impact of ALMP most studies apply a control group methodology to assess the effects of individual ALMP measures on the labour market position of the participants, using individual data. In Europe effectiveness is usually measured by employment status and the non-experimental version of the control group method is generally used to assess impacts, whereas income is the usual impact indicator in US studies, many of which use experiments. The control group method, particularly the experimental version, has the merit of producing reliable results. However, an important limitation of this approach is that it is unable to deal with displacement, substitution and indirect effects of ALMP measures. Thus, we cannot draw conclusions about the impact of ALMP on an aggregate level on the basis of these studies alone. Since ALMP is only effective when it helps to reduce the overall unemployment rate or the inequality between the unemployment rates of various groups, knowing the aggregate impact of ALMP is essential. Currently, however, the number of aggregate studies is relatively small, and little can be said about the aggregate impact of ALMP on the basis of these studies (see de Koning, Chapter 1 in this volume). Given the importance of aggregate effects and the fact that we know so little about them, we focus on aggregate impact analysis of ALMP in this book. The assessment will be based on econometric models and is therefore non-experimental.

Even when ALMP has potentially positive effects, these policies may have no impact in practice because of shortcomings in implementation. While even less is known about the impact of ALMP implementation, it seems likely that it is an important determinant of ALMP results. Implementation of active labour market policies is, therefore, the second focus of the evaluation studies in this volume. Implementation is relevant on different levels (see Mosley and Sol, Chapter 6 in this volume). The studies reported in this volume address the following themes: decentralization, targeting, and co-operation in ALMP implementation at the local level.

Part I of the book deals with aggregate impact analysis. For five countries (France, Germany, the Netherlands, Spain and Sweden) an attempt has been made to estimate the impact of ALMP on the transitions from unemployment to employment using aggregate data at the regional level. Although quantitative in nature, these contributions also take into account qualitative aspects such as the socio-economic context in the countries concerned and the structure of ALMP. Part II focuses on the implementation of ALMP. Implementation studies have been carried out in three countries (Germany, the Netherlands and Sweden). The qualitative element plays a more important role in these contributions, which rely on case studies and surveys in addition to statistical data. A distinctive feature of all the evaluation studies in this volume is that they are based on regional-level data and analysis.

The research reported in this volume is a product of the project 'Social Integration through Transitional Labour Markets (TRANSLAM)' co-ordinated by the Social Science Research Centre, Berlin (WZB), Research Unit Labour Market Policy and Employment in 1996–9. Many persons were involved in the production of this book. First, we would like to acknowledge the contributions of all participants in the international ALMP team of the TRANSLAM project, who co-operated intensively over the three years of the project: María A. Davia, Carlos García-Serrano, Virginia Hernanz, Miguel Malo, Luis Toharia Cortés, Universidad de Alcalá de Henares; Els Sol, and Martijn van Velzen, Hugo Sinzheimer Institute, University of Amsterdam; Marike Arents, Netherlands Economic Institute, Rotterdam; Jaap de Koning, Social Economic Research Institute (SEOR), Erasmus University, Rotterdam; Dominique Anxo, Centre for European Labour Market Studies, Göteborg University; Stéphane Carcillo, Christine Erhel, Bernard Gazier, MATISSE, Université de Paris 1; Frans Kerstholt, Adriaan van Liempt, Jan A.M. van Wezel, WORC, Tilburg University; Lars Behrenz, Lennart Delander, Harald Niklasson, Växjö University; Christoph Hilbert, Hugh Mosley, Günther Schmid, Holger Schütz, Stefan Speckesser, Labour Market and Employment Research Unit, Wissenschaftszentrum Berlin für Sozialforschung (WZB). It was Günther Schmid who developed the idea of an internationally comparative ALMP evaluation project using aggregate data at the regional level. Hugh Mosley and Günther Schmid acted as project co-ordinators at the WZB. The editors are grateful to Miriam Hils for her conscientious and thoughtful editorial improvements and to Robyn

Wiesener, who managed expertly the preparation of the manuscript for publication.

This book is one of four volumes published by Edward Elgar based on the TRANSLAM project. The other titles are: 1) Jacqueline O'Reilly, Immaculada Cebrián, Michel Lallement, *Working-time Changes: Social Integration Through Transitional Labour Markets*; 2) Klaus Schömann and Philip O'Connell *Education, Training and Employment Dynamics: Transitional Labour Markets in the EU*; 3) Günther Schmid and Bernard Gazier, *The Dynamics of Full Employment: Social Integration through Transitional Labour Markets*.

We would like to thank Jacqueline O'Reilly and Christoph Albrecht at the WZB for their very competent and efficient management of a complex international project with 11 teams from seven countries. Karin Reinsch and Hannelore Minzlaff provided indispensable administrative support throughout and were primarily responsible for the successful organization of four large TRANSLAM conferences during the course of the project 1996–9. Special thanks are also due to Bernard Gazier (Paris), Jaap de Koning (Rotterdam), Harald Niklasson (Växjö), Luis Toharia Cortés (Alcalà de Henares), Jan van Wezel (Tilburg) and their collaborators for hosting interim meetings of the ALMP team.

The research reported in this volume was conducted with the financial support of the European Commission, Directorate General for Science, Research and Development (DG XII), Project Number: CT 953007 (PL 953442) (SC) 'Social Integration through Transitional Labour Markets (TRANSLAM)'.

Jaap de Koning
Hugh Mosley

1. Introduction: active labour market policies, social exclusion, and transitional labour markets

Jaap de Koning, Hugh Mosley and Günther Schmid

This introductory chapter addresses the broader issue of the role active labour market policy (ALMP) can play in combating social exclusion, which is the central policy question addressed in this book. First, we discuss the concept and objectives of active labour market policy as a distinctive form of policy intervention in the labour market. Second, we consider the meaning and measures of 'social exclusion' and the extent to which it is affected by labour market outcomes, especially long-term unemployment. Finally, we discuss the concept of transitional labour markets, its diagnosis of the changing nature of modern labour markets, and its implications for active labour market policies.

1 ACTIVE LABOUR MARKET POLICY

Active labour market policies are a subset of labour market and employment policies which are aimed primarily at either preventing unemployment among at-risk individuals; or, if these individuals do become unemployed, at promoting their reintegration into the labour market and their career advancement. The International Labour Organization (ILO), for example, defines ALMP as 'purposive, selective interventions by the government in the pursuit of efficiency and/or equity objectives, acting indirectly or directly to provide work to, or increase the employability of people with certain disadvantages in the labour market'.

It should be noted that active labour market policies represent only one of several types of intervention designed to affect supply or demand in the labour market. Other labour market policies not examined here are also very important, including 'passive' income maintenance programmes, measures aimed at reducing the existing supply of labour (for example, early retirement, reductions in working time), regulatory interventions in the labour market (for example, employment protection regulations, equal opportunity regulations), as well as wage policies.

In recent years, European countries have experienced very high levels of unemployment and long-term unemployment and expenditure for active measures has been substantial. Among the countries studied in this book (France, Germany, the Netherlands, Spain and Sweden), unemployment was lowest in the Netherlands (5.2 per cent) and highest in Spain (20 per cent). In the EU as a whole, 10.6 per cent of the labour force was unemployed in 1997, and about 50 per cent of unemployed people had been out of work for more than one

Table 1.1 Active labour market policies and unemployment, France, Germany, the Netherlands, Spain and Sweden

		Standardized unemployment rate	Long-term unemployment (>12m)[a]	ALMP expenditure (% GDP)	ALMP participants (% labour force)
France	1997	12.4	41.2	1.32[b]	11.3[c]
	1990	9.0	38.0	0.8	7.6[d]
	1985	10.2	46.8	0.7	–
Germany[e]	1997	9.7	47.8[f]	1.3	3.6
	1990	4.8	46.8	1.0	3.4[g]
	1985	7.2	47.9	0.8	–
Netherlands	1997	5.2	49.1	1.5	14.2
	1990	6.2	49.3	1.1	2.9
	1985	10.6	58.7	1.1	–
Spain	1997	20.8	55.5	0.5	2.9
	1990	16.2	54.0	0.8	7.2
	1985	21.4	56.8	0.3	4.3
Sweden	1997	10.2	29.6	2.1	13.5
	1990	1.8	4.7	2.1	3.6
	1985	2.8	11.4	2.1	–
EU[h]	1997	10.7	47.4	–	–
	1990	–	48.6	–	–

Notes:
a Persons unemployed more than 12 months as percentage of all registered unemployed.
b 1996.
c 1995.
d 1989.
e 1980 and 1990 only western Germany.
f 1996.
g 1989.
h EU unemployment rates for 1997 are estimates.

Source: OECD Employment Outlook, various years.

year. Expenditure for ALMP ranged from 0.5 per cent of GDP in Spain to 2.2 per cent in Sweden in 1997 and a large percentage of the unemployed participate in active measures in all five countries (Table 1.1).

The role of active labour market policy has undergone a fundamental transformation. Active labour market policy as a set of instruments for direct state intervention in the labour market has a long history. It developed gradually during this century. Public employment offices were established in most countries around the turn of the century and in some countries even earlier. Specific measures such as job-creation schemes were introduced on a large scale during the great depression in the 1930s. Training for the unemployed was applied on a wide scale after World War II, when there was a shortage of skilled labour. However, active labour market policy as an integral part of socio-economic policy as a whole was first conceived and applied in Sweden and widely disseminated by the OECD in the 1960s (OECD, 1964). At that time, ALMP was considered to be an integral part of a broader economic strategy of facilitating geographic and occupational mobility, thus accelerating structural change. It was also seen as an alternative to exclusive reliance on macroeconomic policies in economies near full employment (Rehn–Meidner model). Today, however, in an era of slower growth and persistently high levels of mass unemployment, the immediate goal is no longer full employment. Instead, European policy-makers in the 1990s view ALMP primarily as a means of ameliorating unemployment – especially long-term unemployment – and of combating social exclusion.[1]

During the past decade increasing doubts about the effectiveness of government intervention in general have led to greater emphasis on the role of the market mechanism in dealing with socio-economic problems. This has also left its mark on labour market policy. In many countries the state monopoly in job brokering has been abolished (see de Koning, Denys and Walwei, 1999), the legal basis for private job placement agencies has been improved, and some public employment service activities are being privatized. There have also been reforms in social protection systems with the goal of enhancing the incentives for the unemployed to accept jobs and for employers to increase employment. However, there will remain a need for active policies for two main reasons. First of all the labour market suffers from a number of imperfections such as imperfect information, wage rigidities and discrimination.[2] Moreover, unemployment is an inevitable by-product of market economies, and, therefore, some level of public intervention will always be needed. Although there are also alternative policies, for example, equal opportunity regulations, active policies seem to be indispensable, and these programmes have in fact been expanded in most countries over the past decade.

It is important to note that ALMP consists of different types of measures with somewhat different purposes.[3] Some measures, such as work-experience schemes or other subsidized labour schemes, are designed to help disadvantaged groups for whom work experience is the first step towards reintegration into the labour market. Therefore, their principal aim is to promote equal opportunity. It could also be argued that, by enhancing the employability of unemployed people, labour market efficiency also improves. In addition, training can be used as a means of increasing the employability of disadvantaged groups. Moreover, this instrument helps reduce mismatch between labour demand and labour supply. While job brokering activities are primarily intended to increase the transparency of the labour market and are usually available to all categories of job seekers and employers, they may, in certain cases, be aimed at specific groups (for example, by attempting to achieve equal representation of target groups in the placement results). For disadvantaged groups, subsidized labour, training and placement activities are increasingly combined in pathways to labour market integration. Thus, all three types of ALMP measures (subsidized labour, training and job placement) are used to promote the reintegration of disadvantaged persons. The same is true for the general information function of ALMP (that is, providing information about job seekers to employers, and about job vacancies to those looking for work). Combating long-term unemployment is given high priority by most, if not all, countries.

Is ALMP really effective in practice, either in reducing the level of unemployment or the incidence of long-term unemployment? This is the central question in the evaluation literature on ALMP, which is addressed in the substantive chapters in this volume. We do not wish to anticipate these findings here; nor is this the place for a detailed discussion of the evaluation literature on ALMP (see Schmid *et al.*, 1996). Nevertheless, some preliminary remarks on this issue are appropriate.

First, ALMP could redistribute job opportunities so that fewer people become long-term unemployed. But when total employment and total labour supply are given, this would imply distributing the unemployment burden among more people.[4] Clearly, an increase in total employment as a result of ALMP would be preferable to a redistribution of unemployment among a greater number of people. It is, however, not at all obvious that ALMP can have a direct effect on total employment.

In economic theory, a positive effect on total employment will emerge directly only insofar as friction between labour demand and labour supply is reduced as a result of ALMP. Yet, as we have experienced in the recent past, excess supply on the labour market tends to be so great that vacancies are usually filled very easily. Thus, ALMP will hardly affect total employment directly. The only exception to this general rule is subsidized job creation. But even in that case, the effect on total employment is uncertain owing to possible displacement and substitution effects.

While it is doubtful and perhaps even improbable that ALMP can have a positive effect on total employment in the short term, it may do so in the long term. Firms are often reluctant to recruit certain categories of unemployed workers, such as long-term unemployed people. When a person is no longer receiving job offers, he or she is virtually excluded from the labour market. But when ALMP succeeds in reintegrating this category of unemployed persons, the effective labour supply increases. This may have a positive effect on employment in two separate ways (Bellman and Jackman, 1996a): wages will be affected negatively, which may eventually have a positive effect on employment, and recruitment will be eased. Moreover, Broersma *et al.* (1997) argue that the wage effect underestimates the total effect of an increased labour supply on employment. First, an increased labour supply will ease the filling of vacancies. Furthermore, supply may become available for types of work for which previously no one was available (latent vacancies or discouraged labour demand).[5] Therefore reintegrating the long-term unemployed and preventing long-term unemployment is certainly worth while. These studies provide circumstantial evidence regarding the aggregate impact of ALMP.

Finally, although the potential impact of ALMP on total employment appears to be limited if labour demand and supply are given, supply and demand on the labour market are in fact complex institutional constructs that can be steered to a certain extent by policy interventions at the micro-level, including ALMP. Thus even if the total volume of employment were given, there is a broad range of conceivable constellations of labour supply and demand and the level of unemployment is not univocally determined by total employment. The concept of transitional labour markets offers an alternative rationale for ALMP which aims to leverage the impact of available employment on unemployment through institutional arrangements to facilitate reduced working hours, individual transitions in working time, and transitions between paid work and other socially useful activities (see section 3 below).

So far, most research regarding the impact of ALMP has been of the type in which micro-data is used to estimate the effect of individual measures on the income and the job chances of ALMP participants. However, the results obtained from micro-studies may not give an adequate picture of the overall impact of ALMP as a whole on the labour market. Aggregate impact analyses are needed to deal with the consequences of displacement and other aggregate effects, which lead to a discrepancy between micro- and macro-outcomes. However, the number of aggregate impact studies, relating aggregate ALMP indicators directly to aggregate employment and unemployment indicators, is relatively small. Furthermore, the attempts made failed to produce convincing results.[6] The ALMP evaluations for France, Germany, the Netherlands, Spain and Sweden reported in this volume address this issue in a methodologically innovative way on the basis of regional-level aggregate impact analyses.

It is, moreover, highly likely that the results of ALMP depend greatly on the way it is organized and implemented. This aspect of ALMP is usually neglected in both micro- and macro-studies on the impact of ALMP.[7]

2 SOCIAL EXCLUSION, POVERTY AND THE LABOUR MARKET

ALMP can play a role in preventing social exclusion by reducing unemployment, especially long-term employment. After discussing the variety of meanings of 'social exclusion', we argue that labour market outcomes are in any case an important determinant. This point is illustrated by selective data available on unemployment as a cause of poverty.

Silver (1998) draws attention to three different features of 'social exclusion'. First, social exclusion is multidimensional: it is not reducible to monetary terms but combines economic and social problems, material and symbolic relations, distributional conflicts and identity politics, class and status orders, social rights and human rights. Second, social exclusion refers to a dynamic process: material want and/or lack of gainful employment can set in motion an individual or group tendency towards social disengagement, disaffiliation, disqualification, or isolation. Third, social rights institutionalized as entitlements to income transfers from insurance or assistance programmes may foster stigmatization, passivity, rejection and feelings of powerlessness.[8]

Kronauer (1997) identifies five principal uses of the term which reflect different national policy discourses. Social exclusion sometimes refers primarily to the special problem situation of an urban ethnic 'underclass', especially in the USA and, to a lesser extent, in the UK, where social exclusion often takes the form of urban ghettos. In France it is used primarily to refer to the problem of unemployed and marginally employed youth, particularly second-generation immigrant youth. The concept is frequently used to refer to the long-term unemployed, especially older workers who have been displaced by structural change from their previous employment and career path. Other authors associate social exclusion with marginal groups at the periphery of society who, for a variety of reasons, are homeless or poor. In an even more restricted definition, social exclusion is applied solely to illegal immigrants.

The heterogeneity of the groups that have, at various times, been labelled 'socially excluded' illustrates the difficulty of defining the term. On the one hand, social exclusion can be defined more restrictively as a situation in which people cannot satisfy their basic needs over a long period of time. This definition is closely related to poverty, which is usually defined in terms of the resources available to a household. On the other hand, social exclusion can be defined more broadly. Although poverty is a core indicator, the emphasis on 'social exclusion' in the European policy discourse since the late 1980s represents a shift away from the use of income measures. Thus, the EU Observatory on National Policies to Combat Social Exclusion has consistently defined social exclusion in terms of social rights (for example, to employment, housing, health care; see Huster, 1997). As Room (1995) points out, it is the word 'social' that makes the difference. While they may not suffer poverty and physical deprivation, being out of work for a very long time may deprive people of social contacts and the personal fulfilment attained from working. In addition, there is evidence that social isolation further reduces job chances because people frequently draw information and motivation for their job search from social contacts and social networks (Anxo and Storrie, 1999).

These two meanings of social exclusion overlap only partially: while some people who are not poor may be socially excluded (for example, the aged or the long-term unemployed in households with sufficient income), people living in poor households may not, in fact, be socially excluded. Indeed, absolute poverty is rare in Europe, where poverty is usually defined on the basis of relative income. Thus, some people classified as poor according to statistical standards may be satisfactorily integrated into social and economic life.[9]

Labour market outcomes, especially long-term employment, are clearly an important cause of social exclusion in the narrow sense of insufficient income and poverty, and in the broader sense of inadequate social integration and lack of self-fulfilment.[10] While no recent systematic data are available at the European level, earlier studies show that unemployment is a major cause of poverty and social exclusion. In the late 1980s in France, 34.8 per cent of the households with an unemployed head of household were classified as poor; in Spain, it was 29.3 per cent, in Portugal 47.5 per cent, in Italy 35.7 per cent, in Greece 24.5 per cent, in Ireland 43.6 per cent, in Belgium 28.3 per cent and in Luxembourg 44.1 per cent (Ramprakash, 1994). Although the methodological problems of international comparisons of poverty are considerable (defined here in terms of the weighted average expenditure for all households), it is evident that poor households tend to be affected by unemployment. This conclusion is also confirmed by more recent national data on reasons for receipt of means-tested social assistance benefits. In Germany in 1997, 39.4 per cent of social assistance beneficiaries over the age of 15 were registered as unemployed, and 24.8 per cent as 'long' long-term unemployed (more than 1 year).[11]

Even short-term unemployment can be a problem when the same person experiences short spells of unemployment frequently, and becomes trapped in the segment of the labour market where low wages, temporary contracts and bad working conditions prevail. Recent German research has also identified 'dynamic unemployment', that is, frequently recurring spells of unemployment that affect more and more persons for longer and longer periods – as a new structural feature of unemployment (Mutz, 1995). In a recent Dutch study, de Koning, van Nes and van der Veen (1999) concluded that, while single spells of long-term unemployment account for most life-cycle unemployment, the importance of shorter spells is growing owing to the increasing share of flexible labour in total labour volume.[12]

Marginalization or exclusion from the labour market does not always result in social exclusion. People may have permanent but low-paid employment that provides an acceptable living standard. Moreover, in all societies labour market outcomes are mediated and cushioned by the intervening welfare state, as well as by societal and, in particular, familial safety nets. Thus, even the same level of unemployment or long-term unemployment will have a very different impact in terms of social exclusion depending on the institutional and societal context. Finally, there are other meaningful activities in addition to paid employment which can be a source of social integration and individual fulfilment. Nevertheless, the prevention of long-term and recurrent unemployment would be a major contribution towards combating poverty and social exclusion. From the previous discussion we can conclude that active policies can be an important tool in combating social exclusion by reducing unemployment and, in particular, long-term unemployment.

3 TRANSITIONAL LABOUR MARKETS AND ACTIVE POLICIES

The labour market has changed considerably since the mid-1970s. Unemployment rates have grown to levels unprecedented in postwar history, and it is highly unlikely that in the near future unemployment will return to the levels of the 1960s. Even in countries with relatively low official unemployment rates, such as the Netherlands, 'true' unemployment is still high when hidden unemployment is taken into account. The current prolonged period of high unemployment has cast serious doubts on the feasibility of full employment as it was traditionally understood (Schmid, 1995).

The level of unemployment is not the only thing that has changed: the underlying dynamics of the labour market are now quite different from the patterns of the past. Until recently, most employees stayed with the same employer during their entire working lives, and very few people switched occupations. Yet increasingly, this pattern is disappearing under the influence of what is sometimes referred to as economic turbulence. Today, things change so quickly that people are less sure of finding and keeping a job. Initial education or training is no longer sufficient to remain employable during working life; continuous training is needed to keep up with the developments in many professions. In addition, because the life cycle of companies tends to be shorter today than it once was, employees may lose their jobs when companies go bankrupt. Finally, occupations may disappear completely as a result of technological progress.

Tables 1.2 and 1.3 show clearly that, in both the Netherlands and Germany, younger generations have been confronted with unemployment to a greater extent than the older generations. The difference is particularly significant for short-term unemployment and unemployment of intermediate duration, although the results may suffer from under-reporting by older generations.[13] Thus the percentage of respondents who report never having been unemployed is markedly lower for the two youngest cohorts (58 per cent and 66 per cent respectively for the Netherlands; 80 per cent and 73 per cent for Germany), despite the shorter duration of their labour force participation. In Germany, it is interesting to observe that women in the oldest cohort were less affected by unemployment than men, whereas women in the younger generations have almost the same risk of experiencing short-term unemployment and the same or a slightly higher risk of long-term unemployment (see Tables 1.2 and 1.3).

There is not only not enough full-time employment for everyone, the available employment is less stable than it was in the past. As a result, the probability of an individual experiencing one or more periods of unemployment during his or her working life has increased considerably. Once people

Table 1.2 Lifetime unemployment according to year of birth, the Netherlands, 1995 (in percentage of cohort)

Number of years in unemployment	Year of birth 1930–38	1940–49	1950–59	1960–69
Never been unemployed	86	79	66	58
0–1 year	6	11	18	26
1–4 year	5	8	12	13
5 years or more	3	3	4	4
Total	100	100	100	100

Source: Statistics Netherlands.

Table 1.3 Lifetime unemployment according to year of birth, Germany 1981–3, 1989 (in percentage of cohort)

Number of years in unemployment	Year of birth 1930–31	1940–41/1949	1950–51/1954–56/1959	1960–61
Never been unemployed	93 (96)	93 (95)	80 (81)	73 (74)
0–1 year	4 (3)	6 (3)	12 (11)	18 (16)
1–4 year	3 (2)	1 (1)	6 (6)	8 (8)
5 years or more	0	0 (1)	1 (2)	2 (3)
Total	100 (100)	100 (100)	100 (100)	100 (100)
(N)	(489)(243)	(717)(352)	(1788)(857)	(641)(321)

Note: Figures in parentheses represent women. Figures may not add up to 100 per cent because of rounding; 0 = >0.5 per cent.[14]

Source: German Life History Study, 1981–83 and 1989, Max-Planck Institute for Human Development, Berlin.

have become unemployed, they risk becoming long-term unemployed. This is particularly true for the low-skilled, for persons of foreign origin, and, to some extent, for women.[15] As was noted in the previous section, long-term unemployment often entails social exclusion.

Active labour market policy cannot alter the higher level of risk in today's labour markets. This increased insecurity is inherent in a number of fundamental changes in the way the economy works, such as changes in consumer preferences, technological development and the globalization of the economy. But it might be possible to prevent long-term unemployment, or at least to minimize its incidence. Increased insecurity for individuals who face a higher risk of encountering unemployment, recurring unemployment, or long-term unemployment during their working lives owing to the changing nature of labour markets implies a much greater need for active policies that maintain labour force attachment and bridge transitions to re-employment.

The traditional forms of active labour market policy are no longer suitable for dealing with the new trends towards social exclusion and the need for reorganizing work. Traditional active labour market policy was, for example, defined as 'manpower' policy, while viewing women as part of a marginal or peripheral labour force. Today, however, the goal of active or proactive labour market policy is equal opportunity for both sexes in the labour market. Moreover, while conventional active labour market policy was closely connected with the idea of coping with structural imbalances on the labour market by regional mobility and of coping with cyclical imbalances by temporary public relief work; new active labour market policy must adjust to the new features of structural change, notably globalization of production or markets and new technologies on the demand side, and individualization, social differentiation or new migration streams on the supply side. Which strategies, policies or policy mixes are suitable to solve the problems arising from these changes is currently being debated.

The concept of transitional labour markets (TLM) hypothesizes that the borderlines between gainful dependent labour market work and other productive activities are becoming more and more blurred. The 'standard labour contract' – that is, full-time, continuous employment – is eroding, but we do not yet know which new standards will develop to replace it. Evidence suggests, however, that people are increasingly moving between different labour market statuses; for example between different working-time regimes, between unemployment and employment, between education or training and employment, between unpaid family work and gainful labour market work, and between work and retirement. Some of these transitions are critical in the sense that they may lead to downward spirals of job careers, ending finally in long-term unemployment, poverty, discouraged withdrawal from the labour market, or violent protest. New kinds of institutional arrangements are necessary to prevent transitions from becoming paths to social exclusion and to transform them into paths of opportunity. 'Making transitions pay' (Schmid, 1998) requires the creation of institutions which provide one or more of the following: *work organizations* which enable people to combine labour market work with other productive activities; *income arrangements* which combine wages or salaries with other income sources such as transfers, equity shares or savings; *entitlements or social rights* which allow choices to be made between different employment statuses according to shifting preferences and circumstances; and *policy provisions* which allow the multiple use of social insurance funds, especially the use of income maintenance programmes (for example, unemployment insurance) for financing measures that enhance employability. It may, however, be necessary in a transitional labour market to accompany the introduction of these various forms of empowerment – especially the creation of new social rights – with the demand for the fulfilment of certain obligations, such as participation in professional further training.

Transitional labour markets are in particular forms of career flexibility in working time through institutional bridges between full-time employment and periods of reduced working time and career breaks for training, family or personal reasons. This paradigm is most directly applicable to employed persons with relatively secure positions in internal labour markets. The facilitation of such transitions through public regulations and programmes, collective agreements, and changes in the personnel policies of enterprises, however, also improves employment opportunities for the unemployed. In some cases programmes to promote transitional labour markets for the employed are explicitly tied to the hiring of a replacement from among the unemployed; for example, the Scandinavian leave schemes.[16] Even where there is no such stipulation, the need to replace 'insiders' who temporarily interrupt their careers or reduce their working time creates additional employment opportunities for 'outsiders'; that is, the unemployed and new entrants.

There are two mechanisms by which these institutional arrangements may improve the chances of the unemployed: 1) a turnover effect, and 2) a labour supply (work-sharing) effect. The first of these suggests that increased turnover between relatively secure positions in internal labour markets and the unemployed reduces the average duration of unemployment. The second proposes that unemployment may not just be redistributed, but could actually be reduced through voluntary reductions in working time or temporary withdrawal from the labour market induced by transitional labour markets. The actual impact of transitional labour markets on unemployment depends on a multitude of factors which must be investigated empirically: to what extent do reductions in the working time of individual employees actually result in replacement hires rather than being offset, for example, by productivity increases or increases in the working time of existing employees? Moreover, are the additional job opportunities taken by the unemployed or by new entrants?

Active measures for the unemployed (for example, training, job creation, wage subsidies) also promote transitions – in this case from unemployment to employment – but are, in fact, qualitatively different from the transitional schemes for the employed. Whereas the latter are relatively secure temporary bridges between employment and other types of activity, the former enhance employability at best, but are not a ticket to regular employment. What is the added value in viewing ALMP for the unemployed from a transitional labour market perspective? One implication is that the priority goal is clearly placement in regular employment. Job-creation programmes should be temporary or counter-cyclical, and the terms and conditions of employment should be less attractive than regular employment. Measures should be as close to the regular labour market as possible (for example, enterprise-based) rather than in a special publicly supported labour market segment (for example, '*zweiter Arbeitsmarkt*'). While the introduction of such measures may increase the likelihood of displacement of employment in competing firms or substitution of programme participants for other employees, this is an acceptable risk if the overall effect is to reduce the average duration of unemployment. Indeed, from the point of view of the unemployed, perhaps the most important implication of a TLM approach to ALMP is that displacement and substitution effects become more tolerable if they increase employment opportunities for the long-term unemployed and other problem groups and thus combat social exclusion. Increased turbulence in labour markets due to the pace of technological development and intensified competition means that individuals will be increasingly confronted with more or less involuntary transitions in their working lives. Therefore, the need for job search assistance and training for people in danger of losing their job or becoming obsolete in terms of their human capital will increase. Preferably, unemployment should be avoided and as far as government policy is needed for this type of measure, one could speak about preventive ALMP for employed persons. But it is possible that, despite an increased effort to prevent unemployment, employment-to-unemployment transitions will occur more frequently than in the past. That would also mean that more has to be done to re-employ displaced workers and to prevent long-term unemployment.

At the same time we should not be overly pessimistic about the possibility of reducing the overall unemployment rate. Countries such as Denmark, Ireland and the Netherlands have shown that policies such as wage moderation, promotion of training, deregulation and social security reforms can have a substantial impact on unemployment, even taking hidden unemployment into account. Nevertheless, the remaining level of unemployment will still be too high from a social point of view, and active policies will be needed to distribute the unemployment burden over more people and to promote 'good' transitions. This will be easier to achieve and to finance insofar as mass unemployment can be mitigated.

NOTES

1. This shift in emphasis does not mean that ALMP is no longer concerned with skill shortages, which can occur even in countries experiencing high levels of unemployment. Moreover, firms have increasingly had problems in filling vacancies in countries like the Netherlands and Denmark in which unemployment has declined markedly.
2. See de Koning (1993b) for an in-depth discussion.
3. The OECD distinguishes the following types of active labour market policy: 1) public employment services (and administration), 2) labour market training for unemployed and employed adults, 3) youth measures, 4) subsidized employed (for example, wage subsidies and direct job creation) and 5) measures for the disabled.
4. Assuming that not the same persons are experiencing more unemployment spells as a result of the policy intervention.
5. According to their results the total labour supply elasticity of employment is almost equal to 1.
6. See Chapter 2 of this volume for a review of the literature.
7. See Chapter 7 in this volume on the importance of implementation.
8. See Leisering (1997) for a recent discussion of 'social exclusion' in the German sociological tradition. For Georg Simmel poverty as a social category is defined not by individual need but by the status of being dependent on public assistance, which in the early-nineteenth century entailed loss of civil and political rights.
9. Berghman (1995) refers to a Dutch study by Muffels *et al.* (1992) according to which only 30 per cent of the poor are also socially excluded (or 'deprived'). Moreover, according to

this study, 8 per cent of the non-poor are socially excluded. The conclusion is that both the poor and the socially excluded amount to 10 per cent of the population, but that the two are only partly overlapping. Their definition of poverty is based on the official subsistence norm, while their social exclusion concept is based on individuals' perception of their own situation.

10. In general the probability of leaving unemployment declines with increasing duration. Thus Ludwig-Mayerhofer (1996), a recent German study based on longitudinal data, concludes that the probability of moving from unemployment to full-time employment is strongly negatively related to the cumulative duration of previous spells of unemployment (but actually positively related to the number of spells!). The extent to which long-term unemployment is explained by personal characteristics or 'path dependence', that is, the impact of unemployment itself is controversial and will not be discussed here (Kiefer, 1988).
11. Forty per cent of all households (*Bedarfsgemeinschaften*) on social assistance have at least one member who is registered unemployed; calculated from Statistisches Bundesamt (1997).
12. A striking result of their analysis is that also from a longitudinal point of view unemployment is highly concentrated among a relatively small group of people. If one would follow a cohort of individuals over their working life, the 10 per cent experiencing unemployment most during their working life account for 50 per cent of the sum total of all unemployment periods experienced by all the people in the cohort during their active lives. In other words, it is more or less the same group of people that is unemployed all of the time.
13. Since most people will have been out of work for a short period, short spells of unemployment may be underestimated and especially older persons may have forgotten.
14. We thank Prof. Karl Ulrich Mayer (Director at the Max-Planck-Institute for Educational Research in Berlin), Heike Solga and Monika Albin who kindly provided these results from the German Life History Study. They note that these figures are based on subjective and retrospective reporting by respondents, which is subject to error. This is especially the case for older cohorts, who may no longer accurately recall earlier experiences of unemployment. Furthermore, the data are derived from two different studies conducted at different times and are thus not strictly comparable. The data in columns 1 and 2 refer to unemployment experiences only until the beginning of the 1980s whereas the data for the younger cohorts (columns 3 and 4) cover the period until the end of the 1980s. Moreover, only persons who have ever been employed were asked about spells of unemployment, which means that students and recent university graduates are not included in the youngest cohort.
15. The share of long-term unemployed for men in EU(15) was 47.4 per cent in 1997, for women 50.6 per cent (Commission 1998, p. 149).
16. For Denmark see Madsen (1998) and Schmid and Schömann (1999).

REFERENCES

Anxo, D. and D. Storrie (1999), 'Employability, jobsearch, employer recruitment strategies, social networks and social exclusion', in B. Gazier (ed.), *Employability: Concepts and Policies*, Berlin: I.A.S.

Bellmann, L. and R. Jackman (1996a), 'Aggregate impact analysis', in G. Schmid, J. O'Reilly and K. Schömann (eds), *International Handbook of Labour Market Policy and Evaluation*, Cheltenham: Edward Elgar, pp. 143–62.

Bellman, L. and R. Jackman (1996b), 'The Impact of labour market policy on wages, employment and labour market mismatch', in G. Schmid, J. O'Reilly and K. Schömann (eds), *International Handbook of Labour Market Policy and Evaluation*, Cheltenham: Edward Elgar, pp. 725–46.

Berghman, J. (1995), 'Social exclusion in Europe: policy context and analytical framework', in G. Groom (ed.), *Beyond the Threshold. The Measurement and Analysis of Social Exclusion*, Bristol: Policy Press.

Broersma, L., J. Koeman and C.N. Teulings (1997), Arbeidsaanbod en werkgelegenheid ('labour supply and employment'), *Economisch Statistische Berichten* 82–4127, pp. 836–40.

European Commission (1998), *Employment in Europe*, Luxembourg: Office of Official Publications.

Huster, E.U. (1997), 'Armut in Europa – ausgewählte Ergebnisse dese Armutsobservatoriums der Europäischen Union', in I. Becker and R. Hauser (eds), *Einkommensverteilung und Armut. Deutschland auf dem Weg zur Vierfünftel-Gesellschaft?*, Frankfurt/M., New York: Campus Verlag.

Kiefer, N.M. (1988), 'Economic duration data and hazard functions', *Journal of Economic Literature*, XXVI, 646–79.

Koning, J. de (1993a), 'Measuring the placement effects of two wage-subsidy schemes for the long-term unemployed', *Empirical Economics*, 8.

Koning, J. de (1993b), 'The Dutch experience', in K. Jensen and P.K. Madsen (eds), *Measuring Labour Market Measures*, Copenhagen: Ministry of Labour.

Koning, J. de, P.J. van Nes and C. van der Veen (1999), *The Distribution of Life-time Unemployment: A Simulation Approach*, Rotterdam: NEI.

Koning, J. de, J. Denys and U. Walwei (1999), 'Deregulation in placement services: a comparative study for eight EU countries', published by the European Commission.

Kronauer, M. (1997), 'Soziale Ausgrenzung' und 'Underclass': Über neue Formen der gesellschaftlichen Spaltung', *Leviathan*, **25** (1), 28–49.

Leisering, L. (1997), 'Soziale Ausgrenzung' – Zur handlungsthoretischen Fundierung eines aktuellen sozialpolitischen Diskurses, in K.S. Rehberg (ed.), *Differenz und Integration. Die Zukunft moderner Gesellschaften*, Band II, pp. 1039–53.

Ludwig-Mayerhofer, W. (1996), 'Was heißt, und gibt es kumulative Arbeitslosigkeit? Untersuchungen zu Arbeitslosigkeitsverläufen über 10 Jahre', in W. Zapf, J. Schupp and R. Habich (eds) *Lebenslagen im Wandel: Sozialberichterstattung* im Längsschnitt, Frankfurt/M., New York: Campus Verlag, pp. 211–39.

Madsen, P.K. (1998), 'A transitional labour market: the Danish paid leave arrangements', in *European Academy of the Urban Environment, New Institutional Arrangements in the Labour Market*, Berlin: Publications of European Academy of the Urban Environment, pp. 68–73.

Muffels, R., J. Berghman and H. Dirven (1992), 'A multi-method approach to monitor the evolution of poverty', *Journal of European Social Policy*, 2, 193–213.

Mutz, G., W. Ludwig-Mayerhofer and E.J. Koenen (1995), 'Diskontinuierliche Erwerbsverläufe. Analysen zur postindustriellen Arbeitslosigkeit, Biographie und Gesellschaft', Bd. 21, Opladen: Leske + Budrich.

OECD (1964), *Recommendations on an Active Manpower Policy*, Paris: Manpower and Social Affairs Committee.

OECD (various years), *Economic Outlook*, Paris.

Ramprakash, D. (1994) 'Poverty in the countries of the European Community. Synthesis of Eurostat's Statistical Research in Poverty', *Journal of European Social Policy*, **4** (2), 117–28.

Room, G. (ed.) (1995), *Beyond the Threshold. The Measurement and Analysis of Social Exclusion*, Bristol: Policy Press.

Schmid, G. (1995), 'Is full employment still possible? Transitional labour markets as a new strategy of labour market policy', *Economic and Industrial Policy*, 16, 429–56.

Schmid G. (1998), *Transitional Labour Markets: A New European Employment Strategy*, WZB Discussion Paper FS I 98-206, Berlin: WZB.

Schmid, G., J. O'Reilly and K. Schömann (eds) (1996), *International Handbook of Labour Market Policy and Evaluation*, Cheltenham: Edward Elgar.

Schmid, G. and K. Schömann (eds) (1999), *Von Dänemark lernen – Learning from Denmark*, WZB Discussion Paper FS I 99-201, Berlin: WZB.

Silver, H. (1998), 'Policies to reinforce social cohesion in Europe', in J.B. Figueiredo and A. de Haan (eds), *Social Exclusion: An ILO Perspective*, Geneva: International Institute for Labour Studies, Research Series 111, pp. 38–73.

Statistisches Bundesamt (1997), *Fachserie 13: Sozialleistungen*, Reihe 2: Sozialhilfe, Wiesbaden: Metzler-Poeschel.

PART I

Aggregate Impact Analysis

2. Models for aggregate impact analysis of active labour market policy

Jaap de Koning

1 INTRODUCTION

This chapter reviews the models which are currently in use for the aggregate impact analysis of active labour market policy (ALMP), or which may be used in the future. The European Commission and the EU member states see ALMP as an important tool in combating the unemployment problem (European Commission, 1996). The OECD is also a strong advocate for this type of policy, but insists that a number of preconditions be met to ensure the effectiveness of ALMP (OECD, 1994). Effective management and implementation of these policies are among the points mentioned by the OECD. One of the main focal points of this book is implementation, which will be addressed in detail later in this chapter.

But while high priority is given to ALMP by policy-makers, surprisingly little is known about the aggregate impact of ALMP on unemployment and other labour market variables. The literature reviews conducted by the OECD (OECD, 1993) and by Bellmann and Jackman (1996a, 1996b) clearly illustrate this point. Most studies in this field use micro-data to assess the impact of a specific programme on the labour market position of the programme participants. But the effect on programme participants is of limited value. In the first place, the positive effects of ALMP measures on the employment chances of participants may be at the expense of non-participants, without having any real effect on the aggregate level. In the reverse situation, it is also possible to have no measurable effect on participants but positive effects on a macro-level. When, for example, unemployed people with good labour market prospects are trained in occupations in which a shortage exists, their job chances may not increase, but other unemployed job seekers may benefit from their transition to other labour market segments. Aggregate impact analysis therefore has added value in comparison with micro-impact studies. While some new research has recently been conducted at the aggregate level, we are still far from being able to reach definite conclusions on this level.

Several models have been used for assessing the impact of active labour market policy on the aggregate level. Before looking at the various models in more detail, we will discuss the possible aggregate effects of ALMP (Layard *et al.*, 1991). These effects can be both direct and indirect. Direct effects are:

- an increase in total employment and a reduction in both total unemployment and unfilled demand due to a more efficient matching process;
- a redistribution of employment opportunities among groups on the labour market;
- an increase in effective labour supply because unemployed persons are made employable;
- an increase in employment and a decrease in unemployment due to the creation of subsidized jobs.

Indirect effects are potentially numerous (see Figure 2.1 for a graphical representation). An increase in effective labour supply will ease recruitment and will therefore have a positive effect on employment. But when more people become available on the labour market, wages will also be affected. Wage increases will be moderated and more employment created, presumably with a certain time lag. When total unemployment decreases, unemployment insurance expenditure will also be reduced; and when unemployment insurance premiums are part of the wage bill, labour will become cheaper and employment will rise. Not all possible effects are, however, positive. For example, due to displacement and substitution effects, job creation need not have a positive effect on total employment. In some cases, participation in ALMP measures may increase reservation wages, thereby delaying the transition to regular jobs instead of speeding up the process (Calmfors and Skedinger, 1995). When employment, unemployment and wages are affected; other macroeconomic variables, such as consumption and investment, will change too. ALMP is, moreover, likely to have an effect on public expenditure since expenditure on ALMP and possible savings on unemployment benefits do not usually break even. Thus the entire macroeconomic system is set in motion, which will, in turn, affect the labour market. We should, of course, be aware that ALMP may also be affected by the labour market situation. Policy-makers will make the level and structure of ALMP expenditure dependent on the type of problems on the labour market and the severity of the problems. Or, in econometric terms, ALMP expenditure is an endogenous variable, not an exogenous variable.

This chapter is structured as follows. In section 2, we treat the u/v-curve and its more elaborated successors as tools for aggregate impact analysis. This class of model is only suited to determining the direct effects on ALMP on the friction between supply and demand and the transitions from unem-

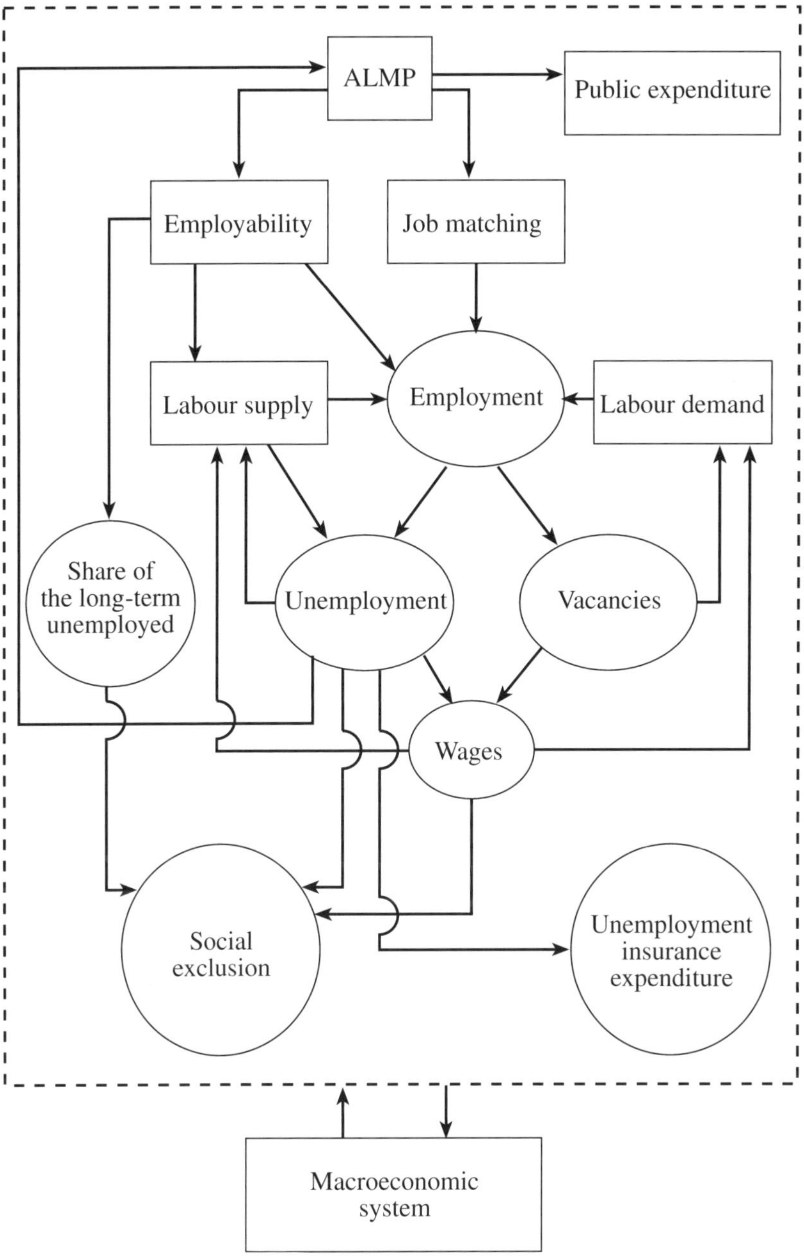

Figure 2.1 Ways in which ALMP can influence labour market outcomes

ployment to employment, and *vice versa*. But this is precisely the type of analysis on which the contributions in this book concentrate. We will also discuss issues relating to the estimation of the models. Models that are capable of studying other aggregate effects are discussed in section 3. We will explain why omitting the latter type of models in the empirical contributions in this book may be less of a problem than one might think. Although this is hardly taken into account in empirical models, the effects of ALMP probably depend on the manner of implementation. Section 4 treats models that incorporate the implementation aspect. In section 5, a summary is given of the empirical results concerning the aggregate effects of ALMP which have been obtained in the literature by using the various models. The final section, section 6, provides a short presentation of the contributions in this book.

2 THE BEVERIDGE CURVE, FLOW MODELS AND RELATED MODELS

2.1 ALMP, the Efficiency of the Matching Process and the Beveridge Curve

It is common knowledge that, most of the time, the labour market is not cleared; that is, that unemployment and unfilled demand co-exist. This implies that there is room for improved functioning of the labour market by bringing employment nearer to the minimum of labour demand and labour supply, thereby reducing both unemployment and vacancies. ALMP can help to reduce the friction between demand and supply mainly by:

- diminishing occupational and spatial mismatch between demand and supply;
- making the labour market more transparent.

Training, information and advice with respect to job search and recruitment, as well as job brokering, are the most obvious ALMP instruments for improving matching.

In order to measure the impact of ALMP on the efficiency of the functioning of the labour market, we must somehow measure efficiency. The so-called Beveridge curve is the oldest attempt to do that. Later the term u/v-curve (where u stands for unemployment and v for vacancies) became more common. It is based on the empirical observation that when the unemployment rate is high, the vacancy rate is usually low, and *vice versa*. Plotting u against v produces a hyperbolic curve, the u/v-curve. The original u/v-curve is a typical example of measurement without theory. Attempts were later made at creating a theoretical foundation for this curve. Two basic explanations have been provided. The first one comes from Holt and David (1966), and is based on the notion that job search and recruitment take time. In their model, the u/v-curve emerges as an equilibrium relation in a flow model of the labour market in which the matching process between labour demand and labour supply is modelled explicitly. The lack of transparency of the labour market is the basic cause behind the u/v-curve in the Holt and David approach. The second approach, developed by Muellbauer (1978), assumes that the labour market consists of many sub-markets, some of which have a supply surplus and others which have a demand surplus. Unemployment and unfilled demand therefore co-exist on a macro-level. Assuming labour demand and labour supply are smoothly distributed over sub-markets, a macro-disequilibrium relation for the labour market emerges which can be rewritten as a u/v-curve.

As will be discussed later in greater detail, the simple u/v-curve and its more sophisticated later versions were used in particular to study changes in the efficiency of the matching process on the labour market. Many studies in various countries found a decrease in labour market efficiency since the mid-1960s. That would certainly call for measures to improve the matching of labour demand and labour supply. ALMP, it was suggested, could play a role in this. Later contributions have, however, challenged this view. The shift of the aggregate u/v-curve may be a mere artefact of aggregation. That would mean that the urgency of ALMP measures to reduce mismatch might be questioned. But, as indicated earlier, ALMP is capable of accomplishing more than just reducing mismatch. It can, for example, help to enhance the job chances of the disadvantaged. This is worth while, even when the improved labour market position of the disadvantaged is achieved at the expense of the short-term unemployed.[1] It is, therefore, important to investigate separately the effects of ALMP on the transition from unemployment to employment for the short-term unemployed and for the long-term unemployed. Unemployment generally becomes a social problem when people remain in it for long periods of time. Since long-term unemployment often leads to social exclusion, reintegrating the long-term unemployed may also contribute to their social reintegration. This brings us back to the issue of social integration, the subject matter of the TRANSLAM project.

In this section, we present an overview of the various approaches to disequilibrium on the labour market described in the literature. In section 2.2, we take a critical approach to traditional u/v-analysis. In sections 2.3 and 2.4 we treat the aggregation approach and the flow model approach to disequilibrium on the labour market, respectively. Modelling implementation is the subject of section 2.4. Finally, in section 2.5, we deal with problems associated with the estimation of the models.

2.2 Traditional u/v-analysis

In empirical research, the u/v-curve was often used in an *ad hoc* way. The simple static relation did not give very satisfactory results in most cases. Typically, highly autocorrelated residuals were found and other variables were added to deal with the problem. Adding lagged values of u and v usually improved the results. Sometimes other variables were added as well, such as demographic variables, replacement rates, indicators of economic structure and the utilization rate of employed labour. The justification for including the latter variable is that open unemployment may temporarily be at a lower level than would be expected on the basis of the going vacancy rate. This is because a large amount of hidden unemployment exists within firms due to a low utilization rate. We will refer to amended u/v-curves in cases where additional variables are included. Both static and amended u/v-curves have been used to study the efficiency of the matching process between demand and supply on the labour market. Shifts in this curve are seen as changes in labour market efficiency. Figure 2.2 may serve as an illustration. In the figure, two u/v-curves have been drawn. It is clear that a given level of unemploy-

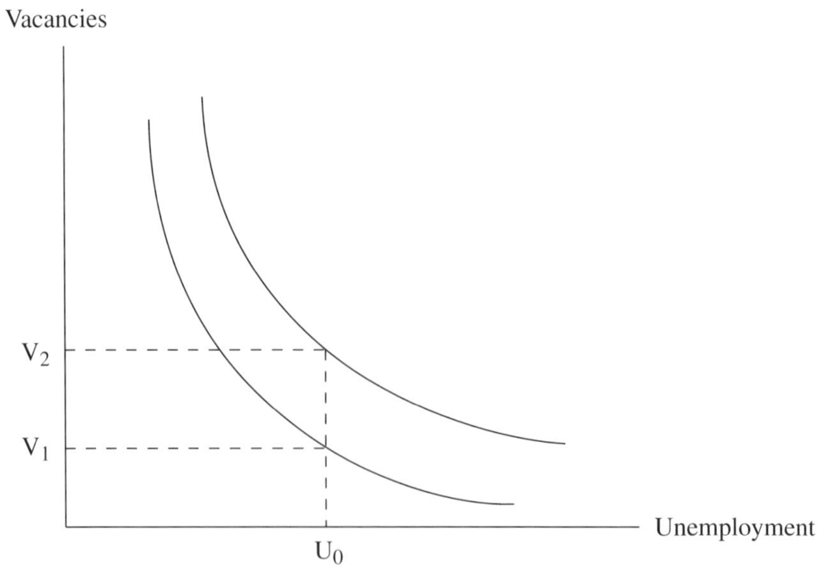

Figure 2.2 Changes in labour market efficiency and the u/v-curve

ment U_0 produces a higher level of vacancies the further the u/v-curve is situated to the right in u/v-space. Dow and Dicks-Mireaux (1958) were the first to use u/v-curves for this purpose.

During the 1960s, 1970s and 1980s, several researchers found clear evidence pointing to a shift of the u/v-curve 'to the right', indicating that the same level of the vacancy rate produced increasing levels of the unemployment rate. The mid-1960s was often found as the starting point of the shift. Examples are Driehuis (1978) for Belgium, the Federal Republic of Germany, France, the Netherlands and the UK; Burch and Fabricant (1968) for the USA; Reid and Meltz (1979) for Canada and Harper (1980) for Australia. Examples of studies which attempt to explain the shift in the u/v-curve from one or more of the factors mentioned earlier are Gujarati (1972) and Foster (1972, 1974) for the UK, Reid and Meltz (1979) for Canada and van den Berg (1982) for the Netherlands. ALMP indicators are usually not included in papers which appeared prior to the 1990s.

Thus several studies in several countries came to the conclusion that the matching between unemployment and vacancies was becoming less and less efficient. It seemed to be a general pattern in the industrialized countries. This view was first challenged by Warren (1980) for both the UK and the US labour markets. He presents a model in which the location of the u/v-curve in u/v-space depends on employment growth, and argues that shifts in this curve originate from changing growth rates in employment instead of a diminishing efficiency of the matching process. The same results were later obtained with the same type of model for the Netherlands by van Ours (1991).

A common characteristic of most empirical studies using aggregate data about unemployment and vacancies is the failure to take the duration aspect into account. Den Butter and van Ours (1990) consider separate matching functions for the various duration classes of vacancies and unemployment. The results of their study reinforce the conclusions drawn earlier by van Ours that the shift of the aggregate u/v-relation is not the result of a labour market which operates less efficiently.

Another criticism of u/v-analysis was made by Kooiman and Kloek (1979). They argue that, while u is usually taken as the dependent variable, no reason is given as to why it is not possible to use v as the variable to be explained and u as the explanatory variable. While it is possible to question the relevance of this observation, the results are not, in fact, the same. Explaining u by v gives other results than explaining v by u. Kooiman and Kloek argue convincingly that employment should be considered the dependent variable, and labour demand and labour supply the explanatory variables. This relation is called the disequilibrium function. In the next section, we examine the Kooiman–Kloek model in greater detail.

2.3 The Aggregation Approach

Since one of the causes of the friction between supply and demand on the labour market is the heterogeneity of labour, a study of the labour market performance on the level of sub-markets would appear useful. Unfortunately, lack of data often forbids such a study. Long time series for employment, vacancies and unemployment according to occupations and educational groups are simply not available; leaving macroeconomic data as a last resort.

The aggregation approach as originally developed by Muellbauer (1978) and Kooiman and Kloek (1979) is based on the following assumptions:

1. The labour market can be divided into a large number of sub-markets to which a minimum condition broadly applies, that is, on which employment is approximately equal to the smaller of supply and demand.
2. The joint size distribution of supply and demand among sub-markets can be approached by a continuous function, corresponding in shape to a (continuous) density function of two random variables.

The first assumption implies that friction is taken to be almost entirely a macro-phenomenon; on sub-markets, unemployment and vacancies are hardly supposed to occur simultaneously. That is, of course, an abstraction from reality. But after reviewing data on unemployment and vacancies on the level of professional groups in regions, some authors have concluded that friction is an important phenomenon on sub-markets as well.[2] The question is whether the concept of professions as operated in statistics is the right criterion for delimiting sub-markets. A portion of the unemployed is known to register under professions for which the individuals lack sufficient qualifications. In such cases the friction apparently existing on a homogeneous sub-market is actually due to the heterogeneity of labour. There is, however a limit to disaggregation. By defining sub-markets more narrowly, we might well end up at the individual level, with each unemployed person and each vacancy constituting a sub-market.

The second assumption made above, according to which the distribution of supply and demand can be approximated by a continuous function, is needed to derive a macroeconomic relation. Assuming a lognormal distribution, Kooiman and Kloek derive the following relation:

$$L = L^s N(Z/\sigma - \sigma/2) + L^d \{1 - N(Z/\sigma + \sigma/2)\} \tag{2.1}$$

where Z is equal to:

$$Z = \ln(L^d) - \ln(L^s) \tag{2.2}$$

N representing the cumulative distribution function of the standard normal distribution. By definition we have:

$$L^s = L + U \tag{2.3}$$

and

$$L^d = L + V, \tag{2.4}$$

where U and V denote unemployment and vacancies, respectively. It can be shown that after substitution of equations (2.3) and (2.4) in (2.1) equation (2.1) can be rewritten as a u/v-function of the type displayed in Figure 2.2.

Kooiman and Kloek do not base their assumption of a lognormal distribution on data from empirical research. Other assumptions are also possible and sometimes lead to a mathematically more tractable disequilibrium function. In his original paper, Muellbauer (1978) uses a uniform distribution and arrives at an employment function that leads to the classical hyperbolic u/v-function UV=constant. Den Broeder (1983) also finds an appealing functional form starting from a Weibull distribution. This results in a CES-type employment relation. In doing so, however, he must assume that supply and demand are distributed independently, which seems hardly realistic. De Koning (1984) presents some empirical material which gives support to the hypothesis of log-normality with respect to the size distributions of labour demand and labour supply. However, equation (2.1) is computationally burdensome, and both the CES function and the Muellbauer function may be good approximations in practice.

Parameter σ from equation (2.1) is a criterion of the friction on the labour market. If this parameter is 'infinitely' large, L is equal to zero, and the friction therefore maximum, supply and demand not teaming up at all. If σ is equal to zero, L is equal to the lesser of supply and demand, and there is no friction at all. In that case, demand matches supply, and *vice versa*.

A possible approach would be to put σ^2 dependent on a number of (macro-economic) variables presumably governing friction on the labour market (including ALMP indicators), and then estimate the model. Estimation can be undertaken in several ways. Kooiman and Kloek take the logarithms of equation (2.1) and add a disturbance term. De Koning (1984), using the same model, takes σ^2 as the dependent variable to which a disturbance term is added.[3] The same options exist using the CES function. The Muellbauer function is the most simple since it allows us to take log (uv) as a function of the x-variables.

De Koning (1984) shows that it is possible to derive the lognormal employment function from assumptions about the way micro-markets work. In his theoretical model, he assumes that on micro-markets, wages react to imbalances between micro-demand and micro-supply.[4] If we assume that all micro-relations are log-linear and that the x-variables determining labour demand and supply are distributed log-normally over sub-markets, we find that σ^2 is a linear function of all the variances and the covariances of the x-variables. The variance of micro-market output is one of the obvious factors determining labour demand, and thus the variance of log (output) over sub-markets would be one of the explanatory variables in the equation for σ^2. One advantage of this approach is that it also explains why lags occur in the equation for σ^2. For example, if the relation between output and labour demand is characterized by a distributed lag pattern, this pattern will also occur in the equation for σ^2.

In a later contribution, Sneessens and Drèze (1986) extended the two-regime approach to three regimes. They distinguish between two forms of labour demand in addition to labour supply: Keynesian demand for labour and capacity demand for labour. By doing so, a connection can be made with the goods market, which can also be in disequilibrium. An earlier attempt to analyse simultaneously disequilibrium on the labour and on the goods market was made by Kooiman and Kloek (1985), elaborating on their earlier paper. Both Kooiman (1984) and Lambert (1984) use business survey data to identify their disequilibrium models. A recent contribution has also been made by Bierens (1996).

It is important to note that, in this generalized approach, identification of the parameters is only possible within the context of the simultaneous estimation of a macroeconomic model. The generalized approach is important in determining to what extent unemployment has a classical or a Keynesian character. The answer will determine which type of macroeconomic policy should be adopted in fighting unemployment. The distinction between the two forms of unemployment may be relevant for ALMP as well. One of the ways through which ALMP may reduce unemployment is that it reactivates unemployed people and thereby strengthens the wage mechanism. But in a situation of Keynesian unemployment, lower wages will not bring about equilibrium, and they may even worsen the unemployment problem. The need for alternative policies like ALMP may, therefore, increase in such a situation.

2.4 The Flow Model Approach

The second approach follows the original Holt and David model. The following presentation is based on an elaboration by Phelps (1970). The basic equation in this model is the employment equation, which defines the change in employment as the result of hirings on the one hand; and quits (Q), retirement (R) and lay-offs (LO) on the other. Thus we have for employment:

$$L = L(-1) + H - Q - R - LO \tag{2.5}$$

If we assume that people quit their jobs only if they have already found other employment, net hirings (total hirings minus quits) will be the result of the matching of unemployed job seekers and vacancies. The following relation could be made:

$$H = f(U,V) \tag{2.6}$$

Functions such as this one have been estimated by Blanchard and Diamond (1989) and van Ours (1991), among many others. De Koning *et al.* (1995) and de Koning and Arents (1997) use this type of hiring function to analyse the impact of ALMP on labour market efficiency.

As for lay-offs and vacancies, the simplest assumption is that both are a fixed proportion of employment at the end of the previous period:

$$LO = \gamma_1 L(-1) \tag{2.7}$$

and

$$R = \gamma_2 L(-1) \tag{2.8}$$

Assuming that the hirings function is linear homogeneous in U and V substituting formula (2.5), (2.6), (2.7) and (2.8) and rearranging terms gives the following equation:

$$f(U/L, V/L) = \Delta L / L + (\gamma_1 - \gamma_2) L(-1) / L \tag{2.9a}$$

In case of a constant growth rate of employment, equation (2.9a) constitutes a static u/v-curve.

Equation (2.9a) can also be written as:

$$\Delta L = f(U,V) - (\gamma_1 - \gamma_2) L(-1) \tag{2.9b}$$

and is used in this form as an employment function in the older literature to analyse shifts in labour market efficiency. Empirically, the advantage of this function is its dynamic character, which is much more in line with the facts than the static u/v-relation.

It should be noted that equation (2.6) can be rewritten as a transition function:

$$H / U = f(1, V / U) \tag{2.10}$$

According to this function, the probability of an unemployed person finding a job is a function of the vacancies/unemployment ratio. This implies that transition functions from unemployment to employment are closely related to u/v-functions. It is not possible to estimate both a transition function and a u/v-relation while pretending to do two separate things. Bellmann and Lehmann (1990), de Koning (1993) and Bellmann and Jackman (1996a) use quasi-flow equations such as (2.10) to assess ALMP or individual ALMP measures. An important limitation of this approach is that it is based on a single equation, and thus fails to take account of the simultaneous nature of the relation between the variables. It may, therefore, produce biased estimates.

We agree with the criticism by den Butter and van Ours that the matching function should be split according to unemployment and vacancy duration classes. In most European countries, however, filling vacancies has hardly been a problem in recent decades. The stock of vacancies is usually a mere fraction of the total yearly inflow of vacancies, indicating that average vacancy duration is not very long. It may, therefore, not be necessary to distinguish between duration classes of vacancies. Our model would then read as follows:

$$H_d = f_d(U_d, V) \tag{2.11}$$

or rewritten as a transition equation:

$$H_d / U_d = f_d(1, V / U_d) \tag{2.12}$$

where:

H_d = hirings from unemployment duration class d;
U_d = stock of unemployed in duration class d.

Hirings from a specific duration class should always be less than total hirings, and the sum total of hirings from the various duration classes should add up to total hirings. For practical purposes, two adaptations may be necessary:

1. Hirings may also result from jobless people who are not considered 'unemployed'.
2. If the unit of time used is relatively long, for example, a year, stock variables should not be used for unemployment and vacancies. Instead, the stock at the beginning of a period plus the inflow during the period should be used.

With respect to equation (2.12), we recommend working with monthly, or even weekly, data. In such a case, the hirings resulting from the unemployed could be linked to a flow model of unemployment. Hirings could then be related to the probability of an unemployed person finding a job, which is directly related to the probability density function of unemployment duration.

It could be argued that, in addition to vacancies and unemployment, employment should be taken as an explanatory variable in the hirings function since vacancies are often filled by workers moving from one job to another. In most cases, however, a worker moving to another job will create a new vacancy. It could, therefore, be argued that filling vacancies with employed people does not contribute to macro-vacancy fulfilment. But in some cases, people move to other jobs because their old jobs are likely to disappear. Moreover, mobility of workers may lead to a better allocation of labour in a qualitative sense. In any case, it may be worth while to try specifications of the hirings function in which (lagged) employment is added.

Lay-offs are the link between the hirings function and the (generalized) u/v-function if we assume that the number of quits is approximately a fixed proportion of employment. ALMP may also target lay-offs. First, measures such as short-time employment may decrease the number of lay-offs. Second, ALMP may be used to help people threatened with unemployment to find a new job. It would, therefore, make sense to estimate a 'separation function' in addition to the hirings functions. When unemployed persons engage in ALMP measures like training, they are sometimes removed from the unemployment figure during participation. The ones who do not find a job directly after ALMP participation will return to unemployment. Thus, it may be advisable to include lagged ALMP in the matching function.

While unemployment duration classes have so far been the only 'sub-markets' we have identified, we will find that other supply characteristics – such as age, gender and age – will also prove important. In principle, the hirings functions for the various duration classes can be differentiated according to supply characteristics. It is also possible to specify hirings functions according to both supply and demand characteristics. By demand characteristics we mean company characteristics, such as size and industry; and job characteristics, such as occupation. However, the very aim of ALMP is to ease the mobility of workers between sub-markets. Therefore, it makes no sense to study the effects of ALMP on a very detailed level of professional and sectoral sub-markets. We propose to study the matter on the level of regions, and to distinguish between duration classes and, where appropriate, other supply characteristics. Segmentation theories could be used to explain why some groups have fewer opportunities to make the transition from unemployment to employment. If we choose the regional level such that cross-regional mobility is relatively low, we could argue that the regional disequilibrium relation is the result of aggregation over many regional sub-markets.

In principle, the flow model approach can be combined with the aggregation approach. Muysken *et al.* (1993) assume that friction between demand and supply also exists on micro-markets. Furthermore, they assume that on each micro-market, the change in employment is the result of hirings and quits/lay-offs. However, the greater realism in assumptions means that the mathematical forms will be less tractable. Moreover, despite the greater realism, the assumptions are still unsatisfactory in some respects. For instance, Muysken *et al.* assume that quits and lay-offs taken together constitute a fixed proportion of employment. Further research will be needed before we can adopt that type of mixed approach.

2.5 Estimation

Even after we put aside the models which simultaneously analyse disequilibrium on the labour and the goods markets, a number of estimation problems remain. Since our main purpose in this book is to measure the aggregate impact of ALMP on labour market transitions, our most important estimation problem is likely to be the so-called endogeneity problem (see, for example, OECD, 1993). When unemployment is rising, governments will decide to spend more on ALMP. The effects of ALMP on unemployment will, however, be relatively small. This suggests that the parameter of the ALMP variable may have the wrong sign, even when ALMP has a reducing impact on unemployment. To solve this problem, instrumental variables techniques must be used. First, ALMP must be explained from a set of factors which include at least some variables that do not influence unemployment. An example of this approach is given by Büttner and Prey (1997), who use regional cross-section data. The political colour of the regional administration is (among other variables) taken as an instrument.

A number of contributions in this book use short time series data for a relatively large number of regions. This type of data set typically requires panel methods. The fixed effect model is probably the most appropriate for our purposes. In this model, it is assumed that unobserved regional factors can be dealt with by including dummy variables for each region (for further details, we refer to Greene, 1993). For cross-national data (or combinations of cross-national and cross-regional data), the same method can be applied.

It is essential to use a broad concept of unemployment. Suppose, for example, that we measure unemployment according to the ILO definition. In that case, the only people included will be those who are actively engaged in looking for a job. Now suppose that the main effect of ALMP is that labour supply (defined as the sum total of employment and ILO unemployment) is increased, which subsequently increases employment. ILO unemployment could then fail to decrease; or may even increase. When, however, as a result of ALMP, people who were previously out of work and have not even looked for work find jobs, ALMP would certainly be considered successful. ILO unemployment is not, therefore, the appropriate variable to use in an aggregate impact analysis of ALMP. Recipients of unemployment benefits who have stopped looking for jobs and other discouraged workers should be included in the unemployment concept which is used to measure the aggregate impact of ALMP. Alternatively, the aggregate impact should be measured on the basis of aggregate employment and labour supply. In the latter option, however, the number of ALMP participants is relatively small, which suggests that detecting an effect on total employment and total labour supply will be difficult.

A related issue is whether participants in ALMP are counted as unemployed. As Calmfors (1994) points out, an observed reducing effect of ALMP on unemployment may be simply due to the fact that, during participation, people are not counted as unemployed. In that case, increases in the number of ALMP participants will increase the flows both out of and into unemployment. The latter effect is due to the fact that participants who do not find a job will become (officially) unemployed again after participation. It may, therefore, be advisable to include ALMP participants in the unemployment measure, although an exception should perhaps be made for job creation measures. When subsidized employment is additional to regular employment and does not displace or substitute it, this must be seen as a positive effect of ALMP – even if it is only for the duration of the project.

3 OTHER AGGREGATE EFFECTS

The focus of this book is the aggregate impact analysis of ALMP on labour market transitions. Yet ALMP may also affect unemployment in indirect ways. While we will not deal with these indirect effects in our empirical models, it is important to state explicitly what effects are not covered.

Using the models discussed above, we can analyse the effect of ALMP on:

- the efficiency of the matching between demand and supply, and
- the distribution of employment opportunities over groups.

We assume, however, that total demand and total supply are given within the framework of the previous section (where supply is based on a broad definition of unemployment). This approach, therefore, tells us nothing about:

- the possible effect of wage subsidies and job creation on total labour demand;

- the possible effect on wage formation, which could then indirectly affect total labour demand;
- the possibility that the productivity–wage ratio of unemployed people improves as a result of ALMP, making marginal economic activities profitable again;
- the possible effect on unemployment insurance expenditure, which may affect wage costs;
- the possible indirect effects on consumption, investment, and so on.

We now look at several contributions which deal with one of more of these indirect effects of ALMP.

3.1 The Layard–Nickell Approach

The Layard–Nickell model was not developed to evaluate the macroeconomic effects of ALMP, but it later proved to be a convenient framework in which to study those effects. Although it is a relatively simple macroeconomic model of the labour market, it contains most of the elements needed to analyse the effects of ALMP. A concise presentation of the model is given by Bellmann and Jackman (1996b).

The Layard–Nickell model can be reduced to two form equations and one structural equation: an employment equation, a wage-setting equation and the Beveridge curve. The first equation shows how many workers firms wish to employ in relation to the real wage rate. The curve of this equation has a downward slope, which depends on factors such as technology and product market competitiveness. The second curve depicts the real wage as an upward sloping function of planned employment. This could be the result of a wage bargain, but it could also follow from wage efficiency considerations of firms. The position of this curve will depend on factors such as capital intensity, benefits and the importance of specific human capital. The third equation, the Beveridge curve, describes the friction on the labour market. Firms will not be able to achieve completely their planned employment goals. The vacancy rate will depend on the ratio between labour supply and planned employment. The higher the ratio, the lower the vacancy rate (and the higher the unemployment rate). In this model, ALMP can influence labour market outcomes in at least three ways:

- by improving the matching between supply and demand;
- by increasing the volume and improving the employability of the labour supply; and
- by providing incentives to unemployed job seekers.

3.2 Incorporating ALMP Effects in Full-scale Macroeconomic Models

The Layard–Nickell model provides a theoretical framework for the ways in which ALMP can influence labour market outcomes on an aggregate level. Yet this model is not sufficient for computing the macroeconomic effects of ALMP because, in principle, ALMP affects not just labour market variables, but other variables as well. Public expenditure is among the variables which will not be left unchanged by labour market policies. Although the implementation of these policies costs money, the policies may also save on unemployment benefits; thus, the result could be either positive or negative. When variables such as employment, wages and public expenditure change as a result of ALMP, the whole macroeconomic system is set in motion. We would, therefore, require a full-scale macroeconometric model to compute the effects.

Although the existing large macroeconometric models do not usually contain ALMP expenditure or ALMP participants as one of the variables, it is theoretically possible to insert into the model the effects of ALMP on unemployment–employment transition, wage formation, mismatch, and so on. Consequently, the macroeconomic effects of changes in ALMP expenditure could be simulated with the help of the model. That would, however, necessitate considerable changes in these models, which do not normally contain elements such as flow equations of the labour market. Whether the potential results are worth the effort of altering these models is questionable. The use of these large econometric models for policy simulations has been severely criticized. Today econometricians generally prefer smaller models which are more general in terms of dynamic structure, such as the VAR models. Yet one virtue of macroeconometric models is that the relevant mechanisms are made explicit, while the VAR approach hardly contains a theoretical component.

3.3 VAR Models Including more than Two Dependent Variables

Time-series analysis is also a possible method for assessing the impact of ALMP on unemployment. Modern methods in time-series analysis use general models in which the number of restrictions on the lag structure is minimized. A popular method is the so-called vector autoregression, or VAR, method (Greene, 1993). To measure the impact of ALMP on unemployment, this method proceeds as follows: for each variable, an equation is specified in which the dependent variable is a linear function of its own lagged values and the lagged values of the other variable. The estimated coefficients in the VAR equation are generally used to generate so-called impulse response functions. These functions reflect how a sudden shock in the residuals of one of the endogenous variables (so-called innovations) affects all other variables. This shock occurs both in the short run and in the longer run, when it gives rise to indirect effects. In other words, the impulse response functions make it possible to analyse both the current and lagged impact of a sudden change in one of the dependent variables (such as a sudden increase in the number of participants in labour market policy programmes, or an increase of unemployment) on the other. These functions can also easily be displayed graphically, showing the time profile for each variable when a sudden shock occurs. VAR models are not restricted to the two dependent variables case, and can be used to study the interaction of more than two variables (see below).

Time-series approaches in the context of employment policy evaluation have been mainly applied in Sweden. Skedinger (1995) adopts a VAR approach on aggregate quarterly time-series data to estimate the crowding-out effects of Swedish youth job-creation programmes. The two estimated VAR equations include as dependent variables youth regular employment and job-creation programmes targeted at youth. In order to control for the level of activity, aggregate unemployment is included as an exogenous variable. The author found empirical evidence that job-creation programmes resulted in considerable displacement of regular employment.

VAR methods have also been recently used to test the direction of causality between economic variables. In an article published in 1995, Forslund and Krueger investigate the displacement effect of Swedish public relief work in the construction and health sectors. They proceed in two steps. By using pooled time series and cross-regional data, they first estimate a traditional employment function for each sector. Their explanatory variables include lagged employment, average real wage, public relief work and a vector of cyclical variables (unemployment and vacancies). They found a negative significant relationship between public relief work and employment in the construction sector, but not in the health sectors. In a second step, they use a VAR model to investigate whether the negative correlation they found between regular employment in the construction sector and public employment programmes reflects a causal relation, or rather a policy response function in which labour market authorities react quickly to the changing situation in the labour market. The results indicate that lagged relief workers and lagged employment have a significant effect in the employment equation, but not in the relief work equation. In light of these results, Forslund and Krueger conclude that Swedish public relief work programmes are associated with substantial displacement effects.

So far, we have discussed two-variable VAR models which could be used to analyse the relation between, for example, ALMP and unemployment. We might also, however, include more dependent variables, which would allow us to take more complicated relations into account. Wages and labour supply are, for instance, obvious candidates for inclusion.

In order to analyse the impact of active labour market policy programmes on the level of unemployment and wage inflation, Ohlsson (1995) estimates a three-variable VAR model. By using the impulse response function, he found evidence that an increase in the number of people in job-creation programmes reduced unemployment in the short run without increasing wage inflation. Ohlsson's results therefore seem to indicate that it is possible to implement an active labour market policy without having a negative impact on wage-setting. In terms of unemployment, Ohlsson found evidence that a sudden increase in the number of job seekers also led to a rapid increase in the number of participants in job-creation schemes. In sum, the results of the estimation indicate that job creation significantly affected the level of unemployment in the short run, but had no impact on wage inflation in the long run. In other words, the Swedish job-creation programmes have been efficient stabilization policy tools, and have shown a clear tendency to react quickly in face of changing conditions in the labour market.

In order to apply VAR models, it is necessary to dispose of long time series; preferably of quarterly data. For most countries, however, only relatively short time series data sets regarding ALMP expenditure or ALMP participants are available, most of them on a yearly basis. Thus the application of time-series analysis will be difficult, if not impossible, in many cases.

What do we miss by failing to take into account other aggregate effects? The contributors to this book focus on assessing the effects of ALMP on mismatch and on unemployment–employment transitions. Since positive indirect effects will usually only occur when ALMP reduces mismatch and/or increases the transition probability from unemployment to employment, our failure to deal with other aggregate effects of ALMP which indirectly affect unemployment may not be that serious.

4 MODELLING IMPLEMENTATION

If we assume that ALMP can influence – at least to some extent[5] – the overall number of jobs and solve problems related to market failure, we must also consider the possibility that ALMP might be wrongly designed and badly implemented; and, as a result, the outcomes of ALMP may even prove to be counter-productive in practice. Typical policy flaws include co-operation failure, unclear or contradicting goals, stop-and-go policies, clientelism, lack of budget constraints and lack of feedback. Schmid[6] describes the conditions under which ALMP management would be most effective. According to Schmid, empirical evidence and theories of co-ordination failure indicate that the management of ALMP must apply a mix of co-ordination mechanisms in which both competition and co-operation are essential elements. In the second part of this book, implementation will be discussed more thoroughly. Our main question here is how we can incorporate implementation into aggregate impact analysis.

4.1 Including Implementation in the Previous Models

The simplest approach is to incorporate implementation variables into the previous models. Suppose, for example, that we want to measure the impact of ALMP on the efficiency of the matching process. The traditional approach would be to include the (relative) number of ALMP participants in a u/v-equation. Alternatively, however, we could add qualitative variables which indicate implementation aspects.

An example of this approach is provided in an article by Jackman *et al.* (1990). They propose an evaluation of the effects of labour market policies on unemployment within the analytical framework of the Beveridge curve.[7] On the basis of international time series data (1970–88, for 14 OECD countries), they investigate whether policy differences between countries – as well as another set of institutional variables – can explain the differences in the location of the Beveridge curve. They find a significant negative effect of labour market policy on unemployment for a given level of vacancies (negative effects were found not only on the unemployment level, but also on the responsiveness of unemployment to vacancies and on its persistence). Corporatism remains the institutional feature with the biggest single impact in sustaining low unemployment rates, but the authors suggest that this variable should perhaps also be thought of as a proxy for unobserved institutional features of labour market policies.

4.2 Measuring the Efficiency of ALMP Implementation

Instead of incorporating ALMP measures directly into the equation that is used for the impact assessment, we might consider taking a two-step approach. In the first step, we relate ALMP output to labour market outcomes; and in the second step, we relate implementation to ALMP output. We might also proceed in the reverse order (see below). Examples of ALMP output indicators include the number of placements and the number of participants in ALMP programmes.

The simplest approach is to examine the residuals of the OLS equation of the equation used for the impact assessment; and then, in a second step, explain the residuals using implementation variables.[8] Suppose, for example, that we have measured the effect of ALMP on unemployment on the basis of cross-regional data. When a region has a large positive residual, this could be seen as an indication that implementation is not efficient in that region. Large negative residuals could point to an efficient implementation strategy. In a second step, we could then explain the residuals from implementation variables and determine whether they are significant and have the expected sign. This is, however, basically the same as directly including implementation variables in the assessment equation.

De Koning (1993), using results from an earlier paper by de Koning and van Nes (1991), explains the number of placements in a region within the framework of a scheme for subsidized placement of the long-term unemployed using a number of implementation variables, including:

- the acquisition strategy of the employment office (passive or active seeking of suitable vacancies for the target group);
- the intensity of cooperation with the municipality;
- the internal organization (whether or not implementation is handled by specialized counsellors).

Indicators of the regional structure of the labour market, such as the share of small and medium enterprises (SMEs) in employment, were also included as control variables.

A somewhat different method is the so-called frontier approach (for an overview see Greene, 1993). The aim of this approach is to measure efficiency. It can be applied to any input–output structure. When we have only one output indicator y which depends on a vector input x the following equation can be specified:

$$y = f(x) + e \tag{2.13}$$

In this equation, e denotes efficiency. Since output is always less than capacity, e always takes negative values. In the frontier approach, e is considered to be a stochastic variable, so that the equation can be estimated using maximum likelihood. Various probability distribution functions have been used for this type of problem, such as the gamma distribution and the half-normal distribution. Models that contain both normal and one-sided error terms – the so-called stochastic frontier models – have also been proposed and applied.

Yet in the case of ALMP, a multi-output approach would be more appropriate. Althin and Beherenz (1995) therefore use a mathematical programming approach which has previously been applied to the study of efficiency in non-profit organizations. It is based on the observation that the employment office is involved in many different activities and its production process can be described as follows: the employment service has at its disposal various officers, computer resources and office space. Ideally, this mix of production factors should fulfil the main purposes of the employment service. These purposes may be described as follows. First, every job seeker should obtain a job that matches his or her requests as closely as possible and within the shortest time possible; and the offices should support those job seekers who are finding it difficult to enter the labour market through job preparation and employment-generation measures. Second, those jobs that are registered at the offices should be filled as quickly and as effectively as possible. An office which uses fewer resources than another office to produce the same services will be classed by the model as more efficient.

5 EMPIRICAL RESULTS OBTAINED WITH AGGREGATE MODELS

In the previous sections, various models were discussed which can be used for aggregate impact analysis of active labour market policy. In this section, we provide a concise overview of the models, the existing applications in the field of aggregate impact analysis of ALMP, as well as the main results and limitations.

We distinguish the following approaches to aggregate impact measurement of ALMP:

1. simple u/v-analysis to measure the impact of ALMP on mismatch;
2. more elaborate variants of u/v-analysis using disequilibrium functions of the labour market;
3. (quasi-)flow equations measuring the impact of ALMP on the transition from unemployment to employment, and *vice versa*;
4. measurement of the aggregate impact of ALMP on wages, unemployment and other variables without using the explicit framework of disequilibrium or flow models of the labour market; and
5. attempts to compute the macroeconomic effects of ALMP by using a full-scale econometric model of the economy.

Implementation aspects could, in principle, be incorporated into each of these approaches.

Table 2.1 provides an overview of aggregate impact studies. For each study, the table supplies information about scope, estimation technique, type of data used and conclusions. From the table it is clear that most contributions can be found in the categories 'simple u/v-analysis', '(quasi-)flow equations' and '*ad hoc* specifications (including VAR-models)'. We can only record one contribution in each one of the two other categories: 'disequilibrium functions' and 'full-scale macroeconometric models'. In the latter case, an effect of ALMP on mismatch is assumed, not estimated econometrically.

Table 2.1 Overview of aggregate impact studies

Author(s)	Scope of the analysis	Type of estimation technique and type of data	Conclusion about the impact of ALMP
Simple u/v-analysis			
De Grip (1987)	Impact of training for the unemployed in the construction sector on mismatch	OLS, using time series data	Weak evidence that training of unemployed workers in the construction sector reduces mismatch
Jackman *et al.* (1990)	Impact of total ALMP expenditure on mismatch	OLS, using time series for a number of countries	No significant effect
Calmfors (1993)	Impact of total ALMP on mismatch	OLS, using time series for a number of countries	No significant effect
Bourdet and Persson (1995)	Impact of total ALMP on mismatch	OLS, using time series for France and Sweden	Significant effect for France No significant effect for Sweden
Disequilibrium functions			
Büttner and Prey (1997)	Impact of training and job creation on mismatch	ML, using pooled time series and cross-section data about German regions. ALMP is endogenized	Job creation reduces mismatch, but training has no significant effect
(Quasi-)flow equations			
Bellmann and Lehmann (1990)	Impact of job creation, wage subsidy and training schemes on flows into and out of unemployment by age and duration	OLS, using cross-regional data for Germany	Positive effect for job creation schemes only

Table 2.1 continued

Author(s)	Scope of the analysis	Type of estimation technique and type of data	Conclusion about the impact of ALMP
De Koning (1993)	Impact of placement subsidy scheme for the long-term unemployed	OLS, using time series data	Deadweight less than 30 per cent Effect on total unemployment limited in size Placements depend on implementation
Lehmann (1993)	Impact of the Restart Programme in the UK on the outflow from unemployment	OLS, using time series data	Increase of the outflow from long-term unemployment, but decrease of the outflow from short-term unemployment Total effect positive
De Koning *et al.* (1995)	Impact of total ALMP expenditure on total hirings from unemployment	OLS, using pooled time series and cross-regional data	No effects on total hirings
De Koning and Arents (1997)	Impact of total ALMP expenditure on the number of hirings from unemployment for different duration classes	OLS, using pooled time series and cross-regional data	Only weak evidence of a redistribution effect between short-term unemployment and long-term unemployment
Ad hoc *specifications, with or without making use of elaborate econometric techniques*			
Peters and Schmid (1982)	Impact of a federal programme in Germany including training and subsidized labour	OLS, cross-section over German regions	Mainly redistributive effects

Layard *et al*. (1991)	Impact of total ALMP expenditure on the unemployment rate	OLS, using cross-country data	Negative sign of the ALMP variable, but significance is very sensitive for the specification
OECD (1993)	Impact of ALMP on wage formation and employment	OLS, using pooled cross-country and time series data	Results suggest that ALMP has been effective in reducing structural unemployment in certain countries
Skedinger (1995)	Estimation of crowding-out effects of Swedish job creation programmes for the young	VAR	Displacement effects are considerable
Forslund and Krueger (1995)	Estimation of displacement effect of public relief work in the construction and health sectors	VAR	Substantial displacement effects
Ohlsson (1995)	Impact of ALMP on unemployment and wage inflation in Sweden	VAR	Job creation has a diminishing effect on unemployment in the short run without affecting wage inflation in the long run
Bellmann and Jackman (1996b)	Impact of ALMP, broken down by type of measure, on various labour market indicators	OLS, using pooled time series cross-country data	Training and job placement have a reducing effect on long-term unemployment and a positive effect on labour supply (for women). Subsidy schemes have adverse effects
Simulations using a full-scale macroeconometric model			
De Broeder *et al*. (1984)	Impact of ALMP on macroeconomic performance	ALMP is assumed to shift the u/v-curve to the origin	Only small effects on macroeconomic outcomes

It is difficult to draw general conclusions from the table. Generally, the studies suggest that the effects of ALMP are minor on a macroeconomic level. There is more evidence that ALMP increases the outflow from long-term unemployment to employment; but, given the former result, at the cost of decreasing the outflow from short-term unemployment to employment. Some studies report a small positive effect on the total outflow from unemployment. But even when this effect on total outflow is zero, a redistribution of job opportunities between the long-term and the short-term unemployment could be seen as a positive result.

Yet many of the studies included in Table 2.1 suffer from the data and estimation problems mentioned in previous sections, and this makes it difficult to judge the validity of the results. ALMP participants may be removed from the unemployment records during participation, thus giving the decrease in unemployment an artificial character. In that case, some of the results regarding the effectiveness of ALMP may even be too optimistic. But many of the studies could also suffer from the endogeneity problem (Büttner and Prey, 1997). Governments will increase ALMP budgets when unemployment is rising. Even when ALMP does have an impact on the level of unemployment, the effect may not be perceptible because unemployment is still higher after the budget increase than it was before. This suggests that some of the studies underestimate the effectiveness of ALMP. A few studies use modern econometric (VAR) techniques which have been introduced to deal with the causality problem. But the economic content of the models used in these contributions is usually overly simplistic, making it difficult to give an economic interpretation to the empirical results.

While it is often assumed (OECD, 1993) that different modes of implementation can explain differences in the outcomes of ALMP in various countries, implementation variables are not included in the models of any of these studies. What is needed is an approach which combines the impact assessment of the studies summarized in this section with the measurement of the efficiency of ALMP implementation.

6 THE MODELS USED IN THIS BOOK

In the ALMP module of the TRANSLAM project, two types of transitions play a central role:

(i) the transition from unemployment (or, more generally, inactivity) to employment;
(ii) the transition from employment to unemployment (or, more generally, inactivity).

ALMP attempts to improve (i) and to prevent (ii). The flow model approach as presented in section 2.4 seems most suited to the study of both transitions. With respect to transition (i), a direct link can be made between the concept of hirings functions and the individual unemployment duration probability density function. It is possible to incorporate into this approach supply characteristics such as age and gender. This framework can therefore be used both for the estimation of more or less *ad hoc* hirings functions, as well as for more elaborate models which explicitly use the concept of a probability density function for unemployment duration. Indicators of ALMP can be easily incorporated into this framework in order to investigate the impact of ALMP on the transition from unemployment to employment. Furthermore, by distinguishing between duration classes of unemployment and other supply characteristics, the link can be made with social exclusion.

It is important to note that once we have functions for (i) and (ii), the u/v-relation is also determined. Therefore, the u/v-function is not independent of the function explaining the transition from unemployment to employment; in fact, the two are closely related.

In most cases, pooled cross-sectional and time series data will be used to estimate the equations.

NOTES

1. And on longer term the displacement effect may not be that big (see Layard *et al.*, 1991).
2. See in particular Hartog (1980).
3. Note that σ^2 is the only parameter in equation (2.1) so that we can compute its value when we know L, L^s en L^d.
4. In one version of the model wage flexibility is restricted by a minimum wage.
5. New job creation is, of course, basically a matter of investment and effective global demand management.
6. See, for example, Schmid (1996a, 1996b).
7. They modify the traditional uv-curve model in their theoretical approach by introducing a vacancy supply curve which takes into account the relationship between wages and job vacancies, as well as the mechanisms determining wages.
8. Peters and Schmid (1982a, 1982b).

REFERENCES

Althin, R. and L. Beherenz (1995), *En effektivitetsanalyse av arbetsfoermedling-kontoren I Sverige*, Swedish Ministry of Labour: EFA Group.

Bellmann, L. and H. Lehmann (1990), *Active Labour Market Policies in Britain and Germany and Long-term Unemployment: An Evaluation*, paper presented to the conference of the European Association of Labour Economists, Lund, Sweden.

Bellmann, L. and R. Jackman (1996a), 'Aggregate Impact Analysis', in G. Schmid, J.

O'Reilly and K. Schömann (eds), *International Handbook of Labour Market Policy and Evaluation*, Cheltenham: Edward Elgar, pp. 143–62.
Bellmann, L. and R. Jackman (1996b), 'The Impact of Labour Market Policy on Wages, Employment and Labour Market Mismatch', in G. Schmid, J. O'Reilly and K. Schömann (eds), *International Handbook of Labour Market Policy and Evaluation*, Cheltenham: Edward Elgar, pp. 725–46.
Berg, D.J. van den (1982), 'The Specification and the Estimation of the Unemployment Vacancy-Curve in the Period 1956–1979,' *Economist*, 397–419.
Bierens, H. (1996), *Mismatches on the Labour Market and Structural Unemployment*, Ph.D. thesis, Rijswijk.
Blanchard, O.J. and P. Diamond (1989), 'The Beveridge Curve', *Brookings Papers on Economic Activity*.
Bourdet, Y. and I. Persson (1995), 'Does Labour Market Policy Matter? Long-term Unemployment in France and Sweden', in J. Johannesson and E. Wadensjö (eds), *Labour Market Policy at the Crossroads*, Stockholm: Ministry of Labour.
Broeder, G. den (1983), 'A Family of Market Transaction Functions', *Series: Foundations of Empirical Economic Research*, Rotterdam: Netherlands Economic Institute.
Broeder, G. den, J.A.M. Heijke and J. de Koning (1984), *Friction between Supply and Demand on the Netherlands Labour Market*, paper presented at the conference on employment and unemployment of the Applied Econometric Association (AEA), Dijon.
Burch, S.W. and R.A. Fabricant (1968), 'A Further Comment on the Behaviour of Help-wanted Advertising,' *The Review of Economics and Statistics*, 69, 278–81.
Butter, F.A.G. den and J.C. van Ours (1990), 'Stock and Flows in the Dutch Labour market: A Quarterly Simulation Model', *Research Memorandum 1990–59*.
Büttner, T. and H. Prey (1997) 'Does Active Labour-Market Policy Affect Structural Employment? An Empirical Investigation for West German Regions, 1986 to 1993', *Diskussionspapier Nr. 42*, CILE, Universität von Konstanz.
Calmfors, L. (1993), 'Lessons from the Macro-economic Experience of Sweden', *European Journal of Political Economy*, 9, 25–72.
Calmfors, L. (1994), 'Active Labour Market Policy and Unemployment – A Framework for the Analysis of Crucial Design Features', *OECD Economic Studies*, 22, pp. 7–47.
Calmfors, L. and P. Skedinger (1995), 'Does Active Labour-Market Policy Increase Employment? Theoretical Considerations and some Empirical Evidence from Sweden', *Oxford Review of Economic Policy*, **11** (1), 91–109.
Dow, J.C.R. and L.A. Dicks-Mireaux (1958), 'The Excess Demand for Labour: A Study of Conditions in Great Britain: 1946–1956', *Oxford Economic Papers*, 10, 1–33.
Driehuis, W. (1978), 'Labour Market Imbalances and Structural Unemployment', *Kyklos*, 31, 638–61.
European Commission (1996), *Employment in Europe*, Luxembourg.
Forslund A. and Krueger A.B. (1995) 'An Evaluation of the Swedish Active Labour Market Policy – New and Received Wisdom', *SNS Occasional Paper*, no. 65.
Foster, J.I. (1972), 'The Behaviour of Unemployment and Unfilled Vacancies: Great Britain: 1958–1971, A Comment', *Economic Journal*, 82, 192–201.
Foster, J.I. (1974), 'The Relationship between Unemployment and Vacancies in Great Britain (1958–72): Some Further Evidence', in D. Laidler and D. Purdey (eds), *Inflation and Labour Markets*, Manchester: Manchester University Press.

Greene, W.H. (1993), *Econometric Analysis*, New York: Macmillan.
Grip, A. de (1987), *Onderwijs en arbeidsmarkt: scholingsdiscrepanties* [Education and Labour-Market: training discrepancies], dissertation.
Gujarati, D. (1972), 'The Behaviour of Unemployment and Unfilled Vacancies: Great Britain, 1958–1971', *Economic Journal*, 82, 195–204.
Harper, I.R. (1980), 'The Relationship between Unemployment and Unfilled Vacancies in Australia, 1952–1978', *The Economic Record*, 56, 231–342.
Hartog, J. (1980), *Tussen vraag en aanbod* [Between demand and supply], Leyden: Stenford Kruse.
Holt, C.C. and M.H. David (1966), 'The Concept of Vacancies in a Dynamic Theory of the Labour Market', in *National Bureau of Economic Research, Measurement and Interpretation of Job Vacancies*, New York.
Jackman, R., C. Pissarides and S. Savouri (1990), 'Labour Market Policies in the OECD Countries', *Economic Policy*, 5.
Koning, J. de (1993) 'Measuring the placement effects of two wage-subsidy schemes for the long-term unemployed', in *Empirical Economics*, **18** (3), 447–68.
Koning, J. de (1994), 'A Micro-to-Macro Approach to the Labour-Market Process', *Series: Foundations of Empirical Economic Research*, Netherlands Economic Institute, 1984/12.
Koning, J. de and P.J. van Nes (1991), 'A Quantitative Approach to Process Evaluation: The Case of the Vermeend-Moor Act', in *Government and Policy*, 9, 111–18.
Koning, J. de, P.A. Donker van Heel, A. Gelderblom, P.J. van Nes and C.T. Zandvliet (1995), 'Arbeidsvoorziening in perspectief. Evaluatie Arbeidsvoorzieningswet 1991–1994', Deelonderzoek B *resultaten en kosten*, Den Haag: Uitgave Ministerie van Sociale Zaken en Werkgelegenheid.
Koning, J. de and M. Arents (1997), *The impact of active labour market policy on the transition from unemployment to employment*, paper for the 9th EALE conference, Aarhus, 25–9 September.
Kooiman, P. (1994), 'Smoothing the Aggregate Fix-Price Model and the Use of Business Survey Data', *Economic Journal*, 94, 899–913.
Kooiman, P. and T. Kloek (1979), *Aggregation of Micromarkets in Disequilibrium: Theory and Application to the Dutch Labour Market 1948–1975*, paper presented at the European Meeting of the Econometric Society, Rotterdam.
Kooiman, P. and T. Kloek (1985), 'An Empirical Two Market Disequilibrium Model for Dutch Manufacturing', *European Economic Review*, 29, 323–54.
Lambert, J.-P. (1984), *Disequilibrium Macro Models Based on Business Survey Data: Theory and Estimation for the Belgian Manufacturing Sector*, unpublished doctoral dissertation.
Layard R., S. Nickell and R. Jackman (1991), *Unemployment: Macroeconomic Performance and the Labour Market*, Oxford University Press.
Lehmann, H. (1993), *The effectiveness of the Restart Programme and the Enterprise Allowance Scheme*, Discussion Paper No. 139, Centre for Economic Performance, LSE.
Muellbauer, J. (1978), *Macrotheory vs Macroeconometrics: The Treatment of 'Disequilibrium' in Macro Models*, paper presented at the European Meeting of the Econometric Society, Geneva.
Muysken, J., H. Bierings and E. de Regt (1993), 'Vacancy Data, the Employment Function and Structural Unemployment in the Netherlands', *Research Memorandum* 93–038, Limburg University.
Ohlsson, H. (1995), 'Job Creation Programmes as Stabilisation Policy Measures', in

J. Johannesson and E. Wadensjö (eds), *Labour Market Policy at the Crossroad*, Report no. 34 from the Expert Group for Labour Market Policy Evaluation Studies (EFA), Ministry of Labour, Stockholm, pp. 29–55.

OECD (1993), *Employment Outlook*, Paris.

OECD (1994), 'Job Study', *Evidence and Explanations*, Paris.

Ours, J.C. van (1991), 'The Efficiency of the Dutch Labour Market in Matching Unemployment and Vacancies', *Economist*, **139** (3).

Peters, A. and G. Schmid (1982a), *Aggregierte Wirkungsanalyse des arbeitsmarktpolitischen Programms der Bundesregierung für Regionen mit besonderen Beschäftigungsproblemen*, WZB Discussion Paper IIM/LMP 82-1, Berlin: WZB.

Peters, A. and G. Schmid (1982b), *Aggregierte Wirkungsanalyse des arbeitsmarktpolitischen Programms der Bundesregierung für Regionen mit besonderen Beschäftigungsproblemen. Analyse der Beschäftigungswirkungen*, WZB Discussion Paper IIM/LMP 82-32, Berlin: WZB.

Phelps, E.S. (1970), 'Money Wage Dynamics and Labour Market Equilibrium', in E.S. Phelps *et al.*, *Microeconomic Foundations of Employment & Inflation Theory*, London: Macmillan.

Reid, F. and N.M. Meltz (1979), 'Causes of Shifts in the Unemployment–Vacancy Relationship: An Empirical Analysis for Canada', *Review of Economics and Statistics*, 81, 470–75.

Schmid, G. (1996a), 'Process Evaluation: Policy Formation and Implementation', in G. Schmid, J. O'Reilly, K. Schömann (eds), *International Handbook of Labour Market Policy and Evaluation*, Cheltenham: Edward Elgar, pp. 198–231.

Schmid, G. (1996b), 'New Public Management of Further Training', in G. Schmid, J. O'Reilly and K. Schömann (eds), *International Handbook of Labour Market Policy and Evaluation*, Cheltenham: Edward Elgar, pp. 747–90.

Skedinger P. (1995), 'Employment Policies and the Displacement in the Youth Labour Market', *Swedish Economic Policy Review*, **2** (1).

Sneessens, H. and J.H. Drèze (1986), 'A Discussion of Belgian Unemployment, Combining Traditional Concepts and Disequilibrium Econometrics', *Economica*, 53, 89–119.

Warren, R.S. (1980), 'Unemployment and Unfilled Vacancies in U.S. Manufacturing: a Search Turn-over View', *Review of Economics and Statistics*, 62, 292–95.

3. Aggregate impact analysis of active labour market policy in France and Sweden: a regional approach

Dominique Anxo, Stéphane Carcillo and Christine Erhel

In their seminal work, Bourdet and Persson (1995) concluded that active labour market policies (ALMPs) were more efficient in Sweden than in France in the 1980s. However, since the beginning of the 1990s (Anxo and Erhel, 1998), policies in these countries have converged. Levels of active expenditure and activity rates are now very similar in France and Sweden. In Sweden, 'mixed' programmes combining training and temporary work, as well as new job subsidies, have been substituted for the traditional tools of ALMP (relief works and mobility grants); while in France, on the other hand, various job-creation programmes have been developed and ALMP has been implemented according to more decentralized management techniques. Consequently, the first question addressed in this chapter is whether these changes have altered the impact of active policies on the respective labour markets. It should also be noted that Bourdet and Persson used aggregate and annual data, which severely reduced the number of observations. Our study uses monthly data aggregated at the regional level, which provides a sounder empirical basis for the evaluation. Moreover, the nature of our data allows us to investigate regional differences, which we deal with in accounting for potential idiosyncratic effects at the regional level – a problem which has so far received relatively little attention in the literature.

In the first section of this chapter, we present the main components and features of active labour market policy in France and Sweden, as well as data concerning exclusion on the labour market. In section 2, we derive the estimated equations from an augmented matching function, and address the theoretical and methodological problems of such aggregate impact evaluations. In section 3, we describe the data and the estimated equation. We present and interpret our results in section 4. Finally, in section 5, we present a summary of our conclusions.

1 ACTIVE LABOUR MARKET POLICIES IN FRANCE AND SWEDEN: AN OVERVIEW

The comparison of French and Swedish employment policies is still strongly influenced by analyses produced in the 1970s and 1980s. These studies highlighted institutional-type differences (integration and a high degree of consensus surrounding active labour market policy in Sweden, versus fragmentation and the absence of participation by employers and trade unions in France); and, in relation to this, differences in the intensity and structure of active policies (higher level of expenditure and rate of activity in Sweden).

This comparative typology is no longer valid for the period covered by our data set (1992–5): this section briefly outlines the most important evolutionary processes which have occurred in the institutional systems and in the national policy mix since the late 1980s. These features provide the background for our evaluation.

1.1 Some Stylized Facts about Labour Market Policy in France and Sweden

The following developments are based on annual financial data, published by the Délégation de l'Animation de la Recherche des Etudes et des Statistiques (DARES) in France, and the national labour market boards (AMS) in Sweden. We may assume that definition of labour market policy expenditure is the same in both countries.[1]

In terms of relative levels, labour market policy expenditure is higher in Sweden than in France (see Figure 3.1). In the 1990s, expenditures in Sweden rose more dramatically than during previous recessions due to the high rate of unemployment: whereas unemployment had been contained at 3 per cent during previous downturns, it reached 8 per cent in 1994. In France, meanwhile, expenditures appeared to follow the economic cycle: a drop in the level of expenditure in 1988–9 was followed by a phase of strong growth up to 1993 and a preliminary reduction in 1994. Overall, we note a rise in the responsiveness of labour market policy to changes in economic activity.

The 1990s show converging activity rates in the two countries (see Figure 3.2). In Sweden, the change in the structure of total expenditure can be seen as a response to a rise in the costs of unemployment benefits, and consequently of passive expenditures. In the French case, the share of active expenditure began to increase starting in 1985. Initially, this change appeared to be the indirect effect of the cut in the amounts devoted to early retirement programmes; and then, from 1990, as the consequence of a real increase in active expenditures.

Source: AMS, DARES.

Figure 3.1 Labour market policy expenditure in France and Sweden, 1973–94 (% GDP)

An analysis of the expenditure by categories highlights structural and functional developments specific to the 1990s (see Figure 3.3). In Sweden, there is a noticeable weakening of the traditional methods of active labour market policy, namely in the areas of job-creation measures (for example, relief works and public sector jobs) and aids for mobility. As part of its 'solidarity wage policy', these two types of programmes were at one time a cornerstone of the Swedish model of active labour market policy. In terms of level of expenditure, job-creation measures have since been supplanted by training programmes. The new measures (such as the 'temporary trainee replacement' measures, youth training programmes and 'work experience' programmes created in 1991 and 1992) are in line with a policy of substituting mixed programmes (which combine temporary employment and training) with 'pure' job-creation measures, such as relief works. At the same time, the definition of the job-creation category continues to evolve owing to the establishment of new measures benefiting firms (General Employment Subsidy (GAS), then Targeted Employment Subsidy (RAS), in 1994 and 1995).

In comparison with Sweden, all expenditure categories are fixed at a lower percentage of GDP in France, except for training measures that show compara-

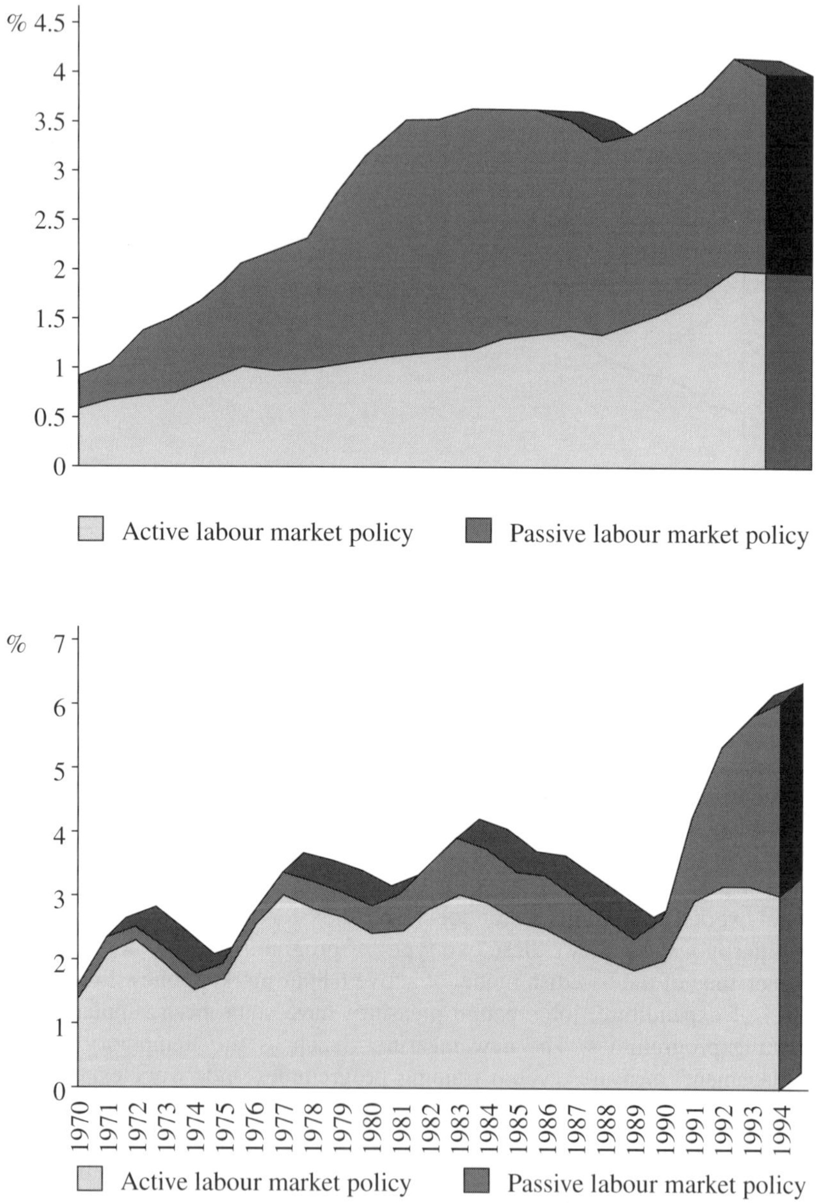

Source: AMS, DARES.

Figure 3.2 Active and passive expenditures in France and Sweden, 1973–94 (% GDP)

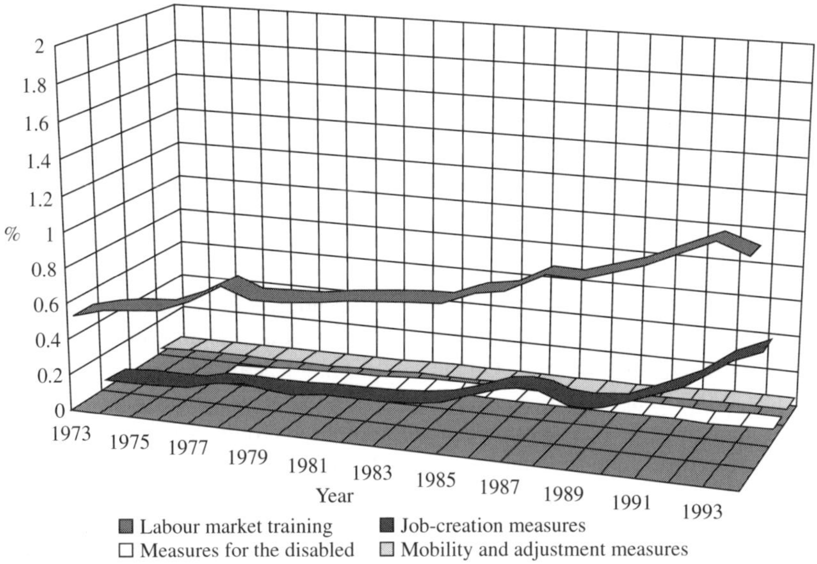

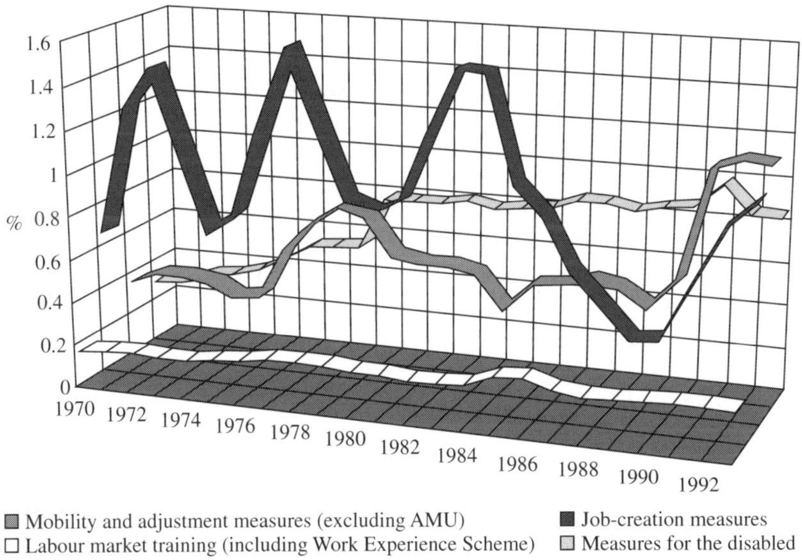

Source: AMS, DARES.

Figure 3.3 Active expenditure by categories in France and Sweden (% GDP)

ble levels at the end of the period (around 1 per cent of GDP). This exception marks the significance of vocational training within the traditional structure of French labour market policy. The most noteworthy development concerns the 'job creation and work promotion' category, which has experienced strong growth since 1989. It should also be noted that this increase is more the result of a succession of new measures than of expanding existing measures. The 'job-creation and work promotion' category includes of a series of heterogeneous interventions in which firms are exempted from social security contributions (for example, 'the first worker in', 'the second worker in' and part-time work); as well as the creation of employment in the non-profit sector (for example, employment-solidarity contracts, return-to-work contracts and, more recently, youth-employment contracts). On the whole, French active labour market policy in the 1990s relied quite heavily on the reduction of labour costs through targeted measures, as well as on general exemptions for less-qualified workers.

These reforms and gradual changes in the national patterns of intervention on the labour market are, of course, related to the economic cycle; especially in the case of Sweden. This effect was accentuated by major changes in the foundations and instruments of the Swedish model. In order to illustrate the evolution of active labour market policy components in France and Sweden, we now provide a brief overview of the organization and implementation of active labour market policy in both countries.

1.2 Institutions and Implementation of Active Labour Market Policy

Rather than presenting a detailed description of the institutional structures responsible for the implementation of active labour market policy, we will instead focus on the organizational principles that underlie their functioning.

Social and political consensus on labour market policy

The unique nature of Sweden's labour market policy is generally attributed to the existence of a broad consensus between industry and government since the establishment of the 'solidarity wage policy' in 1957. The application of the wage-setting principle 'equal pay for equal work', irrespective of industry or firm profitability, required the use of mobility measures to encourage an efficient reallocation of the labour force. Thus active labour market policy was – alongside macroeconomic or wage policies – an important component of the 'Swedish model' (Anxo, 1994). From an institutional perspective, this consensus on state intervention in the labour market took the form of a tripartite administration at every institutional level (national, regional and local) of labour market policy.

In France, on the other hand, employment policy was not established as part of a coherent model, but arose in successive stages in response to the need to counteract the increase in unemployment. Moreover, the French government took the initiative in instituting employment policy, while employers and unions confined themselves to the management of contributory systems (unemployment insurance and some early retirement programmes). Thus, until the early 1990s, an important difference between the French and the Swedish institutional systems was the respective levels of active involvement of employers and unions in the design and implementation of active labour market policies. However, developments since the beginning of the 1990s make it necessary to qualify this distinction.

The move in Sweden towards a decentralized wage-bargaining system is an illustration of the way in which the solidarity wage policy model came to be questioned. Although an important feature of Swedish labour market policy has been the strong involvement of the social partners, the deterioration of the Swedish model of regulation became apparent when tripartite representation ceased in 1993 following a decision by the employers' confederation (SAF) to leave the directorates of the national and county labour market boards. None the less, employers still participate at the local level.

An opposite trend is found in France, where the involvement of employers and unions in matters of active labour market policy is increasing. This does not, however, stem from a structural modification of the institutional system, but from a tendency towards greater cooperation in the management of unemployment insurance system and active policies. Some new programmes aimed at promoting employment – and which therefore should come under the heading of active expenditures – are now financed by the unemployment insurance funds (for example, allowances for training and redeployment and cooperation agreements). These new developments indicate an acceptance by both employers and unions of the legitimacy of active labour market policies.

A decentralization trend

In both countries, an increase in decentralization of the implementation of active measures can be observed.

The high level of decentralization and autonomy in the organizational structure of the labour market authority (AMS) appears to be one of the salient features of Swedish labour market policy. In Sweden the role of the government and parliament is limited to preparing legislation and the budget, developing general policy guidelines and exercising general supervision over the AMS; while responsibility for the implementation of labour market policy, as well as the preparation of the initial budget proposals, lies with the AMS. The central administration determines the division of the budget for programmes in different counties. The various schemes within the programmes are chosen at the county level. Finally, the operational responsibility of implementation – particularly decisions regarding the assignment of participants to the various ALMP schemes – lies with each local employment agency. The Swedish system thus allows for a significant degree of autonomy at both the regional and local levels. The Swedish labour market policy administration furthermore relies on management by objectives (MBO), and not on administration based on regulations and directives. On the whole, the system is characterized by real decentralization and flexible management. This decentralized infrastructure has created a favourable institutional framework for a flexible and efficient labour market policy (see also Chapter 9).

In comparison with the degree of integration of the Swedish institutions, the French system appears fragmented and – despite tendencies towards decentralization[2] and greater flexibility in management techniques – continues to be characterized by hierarchical administrative structures. In practice, eligibility requirements for the programmes, as well as the financial means allocated to them, are determined at the national level. The core institutions in the field of active labour market policy implementation are the labour and employment central offices at the *département* level, and the local employment agencies. The local agencies are headed up by the national employment agency (ANPE), which is responsible for registering the unemployed and helping them in their job search. Some recent studies (Bessy *et al.*, 1995) have shown that, despite the continued hierarchical control of the labour and employment ministry, the labour and employment offices in the *départements* are no longer satisfied with managing employment measures as a purely administrative task. Increasingly, they are taking part in local cooperation networks involving various local political authorities (municipalities, *département* and regional councils). Besides reinforcing and improving the functioning of labour administration, these forms of local management permit greater flexibility in meeting local needs.

Despite important formal and functional differences in the institutional frameworks of active labour market policies, the decentralization of implementation appears to be a common tendency in both national systems. An examination of trends in institutional systems in the 1990s thus highlights converging features in the two countries.

1.3 Social Exclusion and Labour Market Policy

Unemployment duration can be interpreted as an indicator of exclusion on the labour market. This subsection will analyse its evolution in France and in Sweden.

In 1998, almost 40 per cent of French job seekers were classified as long-term unemployed (more than one year), compared with about 30 per cent in Sweden (see Tables 3.1 and 3.2). In both countries, the share of long-term unemployed is on the rise. From the mid-1970s to 1998, the share of long-term unemployment increased more that twofold in France and six times in Sweden. But there are differences between the two countries: until the end of the 1980s, long-term unemployment in Sweden remained much lower than in France. While the sharp increase in long-term unemployment in Sweden coincided with a dramatic rise in overall unemployment in the early 1990s, long-term unemployment in France started to climb in the early 1980s. In 1998, the average duration of unemployment was much longer in France than in Sweden (16 months in France, versus 4.5 months in Sweden; see Table 3.2). While the average unemployment duration increased sharply in France during the period studied (from eight months in 1980 to 16 months in 1998), the average duration in Sweden remained stable at around four months. These diverging trends suggest that social exclusion is more pronounced in France

Table 3.1 *Share of long-term unemployed (more than one year), by age and sex (%)*

France	1975	1980	1985	1990	1995	1998
Total	**16.7**	**32.5**	**46.8**	**35.3**	**39.5**	**41.1**
Men (total)	**13.7**	**30.4**	**42.7**	**32.9**	**38.7**	**40.1**
15–24	8.4	15.0	32.0	14.7	19.0	21.4
25–49	11.3	30.5	44.1	36.3	40.7	40.5
50+	30.0	55.6	64.0	55.9	57.8	60.3
Women (total)	**19.0**	**34.0**	**50.5**	**37.0**	**40.3**	**41.9**
15–24	12.7	24.3	42.0	20.4	23.3	20.0
25–49	20.2	36.6	52.9	38.1	42.5	43.7
50+	35.2	58.0	71.3	66.9	60.6	61.7
Sweden	1976	1980	1985	1990	1995	1998
Total	**5.4**	**5.6**	**11.4**	**4.4**	**23.9**	**28.6**
Men (total)	**5.2**	**6.8**	**11.1**	**5.1**	**27.0**	**30.7**
16–24	0.0	1.9	1.0	0.7	14.0	11.9
25–44	4.2	5.1	5.7	3.4	24.9	28.6
45+	12.5	18.4	28.1	8.5	37.5	45.9
Women (total)	**5.6**	**4.5**	**11.7**	**3.7**	**19.8**	**25.9**
16–24	2.6	1.1	2.1	1.6	8.6	9.3
25–44	3.9	4.0	6.5	2.2	17.4	24.5
45+	27.3	22.9	52.5	8.5	39.1	45.0

Source: INSEE, Enquêtes Emploi, Données Sociales 1999 (unemployment definition BIT); Labour Force Survey (AKU), Statistics Sweden.

Table 3.2 Average unemployment duration for registered unemployed (in months)

France	1975	1980	1985	1990	1995	1998
Men	6.7	10.6	14.6	13.5	14.3	15.5
Women	8.3	12.3	17.3	14.3	14.9	16.4
Total	**7.6**	**11.7**	**16.0**	**13.9**	**14.6**	**16.0**
Sweden	1976	1980	1985	1990	1995	1998
Men	3.6	3.7	4.0	4.2	4.2	4.5
Women	3.8	3.7	3.7	3.7	3.8	4.3
Total	**3.7**	**3.7**	**3.8**	**3.9**	**4.0**	**4.4**

Source: INSEE, Enquêtes Emploi, Données Sociales 1999 (unemployment definition BIT) and Labour Force Survey (AKU), Statistics Sweden.

than in Sweden. Moreover, long-term unemployment in France appears to be characterized by a higher degree of selectivity. Although long-term unemployment varies significantly with age and educational attainment in both countries, the share of long-term unemployment among older workers and women remains higher in France, despite some tendencies towards convergence in the 1990s (see Table 3.1.)

In this context, it is possible to argue that, despite the presence of labour market policy, the French labour market has displayed an increasing tendency towards social exclusion over the last two decades. While some programmes have been targeted at the long-term unemployed (for example, employment solidarity contracts, reintegration contracts and, more recently, employment initiative contacts), empirical evidence shows that their impact on the unemployment structure has been limited. In Sweden, on the other hand, the share of long-term unemployment and the average duration of unemployment – in spite of the sharp employment downturn in the early 1990s – is much lower than in France, indicating a lower degree of social exclusion. The fact that unemployed job seekers have the right to be enrolled in active labour market schemes after an unemployment period of six months may partly explain the contrasting developments in the two countries, and the relatively limited increase of average unemployment duration in Sweden.

2 A MODEL OF AGGREGATE IMPACT EVALUATION

2.1 Matching Technology and ALMPs

Our evaluation relies on a flow approach of the labour market. As such, we consider hirings as the outcome of a matching technology which, in the spirit of Blanchard and Diamond (1989), is represented by a constant returns matching function:

$$h_t = \gamma \cdot m(U_t, V_t) \tag{3.1}$$

$$\text{with } m = (V_t)^{\alpha} \cdot (U_t)^{(1-\alpha)}$$

where h_t is the outflow of hirings at time t, V_t the stock of vacancies and U_t the stock of unemployed. γ is a constant which represents factors influencing the technology.

Drawing on Bellmann and Jackman (1996a), we introduce the effect of ALMPs by augmenting the matching function as follows:

$$h_t = \gamma \cdot c_t \cdot m(U_t, V_t) \tag{3.2}$$

where c_t is the part of the influencing factors specifically due to ALMP programmes over time. This form supposes that such programmes have an impact on the overall matching technology, and particularly on the research intensity of job seekers and the degree of mismatch between supply and demand.

From (3.1) we obtain the hiring probability for an unemployed person:

$$\frac{h_t}{U_t} = \gamma \cdot c_t \cdot m\left(\frac{V_t}{U_t}, 1\right) \tag{3.3}$$

that is:

$$\frac{h_t}{U_t} = \gamma \cdot c_t f\left(\frac{V_t}{U_t}\right) \tag{3.3$'$}$$

with $f(-) = m(-, 1)$.

At the steady state equilibrium $\delta U_t/\delta t = 0$ and $\delta h_t/\delta t = 0$, which implies:

$$\frac{h}{U} = \gamma \cdot c \cdot f\left(\frac{V}{U}\right) \tag{3.3$''$}$$

or, equivalently:

$$\ln\left(\frac{h}{U}\right) = \ln(\gamma) + \ln(c) + \alpha \ln\left(\frac{V}{U}\right) \tag{3.4}$$

Now, c is made of the effect of several types of programmes on matching:

$$c_t = \left(1 + \sum_{j=1}^{p} k_j M_j\right)$$

where M_j, $j \in [1, p]$ measures the intensity of the programme j, relative to unemployment (programme inflows/unemployment). These ratios being quite small, equation (3.4) becomes:

$$\ln\left(\frac{h}{U}\right) = \ln\gamma + \sum_{j=1}^{p} k_j M_j + \alpha \ln\left(\frac{V}{U}\right) \tag{3.5}$$

We will base the equation we estimate on the latter.

2.2 Theoretical and Methodological Considerations in Aggregate Impact Analysis

The use of this kind of model to evaluate labour market policies raises several problems, including difficulties in identifying the exact nature of the measured effect. Bellmann and Jackman (1996a) propose this methodology as a measurement tool of the net effect of labour market policies (that is, given windfall, substitution and displacement effects on outflows from unemployment). Considering, however, Calmfors' (1994) distinction between cosmetic and productive effects on the one hand, and the risk of simultaneity bias in the estimation on the other, this goal appears to be empirically questionable. These problems cannot be ignored and must be answered before we can continue.

Cosmetic versus productive effects

According to Calmfors (1994), the effect of ALMP on unemployment as measured by macroeconometric studies could be merely a statistical effect if the observed decrease in unemployment equals the rise in programme participants. As such, ALMP is efficient only if the various measures induce a decrease in overall unemployment, that is, the sum of unemployed and programme participants. Moreover, the vacancies variable in the Beveridge curve framework should only account for regular job offers, excluding ALMP measures. Where this is not the case, it is impossible to assess the net effect of the former.

The application of Calmfors' criticism to our matching model results in the following requirements:

- unemployment (*U*) should be defined as the sum of registered unemployed and measures participants;
- vacancies (*V*) should exclude job offers related to measures; and
- logically, hirings (*h*) should only include regular matchings and exclude those directly linked to measures.

According to Calmfors, the probability of a programme participant matching a regular vacancy is the principal criterion by which the measured impact of ALMP should be assessed. Despite its analytical virtues, this approach not only rests upon questionable assumptions, but also seems impossible to apply to the existing data.

On theoretical grounds, Jackman (1994) questions the integration of training or job help scheme participants to the unemployment variable, since there is no reason for these participants to behave like unemployed people. Besides the problem of heterogeneity of behaviours of unemployed people as defined by Calmfors, there are no empirical grounds on which to base the difference in nature between scheme and non-scheme hirings. Microeconometric studies generally identify considerable similarities between scheme and non-scheme hirings. As such, the selectivity effect of ALMP programmes tends to reproduce a normal feature of the labour market (Bonnal *et al.*, 1994; Saucier and Sofer, 1995). Finally, Calmfors' definitions do not apply to aggregate data either in France or in Sweden, where scheme and non-scheme vacancies and hirings are not distinguishable.

ALMP impact and simultaneity bias

In aggregate impact evaluation methodology, simultaneity bias stems from the relationship between the assumed impact of measures on the labour market functioning (dependent variables) and the intensity of ALMP schemes, measured either in terms of expenditures or number of participants. Indeed, if a fall (or a rise) in job seekers' hiring probability leads to an increase (or a decrease) in the number of participants in the various ALMP schemes, then positive estimated coefficients within the matching function framework cannot be interpreted as the effect of ALMP on hiring probability. This could be considered a serious limitation to the evaluations based on aggregate data, although it is doubtful such a bias exists in our case for several reasons.

First, the evaluation does not rest on an unemployment equation, but on a matching function. A simultaneity bias would have a greater effect on unemployment equations than it has on flow models (Jackman, 1994) since in the latter – but not in the former – case, the dependent variable is not the direct object of political decisions. In addition, Calmfors and Skedinger (1995) maintain this problem is more likely to be found when variables for the intensity of ALMP are normalized by the labour force. In that specific case, these variables are seemingly negatively correlated to the rate of unemployment from an international comparison perspective.

Moreover, empirical evidence does not support the assumption of reversed causality for the 1992–5 period: the Swedish reaction function is no longer counter-cyclical and it is impossible to detect joint variations between unemployment and the number of scheme participants in France (Erhel, 1998). This conclusion is not, however, straightforward in cross-sectional terms. Calmfors and Skedinger (1995) make two assumptions in the regional determination of the number of participants: first, they assert that this number may be linked to the number of parliamentary seats assigned to left-wing parties; second, they suppose the existence of implicit national standards for the accommodation rate.[3] The first of these assumptions is quite improbable despite the historical link between the development of employment policies and the social democratic party in Sweden. Indeed, the implementation of ALMP is the responsibility of the AMS, not the Swedish parliament. Finally, Calmfors and Skedinger fail to submit their hypothesis to empirical assessment.

3 THE DATA AND THE ESTIMATED EQUATION

The evaluation model introduced above requires aggregate data relating labour market functioning in terms of flows and stocks, including in- and outflows from ALMP measures. The data we have used are regional and monthly, which allows us to extend the evaluation literature on the subject, but imposes some availability limitations given the data requirements of equation (3.5) and specific econometric methods for their treatment.

3.1 Availability

Table 3.3 compares the model requirements and the data actually used in our estimations. For both countries, we used administrative data issued by DARES for France and AMS for Sweden. First, it is important to note that the dependent variable is a proxy: unemployment outflows towards employment underestimate transitions from unemployment towards employment. This is because these outflows exclude control absentees, which account for a significant portion of hiring occurring independently of employment agencies. Given the availability of aggregate time series, this variable appeared to be the best among several possibilities.

Table 3.3 Data description for France and Sweden

Model variables	France	Sweden
Dependent variable: Outflow from unemployment (towards employment) = *L_HU* = ln [unemployment outflow towards employment/stock of registered unemployed people]	*Variable used in estimations*: *L_HU* = ln [employment demand decrease due to hirings/stock of employment demands at the end of the month (*DEFM*)] Source: ANPE Availability: 01/1988–05/1995	*Variable used in estimations*: *L_HU* = ln [number of unemployed people leaving unemployment towards employment/unemployment stock at the end of the month] Source: AMS Availability: 10/1991–12/1995
Independent variable: *'Tightness on the labour market'* = *L_VU* = ln [registered employment vacancies (flow or stock)/stock of registered unemployed people]	*Variable used in estimations:* *L_VU* = ln [job offers registered at the end of the month (stocks)/*DEFM*] Source: ANPE Availability: 10/1986–03/1995	*Variable used in estimations:* 1. *L_VU* = ln [employment vacancies at the end of the month/unemployment stock at the end of the month] 2. *L_VU*1 = ln [new vacancies inflows/stock of unemployment at the end of the month] Source: AMS Availability: 01/1979–12/1995
Independent variables: *ALMPs* For each scheme, the built variable = scheme inflow/stock of registered unemployed people	*Variable used in estimations:* – 3 types of measures (aggregation of flows by type of measures) – registered unemployment = *DEFM* Sources: ANPE/DARES Availability: 01/1992–12/1996 Global data on training not available	*Variable used in estimations:* – 3 types of measures (aggregated by AMS) – registered unemployment = stock at the end of the month Source: AMS Availability: 01/1979–12/1995

Second, the job vacancies variable is not exactly the same in both countries, although the nature of the underlying data is identical. For Sweden we have available both flows and month-end stocks; whereas in France, only stocks were observed.[4] More serious, however, is the risk that French data on vacancies are biased, given the market share of *Agence Nationale Pour l'Emploi* (the National Agency For Employment, *ANPE*).[5] We will therefore assume that the influence of the vacancy variable is underestimated in our results for France, both in absolute terms and in comparison with Sweden.[6]

Finally, the ALMP flow variables are pooled according to the following classical typology:[7] employment creation schemes are distinguished from subsidies schemes and training schemes (see Table 3.4). The training categories are not, however, comparable between the two countries. In France, the data takes into account alternate training programmes (combining classroom training and a subsidized job), including apprenticeship (*apprentissage*); whereas the Swedish data encompass all the training schemes designed for the unemployed registered with the AMS, including classroom training. The samples are comparable in size (between three and four years). For France, the change in the definition of unemployment categories operated by the ANPE from May 1995 fixed the upper bound of the sample, which starts in 01/1992 and ends in 02/1995 (the last two months suffered from missing data). For Sweden, the period runs from 10/1991 to 12/1995; the lower bound being the availability limit of unemployment outflows series.

Table 3.4 ALMP variables for France and Sweden

France	Sweden
DPUBU: employment creation schemes, public and non-tradable sector, inflows/*DEFM;*	*DPUBUF*: relief works, inflows/ unemployment stock
JTRU: alternate training schemes, inflows/*DEFM*	*USUPF*: training schemes, inflows/ unemployment stock
DPRU: employment subsidies schemes, tradable sector, inflows/*DEFM*	*OTHERU*: other ALMPs, inflows/ unemployment stock

The level of aggregation is the county in Sweden (Län) and the region in France. These levels of aggregation fit administrative levels, but do not coincide *a priori* with consistent functioning labour market areas. This could induce a supplementary bias in the estimations. It is, however, reasonable to assume that this will not be a problem in Sweden, where inter-county worker

Table 3.5 Descriptive statistics

Variable	Mean	STD	Minimum	Maximum
France				
HU	0.0459	0.0121	0.0200	0.0969
VU	0.0150	0.0071	0.0055	0.0645
DPRU	0.0096	0.0039	0.0016	0.0246
DPUBU	0.0192	0.0063	0.0027	0.0518
JTRU	0.0086	0.0055	0.0021	0.0496
N=819				
Sweden				
HU	0.1211	0.0441	0.0352	0.4372
VU	0.0371	0.0344	0.0050	0.3518
DPUBU	0.0101	0.0067	0.0004	0.0497
USUPF	0.0385	0.0309	0.000	0.2424
OTHERU	0.0338	0.0300	0.000	0.2405
N=1173				

mobility is low. For France, we have chosen the regional rather than *département* level to cope with this possible bias. Consequently, the number of observation units is 21 for France and 23 for Sweden. Descriptive statistics for all 819 French and 1173 Swedish observations are reported in Table 3.5.

3.2 The data profiles

Variations

The dependent variable follows a decreasing trend in both countries, which is consistent with the global worsening in labour markets functioning over the period (see Figures 3.4 and 3.5). From 1993 onwards, the situation improved slightly in France but not in Sweden. Overall, the hiring probability for unemployed people is higher in France than in Sweden. Moreover, this variable displays a clear seasonal pattern in both countries; with an increase at the beginning of the year, followed by a drop at mid-year (July in Sweden and August in France), and a peak in September. This seasonal pattern coincides with the hiring behaviour of firms.

With the exception of job-creation programmes, there is a significant gap between the national levels of scheme participation probability. This can be largely explained by differences in ALMP intensity which persisted through the 1990s, although such policies were challenged in Sweden during this

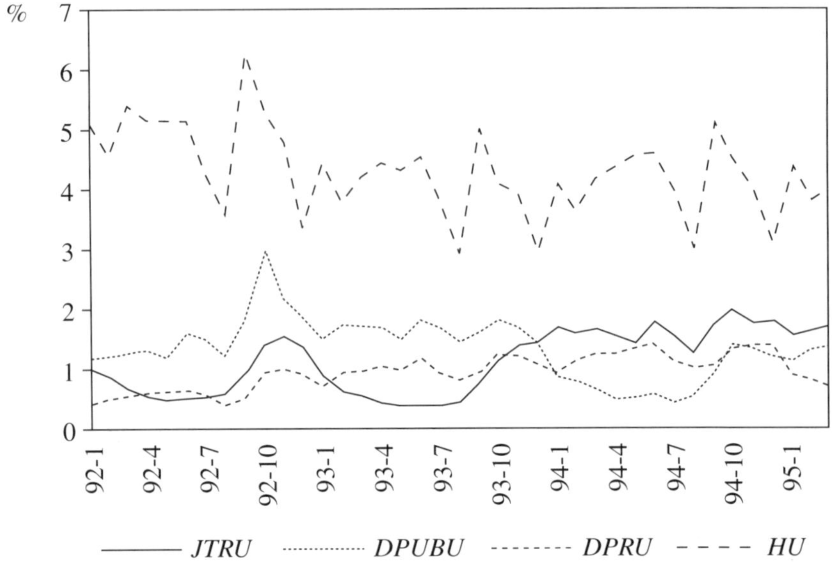

Notes: *DPUBU* = employment creation schemes, public and non-tradable sector, inflows/Stock of Employment Demands at the End of the Month; *JTRU* = alternative training schemes, inflows/Stock of Employment Demands at the End of the Month; *DPRU*= employment subsidies schemes, tradable sector, inflows/Stock of Employment Demands at the End of the Month; *HU* = outflow from unemployment (towards employment).

Figure 3.4 Outflows from unemployment and participant inflows into the various labour market programmes (10/1991–12/1995), (% of unemployment), France, 1992–1 to 1995–3[8]

period. While the trend in France, where active policies continued to expand throughout the 1990s, is clearly positive, Sweden experienced a symmetrical evolution during the same period. Moreover, training and subsidy schemes display a strong seasonal pattern in France and Sweden.

The observed seasonality of the dependent and some of the independent variables means we have corrected our series using the X11 procedure in SAS. This treatment allows us to increase the degree of freedom of the final model, which will not include seasonal dummies.

Structure

The regional data are pooled to form a single large sample with cross-sectional (i=1…N, N=21 for France and N=23 for Sweden) and longitudinal dimensions (t=1…T, T=39 for France and T=51 for Sweden). In order to deal with unobserved individual and time-specific effects, we have introduced

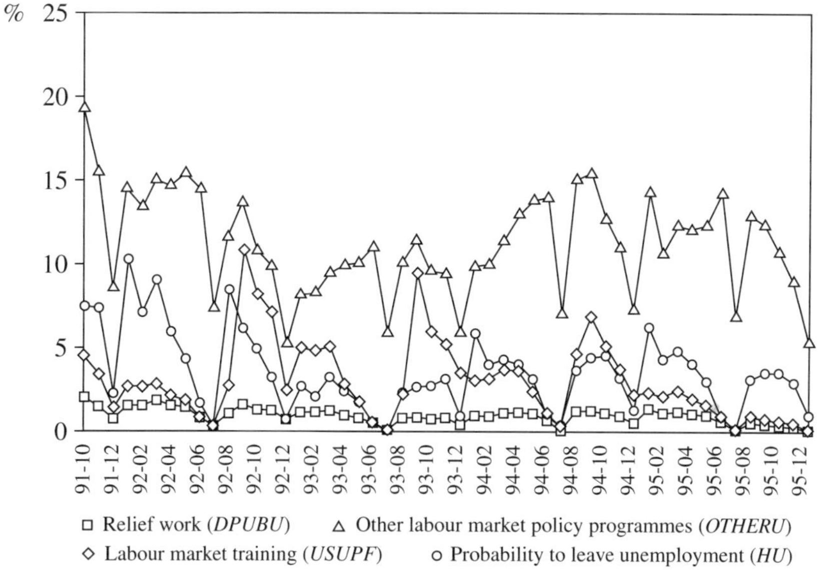

Figure 3.5 Outflows from unemployment and participant inflows into the various labour market programmes (10/1991–12/1995), (% of unemployment), Sweden

dummy variables: R_i equals one for region i and zero elsewhere, and DT_t equals one at period t and zero elsewhere.

The use of pooled data has two advantages (Hsiao, 1985). First, it provides us with a much larger sample and probably increases the accuracy of estimations. Second, this approach minimizes the risk of regarding exogenous variables as explanatory that would only be significant by accident.

3.3 A Double Fixed Effect Model

Since our sample is exhaustive (and not a random draw in a larger population) and theoretically contains all the information required and all the investigated inferences from every region of both countries, the fixed effect model seems more suitable (Balestra, 1992; Hsiao, 1995). In addition to the existence of regional ('individual') effects, we consider in the fixed effect model the possibility of period heterogeneity, which can be accounted for by a time fixed effect through period dummies. This allows us to deal with the specificities of some periods of time in our samples.

The basic calculable form of equation (3.5) is:

$$L\_HU = aL\_VU + b_1 DPUBU + b_2 DPRU + b_3 JTRU + u \qquad (3.5')$$

Including the regional and time dummies, according to the double fixed effect assumption, equation (3.5′) becomes:

$$L\_HU = aL\_VU + b_1 DPUBU + b_2 DPRU + b_3 JTRU + \sum_1^N c_i R_i + \sum_1^T d_t DT_t + u \qquad (3.6)$$

Equation (3.6) is the estimated form of our model.

4 RESULTS

We began with an estimated equation (3.6) on the basis of the de-seasonalized data with OLS. However, in order to deal with heteroscedasticity, inter-regional correlation and auto-correlation, we also carried out estimations using the Parks (1967) method. When we compared it with the model without dummies or a simple regional fixed effect model, we concluded that the double fixed effect model gave the best possible results. The estimated elasticities for the two countries allow us to interpret the results on a comparative basis.

4.1 Double Fixed Effect Results

On the basis of seasonal adjusted series, the best estimations rest on a double fixed effect model with regional and time dummies. For Sweden, we used two definitions of the vacancies variable (see Table 3.3): one based on the stock of vacancies at the end of the month, which is similar to the definition of this variable for France, and another based on the flow of vacancies. Tables 3.6 and 3.7 show the estimated variable coefficients obtained with the OLS and Parks methods.

The results of Fisher tests indicate that regional and time groups of dummies are significant overall. Except for the Parks estimation for Sweden using the stock data for vacancies (*L_VU*), all the coefficients of the explanatory variables are positive and significant. Because the stock data for Sweden are not as reliable as the flow data, the *L_VU* for Sweden is problematic. The coefficient estimates in the same region do not change signs from OLS to Parks methods. A Durbin–Watson test reveals the existence of auto-correlation using OLS, which speaks in favour of the Parks estimation. In the latter, and for Sweden, the employment-creation scheme coefficient is larger, and the coefficients for the other measures decrease compared to OLS. The effect

Table 3.6 Estimation of the double fixed effects model for Sweden (dependent variable L_HU*)*

Variables	OLS with *L_VU* (I)	Parks with *L_VU* (II)	OLS with *L_VU*1 (III)	Parks with *L_VU*1 (IV)
*L_VU/L_VU*1	0.03	0.01	0.15	0.10
	(2.461)	(0.988)	(10.329)	(10.856)
DPUBFU	7.53	8.63	7.01	8.31
	(11.035)	(17.099)	(10.702)	(16.436)
USUPF	1.31	0.6691	1.16	0.69
	(8.894)	(7.2347)	(8.214)	(7.467)
OTHERU	0.69	0.11	0.66	0.16
	(4.060)	(1.2785)	(4.090)	(1.839)

Notes: t-statistics in parentheses. I: ADJ-RSQUARE = 0.9984; all coefficients significant at 1% (including regional dummies). II: RSQUARE = 0.9999; all coefficients significant at 1% (including regional dummies) except *L_VU*; *OTHERU* not significant at usual thresholds. III: ADJ-RSQUARE = 0.9985; all coefficients significant at 1% (including regional dummies). IV: RSQUARE = 0.9999; all coefficients significant at 1% (including regional dummies) except *OTHERU* significant at 6 %.

Table 3.7 Estimation of the double fixed effects model for France (dependent variable L_HU*)*

Variables	OLS (I)	Parks (II)
L_VU	0.05	0.04
	(4.242)	(5.092)
DPRU	9.29	4.20
	(7.503)	(7.314)
DPUBU	3.14	2.95
	(4.285)	(8.745)
JTRU	5.60	3.95
	(4.396)	(7.538)

Notes: t-statistics in parentheses. I: ADJ-RSQUARE = 0.9987; all coefficients significant at 1% (including regional dummies). II: RSQUARE = 0.9999; all coefficients significant at 1% (including regional dummies).

is significantly different for France when we skip from one to the other method: the coefficient for the private employment subsidies increases at the expense of the coefficients of the other variables. Overall, these results confirm the interest in panel data regarding the stability and the quality of the estimations.

4.2 Elasticities

On the basis of equation (3.5), the elasticities of *L_VU*1 (for Sweden) and *L_VU* (for France) are a direct interpretation of the estimated coefficient (as in a Log-Log model). As for the other variables, elasticities are easily computed from the following equation:

$$e_{Y/X} = \frac{\partial \ln Y}{\partial \ln X} = \frac{\partial \ln Y}{\partial X} \cdot \frac{\partial X}{\partial \ln X} = b \cdot X \tag{3.7}$$

where Y is the dependent variable, X the independent variable and b the actual coefficient. A reliable estimation of the elasticity is then based on a reliable estimation of b and the median of X. Such an estimation is called elasticity around the average point. The results are given in Tables 3.8 and 3.9. Since it

Table 3.8 Elasticity of the hiring probability relative to independent variables, France

	Independent variable			
	L_VU	*DPUBU*	*JTRU*	*DPRU*
Elasticity at the average point (based on OLS)	0.049	0.060	0.047	0.087
Elasticity at the average point (based on Parks)	0.037	0.056	0.033	0.040

Table 3.9 Elasticity of the hiring probability relative to independent variables, Sweden

	Independent variable			
	*L_VU*1	*DPUBFU*	*USUPF*	*OTHERU*
Elasticity at the average point (based on OLS)	0.152	0.063	0.038	0.018
Elasticity at the average point (based on Parks)	0.102	0.075	0.022	0.004

is always difficult to assess what is measured by such elasticities, these results should be interpreted with care. These figures should only be interpreted as elasticities within our particular framework. For this reason, it seems hazardous to give any interpretation of their absolute estimated values.

4.3 Interpretation

These results suggest interpretations at two different levels. First, they validate the conclusion that active labour market policies have a positive impact on outflows from unemployment to employment; and second they support the concept of regional heterogeneity in the functioning of the labour market. Moreover, the results of estimation tend to indicate that the efficiency of ALMP on unemployment outflows is quite similar in France and Sweden.

The impact of ALMP on unemployment outflows

Our estimations confirm the augmented matching model assumption of a positive impact of ALMP on unemployment outflows. This result is consistent with other evaluation studies founded on matching functions, including Bellmann and Lehmann (1992), Lehmann (1992) and Rantala (1995), who also use flow variables.[9] Compared with these studies, our contribution lies in the structure of the data used. Previous empirical research on the subject suffered from a lack of reliability due, in part, to an insufficient number of observations, which showed in weakly significant coefficients estimates. The impact we have measured is, however, global; and there is no way to break down this gross effect into cosmetic and productive effects.[10] At this point we reach the classical limits of macroeconomic evaluations, which are based on partial equilibrium models and are limited by the quality of available aggregate data.

In terms of elasticities, employment creation schemes in public and non-trading sectors turn out to be the most efficient measures in France and Sweden, and have similar scales. On the contrary, subsidies and training would have smaller aggregated impacts. Again, these results are consistent with previous studies: for Germany, Bellmann and Lehmann (1992) estimate a positive impact of public job-creation schemes on unemployment outflows, and a non-significant negative effect of training schemes. While using a different methodology (unemployment equation), Calmfors and Skedinger (1995) find a positive impact for relief works, but unsteady coefficients for training measures in Sweden. Such aggregate results, especially for subsidies, can probably be explained by the existence of substitution and windfall effects. Because training schemes are generally heterogeneous, the analysis of their global effect is more complex. As such, alternate training (including job subsidies), sets apart from out-of-the-firm schemes (our classroom training).

In the former (Ermakoff and Tresmontant, 1990), the intensity of substitution and windfall effects depends on the similarities between subsidized jobs and normal jobs: the more these types of jobs resemble each other, the smaller the net effect on employment. The coefficient obtained for France is the result of the aggregation of the many effects of alternate training, and suggests that the impact of this kind of training is less than that of subsidies. This result differs from the Swedish case, where the training variable also comprises out-of-firm training schemes. It is also possible that the effect of training may be underestimated, for these measures have only an impact in the medium or long term, whereas our model is instantaneous.[11]

From a comparative point a view, our results do not confirm conventional assumptions about the difference in efficiency between France and Sweden: the magnitude of the estimated elasticity is quite similar in the two countries (although the employment creation scheme elasticity is marginally bigger in Sweden). Thus there is no evidence to support assertions that the acknowledged superior efficiency of Swedish ALMP compared with that of France in the 1980s still holds true in the 1990s.

Regional heterogeneity of augmented matching functions

Beyond the obvious advantages of panel data in terms of number of observations and increased sample variance, the use of regional data may reveal the existence of significant regional differences in the functioning of the labour market. Indeed, the assumption of regional fixed effects is confirmed in our estimations, which features stable and significant coefficients for the dummy variables for both France and Sweden. How can we understand the existence of such regional differences in the relationship between hirings, vacancies and participant inflows in the various ALMP programmes?

There are few studies which estimate matching functions on local data, but those which do exist confirm the presence of distinctive territorial features. For France, Aggulo and Skourias (1996) used monthly departmental data to estimate a matching function. They verify the existence of departmental fixed effects, which are interpreted as local specificities in the functioning of the labour market. Burda (1993a, 1993b) reaches the same conclusion for Germany and the Czech and Slovak Republics; as did Belderbos and Teulings (1989) for the Netherlands. Thus it appears that the higher the fixed effect, the more efficient the local labour market is in its matching process. Fixed effects can be interpreted as unobserved local heterogeneity that help to explain hirings.

In the Swedish case, regional heterogeneity is not large, and the coefficients for the dummy variables do not depart significantly from each other. Hence, the existence of regional specificity in Sweden is not clearly evidenced by our results.

In France, on the other hand, we found a greater degree of variation between the estimated coefficient for the regional dummies. In particular, the eastern regions of France appear to perform better relative to other regions. The estimated relative efficiency of these regions is consistent with the results of Aggulo and Skourias (1996). Institutional and historical characteristics could explain these differences. The role of ALMP in these differences cannot, however, be assessed from our results since we did not allow the variables coefficients to vary across regions in order to estimate an aggregate impact. None the less, Benayoun *et al.* (1995) conclude that strong regional differences also exist in the intensity of schemes and in the way in which schemes are implemented. From that point of view, the eastern French *départements* appear to favour alternate training schemes combined with intensive employment creations in the non-profit sector.

5 CONCLUSION

This evaluation study confirms the value of matching models in the aggregate impact analysis of ALMP. Moreover, the use of the flow approach of the labour market based on regional data substantially improves the reliability of the results. Our comparison of France and Sweden has shown that no significant difference in the efficiency of the labour market policy programmes exists between the two countries. This conclusion is consistent with the converging evolution of ALMP, and of the way in which policies are implemented in both countries.

Active labour market policy is found to have a positive impact on the outflow from unemployment towards employment, but the size of the estimated impact is small. This limited efficiency in terms of flows on the labour market should be complemented by results for the different groups of unemployed, and especially for the long-term unemployed. Given the development of long-term unemployment in France, it is possible to assume that the impact on the degree of selectivity of the labour market is limited. If data were available, it would thus be necessary to extend this analysis to the various groups of participants (the long-term unemployed, young people, and so on), the hiring probability of which may be differently influenced by the programmes.

Moreover, the estimations confirm the existence of fixed regional effects, thus evidencing unobserved differences in the functioning of local labour markets. However, these results suffer from the classic drawbacks of aggregate impact analysis: the availability and the quality of the data (especially for job vacancies) on one hand; and, on the other, the difficulty in interpreting gross effects in terms of efficiency in the absence of information about substitution and windfall effects. Finally, this study calls for additional research on local labour markets and the role of ALMP at this level.

NOTES

1. A detailed discussion on these problems of comparability can be found in Erhel (1998) and Anxo and Erhel (1998).
2. The French laws on decentralization were enacted in 1982.
3. The accommodation rate is usually defined as the ratio of the number of participants to the 'total' number of unemployed (according to Calmfors' definition).
4. Stock data seem more appropriate to our matching model. See Blanchard and Diamond (1989).
5. Which is estimated to be one quarter in France compared with two-thirds in Sweden (OCDE, 1990; Walwei, 1996).
6. In the absence of reliable data on regional market shares of employment agencies, we forgo correcting the vacancies variable. Bourdet and Persson (1995) corrected for this bias, but they used national data, not regional, and then could apply a global coefficient. But even in that case the reliability of the correction we carried out is questionable.
7. Following AMS. We had to reconstruct the series for France.
8. The peak in the number of participants to non-tradable job-creation schemes in 1992–5 corresponds to the development of the *contrats emplois-solidarité* at the time this scheme was implemented for the first time.
9. Arents and de Koning (1997) find a small positive impact of ALMPs on unemployment outflows on the basis of financial data, which makes any comparison with our results difficult.
10. For Sweden we have estimated our equation with an unemployment variable consistent with Calmfors' definition; our results were not modified. But the correction was only partial, since we lack data on non-scheme vacancies and unemployment outflows.
11. Accounting for mid- or long-term targets of training schemes would have required the introduction of lags to the estimated equation, which turned out to be impossible, given the length of our sample.

REFERENCES

Aggulo, M.-H. and N. Skourias (1996), 'Processus d'appariement sur le marché du travail: une analyse économétrique sur données locales', LIIe Colloque International de l'Association d'Econométrie, Göteborg, 9–11 May.

Anxo, D. (1994), 'Les années 1990, où la fin du modèle suédois', in B. Gazier (ed.), *Trajectoire de l'Emploi*, Paris: Economica.

Anxo, D. and C. Erhel (1998), 'Institutional Systems and Financing of ALMPs in France and Sweden: What are the Evolutions for the Nineties?', *Rencontres France – Pays Nordiques*, MIRE, Copenhagen, September.

Arents, M. and J. de Koning (1997): 'The Impact of Active Labour Market Policy on the Transition from Unemployment to Employment', Conférence EALE, Aarhus, 25–8 September, p. 11.

Balestra, P. (1992), 'Introduction to Linear Models for Panel Data', in L. Matyas and P. Sevestre (eds), *The Econometrics of Panel Data*, Dordrecht: Kluwer Academic Publishers, pp. 21–9.

Belderbos, R. and C. Teulings (1989), 'A New Interpretation of the Relation between

Unemployment and Vacancies', SEO research memorandum 8904, Université d'Amsterdam, Août.
Bellmann, L. and R. Jackman (1996a), 'Aggregate Impact Analysis', in G. Schmid, J. O'Reilly and K. Schömann (eds), *International Handbook of Labour Market Policy and Evaluation*, Cheltenham: Edward Elgar, pp. 143–60.
Bellmann, L. and R. Jackman (1996b), 'The Impact of Labour Market Policy on Wages, Employment and Labour Market Mismatch', in G. Schmid, J. O'Reilly and K. Schömann (eds), *International Handbook of Labour Market Policy and Evaluation*, Cheltenham: Edward Elgar, pp. 725–43.
Bellmann, L. and H. Lehmann (1992), 'British Policies: A Fresh Evaluation', in R. Disney (ed.), *Helping the Unemployed: Active Labour Market Policies in Britain and Germany*, Anglo-German Foundation, London, pp. 226–51.
Benayoun, G., C. Cayol and Y. Lazzeri (1995), 'Critères de territorialisation des politiques de l'emploi', Rapport de synthèse pour le Ministère du Travail, de l'Emploi et de la Formaton Professionnelle, Mars, vol. 1, p. 88.
Bessy, C., F. Eymard-Duverney, B. Gomel and B. Simonin (1995), 'Les politiques publiques d'emploi et leurs acteurs', *Cahiers du CEE*, 34, p. 349.
Blanchard, O.J. and P. Diamond (1989), 'The Beveridge Curve', *Brookings Papers on Economic Activity*, 1, pp. 1–76.
Bonnal, L., D. Fougere and A. Serandon (1994), 'L'impact des politiques d'emploi sur le devenir des jeunes chômeurs: une étude économétrique sur données longitudinales', *Economie et Prévision*, 115, pp. 1–29.
Bourdet, Y. and I. Persson (1995), 'Does Labour Market Policy Matter? Lessons from the Eighties for the Nineties', in J. Johannesson and E. Wadensjö (eds), *Labour Market Policy at the Crossroads*, Stockholm, pp. 117–49.
Burda, M.C. (1993a), 'Modelling Exits from Unemployment in Eastern Germany: A Matching Function Approach', Discussion Paper no. 800, *Centre for Economic Policy Research*, London, May.
Burda, M.C. (1993b), 'Unemployment, Labour Market and Structural Changes in Eastern Europe', *Economic Policy*, 16, 101–28.
Calmfors, L. (1994), 'Politiques actives du marché du travail et chômage – cadre d'analyse des aspects cruciaux de la conception des mesures', *Revue Economique de l'OCDE*, 22, 8–51.
Calmfors, L. and P. Skedinger (1995), 'Does Active Labour Market Policy increase Employment? Theoretical Considerations and some Empirical Evidence from Sweden', *Oxford Review of Economic Policy*, **11** (1), 91–108.
Erhel, C. (1998), *L'évaluation des politiques actives de l'emploi: une perspective européenne*, Ph.D. Dissertation, Université Paris 1 Panthéon-Sorbonne, September, p. 376.
Ermakoff, I. and R. Tresmontant (1990), 'L'impact de la politique de l'emploi: une estimation quantitative de certains dispositifs', *Economie et Prévision*, no. 92–3.
Hsiao, C. (1985), 'Benefits•and Limitations of Panel Data', *Econometric Review*, **4** (1), 121–74.
INSEE (1999), *Données Sociales*, Institut National de la Statistique et des Etudes Economiques, Paris.
Jackman, R. (1994), 'What can Active Labour Market Policy do?', *Swedish Economic Policy Review*, 1, 221–57.
Koning, J. de (1997), '*Training for the Unemployed: the Dutch Experience*', Paper for the TRANSLAM Project, Netherlands Economic Institute, Rotterdam, p. 27.
Lehmann, H. (1992), 'German Policies: A Fresh Evaluation', in R. Disney (ed.),

Helping the Unemployed: Active Labour Market Policies in Britain and Germany, Anglo-German Foundation, London, pp. 132–49.

OCDE (1990), *Labour Market Policies for the 1990s*, Paris.

Parks, R.W. (1967), 'Efficient Estimation of a System of Regression Equations when Disturbances are both Serially and Contemporaneously Correlated', *American Statistical Association Journal*, 500–509.

Rantala, J. (1995), '*Effects of Active Labour Market Programmes on Youth Employment'*, Conférence AELE September, p. 13.

Saucier, P. and C. Sofer (1995), 'L'accès des jeunes aux politiques d'insertion et à l'emploi', *Revue Economique*, **46** (3), 561–71.

Walwei, U. (1991), 'Job Placement in Europe: an International Comparison', *Intereconomics*, September/October, 248–54.

Walwei, U. (1996), 'Improving Job Matching through Placement Services', in G. Schmid, J. O'Reilly and K. Schömann (eds), *International Handbook of Labour Market Policy and Evaluation*, Cheltenham: Edward Elgar, pp. 402–27.

4. Does active labour market policy matter? An aggregate impact analysis for Germany

Günther Schmid, Stefan Speckesser and Christoph Hilbert[1]

INTRODUCTION

This chapter investigates the impact of German active labour market policy (ALMP) on long-term unemployment. Extended periods of unemployment frequently lead to social exclusion. We are therefore interested in finding out whether ALMP can prevent social exclusion and contribute to social integration. Our empirical analysis is based on two methodological approaches: a structural equation model and a matching model based on the aggregate impact analysis (AIA) model outlined in Bellmann and Jackman (1996a). It uses regional employment offices (REO) in Germany as units of observation. The effect of ALMP is measured on aggregate indicators such as the level, structure or change in long-term unemployment and the outflow rate of unemployment in the regions. REO are the operative units of the German federal employment office (FEO) in Nuremberg, which is responsible for administering unemployment insurance and ALMP. Despite central regulation, REO have considerable discretion both in choosing the mix of policies ('portfolio') as well as in implementing them. Our objective is to operationalize these variations and to test whether they matter in the fight against long-term unemployment. We are seeking the 'intelligent portfolio' or policy mix of ALMP for regional labour markets. A further advantage of AIA compared with individual impact analysis is that to some extent (at least indirectly) it captures displacement, substitution, deadweight and multiplier effects.

We will begin with a brief report on the ALMP portfolio for the years 1994–7, and its variation across the 181 REO in Germany (section 1). We then use a pooled cross-section analysis and a fixed effect model to assess the impact of ALMP on the level, structure and change in long-term unemployment (section 2). This approach is complemented by a matching model which estimates the impact of ALMP on outflows from unemployment (section 3).

Policy considerations and suggestions for further analysis conclude this chapter (section 4).

1 ALMP IN GERMANY AND ITS REGIONAL VARIATION

REO have at their disposal various measures designed to prevent long-term unemployment or to reintegrate the long-term unemployed into the labour market. We briefly describe these options (1.1), and show their relative importance and variation in policy mix in western and eastern Germany (1.2).

1.1 The instruments of ALMP

The German labour promotion act (*Arbeitsförderungsgesetz*)[2] provides three basic instruments designed to prevent or reduce long-term unemployment: further training and retraining, temporary public job creation and wage cost subsidies.[3] In theory, further training or retraining is aimed at the total dependent labour force; but in practice, it is used mainly to assist the unemployed and those at risk of becoming unemployed. The FEO bears the costs for the training measures, and pays qualifying participants a subsistence allowance (*Unterhaltsgeld*) amounting to 60 or 67 per cent of the previous net wages (which is equal to the unemployment benefit). REO usually purchase training services from private or semi-private training centres offering programmes for specified target groups and market segments (for example, office workers, data processing, welding). In the process of implementation, REO and the training centre adjust the individual course design in a bargaining process. With the exception of those who are employed, the participants themselves are not involved in the process. The duration of programmes can vary between rather short periods of orientation and upgrading (one to three months) and long periods of complete retraining in another occupation (up to two years). To a limited extent, the programmes also support on-the-job training if a firm is reluctant to hire from the stock of the unemployed because of the high costs of initial on-the-job training (*Einarbeitungszuschüsse*). Since the regional offices are allowed considerable discretion in acquiring suitable training courses, bargaining with training centres or employers, and in making decisions about duration, scope or content of the courses, we expect to find significant regional variation in training measures – even given the same level of unemployment.

Temporary public job creation (*Arbeitsbeschaffungsmaßnahmen* or ABM) aims at creating intermediate jobs for workers in need of assistance, particularly for the long-term unemployed (more than 12 months) entitled to unemployment assistance. The work offered must be ‘additional’ and ‘useful to the community', which means that the jobs would not have existed without the support of the programme. Carriers in both the private and public sectors can claim a subsidy ranging from 30 to 75 per cent – and, in exceptional cases, 100 per cent – of the wages. Non-profit organizations, intermediate employment or training agencies and municipal governments are the main providers of ABM jobs. Formerly based on the wage level set by collective agreements, the subsidy is now limited to jobs with a remuneration of 80 per cent of that for unsubsidized employees. The jobs are temporary, lasting between nine and twelve months; or, in exceptional cases, up to two years. As in the case of further training, the FEO sets standards for the programme design at the national level.

ABM programmes are designed to stimulate the creation of permanent jobs, prepare measures for structural improvements, improve the infrastructure and environment, and provide work experience for extremely difficult-to-place persons. The more limited goal is to redistribute the burden of unemployment among the people who become unemployed, that is, to avoid the creation of individual cases of long-term unemployment wherever possible. Despite the rather strict regulations the REO retains a degree of latitude in interpreting the criteria of 'additionality' or 'public interest' in the direction of projects and in the selection of unemployed. Variation also occurs as a result of the structure of regional providers, which usually offer a subsidized vacancy and are responsible for the fulfilment of the programme norms. In addition, ABM are highly dependent on other local bodies which determine the standards for 'usefulness' for the community (municipalities, networks) and offer suitable employment opportunities, often with co-financing.[4] Significant variation between the regions concerning the design and implementation of ABM measures and corresponding differences in the effectiveness of labour market policy are therefore to be expected. Since the initiative, cooperation and co-financing of local authorities are crucial to programme success, the effectiveness of ABM measures appears to vary across regions to a greater extent than that of training measures. Thus, efficient networks – which will presumably function better in smaller communities than in large and agglomerated areas – are required.

A range of wage cost subsidies is available to support the reintegration of the hard-to-place unemployed.[5] Recruitment subsidies (*Eingliederungsbeihilfen*) provide subsidies of 30–50 per cent for the hard-to-place unemployed for up to one year. Since 1988, a special federal aid programme (*Bundeshilfeprogramm*) financed by the federal government offers subsidies in the same range for the recruitment of long-term unemployed. In implementing this programme for particularly disadvantaged persons – that is, those who have been jobless for at least two years and those with at least three high barriers to reintegration (such as drug addicts and persons with psychiatric disorders or health restrictions) – REO can experiment to some extent and count on additional support. Long-term and degressive subsidies are available to stimulate the recruitment of the elderly long-term unemployed. Finally, 'productive wage cost subsidies', recently renamed 'structural adjustment measures' (*Strukturanpassungsmaßnahmen* or SAM), were introduced as an innovative instrument in eastern Germany in 1993 and extended with some changes in the rules to western Germany in 1995. SAM offer a lump-sum subsidy equivalent to average unemployment benefits for three years (up to four years for small enterprises) to non-profit organizations or private enterprises which create additional jobs for the unemployed (more than three months) in the areas of environmental protection, social services, youth aid and some elements of urban renewal. Since this subsidy covers only 25 to 40 per cent of the costs for a new job, co-financiers are required to join the venture. These include the federal privatization agency (*Treuhandanstalt*), the state government (*Land*), the local community, other agencies or the firm hiring the unemployed. Employment authorities expect this new programme to encourage the development of a rich and interactive local network. Again, this set of wage subsidy programmes gives placement managers of REO considerable room to manoeuvre, so that sizeable regional variations in the programme portfolio are to be expected. We turn now to the size and structure of the ALMP portfolio in Germany and its regional variations.

1.2 The ALMP Portfolio and its Regional Variations

The overall participation rate in ALMP measures[6] in western Germany's 142 REO was 14.2 per cent in 1994 and 10.4 per cent in 1997, varying between 8.6 and 20.8 per cent across the regions in 1994 and between 6.8 and 19.7 per cent in 1997 (Table 4.1). The policy mix shows a strong bias towards training measures. With an average of 1.3 per cent, wage subsidy beneficiaries make up only a small portion of all programme participants. Even temporary public job creation plays a relatively minor role (2 per cent on average), but with a higher standard deviation compared with wage subsidies. Total participation in eastern Germany's 35 REO varies at a much higher level, ranging from 19.4 to 29.2 per cent in 1997 with a strong falling trend. In 1994, the participation rate was almost 38 per cent, compared with 24.8 per cent in 1997 (Table 4.2). The portfolio is also quite different compared with that of western Germany. Although training makes up again the bulk of measures, demand-oriented temporary public job creation and wage subsidies also play an important role. This obviously reflects the different character of the employment problem in the two parts of Germany. Given the highly skilled workforce (including the unemployed) in eastern Germany, the high numbers of participants in training measures

*Table 4.1 Participation in ALMP programmes in western Germany as a percentage of regional extended unemployment**

	Year	Mean	Std.	Min.	Max.	N
ALMP total	1994	14.12	2.55	8.62	20.83	142
	1995	14.9	2.93	9.7	27.27	142
	1996	13.26	2.25	9.49	23.74	142
	1997	10.4	1.82	6.77	19.69	142
Job creation (ABM)	1994	1.72	1.17	0.28	6.42	142
	1995	2.13	1.24	0.49	7.02	142
	1996	1.95	1.06	0.61	5.4	142
	1997	1.52	0.85	0.35	4.1	142
Training (FT)	1994	11.4	2.32	5.52	17.93	142
	1995	11.08	2.37	6.21	19.73	142
	1996	10.06	1.76	6.64	16.9	142
	1997	7.72	1.4	4.7	14.16	142
Targeted wage subsidies**	1994	1.0	0.39	0.28	2.33	142
	1995	1.69	0.48	0.9	3.61	142
	1996	1.25	0.48	0.36	3.94	142
	1997	1.16	0.49	0.47	3.73	142

Notes:
* The participation rate is calculated by dividing the stocks of programme participants in the target group-oriented schemes through the regional extended unemployment (that is, unemployment plus participants in ABM, FT and targeted wage subsidy programmes).
** Target group-oriented programmes are wage subsidies for older and long-term unemployed persons (*Bundeshilfe* excluded due to missing data).

Source: Regional data work-file WZB, *Bundesanstalt für Arbeit*, own calculations.

may appear curious. In eastern Germany, the main problem seems to be a lack of jobs and not a lack of qualified people. Another interesting fact is the high regional variation and its decline, which may be the result of experience gathered over time and the accompanying adjustment in implementation. Regional variation in the participation rates of ALMP, both in western Germany and in eastern Germany, might be a simple reflection of their respective case loads and not of differences in policy choice and implementation. Figure 4.1 explores this possibility. If we compare the total participation rates in the regions with the respective unemployment

*Table 4.2 Participation in ALMP programmes in eastern Germany as a percentage of regional extended unemployment**

	Year	Mean	Std.	Min.	Max.	N
ALMP total	1994	n.a.	n.a.	n.a.	n.a.	35
	1995	37.93	4.13	29.71	46.8	35
	1996	31.76	2.92	25.92	38.06	35
	1997	24.76	2.18	19.4	29.18	35
Job creation (ABM)	1994	n.a.	n.a.	n.a.	n.a.	35
	1995	12.15	2.63	7.93	18.56	35
	1996	11.31	2.93	6.54	19.01	35
	1997	8.85	2.07	5.75	14.13	35
Training (FT)	1994	n.a.	n.a.	n.a.	n.a.	35
	1995	15.28	2.08	11.29	21.44	35
	1996	14.12	1.63	11.37	18.74	35
	1997	10.43	1.16	8.31	13.26	35
Targeted wage subsidies**	1994	n.a.	n.a.	n.a.	n.a.	35
	1995	10.5	4.21	3.66	22.56	35
	1996	6.33	2.04	2	11.18	35
	1997	5.48	1.41	1.82	8.07	35

Notes:
* The participation rate is calculated by dividing the stocks of programme participants in the target group-oriented schemes through the regional extended unemployment (that is, unemployment plus participants in ABM, FT and targeted wage subsidy programmes).
** Target group-oriented programmes are wage subsidies for older and long-term unemployed persons (*Bundeshilfe* excluded due to missing data).

Source: Regional data work-file WZB, *Bundesanstalt für Arbeit*, own calculations.

rates (restricted here to western Germany), we find no correlation at all. REO with high unemployment, as well as REO with low unemployment, show high participation rates, and *vice versa*. However, this zero correlation hides two contrasting relationships. There is a clear positive correlation between temporary public job creation and unemployment, whereas participation in training measures declines with increasing unemployment. The pattern for eastern Germany (not shown here) appears to be similar. This finding seems reasonable since the higher the level of unemployment, the higher the probability that the problem is related to a lack of jobs or demand deficiency. The reinsertion of the long-term unemployed also becomes more difficult, which would seem to justify increasing efforts to compensate their disadvantage through the bridge of temporary public jobs or through wage cost subsidies. Further training efforts would probably be a waste of money since such measures would merely redistribute the unemployment stock between more and less skilled people. At persistent low and medium levels of unemployment, it seems plausible to assume the presence of a relatively higher share of mismatch unemployment owing to lack of skills and competencies or to outdated qualifications. However, as both figures show, there is still tremendous regional variation at equal levels of regional unemployment. Even when we assume that the general direction of ALMP is correct, we still do not know whether it really improves the chances of the (would-be) long-term unemployed. We will address this question in the next section.

2 THE IMPACT OF ALMP ON THE LEVEL, STRUCTURE AND DYNAMIC OF UNEMPLOYMENT

Before measuring the impact of ALMP on long-term unemployment, we will briefly describe the structural equation model (2.1), explain the selection of variables (2.2) and provide the basic descriptive analysis of the variables considered in the equation (2.3). The results of the regression analysis are presented in the final subsection (2.4).

2.1 The Structural Equation Model

For the following part of this study we use a structural equation model based on the following simple function:[7]

$$SE = f(ALMP, IMPL, CONT)$$

where *SE* represents indicators for social exclusion, *ALMP* indicators for active labour market policy, *IMPL* indicators for policy implementation, and *CONT* indicators for control variables. We have used a pooled cross-section analysis with 142 REO in western Germany[8] for 1994–7. The analysis is based on a fixed effect model which, in contrast to the random effect model, assumes for each unit of observation a fixed and unit-specific constant term which is approximated by a regional dummy variable. The fixed effect model is a reasonable approach when we are certain that the differences between the units can be viewed as parametric shifts of the regression function (Greene, 1996, p. 623). This is typically the case when the units of research represent a

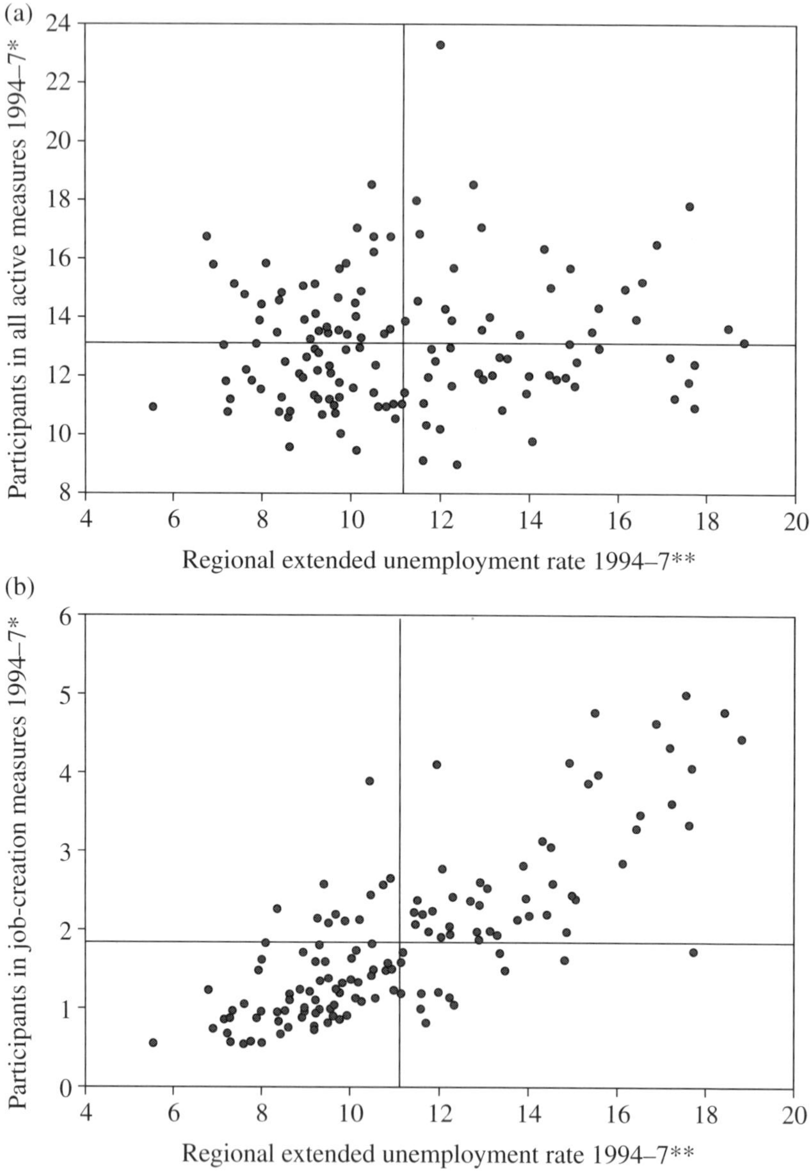

Notes:

* Participants are measured in percentage of the regional extended unemployment.

** Yearly average 1994–7.

Figure 4.1 Responsiveness of ALMP to unemployment in 142 REO in western Germany

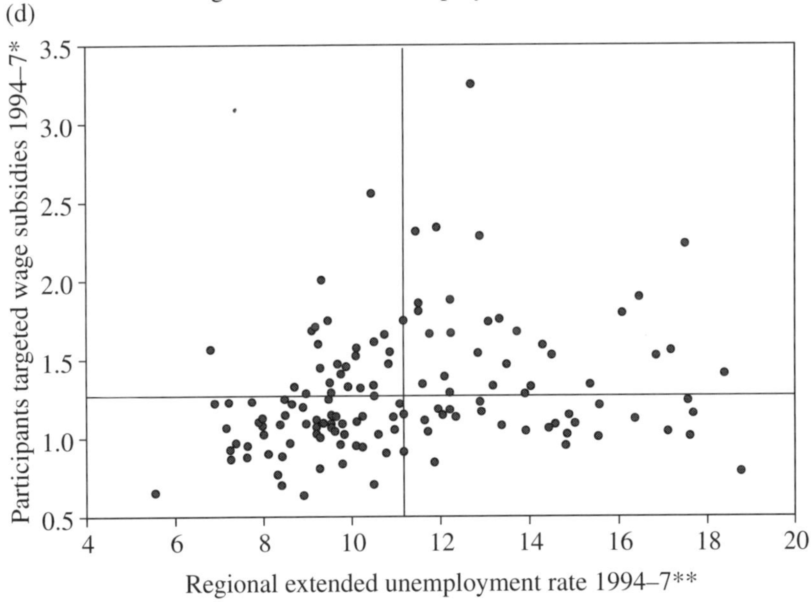

Figure 4.1 *continued*

particular population group in a single national setting. Random effect models are appropriate when the units of research have been drawn from a large population. The model to be estimated therefore has the following form:

$$u_{it+1} = a + \mathbf{b}\boldsymbol{x}_{it} + \mathrm{z_i} + \mathbf{e_{it}}$$

As dependent variable (u_{it+1}), we have used the long-term unemployment rate, the share of long-term unemployed, and the change of long-term unemployment. The dependent variables enter the equation with a time lag of one year to control for endogeneity;[9] '*a*' is a constant term, $\boldsymbol{x}_{it}$ is a vector of economic and policy variables varying over time, **b** is a vector of parameters to be estimated, $\mathrm{z_i}$ is a separate constant term for the i-th region, and $\mathbf{e_{it}}$ is a vector of disturbances varying for each region and over time, t = 1–4 (1994–7).

2.2 Selection of Variables and Hypotheses

As dependent variables we have selected three indicators. First, the level of long-term unemployment has been measured as a percentage of the civil labour force. Although long-term unemployment does not necessarily lead to social exclusion, the probability of transition into very long-term unemployment – or even into permanent exclusion from the labour market – is high. The second model explains the share of long-term unemployed as a percentage of total unemployment. This indicator reflects the negative 'structuralization' impact of unemployment on weaker groups in the labour market – for example, the elderly, the unskilled, the handicapped and women with family obligations in traditional role models. This indicator is formally independent of the size of total unemployment. Because, however, the probability of transition to long-term unemployment corresponds to an increase in competition between the unemployed for a decreasing number of jobs, a strong correlation between both indicators can be expected.[10] The third model takes change in long-term unemployment as a dependent variable measured as the change rate from one year to the next.

All three variables have been tested in two operational forms: first for the 'short' long-term unemployed (that is, people who have been unemployed for longer than six months), and second for the 'long' long-term unemployed (that is, people who have been unemployed for longer than two years) (Table 4.3). The latter group represents those persons who are clearly near social or economic exclusion and who have, in most cases, lost entitlement to regular unemployment benefits. Members of this group may, however, receive unemployment assistance, which is means-tested in Germany and financed by the central state budget (Schmid *et al.*, 1996), and/or social assistance, which is

Table 4.3 Possible impacts of labour market policy on long-term unemployment (LTU)

Independent variables	Dependent variables (t + 1) Level of LTU	Structure of LTU	Change of LTU
Demand conditions			
– change of employment	– –	?	– –
Structure of the labour market			
– level of unemployment < 6/24 months	++	++	++
– level of previous long-term unemployment	###	###	–
– mismatch: duration of vacancies	+	++	+
– unskilled as % of employment	++	++	+
– part-time work as % of employment	–	–	–
– regional attraction	–	–	–
Policy intervention			
– public job creation (t and t+1)	–	–	– –
– training measures (t and t+1)	–	– –	–
– wage subsidies (t and t+1)	–	– –	–
Implementation			
– duration of job creation	–	–	–
– duration of training measures	+	+	+
– duration of wage subsidies	–	–	–
– diversity of portfolio	–	–	–

Notes: +/++/+++ = small/strong/very strong positive impact; –/– –/– – – = small/strong/very strong negative impact; ? = unclear or mutually contradicting influences; ### = not included in the model.

financed by the counties or cities. The 'long' long-term unemployed may, therefore, also be counted as recipients of local labour market policy 'treatment'(see Chapter 8 in this volume).

(1)

In the left hand side of the equation, we distinguish among four groups of independent variables. First, we assume that level, structure and change of long-term unemployment (LTU) are determined by demand conditions, which are represented here by the change of employment. Since growth rates of GDP are not available at the regional level, we experimented with various demand indicators and finally chose change of employment as the best substitute. Because they are difficult to interpret, we discarded hiring or changes in hiring as indicators. They reflect both demand and labour (or job) turnover. We also rejected the vacancy rate (that is, registered vacancies as a percentage of the labour force) since this indicator reflects only part of demand and is cyclically sensitive. Whereas increasing demand should strongly reduce the level or the further increase of LTU, the sign of coefficient related to the share of LTU is left open since mutually contradicting influences are to be expected. Since the short-term unemployed will be the first to profit from a rise in demand, 'structuralization' may even increase in the short term. Given continuing favourable demand conditions, the long-term unemployed will also be affected in the long run (Table 4.3).

(2)

In the next step, we look at the structure (or context) of the regional labour markets, which influences the speed of adjustment to structural change or demand or supply shocks and, thereby, LTU. First, we take the previous level of short-term unemployment (less than 6 months and less than 24 months, respectively) as an important determinant which will strongly increase the probability of long-term unemployment because of the higher competition between the unemployed for scarce jobs.[11] Because policy will respond with higher activity if short-term unemployment rises, we also intend to control for the problem of endogeneity through the inclusion of this variable. In the model explaining the change in long-term unemployment, we will also include the previous level of long-term unemployment to control again for endogeneity and for the base effect: the higher the previous level of long-term unemployment, the lower the rate of change (Table 4.3).

Second, we expect that mismatch between vacancies and unemployment will increase long-term unemployment.[12] After experimenting with various measures, we decided to use the average duration of registered vacancies (which is 2.9 months; see descriptive statistics) as a proper indicator. We expect that – other things being equal – mismatch will still have an independent effect by increasing LTU, especially the structural component of LTU.[13]

Third, we assume that the less qualified the active labour force (in the previous year), the higher the chance that a given inflow into unemployment will turn into long-term unemployment. As an indicator, we use the number of blue-collar workers (*Arbeiter*) lacking formal vocational qualifications as a percentage of total employment. This indicator has a strong positive correlation with the share of employment in the manufacturing industry (0.78), and a negative correlation with the share of employment in services (–0.78). We can, therefore, also use this variable as an indicator for the regional adjustment load. Regions which continue to have a high share of manufacturing (and a correspondingly low share of service industries) will struggle to find a solution to the unemployment problem. Thus we expect the regression coefficient to produce a positive sign for all three of our dependent variables, thereby demonstrating the impact of increasing LTU.

The fourth group of variables are indicators for the flexibility of the labour market which should reduce LTU. We use as a proxy the share of workers in part-time work as a percentage of the total labour force.[14] In theory, however, the impact of this variable on the dynamics of long-term unemployment is ambivalent. On the one hand, part-time work could serve as a bridge to 'regular' full-time employment, making it easier for companies (especially small- and medium-sized firms) to hire additional employees. This argument would be in line with the neo-classical assumption. On the other hand, however, flexibility could reduce incentives to invest in long-term relationships or in human capital, and may also increase transaction costs due to the costs associated with high turnover. We would not, therefore, be altogether surprised if this indicator turns out not to have a significant coefficient in the model. We none the less expect the indicator to produce a negative sign, demonstrating that part-time work is capable of independently reducing LTU.

Finally, we must control for regional attractiveness in terms of work-place capacities. Since our regional units are relatively small, we observe varying degrees of spatial labour mobility between our units of observation. People move daily (or even weekly) between their home and the work-place, that is, between our regional units. Their employment is counted at the work-place, but their eventual unemployment is counted at their place of residence, that is, the community where they live. Owing to the lack of commuting data, we solved this problem by simply dividing the number of dependent employees counted at the work-place by the active civil labour force (minus the unemployed) counted at the place of residence.[15] Regions with high work-place capacities will have fewer difficulties in fighting LTU than regions with lower work-place capacities.[16]

(3)

A third group of independent variables we are especially interested in is the impact of various forms of policy interventions. First, Keynesian theory suggests that demand-oriented measures such as temporary public job creation (usually explicitly directed towards the long-term unemployed) tend to reduce the level of LTU more than supply-oriented training measures. According to this theory, demand-oriented ALMP can increase the level of employment (and thus reduce long-term unemployment) in two ways: through an income effect (higher consumption power of the participants) and through a (Keynesian) multiplier effect. In practice, however, such measures can also lead to displacement, substitution or deadweights. Neo-classical theory would also predict the presence of a 'moral hazard', for example, lower search intensity due to the availability of subsidized jobs. Thus, in theory, the impact of demand measures such as ABM is not at all clear. After considering the arguments, we have come to view temporary public jobs as measures that potentially reduce LTU in all respects: they halt the further increase (change) of LTU, and are assumed to be most effective for the very long-term unemployed.

Supply-oriented policies, here measured as the number of yearly participants in training (stock) as a percentage of the civil labour force, are expected to have little, if any, impact on the level of LTU by reducing skill bottlenecks. We expect, however, supply-oriented measures to have a stronger impact on the structure of LTU than demand-oriented measures. This is because the main objective of such measures is to maintain or to repair the individual employability, and thereby redistribute employment chances. However, an additional means of influencing both level and structure of unemployment should not be neglected. If training measures properly fulfil their primary function, they also increase overall competition within the labour supply, thereby reducing wage pressures and providing a favourable climate for job creation. We consider training to be most effective for the 'short' long-term unemployed, and less useful for the very long-term unemployed.

We will also test the effectiveness of 'structural' policies, measured as the participation rate in wage subsidy programmes other than the temporary public job-creation scheme. Because they serve different objectives, we place these measures between 'demand' and 'supply'. Some are aimed exclusively at redistributing employment chances, while others combine this goal with industrial policy objectives, such as improving the regional infrastructure in terms of social services or environmental protection. Because these measures are very small, we expect them to have little impact on LTU. We also expect wage subsidies to prove more effective for the very long-term unemployed than for the 'short' long-term unemployed.

To control for the trivial effect that each (formerly long-term unemployed) participant will automatically reduce the level of long-term unemployment, all policy variables enter the equation with a time lead of one year (and the dependent variables with a time lag of one year). If the participants again become unemployed (according to the 'revolving door' theory) or displace other unemployed, they will either add to the inflow of unemployment or reduce the outflow of unemployment, thus having no – or even a negative – effect on LTU.[17] All policy variables enter the equation by taking the average of the participation level in the previous and in the current year. We look at the policy activity of both years because the unsuccessful participants would, in both cases, re-enter the stock of unemployment, thereby feeding once again into the stock of long-term unemployment or increasing the competition between short- and long-term unemployed.

(4)
A fourth group of independent variables explaining LTU is the policy mix (portfolio) and its implementation. The placement officers in the regional employment offices (REO) have various choices in selecting and implementing the measures. If the measures are badly targeted, they may have no impact, or even a reverse impact. The same holds true if the measures are badly implemented; for example, if the wrong training curriculum is chosen, interaction tends to occur with ineffective partners, or follow-ups and controls are neglected (see Chapter 8 in this volume). The impact of these choices is difficult to assess because the intensity and quality of interaction can hardly be measured.

We have none the less computed two proxies to measure these influences. First, the duration of measures can serve as an indication of whether placement officers have followed the strategy of large numbers and short duration (with the likelihood of lower quality), or small numbers and longer duration with careful personal selection. We expect that, on average, training measures will be more effective when they take place over a short period of time, while temporary public jobs and wage subsidies will be more effective with a longer duration and in carefully selected cases. Second, portfolio diversity might have an impact on the effectiveness of policy measures. We operationalize portfolio diversity by measuring the deviation of the individual region from the average policy mix of all regions. The indicator varies from zero (if a region has exactly the same mix as the average) and one (if the region has a totally different mix). Early identification of the risk of LTU and a corresponding differentiation of the policy measures according to the regional specificities would, for instance, increase the chances of keeping long-term unemployment low. We assume that proper targeting of policy measures according to the specific regional problems is reflected in a high deviation from the average policy mix. If this deviation loads negatively with our dependent variables, the targeting would have had an impact in the expected direction. If, however, we detect no significant sign or even a significant positive coefficient, such a result would indicate ineffective or inappropriate targeting.[18]

2.3 Regional Characteristics

As the descriptive statistics show, long-term unemployment varies considerably among the 142 western German REO (Table 4.4). The average rate of 'short' long-term unemployment (less than six months) was 5.1 per cent, with a minimum of 1.5 per cent and a maximum of 11.6 per cent. 'Long' long-term unemployment (more than 24 months) was at an average level of 1.5 per cent, varying between 0.2 per cent and 4.8 per cent. The structuring effect of high unemployment is reflected in the share of long-term unemployment. At any given point in time (in this case, September of each year), over 50 per cent (up to 71 per cent in extreme cases) of the unemployed have been out of work for longer than six months on average; while 15 per cent (or up to 30 per cent in extreme cases) of the unemployed have been out of work for an average of more than 24 months. These figures clearly demonstrate the detrimental selection impact of high and increasing unemployment on the weaker groups of the labour market.[19] They also confirm the assumption that regional specificities, whether 'structural' or 'political', are strong determinants of long-term unemployment.[20] The change in the registered number of long-term unemployed also varies enormously. During the period of observation, only a few regions enjoyed a decline in long-term unemployment; while in most regions, long-term unemployment increased, and even rose dramatically in some REO (Table 4.4).[21] As the modest negative correlations with our demand indicator 'change of employment' illustrate (–0.39; –0.31), these differences cannot be entirely explained by the overall development of the labour market situation.

Before turning to our estimates of the impact of policy variables on such differences (for their description see section 2, and Tables 4.1 and 4.2), we would like to make several observations regarding the 'structural' variables. Registered vacancies remained open an average of 2.9 months before being filled. The time span for vacancies in the 142 REO varied between 1.4 and 8.6 months. But three factors diminish the validity of this indicator:[22] first, the registered vacancies reflect only part of all vacancies; second, the degree of vacancy registration varies between regions and business cycles; and third, the duration of registered vacancies is affected, to some extent, by policies. Because the correlation with the level of long-term unemployment is small or even negative (around –0.3), we still take this variable as a fairly good indicator of structural mismatch. Search theory would predict that the duration of vacancies will increase with the level of vacancies, which is confirmed by highly significant positive correlations (between 0.4 and 0.5). Thus, a control for this relationship seems to be necessary or must be taken into account in interpreting the estimation results.

It is interesting to note that the share of 'unskilled' blue-collar workers varies between 11 per cent and 31 per cent among the 142 REO (average 20.1 per cent). As previously mentioned, this indicator correlates highly with employment in manufacturing. There is an important flaw in this indicator because it also includes (formally) skilled craft workers if they are in pay grades normally filled by unskilled blue-collar workers.[23] Such jobs would be exposed to structural change, but the workers in those positions would not necessarily have great difficulties in finding new jobs. Nevertheless, we assume that most unskilled blue-collar workers who become unemployed will

Table 4.4 Descriptive statistics for variables

	Min.	Max.	Mean	Std. dev.
Level of UE > 6 months	1.52	11.61	5.10	1.96
Level of UE > 24 months	0.23	4.77	1.54	0.875
Change of UE > 6 months (t, t+1)	–15.89	44.02	5.02	10.64
Change of UE > 24 months (t, t+1)	–7.44	78.33	20.05	13.50
Structure of UE > 6 months	35.28	71.26	51.75	6.21
Structure of UE > 24 months	5.32	29.26	15.04	4.68
Change of employment (t, t+1)	–7.71	5.74	–0.817	1.26
Level of unemployment < 6 months	2.59	7.06	4.32	0.810
Level of unemployment < 24 months	4.03	13.23	7.66	1.81
Mismatch: duration of vacancies	9.01	72.54	29.76	10.63
Unskilled as % of employment	10.58	31.29	20.57	3.41
Part-time work as % of employment	9.10	18.76	12.97	1.78
Regional attraction	59.61	132.94	86.36	11.85
Public job creation (t and t+1)	0.03	2.23	0.326	0.288
Training measures (t and t+1)	0.55	3.22	1.39	0.456
Wage subsidies (t and t+1)	0.02	0.55	0.134	0.076
Duration of job creation	0.46	1.64	0.862	0.120
Duration of training measures	0.38	4.14	1.18	0.462
Duration of wage subsidies	0.29	1.88	0.7637	0.225
Diversity of portfolio	0.01	0.49	0.152	8.93

Source: Regional data work-file WZB, *Bundesanstalt für Arbeit*, own calculations.

have a low probability of leaving unemployment. This is because most new jobs are created in services, and high barriers exist between low-skilled 'manufacturing jobs' and 'services jobs'.[24]

The share of part-time employment varies between 9.1 per cent (minimum) and 18.8 per cent (maximum), and averages at around 13 per cent. Thus, part-time employment displays a modest variation in comparison with most other variables in the model. The variable 'regional attractiveness' varies between 60 per cent and 133 per cent, thereby indicating that the number of available jobs in a region can be as much as 40 per cent lower than the number of total job seekers in that region. At the other extreme, the number of jobs may be about 33 per cent higher than the number of job seekers living in the same regions. Thus, in some regions, a substantial amount of commuting takes place.

2.4 Results of the Structural Equation Model

Tables 4.5 to 4.7 contain the results of the structural equation model. We have estimated three models for each dependent variable: the first model estimates only the influence of the three policy interventions – training, temporary public job creation and wage subsidies – by controlling for demand and structural variables; the second model tests only the implementation variables; and the third model presents the results of the full model. In the following interpretation, we concentrate on the estimations of the full model and refer to the other models only in the case of important differences. The coefficients of the control variables will only be interpreted if they contradict the hypotheses (see Table 4.3). We begin with the models related to 'short' long-term unemployment (more than six months, SLTU), and then turn to the models explaining 'long' long-term unemployment (more than 24 months, LLTU).

(1)

Policy intervention has the expected impact on the level, structure and change of SLTU. In the level case, it is temporary public job creation which has a significant impact in reducing SLTU;[25] training shows the correct sign but is only significant at the 10 per cent level. In the structural case (share of long-term unemployment), only training has the expected effect. Thus, as expected, training makes a difference, especially in preventing the 'structuralization' of unemployment. Wage subsidies have no impact at all. In the change case, all policy variables have no significant impact, although training does approach expectations.

Implementation matters, too, but in an ambivalent way. With longer duration, training and wage subsidies reduce the level of SLTU. This effect tends, however, to reverse in the structural case, which supports the suspicion that the favourable sign with respect to the level might be nothing more than a cosmetic effect. Long duration of wage subsidies significantly increases the change of SLTU. The duration of temporary public job creation has the consistent tendency to increase the level and structuralization of SLTU, but has no effect on the change of SLTU. However, given the specification of the model, we cannot be entirely certain whether the direction of causation runs the other way round (problem of endogeneity): it could be the case that, with increasing SLTU, placement officers are obliged to prolong their offers of public or private wage cost subsidies in order to get the unemployed into subsidized employment of any kind. The diversity of the portfolio shows no significant impact in all three cases.

With respect to the control variables, our demand indicator affects level and change of SLTU in the expected direction, but has no impact on the

Table 4.5 Estimates of the effect of ALMP on the level of long-term unemployment, western Germany, 1994–7

	Long-term unemployment > 6 months						Long-term unemployment > 24 months					
	Model 1		Model 2		Model 3		Model 1		Model 2		Model 3	
Variables	Coeff.	t-ratio	Coeff.	t-ratio	Coeff.	t-ratio	Coeff.	t-ratio	Coeff.	t-ratio	Coeff.	t-ratio
Constant	2.50	6.0**	2.45	3.9**	2.43	3.9**	1.29	3.6**	1.28	2.3*	1.25	2.1*
Change of employment	–0.05	5.1**	–0.05	4.5**	–0.05	5.0**	0.01	1.1	0.02	1.6	0.02	1.8
Level of SLTU	0.39	11.7**	0.39	12.6**	0.36	11.2**	0.08	1.7	0.18	4.2**	0.13	3.0**
Mismatch	–0.01	0.4	–0.03	2.5**	–0.02	2.0*	–0.00	0.1	–0.02	1.2	–0.02	1.1
Unskilled	–0.02	0.2	–0.16	1.7	–0.15	1.6	–0.07	0.6	–1.18	1.7	–0.13	1.3
Part time	0.47	9.1**	0.36	7.0**	0.36	6.9**	0.53	9.6**	0.39	6.7**	0.37	6.5**
Reg. attract.	0.51	4.3**	0.36	3.3**	0.40	3.6**	0.36	2.8**	0.25	2.0*	0.25	2.0*
Public jobs	–0.05	1.0	–	–	–0.09	2.1*	0.01	0.1	–	–	–0.03	0.6
Training	–0.08	2.3*	–	–	–0.06	1.7	–0.12	3.2**	–	–	–0.06	1.8
Wage subs.	0.03	1.2	–	–	0.01	0.2	–0.04	1.6	–	–	–0.08	3.0**
PJ-duration	–	–	0.02	1.9	0.02	2.1*	–	–	0.01	0.5	0.13	1.1
Training duration	–	–	–0.02	1.7	–0.02	2.0*	–	–	–0.03	2.9**	–0.04	3.6**
WS-duration	–	–	–0.05	5.8**	–0.05	5.5**	–	–	–0.05	4.6**	–0.04	4.0**
Diversity	–	–	0.00	0.00	0.01	0.5	–	–	–0.04	2.0*	–0.03	1.6
R^2	0.99		0.99		0.99		0.99		0.99		0.99	
Adj. R^2	0.98		0.98		0.98		0.98		0.98		0.98	
F-statistics	158.3		181.1		181.9		130.7		142.5		147.6	
No. of observations	426		426		426		426		426		426	

Notes:
* Denotes that the corresponding coefficient is significant at the 5% level.
** Denotes that the corresponding coefficient is significant at the 1% level.

Table 4.6 Estimates of the effect of ALMP on the structure of unemployment, western Germany, 1994–7

	Share of long-term unemployment > 6 months						Share of long-term unemployment > 24 months					
	Model 1		Model 2		Model 3		Model 1		Model 2		Model 3	
Variables	Coeff.	t-ratio	Coeff.	t-ratio	Coeff.	t-ratio	Coeff.	t-ratio	Coeff.	t-ratio	Coeff.	t-ratio
Constant	13.09	4.2**	13.8	3.7**	13.74	3.6**	9.71	0.8	9.71	0.8	9.70	0.9
Change of employment	0.01	0.4	0.01	0.6	0.01	0.6	0.09	5.3**	0.08	5.2**	0.09	5.3**
Level of SLTU	0.75	13.7**	0.80	14.9**	0.75	13.3**	0.22	3.5**	0.34	5.7**	0.31	4.9**
Mismatch	–0.05	2.2*	–0.05	2.3*	–0.04	1.9*	–0.01	0.6	–0.01	0.7	–0.01	0.7
Unskilled	–0.29	1.9	–0.23	1.4	–0.22	1.4	–0.12	0.8	–0.10	0.7	–0.06	0.4
Part time	0.20	2.4	0.24	2.7**	0.22	2.4*	0.29	3.7**	0.21	2.6**	0.19	2.3*
Reg. attract.	–0.34	1.8	–0.38	2.0*	–0.32	1.6	–0.02	0.1	–0.03	0.2	–0.02	0.1
Public jobs	–0.06	0.9	–	–	–0.08	1.1	0.07	1.0	–	–	0.03	0.4
Training	–0.11	2.0*	–	–	–0.11	1.9*	–0.12	2.3*	–	–	–0.06	1.2
Wage subs.	0.04	1.2	–	–	0.03	0.5	0.01	0.3	–	–	–0.05	1.5
PJ-duration	–	–	0.03	1.7	0.03	1.8	–	–	0.00	0.1	0.01	0.3
Training duration	–	–	0.00	0.2	0.03	0.2	–	–	–0.07	4.0**	–0.07	4.2**
WS-duration	–	–	0.03	1.8	0.03	1.9*	–	–	0.01	1.0	0.02	1.4
Diversity	–	–	0.01	0.3	0.02	0.7	–	–	–0.06	2.1*	–0.06	1.9*
R^2	0.97		0.97		0.97		0.97		0.98		0.98	
Adj. R^2	0.95		0.95		0.95		0.96		0.96		0.96	
F-statistics	58.8		58.2		57.8		65.5		70.1		70.0	
No. of observations	426		426		426		426		426		426	

Notes:
* Denotes that the corresponding coefficient is significant at the 5% level.
** Denotes that the corresponding coefficient is significant at the 1% level.

Table 4.7 Estimates of the effect of ALMP on change in long-term unemployment, western Germany, 1994–7

	Change in long-term unemployment > 6 months						Change in long-term unemployment > 24 months					
	Model 1		Model 2		Model 3		Model 1		Model 2		Model 3	
Variables	Coeff.	t-ratio	Coeff.	t-ratio	Coeff.	t-ratio	Coeff.	t-ratio	Coeff.	t-ratio	Coeff.	t-ratio
Constant	65.03	0.2	65.27	2.0*	65.60	2.1*	77.83	3.1**	81.00	3.5**	79.95	3.2**
Change of employment	–0.09	1.6	–0.12	2.4*	–0.12	2.3*	–0.03	0.6	–0.03	0.7	–0.03	0.5
Level of SLTU	1.46	9.0**	1.61	10.5**	1.52	9.6**	1.48	7.9**	1.5	8.4**	1.35	7.1**
Level of LTU	–0.48	1.5	–0.26	0.9	–0.28	0.9	–2.22	14.8**	–1.95	11.9**	–2.07	12.4**
Mismatch	–0.23	4.0**	–0.18	3.2**	–0.16	2.9**	–0.02	0.3	–0.01	0.1	–0.01	0.2
Unskilled	–1.60	3.6**	–1.04	2.4*	–1.07	2.4*	0.17	0.4	1.96	0.4	0.24	0.5
Part time	0.39	1.6	0.77	3.0**	0.75	3.0**	–0.02	0.1	0.02	0.1	0.09	0.4
Reg. attract.	0.13	0.2	0.49	0.9	0.63	1.2	1.55	3.0**	1.64	3.2**	1.53	3.0**
Public jobs	–0.28	1.4	–	–	–0.16	0.8	–0.29	1.5	–	–	–0.25	1.2
Training	–0.16	1.0	–	–	–0.25	1.6	0.13	0.8	–	–	0.04	0.3
Wage subs.	0.09	0.9	–	–	0.16	1.5	–0.46	4.7**	–	–	–0.35	3.4**
PJ-duration	–	–	0.02	0.3	0.01	0.2	–	–	0.00	0.1	0.04	0.9
Training duration	–	–	0.07	1.6	0.09	1.8	–	–	0.20	4.2**	0.15	3.0**
WS-duration	–	–	0.21	4.9**	0.21	4.8**	–	–	–0.01	0.2	0.00	0.1
Diversity	–	–	0.07	0.8	0.08	1.0	–	–	0.12	1.5	0.14	1.7
R^2	0.76		0.79		0.79		0.79		0.79		0.80	
Adj. R^2	0.63		0.67		0.67		0.68		0.68		0.69	
F-statistics	5.8		6.5		6.5		6.9		6.8		7.0	
No. of observations	426		426		426		426		426		426	

Notes:
* Denotes that the corresponding coefficient is significant at the 5% level.
** Denotes that the corresponding coefficient is significant at the 1% level.

structure of unemployment. Assigning a question mark to our prediction (see Table 4.3) was therefore justified. In all three cases, our mismatch indicator has the reverse sign compared with our prediction, which might reflect the fact that we did not control for the level of vacancies.[26] Contrary to our expectations, the skill indicator has either no effect or the reverse effect. Thus, the higher the share of low-skilled blue-collar workers, the lower the change in SLTU appears to be. In other words, regions with a high share of low-skilled workers faced (in our period of observation) a lower risk of increasing SLTU. This may be because the small economic upswing in the middle of the 1990s was mainly driven by a rise in the export of manufacturing goods. The positive sign of part-time work also runs contrary to expectations: in all three cases, part-time work contributes positively to the level, structure or change of SLTU. This explanation might be a corollary to the low-skill or industrial indicator. Part time as an indicator for service-centred regions may simply reflect the fact that the employment crisis in the middle of the 1990s was a phenomenon of rationalization in services. This interpretation is supported by the unexpected positive sign of regional attractiveness in the level case; that is, the level of SLTU is concentrated in regions of high attractiveness in terms of jobs. In the structural case, however, regional attractiveness shows the expected sign.

(2)

Policy intervention is also effective in the case of 'long' long-term unemployment (LLTU). Surprisingly, however, temporary public job-creation measures have no impact at all in all three cases – level, structure and change in LLTU. None the less, training again had the expected impact in the level and structure case; albeit with low significance. In contrast to their ineffectiveness with respect to SLTU, wage subsidies significantly reduce, as anticipated, the level of LLTU. Subsidies also have a small dampening effect on structuralization (but with low significance), and are very useful in slowing down the (further) increase of LLTU.

Implementation matters, too, but again in an ambivalent way. With longer duration, training and wage subsidies reduce the level of LLTU. In the structure case, the favourable impact of training remains, whereas the impact of wage subsidies disappears (or it does not, at least, reverse significantly as in the case of SLTU). As expected, the coefficient for training measures with long duration loads significantly positive with the change of LLTU. Long-term training measures can contribute to a further increase of LLTU because of the opportunity costs involved; they reduce the participation level of the 'short' long-term unemployed, who later go on to become 'long' long-term unemployed.[27] Again, however, the causation could run the other way round: the rapid increase of LLTU may lead placement officers to implement long-lasting retraining measures in an effort to adjust to structural change. The implementation indicator for temporary public job creation is never significant. Diversity of portfolio, however, had the expected effect in the level as well as in the structural case: the higher the diversity of portfolio, the lower the level and share of LLTU.

With respect to the control variables, the demand indicator has no effect on level and change of LLTU, and even has a positive effect on the structure of LLTU. In other words: in regions with a favourable development of employment, LLTU was not reduced, and the share of LLTU actually increased. This – at first glance – counter-intuitive result can be explained by the well-known phenomenon that 'structuralization' – in the sense of negative selection – is stronger in the case of hiring than in the case of firing. If the economic situation improves, the strongest among the stock of unemployed will be selected for hiring and the weakest will remain unemployed, thus leading to a higher share of LLTU. For the other control variables, we find no remarkable differences from the models related to SLTU.

In sum, ALMP matters on the aggregate level, but has a significant impact in only certain cases, and its overall effect is marginal. Training appears to be the most effective instrument but, for implementation, our results have been unsatisfactory. However, before we interpret this outcome in the light of the broader aims of this study, we will supplement our analysis by making use of another model of AIA designed to measure the impact of ALMP. This model focuses on the dynamics of unemployment, and is used in this context to assess the outflow rate of unemployment.

3 AGGREGATE EFFECTS ON UNEMPLOYMENT OUTFLOWS

The basis for this part of the analysis is a model by Bellmann and Lehmann (1993) and Bellmann and Jackman (1996a) which assumes that ALMP increases individual search efficiency in the matching process.[28] Before developing the model, we briefly present some descriptive information. As Table 4.8 demonstrates, we generally observe decreasing outflow rates from unemployment in the period of observation. In 1994, the outflows from unemployment were 2.75 times the average unemployment stock, decreasing to 1.72 in 1997. Around this mean value, the unemployment outflows vary widely; between 415 per cent and 203 per cent of the stocks in 1994, and between 103 per cent and 270 per cent in 1997. The outflow data cited include new entrants in programmes. For the following analysis, we therefore adjust the data by subtracting the inflows into programmes from the unemployment outflows. However, the falling trend, as well as the variation across the regions, remains.

Table 4.8 *Unemployment outflows as a percentage of average regional unemployment*

	Year	Mean	Std.	Min.	Max.	N
Western Germany						
Total	1994	275.94	38.34	203.19	415.34	142
	1995	199.94	43.81	119.14	341.52	142
	1996	181.98	36.38	112.47	302.05	142
	1997	172.23	33.23	103.43	269.83	142
Adjusted*	1994	258.21	35.83	188.08	390.76	142
	1995	178.03	40.53	101.73	318.7	142
	1996	163.42	33.94	96.47	281.3	142
	1997	159.39	31.85	90.04	255.59	142
Eastern Germany						
Total	1994	n.a.	n.a.	n.a.	n.a.	n.a.
	1995	172.95	25.91	119.69	238.7	35
	1996	179.57	20.8	134.23	244.63	35
	1997	156.25	20.29	130.22	216.5	35
Adjusted*	1994	n.a.	n.a.	n.a.	n.a.	n.a.
	1995	119.41	25.88	52.92	173.25	35
	1996	130.47	20.16	82.42	193.44	35
	1997	124.39	20.06	98.23	195.74	35

Notes: * Data adjusted by subtracting the inflows in programmes from total outflows from unemployment.

Source: Regional data work-file WZB, *Bundesanstalt für Arbeit*, own calculations.

3.1 A Matching Model

Bellmann and Lehmann (1993) explain the exits from long-term unemployment as a function of the number of (registered) vacancies V, the search efficiency c^* of the unemployed and their total amount U (4.1). We modify this approach by assessing the impact of ALMP on the outflow from total unemployment. The basic equation shows that A (that is, outflows from unemployment) is a non-specified function of regional unemployment, vacancies and the search efficiency of the unemployed, c^*:

$$A = f(V; c^*U) \tag{4.1}$$

The theoretically expected effect of active labour market policy is an increase in the search efficiency by the vector of measures ($\boldsymbol{M}$) times the net effect of these measures on the search efficiency k, which means that:

$$c^* = c^0(1 + k\boldsymbol{M}) \tag{4.2}$$

with $k\boldsymbol{M} = \Sigma d_i E_i$ denotes the sum of participants in measure i times the effect of the measure i.

The assumption that the function f exhibits constant returns to scale is reasonable and supported by empirical studies (Bellmann and Jackman, 1996a, p. 159). The equation can therefore be rewritten as:

$$\frac{A}{U} = c^* f\left[\frac{V}{c^* U}\right] \tag{4.3}$$

Assuming that $f[V/c^*U] = [V/c^*U]^b$ and by taking the natural logarithm, this function can be transformed into the following additive function:

$$\ln\left[\frac{A}{U}\right] = \ln c^* + b\ln\left[\frac{V}{c^* U}\right] \tag{4.4}$$

We see a function where the outflows from unemployment is an additional function of the log of the search efficiency and b times the available vacancies on regional labour markets over the unemployed. As we suppose in equation (4.2) c^* as a function of c^0, the (at last theoretically) search efficiency without any measures and the quantity of measures $k\boldsymbol{M}$. By substituting this we get:

$$b\ln\left[\frac{V}{c^* U}\right] = b\ln\left[\frac{V}{U}\right] - \ln[c^0(1 + k\boldsymbol{M})] \tag{4.5}$$

By substituting this result into equation (4.4) and through some transformations, we get a function in which (at least theoretically) the search efficiency without the ALMP measures c^0 and the influence of the measures on this value ($1 + k\boldsymbol{M}$) can be estimated:

$$\ln\left[\frac{A}{U}\right] = (1 - b)\ln[c^0(1 + k\boldsymbol{M})] + b\ln\left[\frac{V}{U}\right] \tag{4.6}$$

After solving this equation, we get (4.7).

$$\ln\left[\frac{A}{U}\right] = (1 - b)\ln c + (1 - b)\ln(1 + k\boldsymbol{M}) + b\ln\left[\frac{V}{U}\right] \tag{4.7}$$

Assuming small values for kM, we can rewrite $\ln(1 + kM) \approx kM$ to find (4.8):

$$\ln\left[\frac{A}{U}\right] = (1-b)\ln c + (1-b)k\boldsymbol{M} + b\ln\left[\frac{V}{U}\right] \tag{4.8}$$

As $\boldsymbol{M}$ is the function of active labour market policy, $k\boldsymbol{M}$ can be substituted in the equation, so that the final model emerges (4.9):

$$\ln\left[\frac{A}{U}\right] = (1-b)\ln c + (1-b)\Sigma d_i E_i + b\ln\left[\frac{V}{U}\right] \tag{4.9}$$

In the following paragraphs, the model is modified and operationalized for our empirical material and must be transformed. This is because we assume that policy input is endogenous from the regional level of unemployment, so that a 'policy response' should be taken into account.

3.2 Policy Responsiveness

For an analysis of the long-term net effects, the model would require time-series data which allow us to control the influence of ALMP on the inflows to unemployment in a later period (Dor *et al.*, 1997 recently calculated these effects for Belgium). Unfortunately, the effects of ALMP on 'recurrent unemployment' caused by back-flows to unemployment after participation in a programme cannot yet be included in the model.

As the data does not allow for the analysis of post-programme effects, we must concentrate on gross effects at a certain point in time. In addition, yearly data make it necessary to operationalize the inverse effects to a later point in time, which could be far removed from the programme's expiration. Given these limitations, we must be cautious in interpreting our results: the explicit goal of a programme is to increase the outflows from unemployment, as each participant in a programme is one less unemployed person at t. What happens after the programme ends and whether a participant is reintegrated into the labour market in the long run cannot be observed with cross-section data, and will be the subject of an estimation in a subsequent work.

Another serious problem lies in the positive relationship between local unemployment development and participation in measures (problem of policy responsiveness or endogeneity, cf. Büttner and Prey, 1998). This problem can be solved to a certain extent by the inclusion of information about the local unemployment structure and its development: Büttner and Prey suggest including the average unemployment duration in the analysis because the long-term unemployed are generally eligible for active measures, and a coherent development of long-term unemployment and active measures could filter the policy responsiveness of ALMP. We also assume that the problem of endogeneity can be solved by a weighting with the long-term unemployed. But this would also imply an evaluation of the measures from the perspective of the long-term unemployed. As we test the model for all unemployment outflows, we allow for this problem by examining the total outflows as dependent on changes in the programme size between the two years, and control for regional aggregate unemployment and vacancies as suggested in the model worked out in the preceding paragraph. For the application of the model in empirical terms, the equation must be transformed in the following way:

$$\ln\left[\frac{A}{U}\right]_{i,t} = (1-b)\ln c_{i,t} + (1-b)\Sigma d_i \Delta E_{it,t-1} + b\ln\left[\frac{V}{U}\right]_{i,t} \tag{4.10}$$

By further elaborating upon this basic model, we estimate the variations in the outflow rate by the change in input variables (policy on). As these programmes were in existence long before our observation began, and have, therefore, already produced various effects, we must concentrate on 'policy change' rather than on 'policy on' in our analysis. Only in the case of newly initiated and implemented programmes can an observation of the total 'policy on' effect be estimated, and then only if we have comparable labour markets which are not simultaneously affected by 'policy on' (quasi-experimental programme evaluation).

3.3 The Influence of Policy Change on Search Efficiency

The search efficiency in the basic model can be seen as a kind of natural matching capability in the total absence of measures. As stated above, a total 'policy off' situation can hardly be observed in the empirical data since most programmes have been in existence for a long period of time, and would thus require an enormous data set. In the earlier study conducted by Bellmann and Lehmann (1993), this problem was solved by taking the average length of time spent by an unemployed person in a specific duration category. In their paper, the increase in the search efficiency was therefore operationalized as the increase in the probability of leaving unemployment in relation to the decrease of survival in the specific groups. Since they are impossible to estimate given the available data, we have chosen not to concentrate on specific groups at this stage or on their probability of survival.

Instead, we have decided to operationalize search efficiency s_i again from the perspective of a given situation with a certain policy implementation. The search efficiency in our analysis will be included as a moving average of the hirings[29] as a percentage of average unemployment in the two previous years.

If longer time series existed, we could pattern this dimension more precisely by smoothing factors such as the influence of the business cycle and regional singularities in order to better estimate the effect of the increases in programme participation on outflows.

Now that our model has been improved in terms of empirical specification, we can enlarge the equation (4.10) by including the search efficiency:

$$\ln\left[\frac{A}{U}\right]_{i,t} = (1-b)\ln s_{i,t} + (1-b)\Sigma d_i \Delta E_{it,t-1} + b\ln\left[\frac{V}{U}\right]_{i,t} \tag{4.11}$$

where search efficiency is defined as $s_i = av_{t-2,t} H/U$.

3.4 Implementation Differences

Labour market policy serves the long-term unemployed in particular. For this target group, German ALMP offers alternative programmes. In line with the operationalization in section 2, we aggregate the individual programmes into three principal categories: training, job creation and targeted wage subsidies. By aggregating these programmes in terms of participation, we can, to a certain extent, also stop too much variation among the programmes from occurring. Some regions could, for example, have more participation in a single programme because of additional funding by EU or regional and local bodies while other regions use alternative programmes as functional equivalents. With aggregation in the three principal categories of ALMP, we can better compare the overall design of the policy mix and the broad orientation of the local implementation structure (whether the local implementation network provides better service in terms of creating additional jobs or in terms of training). We therefore specify the term of 'policy increase' from equation (4.12) to

$$\Sigma d_i \Delta E_{it,t-1} = d_1 \Delta E_{1t,t-1} + d_2 \Delta E_{2t,t-1} + d_3 \Delta E_{3it,t-1} \tag{4.12}$$

where ΔE_1, ΔE_2, ΔE_3 are the changes in the participation entries in the three principal forms of measures (the aggregates of some programmes, see section 2).

The dimension of implementation is additionally included with two binary variables: first, we construct a relative importance of the demand- or supply-oriented policies in the region, that is, whether or not the local employment office has a higher share of demand-oriented measures than the national average ($D_1 = 1$). A second variable describes the implementation of labour market training, with the value of one if the local district has a share of internal training among all training measures which is higher than the national average:

$$\Sigma e_i 1_{it,t-1} = e_1 D_{1i} + e_2 D_{2i} \tag{4.13}$$

3.5 Regional Labour Market Trends

Given the present data set, the analysis must be restricted to a cross-section analysis where the integration of the dimension of time cannot be performed. We assume, however, that the regional developments over time have a notable influence on the impact of changes in ALMP. We therefore wish to cover these items with a set of regional control variables. These measures indicate a) the changes in the employment structure, especially the shift of employment from mature industrial sectors to service sectors as a factor which enhances the effectiveness of ALMP; b) the regional labour market dynamic represented by the new entries into the (regular) labour market as an average of the last years (alternatively, a trend variable could be included, although we have not yet adequately explored this possibility); c) the regional development of part-time work based on the assumption that a dynamic development of part-time work promotes flows from unemployment to employment. If we had access to time series data, we could cope with these regional and time effects by setting up a fixed-effects model which would allow us to isolate regional singularities in its fixed-effects variables. It is not, however, possible to estimate such a model using the present data. None the less, data is available on long-term time series for employment and unemployment (since the end of the 1970s for West Germany, and since the start of 1990s for unified Germany), so that the regional control variables included provide extended structural information on regional items.

Thus, the empirical application specifies the basic model in:

$$\ln\left[\frac{A}{U}\right]_{i,t} = (1-b)\ln s_{i,t} + (1-b)\Sigma d_i \Delta E_{it,t-1} + b\ln\left[\frac{V}{U}\right]_{i,t} + \Sigma a_i c_i \tag{4.14}$$

with $\Sigma a_i c_i = a_1 c_1 + a_2 c_2 + a_3 c_3$

and $c_{1i} = \Delta e_{1i} \quad c_{2i} = \Delta n_i / e_i \quad c_{3i} = \Delta p_i / e_i$.

Tables 4.9 and 4.10 show definition and descriptive statistics of the operationalized variables estimated in the multivariate analysis.

3.6 Empirical Analysis and Results

The model elaborated in the previous section is tested using the data of 142 western German employment districts. There are two reasons for our concentration on western Germany. First, as mentioned previously, the labour market

Table 4.9 Summary of the operationalization of the variables used in the model test

Changes in unemployment (dependent variable)	Log of the outflow rate of unemployment adjusted by participants in measures
Vacancies	Log of vacancies as percentage of the extended unemployment (including participants in active measures)
Search efficiency	Log of the moving average from hiring of the two quarters of *t-1* and the four quarters in *t* as percentage of the unemployment rate in *t* (1993 < *t* < 1997)
ABM change	Change of participants in job-creation measures, 1994–6
Further training (FuU) change	Change in participation of further training 1994–6
Wage subsidies change	Participants in different measures of wage subsidies
Employment growth in industry	Change in employment in the industry sector, 1991–6
Employment growth	Change of the overall employment, 1991–6
Part-time growth	Change of part-time employment contracts, 1994–6
ABM duration	Duration of job-creation measures, 1996
Duration further training	Duration of further training, 1996
Internal training	Dummy variable of the relative importance of the average participation rate in internal measures divided by all participants, 1995–6. The variable has the value 1, if the ratio is above the average.
Demand orientation	Dummy: relative importance of the 1995–6 average in respect to supply measure participants. The variable has the value 1, if the ratio is above the average.

situation in western Germany differs from that of eastern Germany. Second, the data available in the two parts of the country are different, which means that the operationalization of the variables would have to be different. We have tested the model for the aggregate unemployment outflows in 1996. The dependent variable is the adjusted outflow rate introduced at the beginning of section 3:

Table 4.10 Descriptive statistics for the variables used in analysis 2

	Min.	Max.	Mean	Std. dev.
Changes in unemployment (dependent variable)	4.57	5.64	5.08	0.203
Vacancies	0.90	3.41	1.99	0.463
Search efficiency	–0.07	1.53	0.812	0.287
ABM change	–36.58	53.72	2.27	15.56
FuU change	–22.62	20.99	–0.414	7.75
Wage subsidies change	–73.54	111.82	–18.25	23.29
Employment growth in industry	–25.53	–0.98	–10.44	3.45
Employment growth	–12.84	21.48	–2.478	5.05
Part-time growth	–2.23	30.85	6.55	4.07
ABM duration	0.00	1.00	0.366	0.484
Duration further training	0.00	1.00	0.401	0.492
Internal training	0.54	1.88	0.855	0.233
Demand orientation	0.46	1.40	0.811	0.161

Source: Regional data work-file WZB, *Bundesanstalt für Arbeit*, own calculations.

$$\frac{A_{t,i}^{*}}{U_{t,i}} = \frac{A_{t,i}}{U_{t,i}} - \frac{E_{t,i}}{U_{t,i}}$$

where $E_{t,i}$ are the total inflows into programmes of ALMP in t. We have chosen this adjusted rate in order to avoid overestimation of outflow due to pure programme effects. Each new programme participant inflow is counted as an unemployment outflow in the statistic.

Table 4.11 presents the results of the regression estimates. In the first model, we have suppressed the implementation variables. By focusing on the variables which we have operationalized theoretically, we can see that the policy variables are hardly significant in the model: neither the increase of ABM nor the targeted wage subsidies have a significant effect on the outflows. The estimators for both variables show that demand-oriented measures have a positive influence on the outflows, but the effect is too small for these measures to matter in this context. We receive a significant negative estimator for further training, which contradicts our assumption that ALMP increases search efficiency.

We must use caution in interpreting this estimator since changes from one year to the next hardly reflect long-lasting labour market problems. This difficulty becomes even more obvious when we look at the estimators of the variables for the regional labour market structure: both the change in regional

Table 4.11 *Aggregate impact of ALMP on unemployment outflows, 1996 (OLS estimation results)*

	Model 1		Model 2		Model 3	
	Coeff.	t-ratio	Coeff.	t-ratio	Coeff.	t-ratio
Search efficiency	0.417	8.639**	0.425	8.967**	0.422	8.617**
ABM change	0.001	0.789	0.001	0.979	0.001	0.866
FuU change	–0.003	–2.478	–0.004	–2.965**	–0.004	–2.795*
Wage subsidies change	0.0002	0.203	–0.0002	–0.411	–0.003	–0.584
Vacancies	0.021	0.803	0.010	0.348	0.008	0.278
Employment growth in industry	0.014	4.780**	0.013	4.456**	0.013	4.320**
Employment growth	0.009	3.509**	0.009	3.502**	0.008	3.154**
Part-time growth	0.004	1.300	0.003	1.150	0.003	1.195
ABM duration			–0.057	–1.412	–0.061	–1.498
Duration further training			–0.166	–2.640*	–0.152	–2.348*
Internal training					0.036	1.864*
Demand orientation					–0.008	–0.373
Constant	4.840	81.121**	5.027	57.928**	5.007	50.644**
R^2	0.74		0.75		0.76	
Adj. R^2	0.72		0.73		0.74	
F-statistics	46.6		39.8		34.1	
No. of observations	142		142		142	

Notes:
* Denotes that the corresponding coefficient is significant at the 5% level.
** Denotes that the corresponding coefficient is significant at the 1% level.

Source: Regional data work-file WZB, *Bundesanstalt für Arbeit*, own calculations.

employment and the development of the industrial sectors have a very significant influence on aggregate unemployment outflows. The overall explanatory power of the model is therefore quite high. The results were nevertheless identical to the most recent analysis by Büttner and Prey (1998), who interpreted the results of their estimation as an indication that further training increases labour market mismatch. While our estimators do not have the same high level of significance, they none the less provide some empirical evidence which tends to support Büttner's and Prey's conclusions.

The two other models which control for implementation variables indicate that implementation strategies bring about significant differences in the overall outflow rate. In the second model, we obtained an interesting result concerning the implementation of training measures indicating that short-term measures should be preferred. This is because the duration of measures is negatively correlated even with the adjusted outflow rate, which is no longer influenced by participation. Moreover, the last extension of the model, including the implementation of training, provides some empirical evidence to support the assumption that internal training leads to higher unemployment outflows. Both extended models have almost the same explanatory power and again indicate that structural development in the regional labour markets (employment growth and development of employment in industry) determines the outflows from unemployment. While the impact of ALMP on the overall outflows from unemployment tend once again to support the conclusions of the previous study by Büttner and Prey (1998), they are not statistically sufficient.

4 CONCLUSION

In sum, we can state with confidence that ALMP matters. Its impact is, however, slight, and difficult to measure using the AIA method. Not all policy measures are effective. As we noted in the descriptive section of this chapter, policy intervention in the form of temporary public job creation (ABM) increases with the level of overall unemployment, and even more strongly with the level of LTU. If we control for this policy response in the structural equation model, we find that this measure had a significant impact on the reduction of long-term unemployment only in the case of SLTU. In the matching model which measures the impact of ALMP on the overall outflows of unemployment, the coefficients are in the right direction, but are not significant. While it may seem disappointing that this measure has no impact on the structure of unemployment, a mere dampening of 'structuralization' processes would be considered a success in terms of the measure's own objectives. Since it is difficult to control for endogeneity (policy response), the reversal of the highly positive binary correlation between measure and goal in the multiple equation model indicates that the model is robust and well specified in principle. ABM may therefore produce small positive effects that disappear in the 'noise' of such an aggregate model.

In the structural equation model, training measures consistently have the expected – and, in some cases, significant – impact on the reduction of LTU, whereas wage subsidies seem to work effectively only for the very long-term unemployed. Training appears to be especially effective in preventing 'structuralization' and in speeding up the reduction of long-term unemployment when the economy is improving. But while the coefficients point in the expected direction, we found no significant impact on the level of LTU. In the matching model, we even found a reverse sign of the expected coefficient related to the overall outflow of unemployment. Yet, due to the model's design, we cannot be certain in this case that we have really solved the problem of endogeneity. Further studies should be extended to include a longer time series since the availability of more empirical material would no doubt allow us to better control for policy responsiveness and the business cycle. In particular, matching which is not influenced by programmes can hardly be operationalized using the data employed for this model test. Further applications of this model would also have to be aimed at more specific target groups among the unemployed, such as the long-term unemployed.

Despite some ambivalent outcomes, the overall results of our study underline the considerable potential of ALMP. The demand measure of temporary public job creation can, if properly implemented, alleviate the level of long-term unemployment. The structural measure of training can prevent the 'structuralization' of unemployment and help to reduce long-term unemployment under favourable economic circumstances. As measures between demand and supply, wage subsidies can be of particular assistance to the very hard-to-place unemployed. These results are corroborated if we take into account the overall restrictions of an aggregate impact analysis. At such levels, implementation of ALMP measures cannot be fully controlled. Thus, because some employment offices apparently fail to use the measures appropriately, the potential of ALMP tends to be underestimated.[30]

Implementation also seems to have an impact, but the results of our study are ambivalent. It is, moreover, unclear whether the model has solved the endogeneity problem in the case of implementation. While it appears that wage cost subsidies work more effectively if they provide longer-term perspectives, we cannot be certain of this. In both cases, however, we found a corresponding significant result in terms of training duration. This indicates that short-term measures may be more effective than long-term measures by inducing effective search earlier. Diversity in the policy mix does not contribute additionally to policy effectiveness, except in the case of the 'long' long-term unemployed. Thus, more research is clearly needed. Case study or numerical comparative approaches,[31] which allow for finer distinctions and a much greater number of indicators covering the variety of regional regimes of coordination and cooperation, are clearly necessary, especially in estimating the impact of different implementation strategies or contextual conditions of implementation (see also Chapter 8 in this volume). It would be especially interesting to measure the impact of ALMP while taking into account and controlling for variations in the financing of the measures.

NOTES

1. Social Science Research Centre Berlin (WZB), Reichpietschufer 50, D-10785 Berlin; Tel. +49-30-25491-130/-132, Fax +49-30-25491-222; e-mail: gues@medea.wz-berlin.de; speckes@rhein.vwl.uni-mannheim.de; christoph_hilbert@de.rolandberger.com. We thank especially Jaap de Koning for continuous advice; we also wish to express our gratitude to the Bundesanstalt für Arbeit in Nuremberg for providing the data.
2. In 1998 the '*Arbeitsförderungsgesetz*' (AFG) was replaced by the '*Sozialgesetzbuch*' (SGB III), which contains some modifications of the ALMP instruments. Some of these modifications were already enacted in 1997, but they are marginally related to our subject. Since we cover empirically the period 1994 to 1997, we refer to the legal situation that existed under the AFG.
3. Placement services and counselling, of course, affect also job search and therefore long-term unemployment. We do not take this instrument explicitly into account since it is related to the whole active labour force; it is partly included since each referral to a programme counts as a placement; for more details see Chapter 8 in this volume.
4. On the increasing importance of community-based labour market policy see Fuchs and Spengler (1997).
5. A wage subsidy for low-wage earners like the US earned income tax credit or other forms of negative income tax does not exist in Germany. For an excellent review of the various forms of wage subsidies see Gautié *et al.* (1994).
6. Related to 'extended unemployment', which means the unemployed plus the number of participants in labour market programmes. In the aggregate impact analysis we will use the total active labour force in the denominator to control for endogeneity.
7. For an early application of this approach see Peters and Schmid (1982), and Schmid and Peters (1982).
8. We excluded the eastern German regions because of their totally different labour market problems in the transition process; also LMP regulations were different in the period of observation. West Berlin, however, is included as one case in our sample.
9. This specification may be questionable; the results, however, do not differ substantially from a specification without a time lag.
10. The correlation, however, is in fact far from perfect, indicating the existence of regional peculiarities stemming from, among other factors, variation in policy and policy implementation. The share of long-term unemployment (more than six months) correlates (0.6) with the short-term unemployment rate (less than three months); the share of long-term unemployment (more than 24 months) correlates (0.54) with the short-term unemployment rate (less than three months).
11. This indicator reflects also to some extent demand conditions; the correlation with the change of employment is around –0.32.
12. The measurement of mismatch is extremely difficult. Research has provided, so far, mixed results; for a general introduction and international comparison see Padoa-Schioppa (1991) and Burda and Wyplosz (1994); for Germany see Franz (1991) and Entdorf (1995). Entdorf has probably developed the most sophisticated mismatch indicator. Using panel data and a matching function he finds (in contrast to the majority of researchers) a drastic decline in the matching efficiency in Germany; in other words an increased mismatch. However, it could be that his measure (using official vacancy and unemployment data) just reflects the fact that more and more transitions between employment and unemployment run through a stage of inactivity. For instance, in Germany only 45 per cent of people leaving unemployment took up employment in 1997; in other words, 55 per cent of the unemployment outflow went into 'inactivity' (parental leave, homework, illness, education, training, retirement, disability, and so on), and about 50 per cent of employment inflows came from 'inactivity'. The inflow of unemployed into employment is affected by cyclical changes, but there is also a general downward trend. The figure for 1985 was 74 per cent, and for 1990 54 per cent (Bundesanstalt für Arbeit, 1998, p. 64).

13. An alternative would have been the share of vacancies registered for longer than three months as a percentage of total registered vacancies; the correlation with the indicator chosen is 0.9.
14. The danger of multicollinearity with the 'low-skill indicator' (and its sectoral implications) is low; the correlation with the low-skill indicator is only –0.29, and with services it is only 0.37.
15. All employment data at the regional level refer to dependent employees who are covered by social insurance; thus, marginal employment not covered by social insurance (employees with a weekly working time below 15 hours), self-employed and civil servants are not included. These employees are counted statistically at the place where they work (principle of the firms' location). The active civil labour force at the regional level of REOs which we are using as unit of observation is an estimation by the FEO; they are used to calculate the unemployment rate and include all persons working or actively seeking work; they recounted where they used to live (the principle of home location).
16. Because regional size as indicator for agglomeration (here operationalized as the number of employees as a percentage of total employment in western Germany) correlates strongly with regional attractiveness (0.47), we disregarded this possibility of including another explicit regional characteristic in the model.
17. To control for possible cosmetic effects, we also corrected the dependent variables by using extended unemployment figures in the nominator, but these experiments did not change the results.
18. Another interesting indicator would be the market share of the PES (see Walwei, 1996). One should expect that PES will be most effective where it has gained a high *market share* in its placement service. The market share is measured by the number of public placements (in employment of at least seven days) as percentage of total hiring. Because each participant in a subsidized job is counted as a placement, the PES market share has to be adjusted by this measure.
19. Another way to measure this impact is to estimate the share of long-term unemployed in the total volume of unemployment. Karr (1997) calculated that of all unemployment spells, 16.8 per cent were over one year, had an average length of unemployment of 792.2 days and made up 58.4 per cent of the total volume of unemployment; 83.2 per cent of all unemployment spells were under one year, had an average length of unemployment of 114.5 days and made up only 41.6 per cent of the total volume of unemployment.
20. A recent study concludes that regional determinants have a stronger impact on the probability to leave unemployment than most of the personal characteristics. Of all new spells of unemployment in the year 1996, 21.2 per cent remained longer than one year unemployed; this measure of risk varied in the western German REO from 9.2 per cent (Traunstein) to 29.2 per cent (Dortmund) (Rudolph, 1998).
21. In western Germany, overall unemployment increased 18 per cent in the observation period 1994 to 1997.
22. Which, in fact, is our own estimation on the basis of duration categories measured in one month of the year.
23. It is estimated that about 25 per cent of 'unskilled' blue-collar workers are in such positions; an often quoted example are formally trained bakers in unskilled positions in the motor car industry.
24. It is to be expected that these barriers are higher for men than for women; a gender differentiation of the estimates would be required to test for this difference, which is beyond the scope of this contribution.
25. We also tested for possible cosmetic effects by correcting the dependent variables by adding an estimated number of the participants in programmes who otherwise would have been long-term unemployed; in the case of temporary public job creation, the weight was 100 per cent; the results, however, did not change significantly.
26. A run of the model testing this hypothesis solved the problem for the change case and the structural case, but not for the level case; in the level case it seems plausible that the causation runs the other way round – high long-term unemployment reduces the share of vacancies with a long duration.

27. This relationship remains, albeit with a lower significance, if we run the model with a combination of participation flows and participation duration. This version of model specification applied to all other models does also not change substantially the other results reported here, which we take as further evidence that the model is rather robust.
28. This part of the study is also inspired by Bourdet and Persson (1991) and (1992); Büttner and Prey (1998); Calmfors (1994); Calmfors and Skedinger (1995); Forslund and Krueger (1995); de Koning (1993); de Koning *et al.* (1991) and Layard *et al.* (1991).
29. The moving average is defined as the average of hiring in the third and fourth quarter of the previous year and of the four quarters in a specific year: $s_t = av_{t-2,t-1,t}\,H/U$.
30. It must be added, however, that the potential of AIA is far from being fully exploited. First, as the monitoring data improve, for example, by adding information on financing, age of participants in programmes and follow-up of participants after programme, the models become more powerful; second, as the data become available in longer time series, the statistical possibilities of model sophistication increase; third, by splitting the sample in various ways (by random procedure or by selective characteristics of the regions), further controlled tests are possible.
31. For instance on the basis of Boolean algebra, see Ragin (1987).

REFERENCES

Bellmann, L. and R. Jackman (1996a), 'Aggregate Impact Analysis', in G. Schmid, J. O'Reilly and K. Schömann (eds), *International Handbook of Labour Market Policy and Evaluation*, Cheltenham: Edward Elgar, pp. 143–62.

Bellmann, L. and R. Jackman (1996b), 'The Impact of Labour Market Policy on Wages, Employment and Labour Market Mismatch', in G. Schmid, J. O'Reilly and K. Schömann (eds), *International Handbook of Labour Market Policy and Evaluation*, Cheltenham: Edward Elgar, pp. 725–46.

Bellmann, L. and H. Lehmann (1993), *Active Labour Market Policies in Britain and Germany and Long-term Unemployment: An Evaluation*, Annual Conference of the European Association of Labour Economists, Lund, Sweden.

Bourdet, Y. and I. Persson (1991), 'Chômage des jeunes et fonctionnement du marché du travail: les cas français et suédois', *Economie et Statistique*, 249, 39–51.

Bourdet, Y. and I. Persson (1992), '*Does Labour Market Policy Matter? Long Term Unemployment in France and Sweden*', Working Paper 6, Department of Economics, University of Lund, Sweden.

Bundesanstalt für Arbeit (1998), '*Arbeitsmarktbericht*', 1997, Nürnberg.

Burda, M. and C. Wyplosz (1994), 'Gross Worker and Job Flows in Europe', *European Economic Review*, 38, 1287–320.

Büttner, T. and H. Prey (1998), 'Does Active Labour Market Policy Affect Structural Unemployment? An Empirical Investigation for West German Regions, 1986 to 1993', in *Zeitschrift für Wirtschafts- und Sozialwissenschaften (ZWS)*, 118, 389–412.

Calmfors, L. (1994), 'Active Labour Market Policy and Unemployment: A Framework for the Analyses of Crucial Design Features', *OECD Economic Studies*, 22, 7–47.

Calmfors, L. and P. Skedinger (1995), 'Does Active Labour-Market Policy Increase Employment? Theoretical Considerations and Some Empirical Evidence From Sweden', *Oxford Review of Economic Policy*, **11** (1), 91–109.

Dor, E., B. van der Linden and M. Lopez-Novella (1997), 'On Labour Market Policies and Aggregate Unemployment Outflows', *Oxford Bulletin of Economics and Statistics*, **59** (1), 109–31.

Entdorf, H. (1995), 'Strukturelle Arbeitslosigkeit in West-Deutschland: Ergebnisse einer Mismatch-Analyse', in W. Franz und V. Steiner (eds), *Der westdeutsche Arbeitsmarkt im strukturellen Anpassungsprozeß*, Baden-Baden, pp. 91–104.

Forslund A. and A. B. Krueger (1995), 'An Evaluation of the Swedish Active Labour Market Policy – New and Received Wisdom', *SNS Occasional Paper*, 65, January.

Franz, W. (1991), 'Match and Mismatch on the German Labour Market', in F. Padoa-Schioppa (ed.), *Mismatch and Labour Mobility*, Cambridge: Cambridge University Press, pp. 105–35.

Fuchs, L. and I. Spengler (1997), 'Kommunale Beschäftigungsförderung. Ergebnisse einer Umfrage von 1997 über Hilfen zur Arbeit nach dem BSHG und dem AFG. Köln', Deutscher Städtetag.

Gautié, J., B. Gazier and R. Silvera (1994), 'Les Subventions à L'Emploi: Analyses et Expériences Européennes', Paris: *La Documentation francaise* (Collection Document Travail et Emploi).

Greene, W. (1996), *Econometric Analysis*, New York: Prentice Hall.

Karr, W. (1997), 'Die Erfassung der Langzeitarbeitslosigkeit. Ein kaum beachtetes Meßproblem', *IAB-Kurzbericht*, 7 August, pp. 1–4.

Koning, J. de (1993), 'The Dutch Experience', in K. Jensen and P.K. Madsen (eds), *Measuring Labour Market Measures. Evaluating the Effects of Active Labour Market Policy Initiatives*, Copenhagen: Ministry of Labour, 265–93.

Koning, J. de, M. Koss and A. Verkaik (1991), 'A Quasi-Experimental Evaluation of the Vocational Training Centre for Adults', *Government and Policy*, 9, 143–53.

Layard R., S. Nickell and R. Jackman (1991), *Unemployment: Macroeconomic Performance and the Labour Market*, Oxford: Oxford University Press.

Padoa-Schioppa, F. (ed.) (1991), *Mismatch and Labour Mobility*, Cambridge: Cambridge University Press.

Peters, A. and G. Schmid (1982), *Aggregierte Wirkungsanalyse des arbeitsmarktpolitischen Programms der Bundesregierung für Regionen mit besonderen Beschäftigungsproblemen. Analyse der Beschäftigungswirkungen*, Discussion Paper IIM/LMP 82–32, Berlin: WZB.

Ragin, Ch. C. (1987), *The Comparative Method. Moving Beyond Qualitative and Quantitative Strategies*, Berkeley, CA: University of California Press.

Rudolph, H. (1998), 'Risiko von Langzeitarbeitslosigkeit frühzeitig erkennen. Berechnung der Verbleibswahrscheinlichkeit von Arbeitslosen', *IAB Werkstattbericht Nr. 14*, Nürnberg, 19 November.

Schmid, G. and A. Peters (1982), 'The German Federal Employment Programme For Regions With Special Employment Problems', *Regional Science and Urban Economics*, 12, 99–119.

Schmid, G., J. O'Reilly and K. Schömann (eds) (1996), *International Handbook of Labour Market Policy and Evaluation*, Cheltenham: Edward Elgar, p. 954.

Walwei, Ulrich (1996), 'Improving Job-matching through Placement Service', in G. Schmid, J. O'Reilly and K. Schömann (eds), *International Handbook for Labour Market Policy and Evaluation*, Cheltenham: Edward Elgar, pp. 402–30.

5. The impact of active labour market policy on job hirings and unemployment in the Netherlands

Jaap de Koning and Marike Arents

1 INTRODUCTION

This chapter focuses on the impact of active labour market policies (ALMP) on job hirings and unemployment in the Netherlands. Using data on the regional level for a number of years, we use simple models to investigate whether ALMP contributes to more job hirings from unemployment and to decreasing unemployment. Since unemployment of long duration is particularly troublesome, special attention is given to long-term unemployment and the transition from long-term unemployment to employment. Long-term unemployment is strongly related to social exclusion. If ALMP contributes to a reduction in long-term unemployment, it would also be effective in combating social exclusion.

During the 1990s the Netherlands came to be regarded as an example of good practice in both economic and labour market policy. Economic growth reached higher levels than in most other industrialized countries and the official unemployment rate dropped to a level which had not been seen since the 1970s. However, when we take a closer look it becomes clear that we are still very far from a solution to the unemployment problem.

First of all it is important to note that the official unemployment figure strongly underestimates the unemployment problem. The reason for this is that many people with an unemployment benefit are not counted as unemployed officially. Beneficiaries over a certain age are not obliged to apply for jobs. Moreover, those who have an obligation to actively search for a job may not always do so in practice and, until recently, most of them could get away with it. As a result, in 1997 the number of people with unemployment benefit was almost twice as high as registered unemployment (see Table 5.1).[1] Furthermore, there is still considerable hidden unemployment among older workers who became 'disabled'. In the Netherlands the relative number of beneficiaries in disability arrangements is much higher than in the other EU countries.

Table 5.1 Key labour market indicators for the Netherlands (in thousands)

	1991	1992	1993	1994	1995	1996	1997
Labour force	6066	6296	6406	6466	6596	6681	6838
Persons with unemployment benefit	563	587	664	777	792	765	701
Registered unemployment[a]	334	336	415	486	464	440	375
Long-term unemployment[b]	176	165	188	244	247	221	195

Notes:
a. Registered unemployment relates to all persons aged 16 to 24 who are registered at the PES, who do not work or who work less than 12 hours per week and who are available for work for 12 hours or more per week. The number of registered unemployed is less than the number of persons receiving a social benefit due to unemployment. This difference has primarily to do with persons who are not or no longer obliged to search actively for a job, for example, lone mothers with children under the age of 5 and persons over 57 years of age.
b. Registered unemployed longer than one year.

Source: Central Planbureau, CEP, 1996 and Enquête Beroepsbevolking (Labour Force Survey) 1997, CBS, 1997.

The second reason why unemployment is still a severe social problem in the Netherlands is that it is highly concentrated among a relatively small group of people. About half (52 per cent in 1997) of the stock of unemployed has been out of work for more than one year. The concentration of unemployment can be even more clearly illustrated by results from a recent study by de Koning, van Nes and van der Veen (1999). According to their results, 10 per cent of the people who, on a lifetime basis, suffer from unemployment most make up half the total number unemployed. About two-thirds of unemployment inequality is explained by gender, ethnic origin and education.

The Dutch government has reacted to the unemployment problem with different measures. Lowering labour costs, particularly the cost of low-skilled labour, has been, and still is, central to the government's strategy. But the government also raised ALMP expenditure considerably, almost tripling it between 1980 and 1995, if we include the new job creation measures introduced in the 1990s. The question to be answered in this chapter is, was it worth while?

The government objectives in expanding ALMP are to improve labour market performance in terms of efficiency and equity. Labour market efficiency means that the simultaneous occurrence of unemployment and vacancies is avoided as much as possible. Given labour demand and labour supply, employment will be higher and unemployment and unfilled demand lower, the more efficiently the labour market operates. Labour market equity means that the unemployment burden is distributed as equally as possible over the labour supply. Given the efficiency of the labour market, more equity will usually mean that the existing jobs are redistributed over the different categories of the supply. As a result some groups will be better off and others will be worse off.

Under certain circumstances some ALMP measures may contribute to both efficiency and equity. For instance, this is the case when long-term unemployed people are trained in professions in which persistent shortages exist. However, until recently the number of unfilled vacancies in the Netherlands was only a tiny fraction of the number of unemployed. In that situation ALMP will hardly have any direct effect on total unemployment, at least in the short run. Active measures will then have a redistributing effect only. For instance the share of long-term unemployment (LTU) in total unemployment could be reduced. More people would become unemployed, but the average unemployment duration would decline. Since unemployment is mainly a social problem when people remain in it for a long time, this could be seen as a positive result, although total unemployment remains unchanged or even increases. Given the fact that during the period studied in the empirical analysis (see next sections) unemployment was high and unfilled vacancies hardly existent, we expect to find mainly redistribution effects.

Regional data over the period 1991–95 is used in our analysis. The regional data refer to regional boards of the Public Employment Service (PES). There are considerable differences in ALMP expenses per unemployed person and in the policy mix between the regions.

The chapter is organized as follows. Section 2 gives a description of Dutch ALMP both in qualitative and in quantitative terms. Then, in section 3, the models are presented which form the basis of the empirical analysis. Data and estimation results are the subject matter of section 4. Finally, in section 5 conclusions are drawn and a number of concluding remarks made which make it possible to identify the impact of ALMP, at least in principle. An alternative way would be to use macroeconomic time series data over a longer period. This approach was recently followed by de Koning and Versluis (1999). The results of their analysis will be discussed briefly in this chapter.

2 DUTCH ALMP

2.1 Policy Developments

Dutch ALMP has gone through a process of rapid change. In 1991 the PES lost its monopoly in job brokering. Private firms, particularly temporary work agencies (TWA), play an increasingly important role in the job placement market. But the position of the PES is not only challenged by deregulation. Perhaps even more important is that the government changed its philosophy about the role of the PES. The tendency is to emphasize reduction in unemployment benefits as the central goal of ALMP and to give the organizations responsible for unemployment benefits more responsibility for ALMP. Consequently, the PES budget was partly transferred to those organizations. They can spend this budget on active measures, but they have to outsource implementation to other agencies. At the moment they are still obliged to involve the PES for a certain amount of money, but in the future they will probably have complete freedom to choose other partners such as TWAs. Already now TWAs and other private agencies are involved in the implementation of ALMP. In a few years time the PES may only be publicly financed to provide a number of so-called ‘basic services’, including registration of job seekers and vacancies. Other PES services will have to be financed by competing for resources with other providers.

There are two kinds of organizations dealing with unemployment benefits. First of all, there is a collective social insurance system, which is implemented by insurance organizations, the so-called *uvis*. The government decides on the eligibility criteria and the benefit levels, but firms can choose between the different insurance organizations. In the future the *uvis* will probably merge into one public organization.

Municipalities are the other organizations dealing with unemployment benefits. Unemployed people who are not eligible for unemployment insurance benefits (any more) have to rely on social assistance, which is provided by municipalities. Because eligibility criteria for unemployment insurance are strict and benefit duration for most people is relatively short, most long-term unemployed people are found among social assistance claimants. This is the main reason why schemes for subsidized labour are usually the responsibility of the municipalities. But here too we find an increasing tendency to separate responsibility and implementation. The implementing agencies often function on a contract basis and their output is monitored. Management principles borrowed from private business are applied. This is also true for the PES, by the way.

The developments described imply that the PES no longer has the central role in the design and the implementation of ALMP it used to have. This situation is by no means typically Dutch. An international comparative study into deregulation in placement services (de Koning *et al.*, 1998) shows that there are similar developments in many other EU countries.

An important implication of the institutional changes, and perhaps a partial explanation for them, is that publicly financed ALMP has become more concentrated on disadvantaged groups. This is particularly true for the policies falling under the responsibility of the municipalities, which have profited most from the re-allocation of ALMP funding.

Deregulation of placement services and re-allocation of ALMP funds go hand-in-hand with decentralization. Since 1991 the regional boards of the PES (called RBAs) have considerable autonomy in choosing their policy priorities and implementation practices. In 1991 28 regional boards were installed; since 1996 some of them have merged which reduces their total number to 18. As far as ALMP measures are directly under the control of the Ministry of Social Affairs and Employment, municipalities are responsible for their implementation in which they have considerable freedom. An important advantage of decentralization is that the regional and local authorities can adapt the policy mix to the needs of the regional or local situation. For instance, the need for training will depend heavily on the discrepancy between the skill structures of labour demand and labour supply, which varies between regions. Furthermore, the most disadvantaged groups are highly concentrated in the big cities, implying that in those regions subsidized labour will be used more intensely than elsewhere. However, the evaluation of the Employment Services Act of 1991 (Dercksen and de Koning, 1996) showed that decentralization may go too far. Clients of the PES, particularly firms with a number of establishments spread all over the country, expect the same kind of services from all the regional boards of the PES. Therefore, in 1996, some changes in the internal organization of the PES were made to improve its cohesion.

At the time of its introduction, a much debated feature of the 1991 Employment Services Act was the tripartite structure: the shared administration by government, unions and employers' organizations. It was expected that a stronger commitment of the social partners would increase the effectiveness of ALMP, and, in fact, as a result of the tripartite structure, more arrangements were made in collective sectoral agreements about inclusion of unemployed people in employment. But, on the basis of scant information (Dercksen and de Koning, 1996), there are doubts whether firms really implement these arrangements in practice. Therefore, the added value of the tripartite structure is not unchallenged.

2.2 Description of ALMP Programme Trends

Most data on Dutch ALMP are on expenditure. Although strictly speaking not correct, we will also refer to these data as ALMP costs. The data relate to expenditure from the PES but also to expenditure of the Ministry of Social Affairs and Employment. The job-creation schemes for youngsters and long-term unemployed, the Youth Work Guarantee Act and the Job-pool, fall under the direct financial responsibility of this Ministry, whereas their implementation is the responsibility of municipalities. The data of the PES allow a breakdown in a number of expenditure-categories, namely:

- budget allocated to training;
- budget allocated to placement subsidies and subsidized labour;
- budget allocated to other specific categories of ALMP measures;
- personnel costs;
- other general costs (housing, material, and so on).

The costs on personnel and other general costs will hereafter be referred to as administrative expenditure. Within this category of costs personnel costs constitute the larger part. These costs primarily arise from job-brokerage activities, which are of course also part of ALMP.

Data over the period 1991–5 (our estimation period) are given in Table 5.2. From the table we can conclude that ALMP expenditure varies over time. It increased until 1993, when it was at its maximum. After 1993 total expenditure fell somewhat. There are also considerable changes in the composition of ALMP expenditure. The share of both job-creation schemes, the Youth Work Guarantee Act (referred to as JWG) and the Job-pool in ALMP expenditure increased dramatically from 9 per cent in 1991 to 36 per cent in 1995. The JWG was introduced in 1990; the Job-pool has been effective since 1991. The inflow into the Job-pool increased substantially after its introduction. The transition to regular, non-subsidized employment was not an objective of this measure and consequently it was not considerably large. The increasing inflow combined with the low outflow explains the large increase in expenditure on this measure.

The share of PES expenditure in total ALMP expenditure fell during 1991 to 1995 correspondingly from 92 to 64 per cent. The decrease in expenditure on specific ALMP measures (such as training) was partly offset by an increase in administrative, mainly personnel costs. This increase reflects the decision of the PES during this period to concentrate more on job brokering and related activities which it considers as its core activities. The budget for training was almost halved between 1991 and 1995. That probably also implied less emphasis on disadvantaged groups. But, within ALMP as a whole, this was compensated for by the increasing expenditure on job-creation schemes, which are fully targeted at disadvantaged groups.

The problem with these financial data is that they do not include the costs of all related activities. For example, the financial data with respect to training include the direct training costs of the institutions providing the training, but not the indirect costs of the PES counsellors involved in training policy. These are included in the general administrative costs. The same holds for placement subsidies and subsidized labour as far as these measures fall under

Table 5.2 Expenditure for ALMP in the Netherlands, 1991–5 (1 000 000 guilders)

Variable	1991	1992	1993	1994	1995
Total ALMP expenditure	2115	2496	3007	2710	2467
Share of training expenditure (%)[a]		35	27	25	20
Share of expenditure on placement subsidies (%)[a, b]	63	13	10	6	4
Share of expenditure on other specific ALMP measures (%)[a]		8	7	4	4
Share of administrative expenditure (including personnel costs) (%)[a]	29	24	33	37	36
Share of expenditure on Job-pool and Youth Work Guarantee measures (%)[c]	9	20	23	28	36
Total (%)	100	100	100	100	100
Total ALMP expenditure per unemployed person (× hfl 1000)	6.3	7.4	7.3	5.6	5.3

Notes:
a PES expenditure.
b Expenditure relating to placement subsidies and subsidized labour.
c Expenditure of the Ministry of Social Affairs and Employment.

Source: PES, different regions and central staff unit, Ministry of Social Affairs and Employment, adapted by NEI.

the responsibility of the PES. As a result, the administrative costs refer not only to activities such as registration, job search assistance and job brokering but, to a certain extent, also to training and placement subsidies.

The job-creation schemes referred to in Table 5.2, JWG and Job-pool, fall under the responsibility of the Ministry of Social Affairs and Employment and are implemented by municipal organizations. The figures in Table 5.2 include only the funds made available by the central government for both job-creation schemes. They do not include additional municipal funding for these schemes. As a result the figures in the table underestimate total ALMP expenditure.

Total ALMP expenditure per unemployed person shows almost the same development as total ALMP expenditure. The large increase in 1997 is, however, remarkable. This can partly be explained by the sharp decrease in unemployment in this year, as was shown in Table 5.1. This suggests a lagged adjustment of ALMP budgets to the labour market situation.

Data with respect to ALMP participants are also available, but mainly on a national level. And since 1994 we do not even have national data concerning the number of trainees. We also have a problem in measuring the number of participants in job brokering and related activities. We only know the number of placements. But the number of job seekers for which the PES has provided placement services will probably be considerably higher than the placement figure. Given the problems with the participant data we decided to use only cost figures as our ALMP indicator.

To what extent does ALMP expenditure and the number of ALMP participants vary between regions? This question is important as PES measures are, to a considerable extent, designed and implemented by its regional boards (RBAs). These boards have a large degree of autonomy; within the budget allocated to them by the Central Board, they are free to fine-tune its allocation to the local labour market situation. But regional differences are also of importance as we intend to study the effects of ALMP by using regional data.

In order to consider the importance of regional differences in ALMP implementation, total ALMP expenditure per unemployed person for each region is plotted against the regional unemployment rate in Figure 5.1 for the years 1991 up to and including 1995.[2] These costs vary considerably between regions. Its minimum value is slightly above 2 700 Dutch guilders (one

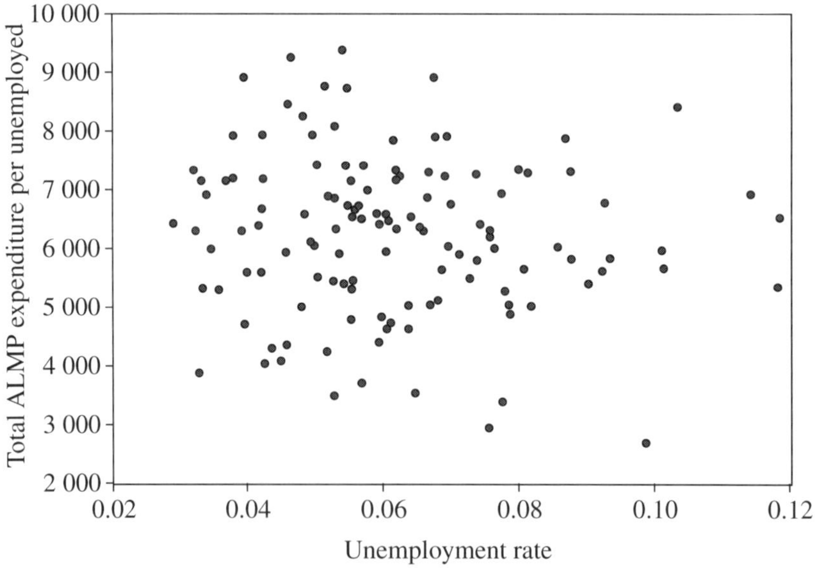

Figure 5.1 Total ALMP expenditure per unemployed person, 1991–5 by RBA region

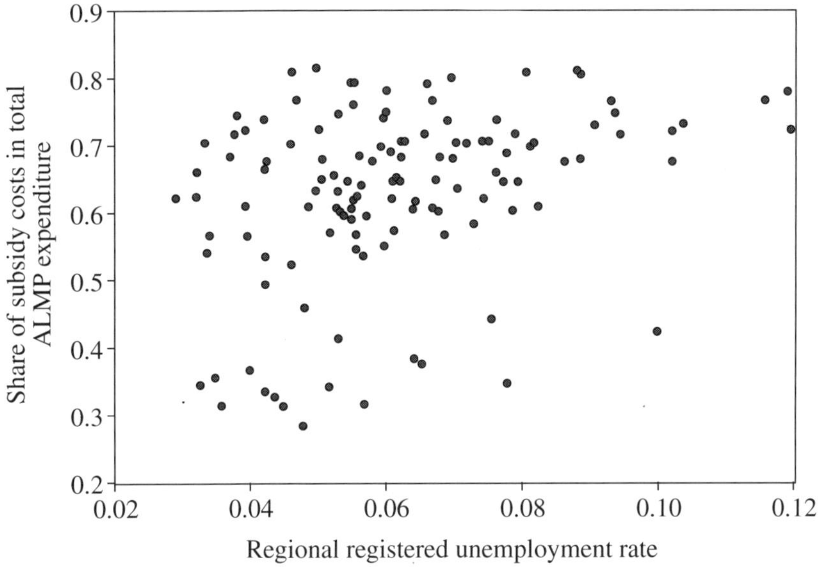

Figure 5.2 The percentage share of subsidy costs in ALMP, 1991–5 by RBA region

guilder is about 0.4 Euro) and its maximum value almost 9 500 guilders. There is not a clear pattern indicating that expenditure per unemployed person neither increases or decreases with the unemployment rate.

Another question is to what extent ALMP expenditure per unemployed person and the structure of ALMP expenses depend on the unemployment level. In Figure 5.2 the share of subsidy costs in ALMP is plotted against the unemployment rate. Again we observe a huge variation. The share of expenditure on placement subsidies, subsidized labour, training and other specific ALMP measures (referred to as subsidy costs in the figure) varies between 25 and 80 per cent of total ALMP costs.[3] There is no correlation between this share and the unemployment rate.

3 MODEL SPECIFICATION

The logical order of things is to specify the theoretically sound model and then look for the relevant data with which to estimate the model. However, given the limitations of the available data the latter determine, to some extent, the model specification in practice. Therefore, in this section we will sometimes refer to the data available.

The *first class of models* we use are so-called hirings functions in which hirings from unemployment (H) are related to the number of vacancies VAC, the number of unemployed job seekers U, $ALMP$ and exogenous factors x_1 (equation 5.1). A more efficient functioning of the labour market results in more matchings and probably also hirings from unemployment. For the theoretical background of the model see the literature overview given in Chapter 2. The model used here has the following form:

$$H = f(U, VAC; ALMP, x_1) \tag{5.1}$$

Earlier in this chapter we argued that the impact of ALMP on long-term unemployment is of particular interest. We know the number of hirings from long-term unemployment and those from short-term unemployment. To investigate the impact of ALMP on both duration classes we use the following equation:

$$\frac{H_d}{H} = g\left(\frac{U_d}{U}, \frac{VAC}{U}; ALMP, x_2\right) \tag{5.2}$$

where:

U_d = unemployment in duration class d;
H_d = hirings from duration class d;
$\boldsymbol{x}_2$ = vector of exogenous variables.

This equation states that the share of hirings from unemployment duration class d depends on the share of this duration class in total unemployment, the vacancy–unemployment ratio, policy variables and exogenous variables.

Both equations can be rewritten as transition probabilities by dividing both sides of the equation by unemployment (equation (5.1)) or the share of duration class d in unemployment (equation (5.2)) respectively.[4]

But ALMP may not only increase the outflow from unemployment; another objective of these policies might be to decrease the inflow into unemployment. Therefore, when analysing the effects of ALMP on unemployment, we should also take the possible impact on the inflow into unemployment into account. However, we do not have both inflow and outflow data with respect to unemployment. Therefore, a quasi-flow model' approach was used according to which theoretical equations were assumed with respect to the flows, which are then substituted to form a reduced form equation for the change in unemployment. Here two separate equations are estimated for both the long-term and the short-term unemployed. This is the *second class of models* we use.

Basically the model is derived from a structural form consisting of an inflow equation, an outflow equation and a definition equation defining the change in the stock of unemployment as the difference between inflow (*IN*) and outflow (*OUT*). A simple linear version of the model looks as follows:

$$IN = \alpha_1 L(-1) + \alpha_2 VAC + \alpha_3 ALMP \tag{5.3}$$

$$OUT = \beta_1 U(-1) + \beta_2 VAC + \beta_3 ALMP \tag{5.4}$$

$$\Delta U = IN - OUT \tag{5.5}$$

Substitution of equations (5.3) and (5.4) in (5.5) gives a reduced form equation in observed variables which can be estimated:

$$\Delta U = \alpha_1 L(-1) - \beta_1 U(-1) + (\alpha_2 - \beta_2)VAC + (\alpha_3 - \beta_3)ALMP \tag{5.6}$$

As indicated earlier, a problem with the data about official registered unemployment is that people with unemployment benefit are not always included. Therefore, we will also estimate equations of the second class of models where the number of unemployment benefits is taken as the unemployment variable. This is the *third class of models* we use. There are two arrangements for unemployment benefits: unemployment insurance benefits and social assistance benefits. The problem is that the data about unemployment benefits do not allow a breakdown according to benefit duration. However, we know that of the two arrangements for unemployment benefits, unemployment insurance benefits are usually of short duration and social assistance benefits of long duration.

A well-known problem in this type of research is that participants in ALMP measures are often excluded from the official unemployment data. Therefore, a negative impact of ALMP on unemployment may simply reflect this artificial effect. In the case of the official unemployment figures it is not clear how this works out. These figures are based on the Labour Force Survey. Therefore, if an unemployed person engaged in an ALMP measure answers that he is actively searching for a job and is, under certain conditions, prepared to accept a job right away, this person is included in the official unemployment figure. But we do not have any information about the way respondents deal with this. Things are clearer in the case of unemployment benefits. Beneficiaries engaged in normal job assistance schemes and those participating in training measures keep their benefits and are still counted as beneficiaries. However, people participating in subsidized labour schemes are not considered beneficiaries any more. It is questionable whether the latter effect should be regarded as artificial. Subsidized jobs are meant for the hopeless cases without any real prospect of a regular job. Therefore, if we were to find that the number of social assistance beneficiaries in a region is lower the more money is spent on subsidized labour, then this would not be a bad outcome. We should only take account of temporary effects due to changes in the number of entrants in subsidy schemes. When entrance in an ALMP scheme implies leaving official unemployment then at least some of the participants will enter unemployment again after some time (those who did not find a job). Therefore, in that case a one-off increase in ALMP entrants will lead to a decrease in official unemployment, but only temporarily.

In the Appendix a flow model is presented which takes the flows between unemployment, employment and participation in ALMP measures into account explicitly. The conclusion is that both current and lagged values of ALMP participation may influence the change in unemployment. The pattern will depend on the type of measure, on the impact of the measure on the transition from unemployment to employment, and on the impact on future transitions.

Finally we have the endogeneity problem. We know that within the PES budgets are allocated on the basis of the regional labour market situation. Both unemployment and employment are taken into consideration, where most weight is given to employment. We do not know the exact formula. But we do know that the formula is applied with lagged values for unemployment and employment, simply because the statistical data becomes available with considerable delay. Therefore, PES budgets depend on lagged unemployment, implying that we do not have an endogeneity problem. However, this may not be the case for the subsidized jobs schemes which do not fall under the responsibility of the PES. There might still be a problem there.

The fact that we have short time series for each region may be of some help in dealing with the endogeneity problem. This enables us to apply the fixed-effects method by which a correction can be made for region-specific factors that are constant in time. However, when the change in unemployment is correlated with the level of unemployment and the latter variable is strongly positive related to ALMP expenditure (high unemployment regions spending more on ALMP than other regions), then we would still have a problem. Unfortunately, we do not dispose of instrumental variables that would be needed for the proper way to deal with the problem: simultaneous estimation of both the impact equation and an equation explaining regional ALMP expenditure.

4 DATA AND ESTIMATION

4.1 Data

As indicated in the previous section, we will estimate the effects of ALMP by using three different classes of models. The dependent variables in these models are, respectively, the number of job finders among the unemployed, the change in unemployment and the change in the number of unemployment benefits or social assistance benefits paid.

The analyses are based on yearly, regional data. The aggregation level is that of the RBAs which are in charge of the administration of the PES. As already illustrated in section 2, the large degree of autonomy of regional boards in designing and implementing ALMP is reflected in differences in the composition of ALMP expenditure.

Next to these policy variables, also some labour market variables, like the *UV*-ratio, are included in the analyses in order to correct for labour market differences between the regions. Furthermore, to be sure that other regional differences do not distort the results of the analyses, we made use of a fixed-effects model by including a dummy variable for each region (RBA).

4.2 Estimation results

In all estimates for the three types of models the current volume of ALMP expenditure is included, next to some labour market indicators. The results will be presented per type of explanatory variable. The analyses have been carried out by using a fixed effects model which allows unobserved regional differences between RBAs to be taken into account.

Job finders

The effects of ALMP on the number of job finders from the pool of unemployed are presented in Tables 5.3–5.7. The estimates are based on 28 RBAs and are made for the years 1991 up to and including 1993, as the figures on the number of job finders are only available for this period. Thus, we have 84 data points. Both the dependent and the independent variables have been scaled by the total number of unemployed defined by the sum total of the stock of unemployed at the beginning of the year plus the inflow into unemployment during the year. It is computed as follows:

Stock beginning year t + inflow during year t = stock at the end of year t + outflow during the year to employment.

This is only an approximation, since inactivity is also a possible destination of people flowing out of unemployment. However, data on outflow to inactivity is not available. We can compute the total number of long-term unemployed and the total number of vacancies in the same way.

In Table 5.3 the total number of job finders from unemployment is taken as the dependent variable. The estimation results indicate that if total expenditure on ALMP is increased, the number of job finders from the pool of unemployed, in comparison to this pool of unemployed, increases. This suggests that ALMP efforts do indeed result in an increased outflow from unemployment to employment. The positive effect of the *VU*-ratio on the number of job finders is intuitively appealing: when the number of vacancies rises in relation to the number of unemployed, the relative outflow from unemployment, approximated by the number of job finders, will increase.

Table 5.3 Explaining the total number of job finders from unemployment, model 1

Variable	Coefficient	Adj. R-square	N
Dependent variable: Log (job finders)/ (Total number of unemployed)		0.789	84
Constant	–0.644*		
(Total PES expenditure on ALMP)/ (Total number of unemployed)	8.487E-05*		
Log (Total number of vacancies + job finders)/(Total number of unemployed)	0.680*		

Note: * The estimated parameters differ significantly from zero at 5% level.

When total expenditure is decomposed into expenditure on training and placement subsidies on the one hand (referred to as ALMP measures) and other expenditure, on the other hand, then the results show that expenditure on ALMP measures no longer influences the number of job finders significantly (Table 5.4). Other expenditure, which consists mainly of personnel costs because of job brokerage by the PES, still has a significant positive influence. If we include additional variables on the labour market situation in the analyses, the coefficients of the ALMP variables do not change significantly. Examples of the included context variables are the share of women or ethnic minorities in the labour force and the share of the industrial or service sector in total employment.

Table 5.4 Explaining the total number of job finders from unemployment: ALMP differentiated by type of expenditure

Variable	Coefficient	Adj. R-square	N
Dependent variable: Log (Job finders)/ (Total number of unemployed)		0.821	84
Constant	–0.478*		
(PES expenditure on ALMP measures)/ (Total number of unemployed)	7.676E-06		
(Other PES expenditure)/ (Total number of unemployed)	2.593E-04*		
Log (Total number of vacancies)/ (Total number of unemployed)	0.850*		

Note: * The estimated parameters differ significantly from zero at 5% level.

Table 5.5 Explaining the total number of job finders from the pool of long-term unemployed

	Coefficient	
Dependent variable: Log (Job finders from LTU[a])/ (Total number of long-term unemployed)		
Constant	–0.386	–0.246
(Total PES expenditure on ALMP)/(Total number of unemployed)	5.529E-05	
(PES expenditure on ALMP measures)/(Total number of unemployed)		–9.632E-06
(Other PES expenditure)/(Total number of unemployed)		1.903E-04
Log (Total number of long-term unemployed)/ (Total number of unemployed)	1.266*	1.301*
Log (Total number of vacancies)/(Total number of unemployed)	–0.313	–0.194
Adj. R-square	0.575	0.572
N	84	84

Notes:

a LTU = long-term unemployment. Long-term unemployment is defined as all people who have been out of a job for more than one year.

* The estimated parameters differ significantly from zero at 5% level.

We also examined the effect of ALMP expenditure on job finders from the pool of long-term unemployed. As can be seen from Table 5.5 total expenditure on ALMP does not have a significant effect on the share of job finders from the pool of long-term unemployed in the total number of job finders. The number of job finders from the pool of long-term unemployed is, however, significantly influenced by the share of long-term unemployment in total unemployment. When the latter is higher, then the share of long-term unemployed among job finders is also larger. The *VU*-ratio does not have any significant influence. These findings do not change when total ALMP expenditure is decomposed into expenditure on ALMP measures and other expenditure of the PES. None of the expenditure variables seems to influence the share of previously long-term unemployed job finders in the total number of job finders. This would indicate that ALMP efforts, when measured in terms of expenditure, do not increase labour market equity.

Unemployment

The effects of ALMP can also be studied by considering relative changes in the level of registered unemployment. The dependent variable is divided by the total labour force in the previous period, which is defined as all employed and unemployed persons together. The data cover the years 1991 up to and including 1995. Table 5.6 gives the results of the equation in which the ALMP variable is lagged one year. Although the coefficient of the ALMP variable has the right sign, it is not significant. A number of alternative specifications have been tried; for instance, one in which only the current ALMP variables were included or one in which both the lagged and the

Table 5.6 Explaining the change in the level of unemployment

Variable	Coefficient	Adj. R-square	N
Dependent variable: Change in total registered U/labour force previous year		0.378	112
Constant	7.072E-02*		
Total PES expenditure on ALMP/U previous year	–7.991E-07		
Vacancies/Labour force previous year	–1.862*		
U previous year/labour force previous year	–0.536*		

Note: * The estimated parameters differ significantly from zero at 5% level.

current variable were included. In none of the cases did the ALMP variable prove to be significant.

Unemployment benefits and social assistance

Another way to study the effects of ALMP is to consider figures on the number of beneficiaries of social security benefits. The number of unemployment benefits paid could be seen as a proxy for the number of short-term unemployed, as most people are only eligible for this type of benefit during a relatively short period. After a longer period of unemployment most people will become reliant on social assistance benefit. Therefore, the number of social assistance beneficiaries can be considered to be approximately the number of those in long-term unemployment.

As dependent variables we took the change in the number of beneficiaries of unemployment benefits and social assistance beneficiaries, respectively. Again we have used fixed-effects models to take unobserved differences between RBAs into account. In both analyses the same variables are included, except one. When explaining the change in the number of beneficiaries of social welfare payments we also included the lagged value of the number of unemployment benefits paid. This is because some people who received unemployment benefit during the previous period might now receive social assistance since their right to unemployment benefit had been exhausted. In both cases the estimation period is the period 1991–5. The results are shown in Table 5.7. ALMP does not have a significant influence. The coefficients involved even have the wrong sign. Other specifications were tried, however, with the same results. Particularly, the equation for the change in the number of social assistance beneficiaries is poor. Only the vacancy variable in this equation is significant.

A closer examination of the data showed that in the period under consideration job-creation measures in general were expanded in reaction to the increase in the number of beneficiaries. As a result, separate inclusion of the job-creation measures in the equation for social assistance even shows a significantly positive relationship. It seems that the endogeneity problem is bothering us here.

Contrary to these results de Koning and Versluis (1999) do find a significant negative impact of active policies on the number of unemployment beneficiaries. According to their findings the increase in PES expenditure after 1980 of about one billion guilders or 0.4 billion Euros leads to a reduction of approximately 25 000 person years in the number of beneficiaries. According to their study job-creation measures introduced in the 1990s were much more effective. The results point to a reduction in the number of beneficiaries of about 100 000 person years. However, for a considerable number of these people the subsidized jobs are dead-end jobs. These people

Table 5.7 Explaining unemployment benefits

Variable	Dependent variable: *Change in total number of beneficiaries of unemployment benefit/labour force in previous period*	Dependent variable: *Change in total number of beneficiaries of social assistance/labour force in previous period*
Constant	3.342E-02*	–2.826E-03
U/labour force previous period	–0.190*	2.864E-02
Vacancies/labour force previous period	–1.700*	–0.314*
Total PES expenditure on ALMP/all unemployment (or in last column: social assistance) beneficiaries in previous period	2.869E-07	9.909E-07
Number of beneficiaries of unemployment benefit previous period/labour force previous period		1.121E-02
Adjusted R-square	0.327	0.054
N	112	112

Note: * The estimated parameters differ significantly from zero at 5% level.

may never find a 'normal' job. Therefore, the impact is artificial to a certain degree, although doing subsidized work is probably better than doing nothing. If we accept the results it would roughly mean that a 200 per cent increase in ALMP expenditure leads to a 20 per cent decrease in the number of beneficiaries, which comes down to an elasticity of 0.10. If we only take PES measures into account the elasticity is even lower (0.05). These figures should, of course, be treated with great caution.

The main difference in approach is that de Koning and Versluis use yearly time series on the macroeconomic level, which cover the period 1979–95. This is a relatively short period for a time-series analysis. However, an important advantage is that, on the macro-level, the participants in the job-creation schemes can be distinguished in the data according to their benefit duration when entering the programmes. Therefore, the analysis could be carried out for each duration class separately. Clearly, this was important for the identification of the impacts, because the effects of the programmes differed considerably between the various duration classes. PES expenditure and the subsidy creation scheme for young people were only relevant for the first duration class (up to one year), while the job subsidy scheme for adults only had an impact for the higher duration classes (three years and over). This is in line with the eligibility criteria for the two job-subsidy schemes. Furthermore, it is quite plausible that PES measures are mostly applied to people of relatively short benefit duration. But the fact that the outcomes of the macro time-series analysis are more in line with our expectations do not of course prove that they are right and that the results found in this chapter are wrong.

5 CONCLUSIONS

In this chapter we have investigated the aggregate impact of active labour market policy on unemployment. Three different independent variables were used: the outflow from registered unemployment to work; the yearly change in the level of registered unemployment; and the yearly change in the number of people with unemployment benefit. We also used data on unemployment benefits because this is a better measure for unemployment than registered unemployment. However, we do not have regional data on benefit duration, while data on the duration of registered unemployment are available. In the case of unemployment benefits we only have a rough indication of duration by distinguishing between unemployment insurance and social assistance benefit. Unemployment insurance benefits are mostly of short duration and social assistance benefits often of long duration.

Simple models were used which were estimated with the fixed-effects method on the basis of regional data over a couple of years. Only in the case of the outflow from registered unemployment was a significant impact of ALMP found. However, according to the results, ALMP does not have a significant impact on the outflow from long-term unemployment. ALMP seems to have no significant effect on the change in the level of registered unemployment either. Although it is difficult to draw any definite conclusions about the relative performance of the various ALMP measures the results seem to indicate that job-brokering activities are more effective than specific ALMP measures such as training.

In the case of unemployment insurance benefits and social assistance benefits, the impact is not only insignificant, but the coefficients also have the wrong sign, which has to do with the endogeneity problem. ALMP expenditure, particularly expenditure on job-creation measures, increased most in regions where the number of beneficiaries increased most. Also, because the impact of ALMP is probably relatively small, a positive correlation between ALMP and unemployment benefits emerges. In this chapter results based on a macroeconomic time-series analysis were discussed which do show a negative impact of ALMP on the number of people with unemployment benefit. In the latter analysis, duration classes could be distinguished, which proved to be essential for the identification of the parameters of the model. The results of this analysis indicate that the job-creation measures introduced in the 1990s had a substantial impact on the number of beneficiaries. However, for many persons concerned the subsidized job is a dead-end job. Therefore, the reduction in benefits is, to a certain extent, an artificial effect. Because the group of beneficiaries only partly overlaps the group of registered unemployed, it is not surprising that the impact of job-creation measures on registered unemployment was limited. This can also explain why, according to the macroeconomic analysis, the impact of the measures of the Public Employment Service (which has the registered unemployed as its main clients) on the number of beneficiaries has been small.

The overall conclusion is that the aggregate impact of ALMP on unemployment is limited. This is particularly true for PES measures. And, as far as PES measures have an impact, the results indicate that it is on short-term unemployment, not on long-term unemployment. Job-creation measures may have a substantial impact on the number of beneficiaries, many of whom are long-term unemployed, but this effect is partly artificial because those involved do not move on to regular jobs.

APPENDIX A FLOW MODEL TAKING ACCOUNT OF THE FLOWS BETWEEN UNEMPLOYMENT AND PROGRAMME PARTICIPATION

In this Appendix we will present a model to illustrate the possible influence of lagged ALMP on current unemployment. It is a simple flow model for unemployment consisting of the following equations.

$$\Delta U = IU - OU \tag{A5.1}$$

The mutation in unemployment is equal to inflow (*IU*) minus outflow (*OU*) by definition.

$$IU = OMU + IUO \tag{A5.2}$$

Inflow in unemployment consists of participants in ALMP measures finishing the project without finding a job in case participants are not included in the unemployment figure (*OMU*), and people flowing in from other directions (from school, from work, and so on, *IUO*).

$$OU = OUJ - DIS + OUM + OMW \tag{A5.3}$$

The outflow from unemployment consists of:

- unemployed people who do not participate in measures to find a job (*OUJ*);
- minus the people flowing into ALMP measures who would have found a job if not participating (*DIS*);
- plus unemployed people engaging in ALMP measures (*OUM*), supposing again that engaging in ALMP measures implies removal from the official unemployment figure;
- plus the participants flowing out of unemployment due to jobs, and so on, as far as they remain unemployed during participation (*OMW*).

Suppose that *OMU* is a fraction of the people engaging in measures last year (*IM*):

$$OMU = \lambda_1 \lambda_2 IM(-1) \tag{A5.4}$$

Where λ_1 is the fraction of participants not finding a job and λ_2 is the fraction of the inflow of participants in measures who were not considered officially unemployed any more.

Suppose further that *DIS* is a fraction of *IM*:

$$DIS = \mu_1 IM \tag{A5.5}$$

By definition we have:

$$OUM = \lambda_2 IM \tag{A5.6}$$

$$OMW = (1 - \lambda_1)(1 - \lambda_2) IM \tag{A5.7}$$

Substitution of the various equations in (A5.1) gives:

$$\Delta U = IUO - OUJ + \lambda_1 \lambda_2 IM(-1) + \{\mu_1 - \lambda_2 - (1 - \lambda_1)(1 - \lambda_2)\} IM$$

Therefore, both *IM* and *IM*(–1) may occur in the reduced form equation for the change in unemployment.

We have to take into account the fact that these parameters will differ between the various measures. In the case of placement activities λ_2 will be zero. In that case lagged values of *IM* are not relevant. In the case of JWG and Job-pool λ_2 is probably 1 and, in the case of training, it may be somewhere in between 0 and 1. Now suppose that the inflow of participants in ALMP measures is a relatively constant fraction of the stock of participants and that this stock is proportional to ALMP costs. This would imply that both the current and the one-year lagged value of ALMP expenditure could be included in the equation for the change in the level of unemployment. Furthermore, the transition probability from employment to unemployment may depend on past ALMP participation of the persons concerned. The same could be said for the case for the transition from unemployment to employment of people who did not participate in measures during the last two years, but did so some years ago. As a result both *IUO* and *OUJ* may depend on two or even three years lagged ALMP. However, our data are not capable of identifying those lag structures.

NOTES

1. The figures on unemployment benefits include social assistance. An unknown number of social assistance beneficiaries consist of people who can probably be considered to be unfit for the labour market. A best guess is that this number is about 100 000. The 'real' unemployment rate 1997 would then be equal to approximately 8.5 per cent compared to the official 5.5 per cent.
2. As the expenditure on the Job-pool as well as the JWG-measure are not available for separate RBA regions for the years 1996 and 1997, we had to restrict the scatterplots to the period 1991–5.
3. In these subsidy-costs expenditure on the Job-pool and the JWG-measure are also included.
4. For equation (5.1) we then have to assume that it is linear homogeneous in *U* and *VAC*.

REFERENCES

Dercksen, W.J. and J. de Koning (1996), 'The New Public Employment Service in the Netherlands (1991–1994)', WZB Discussion Paper FS I 96-201. Berlin: WZB.

Koning, J. de and H. Versluis (1999), 'Did Active Measures and Social Security Reforms Reduce the Number of Unemployment Beneficiaries in the Netherlands?', NEI Working Papers, No. 1999/2, NEI, Rotterdam.

Koning, J. de, J. Denys and U. Walwei (1998), 'Deregulation in placement services: a comparative study of eight EU countries', NEI/HIVA/IAB, Rotterdam.

Koning, J. de, P.J. van Nes and C. van der Veen (1999), *The Distribution of Life-time Unemployment: A Simulation Approach*, Rotterdam: NEI.

6. Do active labour market policies matter in Spain?

María A. Davia, Carlos García-Serrano, Virginia Hernanz, Miguel A. Malo and Luis Toharia Cortés

1 INTRODUCTION

Policy actions designed to combat unemployment in Spain have focused on legislative reforms and on income maintenance policies (usually known as passive policies). The latter have had a predominant role in labour market policy in terms of public resources devoted to unemployment benefits and in terms of public interest. Policies oriented towards improving the re-entry probability of unemployed workers – namely active labour market policies (ALMP) – have received lower priority compared with passive policies. In principle, however, the marginal role of ALMP in expenditure and public opinion should not have prevented such policies from being effective tools in combating unemployment and, in particular, long-term unemployment.

This is important since it is widely agreed that the main objective of economic policy during the 1990s has been to reduce the persistently high Spanish unemployment rate and long duration of unemployment spells. This is connected with the concept of 'transitional labour markets', which are defined as institutionalized arrangements supporting the change of employment status or the combination of labour market work with other socially useful activities (Schmid, 1998). Since high and persistent long-term unemployment is one of the chief causes of social exclusion, institutional arrangements such as active labour market policies that reduce the inflow into and speed up the outflow from long-term unemployment should be considered essential. It is therefore important to evaluate ALMP programmes to find out whether they have helped reduce social exclusion through the reduction of long-term unemployment.

In this chapter we first describe the main ALMP programmes in Spain to combat unemployment. These include labour market training for the unemployed, employment promotion and (public) employment-creation policies, as well as measures designed to foster entrepreneurial initiatives and employment creation in the private sector. We then carry out the first macroeconomic evaluation of Spanish ALMP. It is widely agreed that macroeconomic evaluation (that is, examining the effects of ALMP on either the overall unemployment rate or the outflow rate from unemployment) is complementary to microeconomic evaluation (that is, assessing the effects of policy on individual unemployment duration). Since the only data available for our analysis is flow data which starts in 1987, the evaluation will be limited to a short period of time. We use an aggregate impact analysis (AIA) approach in order to estimate the likely effects of ALMP measures on some basic indicators of labour markets' performance and social exclusion (conducted at the regional level and controlling for other variables). These indicators include the overall unemployment rate, the long-term unemployment rate, the overall outflow rate from unemployment to employment and the outflow rate from long-term unemployment to employment. We pay special attention to the analysis of long-term unemployment in the belief that social exclusion may be reduced through ALMP.

The remainder of the chapter is structured as follows. In section 2, we describe ALMP programmes currently operating in Spain. In section 3, the empirical analysis and macroeconomic evaluation of those programmes is shown using panel data at the regional level (for the 17 so-called 'autonomous communities') for the period 1987–95. Finally, section 4 provides a summary of our conclusions.

2 ACTIVE LABOUR MARKET POLICY PROGRAMMES IN SPAIN[1]

According to the OECD classification, ALMP consists of labour market training, measures directed towards young people, subsidies for direct job creation and for hirings (which may be either direct or implicit subsidies), and measures for the handicapped. Current efforts at reforming the public employment services should also be considered active labour market policies.[2] In particular, ALMP in Spain consists of the following measures:

- labour market training: for the unemployed (so-called occupational training) and for the employed (hereafter referred to as continuing training);
- employment promotion and creation policies: contracts without direct economic incentive (fixed-term contracts, part-time contracts), contracts with direct economic incentive (practice and training contracts; as well as permanent contracts for several groups of workers, including

Table 6.1 Public expenditures and participant inflows in labour market programmes in Spain, 1990, 1994 and 1997

	Public expenditures as a percentage of GDP			Participant inflows as a percentage of LF		
	1990	1994	1997	1990	1994	1997
Public employment services and administration	*0.13*	*0.10*	*0.08*			
Labour market training	*0.17*	*0.22*	*0.14*	*1.9*	*0.7*	*0.8*
Training for unemployed adults and those at risk	0.14	0.17	0.11	1.5	0.4	0.6
Training for employed adults	0.03	0.06	0.04	0.4	0.2	0.3
Youth measures	*0.07*	*0.09*	*0.07*	*0.3*	*0.4*	*1.9*
Subsidized employment	*0.45*	*0.17*	*0.20*	*5.4*	*1.2*	*1.5*
Subsidies to regular employment in private sector	0.14	0.11	0.11	3.5	0.1	0.0
Support to unemployed persons starting enterprises	0.19	0.02	0.11	0.5	0.2	0.2
Direct job creation	0.12	0.04	0.06	1.4	1.0	1.3
Measures for the disabled	*0.00*	*0.01*	*0.02*	*0.1*	*0.1*	*0.2*
Total active measures	**0.76**	**0.59**	**0.51**	**7.6**	**2.4**	**4.4**
Unemployment compensation	2.42	3.09	1.87			
Early retirement for labour market reasons	0.00	0.00	0.00			
Total passive measures	**2.42**	**3.09**	**1.87**			

Note: Figures are rounded.

Source: OECD (1996, 1998).

people under the age of 26, older workers, women in occupations in which they are under-represented and the disabled) and direct employment creation in the public sector (through collaboration between the Spanish public employment service (INEM) and the various public administrations, the rural employment programme (PER) and projects of social interest);
- measures encouraging entrepreneurial initiatives and employment creation: promotion of self-employment, co-operatives and worker-owned firms, local employment initiatives and capitalization of unemployment benefits.

Table 6.1 gives basic quantitative information about developments in ALMP programmes. As can be seen, expenditures on active measures represent around 0.5 per cent of GDP, although they have been reduced during the 1990s owing to a decrease in the resources devoted to public employment services and to subsidized employment. Resources aimed at providing labour market training have, however, increased somewhat. Overall, active measures represent less than 20 per cent of total public labour market expenditures, with the proportion varying from year to year because of the high sensitivity of passive measures to the business cycle.

2.1 Labour Market Training

The main scheme for labour market training in Spain has been the FIP plan (*Plan Nacional de Formación e Inserción Profesional*, or National Plan for Labour Market Training and Integration).

The goal of the FIP plan is to widen and renew the qualification and professional recycling of unemployed workers, especially the least employable groups. The plan is managed by INEM. The latest regulation dates from 1993, when the training of employed workers was transferred to a private foundation (FORCEM, *Fundación para la Formación Continua en las Empresas*) managed by the social partners and funded by the government. Since then, the management of FIP activities has been transferred to most regions.

While training for the unemployed is managed by INEM (or the regions to which it has been transferred), the agency is only partially involved in training itself. 'Practice training' is generally carried out either by private firms or a public centre recognized by INEM or the regional government. As for the assessment of the FIP plan, no evaluations of these programmes with the use of proper control groups have yet been carried out.[3]

In addition, two other policies may be regarded as labour market training measures. The first is the workshop-schools and trade houses programme

(*Programa de Escuelas-Taller y Casas de Oficios*). Although it is currently part of the FIP plan, this programme, aimed at the young unemployed, is generally analysed independently because of its special characteristics. While practice and apprenticeship (formerly training) contracts may also be placed under the heading of labour market training policies, we shall consider them below as employment contract policies.

2.2 Employment Promotion Measures

One of the main labour market policy strategies pursued in Spain during the 1980s and 1990s has been the creation of various types of labour contracts. These contracts may involve either direct incentives (through subsidies, tax deductions and social charges deductions or exemptions) or indirect incentives (evading the regulatory framework for 'usual' permanent contracts). They may also affect either specific groups of workers or all of them. Although it is debatable whether this kind of policy may be considered an 'active' policy, it has been clearly interpreted in this way by Spanish policy-makers, and thus deserves attention here. As previously mentioned, we have identified three types of contracts: contracts with economic incentive, contracts without economic incentive and public sector jobs.

a. Contracts with direct economic incentive

a1. Permanent contracts for specific groups of workers Since 1992, a flat-rate subsidy of 400 000 pesetas (roughly equivalent to three months' wages) has been paid to firms hiring long-term unemployed under 25 years of age and unemployed people between the ages of 26 and 30 with less than three months of job experience; or to firms giving a permanent status to training, apprenticeship or other fixed-term employment contracts. Similar subsidies are paid when the person hired is either over the age of 45 or disabled. The numbers involved in this type of contract have never been very large, with the exception of the programme for young people under 26 years of age.

a2. Permanent contracts for women who are in occupations in which they are 'under-represented' or who are returning to the labour market Although a subsidy of 500 000 pesetas is paid to employers, uptake of this programme by firms has been low.

a3. Relief contracts, such as replacement contracts tied to retirement schemes Firms can hire a relief worker within 15 days of the start of the phased retirement of an older employee. The new employee must be registered as unemployed and will be hired for a period lasting until the date of retirement of the older worker (up to three years). If the new worker is hired on a full-time basis at the end of the contract term, the employer has the right to a 50 per cent reduction of social security contributions during a period equal to that of the prior relief contract.

b. Contracts without economic incentive

b1. Apprenticeship contracts These contracts, introduced in 1993 to replace the former 'training contracts', are aimed at people under the age of 25 with low-skill levels. Social security contributions are substantially reduced (the entitlements of the workers are also reduced accordingly, in particular unemployment compensation), wages may be below statutory minimum wage (unless otherwise regulated in collective agreements) and at least 15 per cent of the total working time will be devoted to theoretical training.

b2. Practice contracts These are contracts designed for people who have recently graduated from various educational and training programmes. The current regulation establishes a minimum period of six months and a maximum of two years (before 1994 the maximum was three years). Before 1992 there was a direct economic incentive for these contracts in the form of a reduction of social security charges. Since 1992 employers can claim a subsidy of 550 000 pesetas if the employee is given permanent status upon expiration of the maximum period of two years.

The number of both types (training/apprenticeship and practice) of contracts increased until the end of the 1980s and levelled off in the period prior to the date when subsidies and social security relief were eliminated (1993). The new apprenticeship contract introduced in 1994 has yet to reach the level of its predecessor. Practice contracts also became less popular with firms because of the cancellation of the subsidy, although uptake has been on the rise again since 1994. The subsidy was dropped because this contract was being used more as a source of cheap labour than as a real training tool.

The labour market reform of 1996 led to changes in the apprenticeship contract. The contract is now aimed at people under the age of 21. The maximum tenure is two years and the social protection for these contracts is equivalent to that of other workers.

b3. Fixed-term employment promotion contracts These contracts were introduced without restrictions in 1984. Their principal characteristic was that they allowed a more or less unrestricted use of workers on a temporary basis for carrying out normal tasks. A significant change took place in 1994 when the use of temporary contracts was restricted to specific groups. Currently the eligible groups are people over the age of 45, disabled workers and the long-term unemployed receiving unemployment benefits.

Although these kinds of contracts do not involve direct outlays from government, they may none the less be considered a policy measure because firms are not obliged to bear the (potential) burden of the dismissal procedures imposed upon companies hiring workers under the normal permanent contracts. (Employment promotion fixed-term contracts involved a small severance payment upon termination, but workers could not sue employers for termination.)

These contracts were used most widely during the period 1985–91. Their high degree of flexibility – together with their minimal requirements – made them the most convenient option, especially for workers over the age of 25. Following the changes in regulation in 1992, the number of contracts of this type sharply diminished. Since 1994 fixed-term contracts have clearly changed in nature, which explains the smaller number of participants. This reduction appears to have been compensated by 'other' temporary contracts (the so-called 'per task or service').

c. Public sector jobs

There are currently two types of programmes creating direct jobs in the public sector for the unemployed. First, INEM has signed various agreements with public administrations (notably municipalities) to provide work for the unemployed in socially useful activities. The other programme is the PER (*Plan de Empleo Rural*, rural employment programme). This is a plan aimed at providing low-skilled jobs in public investment projects.

2.3 Other Measures to Support Entrepreneurial Activities and Job Creation

We now turn to various programmes aimed at fostering job creation, mostly through various forms of self-employment:

a. Unemployment benefit capitalization

Workers entitled to unemployment benefits may request an advance payment of the full benefit to start up their own business. Before 1992, eligible businesses included self-employment and employment in cooperatives and worker-owned firms. Since 1992, however, only the latter category of project is eligible for this programme.

b. Promotion of self-employment

The purpose of this programme is to promote and financially support self-employment projects submitted by workers registered as unemployed. The costs of feasibility studies, auditing and counselling are partly or fully subsidized.

c. Promotion of employment in cooperatives
The objective of this programme is to grant financial assistance to the investments in the creation or maintenance of jobs in worker-owned firms or other cooperative firms.

d. Promotion of local employment
This programme is geared towards the creation of small- and medium-sized enterprises which demonstrate an innovative approach to economic activity and self-employment in a local setting. Priority is given to projects which create steady employment for individuals under 25 years of age or long-term unemployed and which are oriented towards community and social services.

e. Labour market integration of the disabled
We have already mentioned previously the subsidies provided to disabled people hired under various contracts. In addition, grants are provided to the so-called special job centres and to handicapped individuals wishing to start their own business.

3 REGIONAL AIA IN A MULTIVARIATE SETTING

3.1 Introduction

In this section, we carry out an application of aggregate impact analysis (AIA) methodology at the regional level. The objective is to estimate an econometric model in order to perform a macroeconomic evaluation of ALMP. The main goal is to find out whether ALMP have any effect on aggregate variables. In other words, are active labour market measures associated with either lower unemployment rates or increased exits from unemployment to employment?

There are two basic problems in answering this question (Jackman, 1994). The first problem stems from the distinction between open unemployment and participation in active labour programmes (Calmfors, 1994). Thus policy can produce more cosmetic effects (to reduce unemployment by reclassifying it as participation in a programme) than productive effects (to increase the number of jobs, thus reducing the number of unemployed). Empirical evidence suggests that the reduction in open unemployment is equivalent to the number participating in active programmes; although the costs of making labour markets more efficient may be large relative to the benefits achieved.

The second problem is that of endogeneity and arises as a consequence of the relationship between policy measures and unemployment variables. Spending on ALMP can affect either the unemployment rate or the outflows from unemployment, but it is also true that the level of unemployment and the level of unemployment outflows can affect the provision of ALMP. This might suggest that a policy reaction function exists: governments alter the spending per unemployed person when unemployment changes significantly. Therefore the validity of this problem appears to depend on the way spending on labour market schemes is actually determined. On the one hand, Layard *et al.* (1991) assume that government policy is defined in terms of spending per unemployed person. This measure of ALMP, however, generates an inverse correlation between the spending per unemployed person and the unemployment rate if total spending on active programmes adjusts less than fully to changes in unemployment. Layard *et al.* maintain that this was the case for some OECD countries during the 1980s. On the other hand, the OECD (1993) suggests that the policy reaction function is different and may be defined as a given proportion of GDP to ALMP over the cycle. Using total ALMP spending as a proportion of GDP, the OECD finds no significant effect of ALMP on average unemployment over the cycle. Thus the difference between those results comes from the assumption made about the policy reaction function of government to unemployment. Jackman (1994) formulates that function explicitly, and suggest that the way to avoid the simultaneity problem is either by examining the effects of policies on the u-v (Beveridge) curve or by using cross-section time series data.

While such a policy reaction function may indeed exist, certain facts lead us to believe that this is not the case for Spain in the period analysed here. First, as can be seen from Figures 6.1 and 6.2, there is a somewhat inverse relationship between regional unemployment rates and participation rates in training measures on the one hand, and between regional unemployment rates and expenditure on employment creation schemes on the other. Thus higher levels of unemployment do not automatically lead to higher levels of ALMP (training and employment creation) measures. Second, since the type of information we have on expenditure concerns spending on employment creation schemes but not on all ALMP programmes, we cannot assume that a typical reaction function exists either at an aggregate level (in the sense that all expenditure is distributed across regions taking into account exclusively the regional unemployment rate) or at a regional level (the employment creation scheme is only one field of ALMP, and regions do not have complete autonomy in controlling their own expenditures). Finally, INEM managers have told us that no explicit means of distributing job-creation expenditures among regions existed until 1992 (when the process of transferring competencies and spending to regions began); in fact, it seems that certain variables

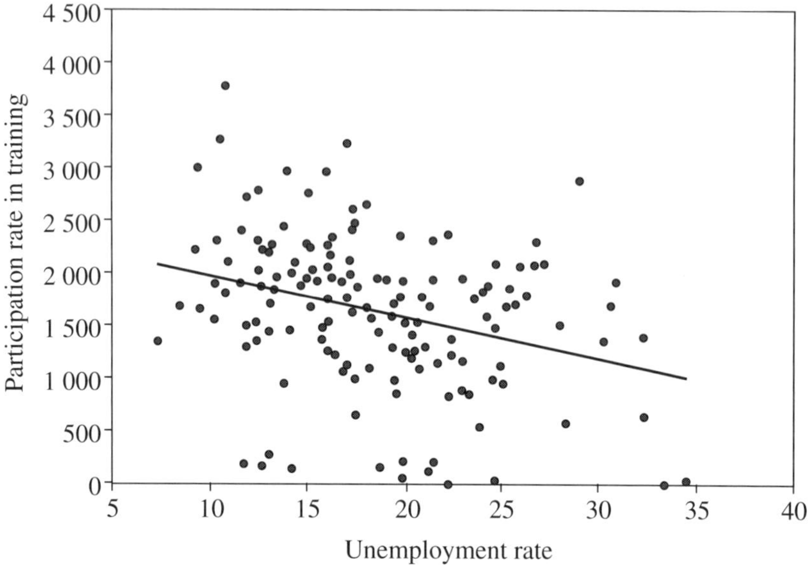

Figure 6.1 *Regional unemployment rates and rate of participation in training measures, Spain, 1987–95*

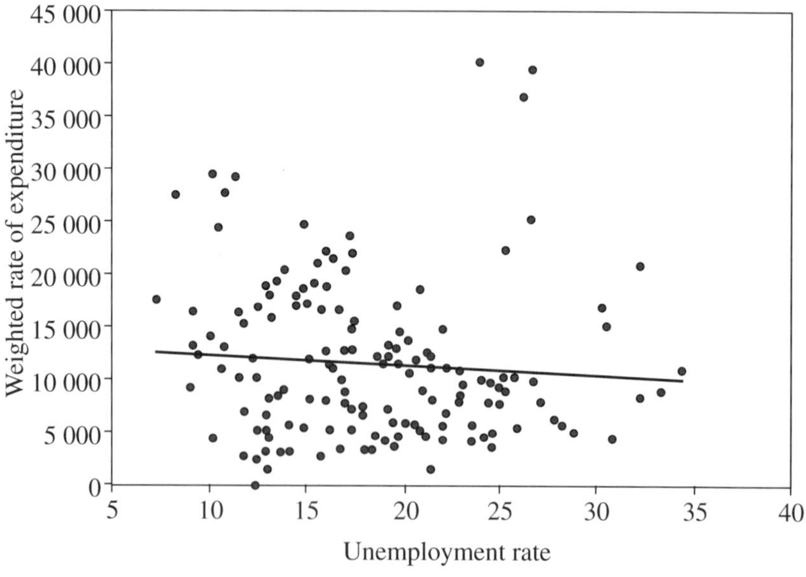

Figure 6.2 *Regional unemployment rates and weighted rate of expenditure on employment-creation schemes, Spain, 1987–95*

such as registered unemployment, labour force figures and administrative management ability were taken into account before that date. Since the last factor (the ability of administrative management) is a very subjective measure, we believe that there is no close relationship between ALMP and unemployment in Spain during the entire time period.

Thus our approach here is to take advantage of a panel (cross-section time series) data set for the 17 Spanish regions over a nine-year period (1987–95), which covers a complete business cycle of the Spanish economy.

3.2 Data and Variables

The data used come from different sources. First, information on various aspects of regional labour markets has been drawn from the Spanish labour force survey: for example, unemployment rates (overall and by gender, age and educational levels), unemployment structure (unemployment by gender, age and spell duration), employment structure (employment by industry and educational levels), and transitions (flows among three possible states: employment, unemployment and inactivity). Second, we also have information from administrative sources on training programmes, the promotion of employment contracts, as well as on employment creation schemes or subsidized employment.

The dependent variables are the overall unemployment rate, the long-term unemployment rate, the overall outflow rate from unemployment to employment and the outflow rates from short-term and long-term unemployment to employment.[4] For ALMP we have defined several variables (subject to data availability) in relation to the programmes described in section 2.

a. The variable *TRAINING* refers to the number of participants in all training programmes in the course of each year.
b. The variable *CREATION* comprises the assistance given to unemployed people in setting up their own businesses. In this case we have data on total expenditure and number of participants for each programme. For econometric purposes, *CREATION* refers to data on total expenditure (all schemes).
c. Data on the number of employment promotion contracts with and without economic incentives (by type of contract) is available. We have constructed two variables (*CONTR.WITH* and *CONTR.W/O*), adding all contracts with and those without direct economic incentives, respectively.[5]

In the estimation, first and third variables are normalized in order to take into account the varying population sizes across regions. Thus the number of participants in training programmes and the amount of the promotion of employment contracts are divided by the labour force.[6]

On the other hand, the second variable (the government expenditure on employment creation schemes) is computed in three different ways. Two of them are based on the definitions used by Layard *et al.* (1991) and the OECD (1993): that is, the ratio of expenditure to GDP and the real expenditure per unemployed person. The third measure is built as a combination of both: it is defined as the ratio of expenditure to GDP times the inverse of the unemployment rate. In this latter case, the measure tries to take into account not only the extent of the problem (the unemployment rate), but also the effort made by the country (the proportion of GDP directed to employment creation schemes). This is the measure of employment creation schemes which we include in the estimation.

We also include other variables in the analysis that can affect the regional unemployment rates and the outflow rates from unemployment to employment. First, there are some variables on the regional employment structure related to differences across regions by industry, educational level, and age distribution of the labour force: the share of agriculture (*AGRICULTURE*) and the service sector (*SERVICES*); the share of the employed with no schooling (*NOSTUDIES*), those with primary (five years) schooling (*PRIMARY*), and those with a university degree (*UNIVERSITY*); and the share of those aged 16–24 (*YOUNG*) and those over the age of 55 (*OLDER*).

While it seems plausible to assume that regions are exposed to the same aggregate shocks, it is equally true that regions differ in their ability to respond to those shocks. Different production and employment growth rates are, therefore, observed across regions. Thus we include the regional GDP growth rate (*GDPCHANGE*) in the regressions as a relevant factor affecting unemployment. In addition, the vacancy rate (*TVACANCY*, the ratio between the number of vacancies and the labour force) has been considered, therefore estimating a sort of u-v or Beveridge curve. Vacancies are measured as the number of unfilled employment positions at the end of the corresponding month in public employment offices. Because employment and unemployment data coming from the Labour Force Survey (LFS) refers to the second quarters, we have decided to use unfilled vacancies in April of each year. Although the unreliability of the vacancy figures is well known, they are the only data available as a proxy for job creation by employers and unsatisfied labour demand. The reliability of official figures regarding the effective level of vacancies is very low because INEM figures only take into account those unfilled employment positions for which INEM is directly responsible; that is, the so-called 'public' or 'generic' vacancies. However, official data also contains information on the number of placements employers communicate to INEM ('private' or 'named' placements), which is larger than the number of generic placements. Since the employment offer and the placement occur simultaneously, those private placements do not, by definition, generate vacancies. Antolín (1994) has devised a method to correct the number of registered vacancies at INEM offices; he estimates a corrected vacancy series (registered generic vacancies plus private vacancies) using a correction factor which inflates the number of official vacancies following a method proposed in Jackman *et al.* (1989). He uses the revised data to estimate an aggregate Beveridge curve for the Spanish economy in the period 1977–91. However, he found that the empirical results do not change when either the original or the corrected series are used. The same conclusion is reached by Dolado and Gómez (1996), who use both series to estimate a u-v curve for the aggregate and for all Spanish regions in the period 1977–94. Both studies find a significant and negative effect of the vacancy rate on the unemployment rate.

Table 6.2 reports descriptive statistics for the variables used in the analysis; including the average, the standard deviation, and the maximum and mini-

Table 6.2 Descriptive statistics for the variables, 1987–97

	Average	Max.	Min.	Deviation
Dependent variables				
Unemployment rate	18.37	34.40	7.30	5.70
Long-term unemployment rate	10.20	18.32	3.31	3.55
U-E rate	28.69	53.43	14.66	6.89
Short-term U-E rate	29.76	54.17	11.86	7.65
Long-term U-E rate	18.37	36.00	11.76	4.94
ALMP variables				
Training	1.68	3.81	0.02	0.73
Contracts With Incentives	1.50	3.87	0.19	0.88
Contracts W/O Incentives	10.47	23.98	4.41	3.82
Creation	11.59	40.12	0.06	7.44
Other variables				
Tvacancy	0.26	0.88	0.02	0.17
Gdpchange	2.67	24.70	–9.13	5.38
Agriculture	13.09	39.34	0.65	8.22
Services	54.96	77.68	37.96	8.40
Young	19.08	26.11	14.99	2.03
Older	32.82	40.26	24.11	3.37
No studies	9.18	23.22	1.89	6.65
Primary	40.41	61.44	26.03	7.55
University	12.27	24.37	6.28	3.14

mum values. These can be taken as indicators of regional variation. For example, the unemployment rate ranges from a minimum of 7.3 per cent to a maximum of 34.4 per cent, and the proportion of trainees in relation to the labour force ranges from a minimum of 0.02 to a maximum of 3.81. Regional variation is, therefore, very large for all variables considered here.

3.3 Model Specification and Results

In Chapter 2 de Koning reviews the models for AIA used in the economic literature. One of them is the u/v-analysis, which, in turn, is also used in other chapters of this book. Therefore, in order to use a similar empirical model to assess the effect of ALMP variables on social exclusion indicators, we estimate the following model:

$$\ln(u_{it}) - a \mid \boldsymbol{b}_1 \ln(v_{it}) \mid \boldsymbol{b}_2 \boldsymbol{x}_{it} \mid z_i \mid \boldsymbol{e}_{it}$$

The dependent variable ln (u) is the logarithm of the unemployment rate, the long-term unemployment rate or the transition from unemployment to employment; a is a constant term; ln (v) is the logarithm of the vacancy rate; **x** is a vector of economic and policy variables; $\boldsymbol{b}_1$ and $\boldsymbol{b}_2$ are vectors of parameters to be estimated; z is either a separate region-specific constant term or a region-specific random disturbance (depending on whether a fixed effects or a random effects model is to be estimated); **e** is a vector of white noise disturbance terms; the index i refers to the i-th region; and the index t refers to time (the years 1987 to 1995).

The model has been estimated using panel techniques and assuming fixed effects (Greene, 1993; Baltagi, 1995). In the case of the fixed effects approach, the estimates are conditional on the sample in that z_i are not assumed to have a distribution but are instead treated as fixed and estimable. Therefore, it should be appropriate if the model is viewed as applying to the cross-sectional units in the study, not to additional ones outside the sample. In addition, its main virtue is that there is no justification for treating the individual effects as uncorrelated with the regressors (*corr* $[z_i, \boldsymbol{x}_{it}]=0$) as the random-effects approach assumes. In this case, $z_i + \boldsymbol{e}_{it}$ is treated as a residual, but if z_i and $\boldsymbol{x}_{it}$ are correlated, the estimator cannot determine how much of the change in u_{it} associated with a change in $\boldsymbol{x}_{it}$ to attribute to b versus how much to assign to the unknown correlation. Therefore, the random effect estimator may be biased and suffer from inconsistency owing to omitted variables.

It should be noted that, while the unemployment related variables and the vacancy rate have been included in logs in this specification, the model has also been estimated with those variables measured in levels (normalized by either the unemployment stock or the labour force). The results do not, in any case, differ from those presented here.

Different specifications of the empirical model have been tried. Tables 6.3–6.6 give the estimates for the effect that ALMP and other variables have on the overall unemployment rate, the long-term unemployment rate, the overall exit rate from unemployment to employment, and the exit rate from long-term unemployment to employment (estimations on the exit rate from short-term unemployment to employment have also been done but are not included here). They also give the four final specifications we have chosen. Model 1 includes only promoting employment contracts with direct economic incentive; Model 2 includes only promoting employment contracts without direct economic incentive; Model 3 takes into account both types of contracts; and Model 4 does not include either type of contract as independent variables.

We begin the discussion of results with the estimates of the overall unemployment rate (Table 6.3). Variables measuring ALMP programmes are always statistically significant at a conventional level. As expected, *TRAINING* and *CONTR.W/O* negatively affect the unemployment rate. That means that training programmes and, above all, employment promotion contracts without economic incentive, help reduce the unemployment rate. A direct relationship is, however, sometimes found between the unemployment rate and *CREATION*. This positive sign on employment creation schemes expenditure may reflect the policy reaction function already discussed: that is, when unemployment rises, the regional authorities increase their expenditure on those programmes. This result holds when other measures of the expenditure on employment-creation schemes (expenditure normalized by the GDP or by the unemployment rate) are used.

Looking at the rest of the variables, there is, as expected, an inverse relationship between the unemployment rate and the vacancy rate; while the GDP growth rate does not affect significantly the unemployment rate (in all specifications, this variable always has the correct sign but it is never statistically significant, even when it is included in an estimation without the vacancy rate). Finally those variables intended to take into account differences across regions are relevant: the share of the population aged 16–24 and over the age of 55, as well as the proportion of employed people in the service sector, positively affect the unemployment rate; but the educational variables are not statistically significant.

Now we turn to the effects of all those variables on the long-term unemployment rate (Table 6.4). In this case the results are similar to those obtained for the overall unemployment rate in that *TRAINING* and *CONTR.W/O* are statistically significant for the reduction of the long-term unemployment rate. These results for training programmes and employment promotion contracts

Table 6.3 Estimates of the effect of ALMP on the overall unemployment rate, Spain, 1987–95

	MODEL 1		MODEL 2		MODEL 3		MODEL 4	
Variables	Coefficient	t-ratio	Coefficient	t-ratio	Coefficient	t-ratio	Coefficient	t-ratio
Constant	–1.316	–1.733	0.442	0.694	0.894	1.420	–1.276	–1.685
TVACANCY	–0.138	–3.288 *	–0.030	–0.881	–0.041	–1.202	–0.147	–3.611 *
GDPCHANGE	–0.003	–0.933	–0.000	–0.002	–0.003	–1.142	–0.005	–1.344
TRAINING	–0.097	–3.165 *	–0.101	–4.124 *	–0.096	–4.058 *	–0.095	–3.123 *
CONTR WITH	–0.022	–0.803			0.082	3.354 *		
CONTR W/O			–0.050	–8.909 *	–0.059	–9.765 *		
CREATION	0.000	0.051	0.003	1.346	0.004	2.094 *	0.000	0.170
AGRICULT	0.015	2.832 *	0.002	0.498	0.007	1.606	0.018	3.675 *
SERVICES	0.006	1.801	0.013	4.550 *	0.015	5.356 *	0.006	1.896 *
YOUNG	0.145	6.202 *	0.095	4.818 *	0.084	4.405 *	0.145	6.198 *
OLDER	0.035	2.753 *	0.022	2.132	0.012	1.162	0.034	2.648 *
NOSTUDIES	–0.009	–1.071	–0.003	–0.413	–0.009	–1.348	–0.011	–1.394
PRIMARY	–0.005	–0.953	–0.004	–0.927	–0.007	–1.531	–0.006	–1.117
UNIVERSITY	–0.002	–0.211	–0.004	–0.380	–0.005	–0.582	–0.003	–0.249
R^2	0.558		0.717		0.738		0.557	
Adjusted R^2	0.520		0.693		0.714		0.522	
F-statistics	14.77		29.57		30.16		16.10	
No. of observations	153		153		153		153	

Note: * denotes that the corresponding coefficient is significant at the 5% level.

Table 6.4 Estimates of the effect of ALMP on the long-term unemployment rate, Spain, 1987–95

	MODEL 1		MODEL 2		MODEL 3		MODEL 4	
Variables	Coefficient	t-ratio	Coefficient	t-ratio	Coefficient	t-ratio	Coefficient	t-ratio
Constant	–2.265	–2.308 *	–0.681	–0.738	0.345	0.403	–2.376	–2.412
TVACANCY	–0.141	–2.603 *	–0.004	–0.073	–0.026	–0.568	–0.118	–2.231
GDPCHANGE	–0.001	–0.190	0.007	1.664	–0.001	–0.176	0.002	0.495
TRAINING	–0.137	–3.465 *	–0.147	–4.145 *	–0.136	–4.218 *	–0.142	–3.563 *
CONTR WITH	0.063	1.706			0.187	5.599 *		
CONTR W/O			–0.049	–6.062 *	–0.070	–8.466 *		
CREATION	–0.002	–0.621	–0.001	–0.195	0.003	1.014	–0.003	–0.872
AGRICULT	0.031	4.405 *	0.010	1.639	0.021	3.573 *	0.026	4.061 *
SERVICES	0.005	1.156	0.011	2.600	0.016	4.073 *	0.004	0.980
YOUNG	0.162	5.336 *	0.113	3.953 *	0.090	3.430 *	0.163	5.328 *
OLDER	0.020	1.205	0.015	0.981	–0.008	–0.557	0.026	1.584
NOSTUDIES	–0.025	–2.296	–0.011	–1.151	–0.025	–2.784 *	–0.019	–1.843
PRIMARY	0.000	0.033	0.005	0.699	–0.001	–0.217	0.002	0.342
UNIVERSITY	0.019	1.181	0.019	1.356	0.015	1.180	0.020	1.254
R^2	0.499		0.595		0.669		0.488	
Adjusted R^2	0.456		0.560		0.638		0.448	
F-statistics	11.61		17.13		21.65		12.24	
No. of observations	153		153		153		153	

Note: * denotes that the corresponding coefficient is significant at the 5% level.

are similar to those reported in Bellman and Jackman (1996). However, no relationship is found between the long-term unemployment rate and expenditure on employment-creation schemes. Finally, while the educational distribution of the employed population makes no difference across regions, the age structure is important: those regions with a higher proportion of young people have higher long-term unemployment rates.

It must be stressed that the estimation results presented so far appear to be sensitive to changes in the specification. In fact what we see is that inclusion/exclusion of employment promotion contracts without economic incentive variable affects the significance of *TVACANCY*. This is the reason why we present four different specifications of the empirical model. From a theoretical perspective, we believe that this type of contract has been used as an important economic policy tool to encourage the exit from unemployment in order to prevent long-term unemployment and, thus, social exclusion. It is therefore reasonable to include those contracts in the estimation procedure. In any case, the likely correlation of this variable with the business cycle may explain its effect on the significance of *TVACANCY*.

Now we discuss the estimates on the overall exit rate from unemployment to employment (Table 6.5). The estimate results show that the only ALMP variables significantly influencing that transition are the number of participants in training courses and the employment promotion contracts (without economic incentive). The other ALMP variables are never statistically significant, although they always show a positive sign. As for the rest of the variables, neither those reflecting the cyclical position of the economy (GDPCHANGE) nor the relative labour market mismatch (TVACANCY) are significant in explaining the outflow rate from unemployment to employment. As for those variables reflecting differences across regions in educational or industry structures, a higher proportion of employed people without schooling or in the service sector negatively affect the outflow rate from unemployment. On the other hand, in specifications 1 and 4, the age structure is statistically significant: a higher proportion of the population aged 16–24 or over the age of 55 negatively affect that aggregate flow.

Finally, Table 6.6 offers the estimates on exit rates from long-term unemployment to employment (we have also performed estimations on the outflow rate from short-term unemployment to employment, but do not present them here for the sake of brevity).[7] The results show that the only ALMP variable significantly influencing those transitions is the number of employment promotion contracts without economic incentive. Another interesting result is that the economic cycle (given by the variable *GDPCHANGE*) is significant in explaining the outflow rate from long-term unemployment to employment, although it is not significant in explaining the outflow rate from short-term unemployment to employment. It therefore seems that, in addition to employment promotion contracts, positive economic conditions are necessary for the very long-term unemployed to enter the workforce. This may be because the short-term unemployed are more likely to get temporary contracts, thus moving quickly between employment and unemployment regardless of the conditions observed in the economy.

In order to provide results that are comparable for the various countries included in the different chapters of the book, we have computed average elasticities from the parameter estimates. These are shown in Table 6.7. As previously stated, the ALMP variables significantly influencing either the unemployment rates or the exit rates to employment are *TRAINING* and *CONTR.W/O*. On average, a 1 per cent increase in the (normalized) number of trainees reduces the overall and long-term unemployment rates by 0.2 percentage points and increases the overall short- and long-term unemployed exit rates by 0.1 percentage points. Similarly, a 1 per cent increase in the (normalized) number of contracts without economic incentives reduces the overall and long-term unemployment rates by 0.5 percentage points; and, at the same time, increases the overall exit rate by 0.15 percentage points and the short- and long-term unemployed exit rates by 0.25–0.29 percentage points. The other two ALMP variables have minor effects and do not significantly influence the dependent variables.

Table 6.7 Average elasticities of ALMP variables on unemployment-related variables, Spain, 1987–95

	Overall unemployment rate	Long-term unemployment rate	Overall U-E rate	Short-term U-E rate	Long-term U-E rate
TRAINING	–0.163	–0.231	0.086	0.094	0.102
CONTR. WITH	–0.034	0.094	0.032	0.062	0.132
CONTR. W/O	–0.525	–0.518	0.138	0.251	0.294
CREATION	–0.002	–0.026	0.036	–0.139	0.012

4 CONCLUSIONS

In the preceding sections, we have reviewed the Spanish experience with active labour market policies. Integral to the Spanish approach are, we believe, those policies with the goal of changing the fringes of the labour market to make hirings cheaper for firms by creating new types of contracts aimed at easing the (re)integration of the unemployed (particularly the long-term unemployed). This active policy without budgetary expenditure has been successful in that the GDP elasticity of employment has increased in Spain.

These types of policies (and, in general, all ALMP measures) can be connected to the concept of 'transitional labour markets' (Schmid, 1998): that is, institutionalized arrangements which support the change of the employment status or the combination of labour market work with other socially useful activities. It is widely acknowledged that high and persistent long-term unemployment is one of the causes of social exclusion. Therefore, institutional arrangements such as active labour market policies that reduce the inflow into and speed up the outflow out of unemployment into employment should be considered essential in fighting long-term unemployment and social exclusion. This implies too that the evaluation of whether ALMP programmes have succeeded in reducing social exclusion by reducing long-term unemployment is an important empirical issue.

The econometric results in this chapter show that, in the estimates for the overall unemployment rate and for the long-term unemployment rate, some ALMP variables (training programmes and promoting employment contracts without economic incentives) are always statistically significant (for all model specifications) and with the expected sign. In other words, those variables reduce both unemployment rates. The estimates for the outflow rates from overall short- and long-term unemployment to employment show, however, that the only (sometimes) significant variable among all ALMP variables is that for promoting employment contracts (the number of trainees and the expenditure on employment creation schemes are never significant, although they have a positive sign; that is, they would positively affect the outflow rate).

If we consider the two results together, they would, surprisingly enough, indicate that ALMP do not greatly affect, at the aggregate level, the outflow from unemployment to employment even though they contribute to the reduction of unemployment. There are two possible explanations for this: on the one hand, there is a lag in the influence that ALMP have on the outflow from unemployment (that is, it takes time for individuals who have participated in ALMP to find a job); on the other, ALMP can influence the entry into unemployment from employment in the sense that those who exit to a job 'stay' for a while in that job and do not return immediately to unemployment (thus the lower the inflows into unemployment, the lower the unemployment rate).

Although previous results persist independently of the econometric specification, it must be stressed that a correlation may exist between the active labour market measures and the variables identifying unemployment, which would imply that there is a policy reaction function. That does not, however, seem to be the case here. First, we have seen that an inverse relationship exists between regional unemployment rates and ALMP (training and employment creation) programmes; thus higher levels of unemployment do not automatically lead to higher levels of ALMP measures. Second, since information on expenditure details spending on employment-creation schemes but not on all ALMP programmes, we cannot assume that a reaction function exists either at an aggregate or at a regional level. Finally, it seems that, at least until 1992 (when the process of transferring competencies and spending to regions began), there was no explicit means of distributing job-creation expenditure among regions; although certain variables such as registered unemployment, labour force figures and administrative management ability were taken into account.

Finally, it is true that the structure and functioning of active labour market measures are quite rigid in Spain. On the one hand, different features of the potential recipients are not considered; and, on the other, there are no linkages between them. These measures thus become quite isolated, which implies a loss of efficiency. Recommendations from the OECD focus on the need for implementing integrated groups of measures for more specific target groups. With respect to policy responsibility, employment policies are carried out by the central government through the Ministry of Labour and Social Affairs and INEM (the public employment service). At the same time, however, the domain of the regional governments must be clearly defined. Sufficient attention must also be paid to the heterogeneity of both the agents offering the programmes and the unemployed workers attending them.

NOTES

1. This section is based on chapter three of Toharia (1997).
2. In 1995, as a consequence of the labour market reform introduced in Spain in 1994, the monopoly situation of the Spanish public employment service (INEM) was ended with the introduction of private, non-profit agencies as well as the creation of so-called 'Integrated Employment Services' (known as SIPEs).
3. In fact, two microeconomic evaluations have been done in relation to the FIP Plan. On the one hand, INEM has selected two samples (stratified in terms of gender, age and level of education), one of trained people and one of not trained unemployed. The comparisons between these two groups show that those having received training had a substantially higher integration rate (between 10 and 15 percentage points) than those who did not receive training. Sáez and Toledo (1996) also report similar results from a study of 10 000 trained unemployed with a control group of 2 000 other unemployed. In both cases, the samples of trained and not trained unemployed were not selected randomly.
4. Participants in ALMP are included in unemployment figures. Therefore, results regarding the effect of ALMP on unemployment in the next subsection are not overestimated because participants are not removed from unemployment during participation.
5. Data on public sector jobs (through work in projects of social interest and the rural employment programme) are not included since these schemes are mainly carried out by municipalities and INEM is not capable of collecting all this data.
6. We have tried other specifications. For instance, the amount of employment promotion

contracts has been divided by either the number of unemployed people or the number of those employed. The first measure was intended to grasp the 'turnover intensity' in the local labour market in terms of the proportion of the flow of employment promotion contracts with respect to the stock of unemployed workers. The second measure tried to give a similar idea (in this case something like 'temporary employment intensity'), thus giving the proportion of employment-promoting contracts with respect to the stock of employed workers. The econometric results do not change when considering those different measures.

7. Estimations on the outflows from short- and long-term unemployment have been done by aggregating the 17 autonomous communities into 10 regions because the number of cases when considering unemployment durations was very low (and, therefore, data representativeness was not reliable) in some (small) regions. We have also repeated the estimation procedure on the overall exit rate from unemployment using the 10-region aggregation; results do not differ substantially from those reported previously.

REFERENCES

Antolín, P. (1994), '*Unemployment Flows and Vacancies in Spain*', Instituto Valenciano de Investigaciones Económicas (IVIE), Working Paper 94–05, Valencia.

Baltagi, B. (1995), *Econometric Analysis of Panel Data*, Wiley: New York.

Bellman, L. and R. Jackman (1996), 'The Impact of Labour Market Policy on Wages, Employment and Labour Market Mismatch', in G. Schmid, J. O'Reilly and K. Schöman (eds), *International Handbook of Labour Market Policy and Evaluation*, Cheltenham: Edward Elgar.

Calmfors, L. (1994), 'Active Labour Market Policy and Unemployment: A Framework for the Analysis of Crucial Design Features', *OECD Economic Studies*, 22, 7–47.

Dolado, J.J. and R. Gómez (1996), 'La relación entre vacantes y desempleo en España: perturbaciones agregadas y de reasignación', mimeo.

Greene, W. (1993), *Econometric Analysis*, Prentice Hall.

Jackman, R. (1994), 'What Can Active Labour Market Policy Do?', *Swedish Economic Policy Review*, 1, 221–57.

Jackman, R., R. Layard and C. Pissarides (1989), 'On Vacancies', *Oxford Bulletin of Economics and Statistics*, 51, 377–94.

Layard, R., S. Nickell and R. Jackman (1991), *Unemployment. Macroeconomic Performance and the Labour Market*, Oxford: Oxford University Press.

OECD (1993), *Economic Outlook*, Paris.

OECD (1996), *Employment Outlook*, Paris.

OECD (1998), *Employment Outlook*, Paris.

Sáez, F. and M. Toledo (1996), 'Las políticas de empleo y del mercado de trabajo en Europa: una visión general', *Economistas*, 70.

Schmid, G. (1998), 'Transitional Labour Markets: A New European Employment Strategy', WZB Discussion Paper, FS I 98–206, Berlin: WZB.

Toharia, L. (1997), 'Labour Market Studies: Spain', *Employment and Social Affaires Series* no. 1, European Commission.

PART II

Implementation Studies

7. Process evaluation of active labour market policies and trends in implementation regimes[1]

Hugh Mosley and Els Sol

This chapter first discusses 'process evaluation' and its relationship to impact evaluation. Whereas impact evaluation attempts to assess the effects of active labour market policy (ALMP) programmes on participants or – in aggregate impact analysis – regional or national labour markets, process analysis is primarily concerned with how ALMP programmes are implemented and how implementation affects programme outcomes. Thereafter three major trends in ALMP policy implementation are discussed: decentralization, co-operative networks, and contracting out.

1 PROCESS EVALUATION: THE IMPLEMENTATION BLACK BOX

Policy-makers and policy researchers have increasingly come to realize that the *organization of policy* influences the final outcome. Traditionally, evaluation research focused on policy effects and the evaluation of labour market policies usually takes the form of impact analysis. Policy contents, that is, the 'treatment', are taken for granted and the institutional context in which policies are generated and transformed into programmes as well as policy implementation (the so-called 'within-puts') are neglected. Process analysis and process evaluation aim at opening the 'black box' of policy implementation. The goal of process evaluation is to contribute to the improvement of policy design in order to obtain better results. It is thus not an alternative to impact analysis but a necessary complement (Palumbo and Calista, 1990; Scheirer, 1994; Schmid, 1996).

Classical evaluation research in labour market policy has been predominantly programme-oriented impact analysis. Using an explanatory model borrowed from medical research, evaluation has focused on the impact of programme 'treatments' on individual participants. The goal of the evaluation exercise has been primarily to assess the net impact of programmes on participants' employment and earnings. The analytical paradigm of this type of evaluation has been to compare programme participants with an experimental or quasi-experimental control group of non-participants (that is, the counterfactual). An elaborate conceptual framework and increasingly sophisticated methodology has been developed for this task, which addresses key analytical issues such as 'selection bias' and various components of programme effects such as 'deadweight', 'substitution', and 'displacement'. This tradition of impact analysis is now the standard in evaluation research and has greatly increased our sophistication in assessing the net effects of labour market programmes. The limitations of this programme-oriented approach to impact evaluation of labour market policy have been addressed elsewhere and need not be repeated here (see Schmid *et al.*, 1996).[2]

From the point of view of implementation research, classical impact analysis of programme effects on participants has two major shortcomings: (1) it tends to assume a simplified input–output model in which the implementation process is automatic and thus underestimates the importance of *programme variation* in the implementation process for programme effects; and (2) by focusing primarily programme effects on individuals, it fails to address a range of other *implementation issues* that are central to policy-making and ALMP policy outcomes (Palumbo and Calista, 1990; Scheirer, 1994).

1.1 Programme Variation

Labour market job-creation, training, or wage-subsidy programmes provide complex services or administer incentives that are in practice very heterogeneous. Labour market programmes in many countries are, by design, framework regulations that permit a great deal of local variation in the organization, content, and even in the terms and conditions for participation in labour market programmes. This is the case, for example, in many European Social Fund programmes which are merely funding instruments for a wide variety of labour market programmes, but also for major national training and job-creation programmes in Germany and in other countries. Moreover, even in programmes in which there is an attempt to specify programme components and implementation in detail, the real quality of programme participation may vary considerably for participants throughout the country.[3] Finally, there is an increasing tendency towards programme diversity inherent in the trend towards decentralization of ALMP and increasingly complex constellations of the actors involved. In sum programme 'treatments' are seldom so standardized as the (misleading) analogy to medical research suggests, and this fact needs to be taken into consideration even in impact analyses at the risk of drawing misleading or false conclusions (Scheirer, 1994).

In principle, these shortcomings can be remedied by giving more consideration to the role of implementation in modelling the impact of ALMP measures and by collecting appropriate data (for example, de Koning and van Nes, 1991). In practice, this is difficult owing to the general scarcity of relevant data. Information on variations in programme delivery is seldom systematically collected in monitoring systems and, moreover, variation may be due to irregular behaviour that will not be reported. Furthermore, the data used in assessing the impact of individual participation are frequently based on national samples, whereas variation in implementation is largely regional and pertains to programme characteristics of which individual participants may not even be aware. Thus, implementation variables could not be taken more into consideration in the aggregate impact analyses in this volume because of the lack of pre-existing administrative data and the difficulties of carrying out the comprehensive survey at the regional level that would have been required.

1.2 Implementation Issues

Process evaluation also addresses a wide range of issues beyond ALMP-programme effects on individuals: uptake, efficiency, targeting, implementation process and their effects on programme performance. Of particular interest are structural issues related to the organization of the public employment service including its financing, governance, management structures, and interaction with other relevant actors at national, regional and local levels. These broader institutional features of the organization of labour market policy pertain not just to individual programmes but span several programmes and set overall priorities.

The methodology of process evaluation is not, in principle, different from impact analysis. For obvious reasons process evaluations rely more heavily on qualitative analyses or case studies than on quantitative analyses, although the three implementation studies presented in this Part combine both qualitative and quantitative approaches. The typical dependent variables are not just the impact of programmes on individuals (as in classical impact analyses) or on regional labour markets (as in the regional aggregate impact analyses in this volume) but rather on processes and organizational outcomes such as co-operation and efficiency. Implementation variables may, however, also be directly related to individual labour market outcomes in the context of an impact analysis (see the Swedish study in Chapter 10).

2 TRENDS IN ALMP IMPLEMENTATION REGIMES

Public employment services (PES) are currently undergoing profound changes in the definition of their goals, their implementation structures, and their relationships with other societal actors (for example, the social partners, local governments, service providers). Traditional hierarchical forms of public employment service organization are being challenged by innovative 'new public management' strategies borrowed from the private sector: decentralization, management by objectives, contracting out, competition even within government, customer orientation and so on. Instead of being monopolistic institutions they are expected to compete and co-operate with other private, public, and non-profit organizations involved in the same tasks.

This section focuses on three interrelated major trends in ALMP policy implementation in recent years:

- decentralization of public employment services especially through reliance on performance indicators and management by objectives;
- contracting out and increased reliance on market forms of co-ordination;
- network-based co-operative approaches to ALMP implementation.

The first two are closely related strategies for increasing the efficiency and effectiveness of public administration associated with 'new public management'. The latter is a response to broader trends towards increased responsibility of local authorities for ALMP and the 'activation' of institutions responsible for social security, which have led to more complex actor constellations and new co-ordination problems in ALMP implementation.

2.1 New Public Management in Public Employment Services[4]

'New public management' (NPM) is the key word for a family of ideas currently transforming public administration and the implementation of ALMP by public employment services. Whereas traditional public administration was built on the idea of a 'highly distinct public sector "group" and a dense "grid" of general procedural rules governing the conduct of business', NPM aims to reduce 'the extent to which discretionary power (particularly over staff, contracts and money) is limited by uniform and general rules of procedure' (Dunleavy and Hood, 1994). It aims to replace 'administrative culture' with a 'management culture' (Richards, 1994; Metcalfe and Richards, 1990) using a quasi-contractual and quasi-market paradigm adapted from the private sector (Osborne and Gaebler, 1992). In the 1990s there was a near universal trend towards NPM in public administration (OECD, 1993a, 1993b, 1993c, 1994, 1995, 1996a).

'New public management' is a very diverse family of theories and reform initiatives that resists precise definition. It is, both in theory and practice, a mixture of different public choice approaches with management theories and concepts of 'managerialism' (see Aucoin, 1991; Gray and Jenkins, 1995; Pollitt, 1990). There are, therefore, alternative NPM approaches from different theoretical backgrounds (Ranson and Stewart, 1994). None the less, all identify a common problem: the shortcomings in efficiency and effectiveness of traditional public administration (Schütz, 1996).

In the following sections we discuss two trends in the implementation of labour market policy that are heavily influenced by the new public management approach: *decentralisation* through management by objectives (MBO) and *contracting out*. Thereafter we discuss *network-based co-operation* in implementation regimes.

2.2 Decentralization and Management by Objectives

By decentralization we mean the extent to which responsibility for the shaping of ALMP is delegated to the regional and local levels. Decentralization entails increased regional and local control over programme design features and targeting, policy mix through flexible budgets, personnel levels and terms and conditions of employment. It is frequently argued that decentralization will enhance the adaptation of labour market policy to local needs and improve efficiency.

The organizational paradigm of management by objectives (or management by results) is the common denominator of diverse efforts to decentralize implementation and thereby to enhance the efficiency and effectiveness of labour market policy in many countries. In the field of labour market policy, Sweden and Norway are the most experienced countries with MBO-systems in Europe introducing them in the mid-1980s (Niklasson and Tomsmark, 1994). Finland and more recently Denmark (in 1994) also attempt to steer PES performance via MBO-systems (OECD, 1996b). Outside of Scandinavia, the UK and the Netherlands have had considerable experiences with quantitative performance indicators during the 1990s (Mosley and Degen, 1994; Sol and Glebbeek, 1998; Moraal, 1994; OECD, 1993d). Austria has been taking considerable steps towards performance management and comprehensive monitoring in the course of the recent AMS reforms. Germany introduced far-reaching decentralization of the PES in January 1998, which entails, *inter alia*, the publication of annual 'reintegration balance sheets' for all regional PES offices as well as the introduction of performance agreements between different levels of the PES (see Chapter 8).

Although management by objectives, like other elements of NPM, has been implemented in different ways and with different degrees of stringency, it can be summarized provisionally in the following six basic elements:[5]

- Goal definition and performance indicators: establishment of clear objectives and development of performance indicators that show the extent to which these goals have been achieved.
- Cost accounting: establishment of accounting systems that permit costs to be known and related to different outputs.
- Delegation: delegation of objectives and resources, in manageable units, to staff at subordinate levels of the organization.
- Policy discretion: operating units are permitted to shift resources between different budget items in order to optimize achievement of performance targets.
- Monitoring: monitoring systems providing detailed information on the progress towards organizational objectives.
- Assessment: regular reviews to assess progress towards achieving objectives, which is the principal criterion for judging their performance.
- New policy cycle: redefinition or adjustment of policy goals and performance indicators and beginning of new planning cycle.

The implications of NPM for decentralization are ambiguous. The mainstream NPM approach does not represent an abandonment of central control of the organization but rather a refinement of central steering. NPM stresses in particular management by objectives or management by results in which operating units are typically given a great deal more discretion in the use of funds and personnel and in the organization of programmes than in more traditional administrative structures but are expected to achieve centrally-set targets or goals in terms of which their performance is assessed. The actual degree of decentralization in policy-making entailed depends largely upon whether organizational goals are defined broadly or restrictively.

2.3 Market Co-ordination through Contracting Out

Contracting out aims at achieving heightened efficiency and flexibility by outsourcing employment services to external market providers. New public management strongly advocates contracting out in the public sector on the assumption that the market sector is more efficient than the public sector. The issue here is not whether or not the public sector should assume responsibility for providing a service but whether a public service should be provided 'in-house' by its own employees or though external providers on a contractual basis. Long practised in many countries in the area of training and job-creation programmes, this approach is now being increasingly used even in placement services, which in most countries is one of the few labour market services that are still provided 'in-house'. Contracting out is, in its various forms, perhaps the most widespread form of privatization in labour market policy, whereby external providers are frequently not private for-profit organizations but other governmental entities or from the non-profit sector.

The issue of when contracting out is appropriate is addressed at a more theoretical level in transaction cost theory (Williamson, 1985). Two characteristics of transactions are considered to be of central importance for the choice of form of governance: uncertainty and transaction-specific investment. As a rule the higher the level of uncertainty in a transaction the more difficult it is to regulate it through a contract with an external provider because the terms and conditions of the transaction cannot be adequately specified in advance. Even more important is the existence of transaction-specific investments, which increase the risk of opportunism. In general, high transaction-specific investments are an obstacle to outsourcing (Barney and Hesterly, 1996).

It is difficult to apply an analysis of this level of generality to the particular problems and choices of ALMP implementation, for example, whether PES labour market training or placement services should be provided in-house by its own personnel and in its own facilities or by external providers, although it does provide some insights. Thus an external training provider may be unwilling to make large investments in plant and equipment to provide highly specialized training services on a contract basis. In practice these issues are resolved more pragmatically by 'market testing' and learning from the experience of other agencies or countries as evidenced, for example, by the gradual substitution of contracting out for PES in-house training facilities over the last two decades in most countries. Placement services appear to be the last core services that are provided directly by the PES in all countries. However, in this case too there is a clear trend towards contracting out of placement activities for special groups, such as the long-term unemployed and social assistance recipients. Moreover, in the recent reform of the Australian PES contracting out to external providers is the usual form of placement service provision.

Agency theory provides an alternative framework for analysing the functional problems of contracting in service provision. In agency relationships one partner to the transaction (the principal) delegates authority to another (the agent) and the welfare of the principal is affected by the choices of the agent (Arrow, 1985). The agency relationship is problematic for the principal because the interests of principal and agent diverge and the principal cannot perfectly, and costlessly, monitor both the agent's actions and the information available to the agent. Arrow (1985) identifies two principal types of agency problems: moral hazard and adverse selection. In the former the actions of the agent are either hidden from the principal or costly to monitor. In the latter case the agent has information that is for the principal either unobservable or costly to obtain and, therefore, the principal cannot fully know whether its interests are served by the agent's decisions (Barney and Hesterly, 1996).

Agency theory provides a useful framework for analysing the functional problems in ALMP implementation regimes that rely heavily on contract models. For example, Courty and Marschke (1995) found that output-oriented contracting with training providers in US Job Training Partnership Act (JTPA) programmes induced gaming behaviour and a problem of moral hazard, that is, 'actions which cannot be eliminated contractually *ex ante* and which the principal cannot detect *ex post*'. 'Gaming' the performance measures was defined as taking action that increases reported performance without improving actual performance at the expense of the organization's objectives. In this case contractors were compensated based on the post-programme employment status of their clients. Training providers used the discretion available to them to manipulate the timing of exits from the programme to coincide with placements, which were frequently short-term jobs. Courty and Marschke (1995) estimate that this practice inflated reported training centre performance by about 20 per cent.

A special case of adverse selection in ALMP programme implementation is the well-known phenomenon of 'creaming', that is, the selection of those eligible persons for labour market programmes who, owing to personal characteristics (qualifications, attitude, and so on), can be prepared in the shortest possible time for achieving programme goals. In this case the selection of programme participants is based on knowledge unavailable to the principal. It is a problem in all labour market programmes but is particularly likely to occur where performance assessment or even performance-based compensation is incorporated in contracts or quasi-contracts. For example, output-related funding arrangements in Training and Enterprise Council (TEC) contracts in the UK clearly produced a tendency towards the selection of participants who can be prepared in the shortest possible time for employment or a National Vocational Qualification, to the neglect of those with special needs (Mosley and Degen, 1994).

2.4 Networks and Co-operation

A major focus of recent trends in ALMP implementation is to improve horizontal co-ordination of labour market policy tasks that belong to different policy domains. This is a response to the fact that the different functions of labour market policy (job placement, active measures, unemployment benefit and social assistance) have evolved into separate policy domains that are frequently under the responsibility of different institutional actors. The co-ordination problem in this regard differs from country to country depending on the national institutional setting. Among OECD countries only nine (Austria, Canada, Germany, Greece, Italy, Japan, Luxembourg, Norway and Spain) have fully integrated regimes in which the three principal labour market policy tasks (job brokerage, management of active programmes, and benefit administration) are located within the same organization, although all three tasks have a common objective, to reintegrate the unemployed as rapidly as possible. In eight other countries the brokerage and ALMP are concentrated within the PES (Belgium, Denmark, Finland, Ireland, the Netherlands, Portugal, Sweden, Switzerland) while benefit administration is the responsibility of separate agencies. In four other countries (Australia, France, UK, USA) responsibility for placement services and active measures are assigned to two or more separate institutions (Mosley *et al.*, 1998).

Co-ordination problems resulting from the institutional fragmentation of these interrelated tasks are evidently an obstacle to the development of coherent and efficient labour market policies to combat long-term unemployed (OECD, 1997):

- a close co-ordination between placement and benefit work is needed in order to apply work tests effectively and hence fulfil one of the key preconditions for benefit entitlement;
- a close co-ordination between job brokerage and ALMP is needed in order to ensure that the unemployed can acquire the attributes necessary to fill available job vacancies;
- a close co-operation between benefit administration and referral to ALMP is needed in order to avoid long-term dependency on benefit receipt and programme participation for the sole purpose of renewing benefit entitlements.

Moreover, the complexity of actor constellations in active labour market policy has been further complicated by the trend towards ‘activation’ of unemployment benefits, that is, giving priority to reintegration of the unemployed versus ‘passive’ income maintenance benefits. This, however, means in practice that institutions previously responsible only for administration of unemployment benefit and social assistance have now become involved in the provision of active programmes for their respective clientèles. Thus the co-ordination problem in labour market policy now goes beyond the classical three functions and includes other policy domains, especially social assistance, which in most countries is the responsibility of still another institution, for example, the local authorities in Germany, the Netherlands, and Sweden in the implementation studies in this volume.

National responses to these structural problems of ALMP policy implementation have varied. At the risk of oversimplification there appear to be two principal strategies: one in which the PES continues to be the central institution co-ordinating different labour market policy tasks and another alternative network-based approach in which the PES is no longer the central ALMP player (Fay, 1997). What is required is an effective co-ordination between the different actors responsible for the different policy domains, employer associations, trade unions and governmental organizations.

In the remainder of this section we discuss co-operation as a collective action problem and then apply these considerations to ALMP implementation. By co-operation we mean voluntary co-ordination of the implementation of ALMP by two or more organizations, such as, between the public employment service and local authorities responsible for social assistance.[6] In most general terms, a collective action problem arises when voluntary co-operation to provide a collective good is inhibited by the existence of externalities and by opportunistic behaviour, that is, the free-rider problem, because the benefits of collective goods cannot be appropriated by or limited to the actors that provide them (Elster, 1989).

In the case of labour market policy the collective action problem is one of inter-organizational co-ordination which is aggravated by the institutional complexity of the public sector (Kooiman, 1993; Mayntz, 1998; Marin and Mayntz, 1991; Sol, 2000; Powell and DiMaggio, 1991). Labour market policies typically involve institutions in a number of different functional areas and government jurisdictions (for example, labour, education, social security institutions, central and local government). An important consequence of this institutional fragmentation is a mismatch between institutions and issues and between the costs and benefits of programmes in the policy process so that external effects for other public sector institutions or levels of government may not be fully taken into account in the policy-making process (Bruche and Reissert, 1985; Hanf and O'Toole, 1992; Rabe, 1995). For example, Schmid *et al.* (1992) argue that 'institutional incongruence' may lead to a suboptimal level of provision of ALMP: if the costs of ALMP programmes are concentrated in one agency or level of government (that is, the PES budget) while the fiscal benefits are more widely dispersed among different levels of government and institutional budgets, the politico-administrative apparatus may be less responsive to demands for active programmes than would otherwise be the case if costs and benefits were more transparent.

More generally, co-operation between organizations in the implementation of ALMP depends on the costs and benefits of co-operation to the parties concerned. Only when the parties expect to realize net benefits is co-operation sustainable. For public sector entities the 'assessment criteria' in terms of which their interests are defined are complex and derived to a large extent from the institutional framework in which they operate (for example, formal or informal performance indicators), which also imposes important constraints on their behaviour (laws, regulations, financial and personnel resources, and so on; see Chapter 10). This suggests that we need to analyse, in the first instance, the incentives for co-operation of the respective parties in the specific national institutional setting.

Overcoming institutional fragmentation in the co-ordination of active policies for the long-term unemployed and social assistance recipients is, in our view, ultimately a question of institutional design and in the last instance of political will. Although the theoretical types of implementation regimes based on hierarchy, markets or networks (Scharpf, 1993; Knoke, 1990, 1993; Miles and Snow, 1992; Van den Bos, 1991; Anheier and Romo, 1992) are useful analytical constructs, real implementation arrangements represent specific combinations of these. Recent developments in the Netherlands may serve as an example. Dutch agencies for social security, social assistance and employment services are separate bodies. Currently there is a network-based co-operative arrangement between them which focuses on reintegrating disadvantaged groups (see Chapter 9): all three organizations have (more or less) the same group of clients and know that they are dependent upon each other to achieve a real integration of their clients. At the same time there is a principal–agent market relation between the PES and the two social agencies, which contract with the employment service to provide labour market services for their clients (that is, disability and social assistance beneficiaries). Elements of a hierarchical co-ordination are also present: the central government establishes the legal framework and sets the conditions for the different parties. Moreover, the parties are in general terms obliged to co-operate. In order to be effective, the combination of forms of co-ordination in an implementation regime must be based on elements that are complementary.

Based on recent experience in Germany, the Netherlands, and Sweden at least three strategies for improving co-ordination between the PES and other social agencies involved in the implementation of ALMP for social assistance beneficiaries and other problem groups can be identified. First, PES governance structures can be changed to include major actors or to give more weight, for example, to the social assistance carriers, who can be expected to represent the interests of 'their' clientèle in PES policy-making. Thus recent Swedish reforms have sought to achieve greater integration of ALMP implementation at the regional level and improved responsiveness to the needs of the municipalities by giving representatives of the latter a majority in regional PES policy committees.

Second, the case of the Netherlands represents a quite different strategy based on the introduction of a purchaser/provider model in which the PES becomes merely a labour market service provider (among others) for the local authorities, who are responsible for social assistance, and the social insurance carriers. These organizations now have their own funds for purchasing services for their clientèles and PES policies are shaped by the introduction of a market mechanism among the actors involved.

A third strategy is through PES management systems: to introduce programme eligibility requirements or performance indicators in active programmes that encourage, or require, local PES offices to give higher priority to the long-term unemployed and social assistance recipients. If such policies are enforced through adequate monitoring mechanisms and appropriate sanctions, PES offices will have sufficient incentive to seek co-operation with social assistance carriers and to include their clientèle in its programmes.

2.5 The Implementation Studies in This Volume

The German, Dutch, and Swedish implementation studies in this volume are all based on analysis of regional level variation in implementation regimes. They differ, however, in important respects both in thematic focus and methodology. Thematically, the principal common focus is on forms of networking and co-operation between the PES and the local authorities in providing labour market services to problem groups, especially social assistance recipients. However, both the German and the Swedish studies also give special emphasis to PES management systems and to issues related to the scope and limits of central direction and local PES autonomy in the implementation of ALMP. In fact, decentralization rather than co-operation is the principal focus of the German study. Among the trends in implementation regimes discussed above, the principal omission is contracting out and purchaser/provider relationships in the co-ordination of local implementation networks.

All three implementation studies represent examples of process evaluation but of somewhat different types. The Dutch and Swedish studies are primarily concerned with the impact of implementation regimes, especially co-operation between the PES and local authorities, on programme performance (the Netherlands) or labour market outcomes (Sweden) at the local level, whereas the German study focuses in particular on the impact of the organization of ALMP, that is, the delivery system, on patterns of ALMP uptake, policy mix and targeting in PES district offices. Thus in the German study patterns of co-operation (and co-operation failure) are interpreted primarily as a product of the institutional framework of the ALMP implementation regime, whereas in the Dutch and Swedish studies the central question is the impact of co-operation on programme and labour market outcomes.

Ideally, the coverage of the implementation studies would include all five countries included in the aggregate impact analyses reported in Part I. For practical reasons this was not possible and studies could be carried out only for Germany, the Netherlands, and Sweden. The conclusion (Chapter 11) contains a synthesis of the implementation studies and their principal findings.

NOTES

1. The authors are grateful for assistance from many members of the ALMP project team. Special thanks are due to Holger Schütz for his helpful comments on earlier drafts.
2. There are also a number of macro-studies based on aggregate data in addition to classical analyses based on individual data. These studies investigate the impact of ALMP, or specific programmes, by comparing different policies in different countries or changing policies within a single country in a cross-section or time-series framework (see Bellmann and Jackman, 1996). The aggregate impact analyses reported in Part I represent a special case of aggregate impact analysis based on regional level data.
3. Schierer (1994) distinguishes between 'aggregate' and 'targeted' programmes.
4. This following discussion of 'new public management' and 'management by objectives' is based on Schütz (1996).
5. This 'ideal type' is adapted from Richards' (1994) account of the UK experience.
6. Voluntary co-operation in this sense is closely related to that in network analysis, although our analysis of co-operation takes as its starting point the institutional framework, that is, the legal and regulatory framework of the PES, social insurance, and social assistance agencies, and so on, which is constitutive for the actors and their field of interaction.

REFERENCES

Anheier, H.K. and F.P. Romo (1992), 'Modelle strukturellen Scheiterns in Policy Netzwerken', *Journal für Sozialforschung*, **32** (1), 33–60.

Arrow, K.J. (1985), 'The Economics of Agency', in J. Pratt and R. Zeckhauser (eds), *Principals and Agents: The Structure of American Business*, Boston: Harvard Business School Press, pp. 37–51.

Aucoin, P. (1990), 'Administrative Reform in Public Management: Paradigms, Principles, Paradoxes and Pendulums', *Governance*, **3** (2), 115–37.

Barney, J.B. and W. Hesterly (1996), 'Organisational Economics: Understanding the Relationship between Organisations and Economic Analysis', in S. Clegg, C. Hardy and W. Nord (eds), *Handbook of Organisation Studies*, Sage: London.

Bellmann, L. and R. Jackman (1996), 'Aggregate Impact Analysis', in Schmid *et al.*, pp. 143–62.

Bruche, G. and B. Reissert (1985), *Die Finanzierung der Arbeitsmarktpolitik: System, Effektivität, Reformansätze*, Frankfurt: Campus.

Dunleavy, P. and C. Hood (1994), 'From Old Public Administration to New Public Management', *Public Money and Management*, **14** (3), 9–16.

Elster, J. (1989), *The Cement of Society: A Study of Social Order*, Cambridge: Cambridge University Press.

Fay, R.G. (1997), *Making the public employment service more effective through the introduction of market signals*, Paris: OECD.

Gray, A. and B. Jenkins (1995), 'From Public Administration to Public Management: Reassessing a Revolution?', *Public Administration*, **73** (1), 75–99.

Hanf, K. and L. O'Toole (1992), 'Revisiting Old Friends: Networks, Implementation Structures and the Management of Inter-organisational Relations,' *European Journal of Political Research*, 21, 163–80.

Koning, J. de and P.J. van Nes (1991), 'A Quantitative Approach to Process Evaluation: The Case of the Vermeend-Moor Act', *Government and Policy*, 9, 111–18.

Knoke, D. (1990), *Political Networks: the Structural Perspective*, Cambridge: University Press.

Knoke, D. (1993), 'Networks of Elite Structure and Decision Making', *Sociological Methods and Research*, 1, 23–45.

Kooiman, J. (1993), *Modern Governance: New Government–Society Interventions*, London: Sage.

Marin, B. and R. Mayntz (1991), 'Introduction: Studying Policy Networks', in B. Marin and R. Mayntz (eds), *Policy Networks: Empirical Evidence and Theoretical Consideration*, Köln/Colorado, Campus/Boulder.

Mayntz, R. (1992), 'Modernisierung und die Logik von interorganisatorischen Netzwerken', *Journal für Sozialforschung*, **32** (1), 19–32.

Mayntz, R. (1998), New Challenges to Governance Theory', *Jean Monnet Chair Papers*. Florence: European University Institute.

Metcalfe, L. and S. Richards (1990), *Improving Public Management*, 2nd edition, London: Sage.

Miles, R.E. and Snow, C.C. (1992), 'Causes of Failure in Network Organisations', *Califonia Management Review*, Summer, 53–70.

Moraal, D. (1994), 'Reorganisation of Labor Market Policy. Further Training for the Unemployed in the Netherlands', WZB Discussion Paper FS I 94–204, Berlin: WZB.

Mosley, H., T. Keller and S. Speckesser (1998), 'The Role of the Social Partners in the Design and Implementation of Active Measures', ILO Working Paper, Geneva.

Mosley, H.G. and C. Degen (1994), 'The Reorganization of Labor Market Policy: Further Training for the Unemployed in the United Kingdom', WZB Discussion Paper FS I 94–205, Berlin: WZB.

Niklasson, H. and L. Tomsmark (1994), 'Zielsteuerung der Arbeitsmarktpolitik in Finnland, Norwegen und Schweden', originally published as: Att malstyra arbetsmarknadspolitik, *TemaNord* 573, Kopenhagen.

OECD (1993a), *Public Management: OECD Country Profiles*, Paris.

OECD (1993b), *Public Management Developments: Survey*, Paris.

OECD (1993c), *Managing with Market-Type Mechanism: Public Management Studies*, Paris.

OECD (1993d), *The Labour Market in the Netherlands*, Paris.

OECD (1994), *Public Management Developments: Update*, Paris.

OECD (1995), *Public Management Developments: Update*, Paris.

OECD (1996a), *Public Management Developments: Update*, Paris.

OECD (1996b), *The Public Employment Service in Denmark, Finland and Italy*, Paris.

OECD (1996c), *The OECD Jobs Strategy. Enhancing the Effectiveness of Active Labour Market Policies*, Paris.

OECD (1997), *Labour Market Policies: New Challenges. Enhancing the effectiveness of active labour market policies: a streamlined public employment service*, Paris.

Osborne, D. and T. Gaebler (1992), *Reinventing Government: How the Entrepreneurial Spirit is Transforming the Public Sector*, Reading, MA: Addison-Wesley.

Palumbo, D.J. and D.J. Calista (1990), 'Opening up the Black Box: Implementation and the Policy Process', in D.J. Palumbo and D.J. Calista (eds), *Implementation and the Policy Process: Opening up the Black Box*, New York: Greenwood Press, pp. 3–16.

Pollitt, C. (1990), *Managerialism and the Public Services. The Anglo-American Experience*, Oxford: Basil Blackwell.

Powell, W.W. and P.J. DiMaggio (1991), 'Introduction', in W.W. Powell and P.J. DiMaggio (eds), *The New Institutionalism in Organisational Analysis*, Chicago: University of Chicago Press.

Rabe, B. (1995), 'Cooperating in Multi-organizational Implementation: Lessons from New Policy Designs in Eastern Germany', paper presented to the 12th EGOS Colloquium, Istanbul, Berlin, unpublished manuscript.

Ranson, A. and J. Stewart (1994), *Management for the Public Domain: Enabling the Learning Society*, New York: St. Martin's Press.

Richards, S. (1994), 'Devolving Public Management, Centralizing Public Policy', *Oxford Review of Economic Policy*, **10** (3), 40–50.

Scharpf, F.W. (1993) 'Coordination in Hierarchies and Networks', in F.W. Scharpf (ed.), *Games in Hierarchies and Networks: Analytical and Empirical Approaches to the Study of Governance Institutions*, Frankfurt a.M. and Boulder Co: Campus and West View.

Scheirer, M.A. (1994), 'Designing and Using Process Evaluation', in J. Wholey, H. Hatry and K. Newcomer (eds), *Handbook of Practical Program Evaluation*, San Francisco: Jossey-Bass Publishers, pp. 40–68.

Schmid, G., B. Reissert and G. Bruche (1992), *Unemployment Insurance and Active Labour Market Policy: An International Comparison of Financing Systems*, Detroit: Wayne State University Press.

Schmid, G. (1996), 'Process Evaluation: Policy Formation and Implementation', in G. Schmid, J. O'Reilly and K. Schömann (eds), *International Handbook of Labour Market Policy and Evaluation*, Cheltenham: Edward Elgar, pp. 198–231.

Schmid, G., J. O'Reilly and K. Schömann (eds) (1996), *International Handbook of Labour Market Policy and Evaluation*, Cheltenham: Edward Elgar.

Schütz, H. (1996), 'Modernisierung der Arbeitsverwaltung – Theoretische und empirische Ansätze im internationalen Vergleich', Diplomarbeit am Fachbereich Politische Wissenschaft der Freien Universität Berlin, unpublished manuscript.

Sol, E. (2000), *Arbeidsvoorzieningsbeleid in Nederland. De rol van de overheid en de sociale partners* (*Labour market policies in the Netherlands. The role of government and social partners*). The Hague: Sdu.

Van den Bos, J.M.M. (1991), *Dutch EC policy making. A model-guided approach to coordination and negotiation*, Amsterdam: Thesis.

Williamson, O.E. (1985), *The Economic Institutions of Capitalism*, New York: Free Press.

8. The implementation of active policies in the German regions: decentralization and co-operation[1]

Hugh Mosley and Holger Schütz

1 INTRODUCTION

Evaluation of active labour market policies typically focuses on the assessment of the impact of programmes on individual participants, especially on earnings and employment. By contrast, studies of the impact of implementation structures and processes – that is, the delivery system for labour market policy – are relatively rare. At present, however, these institutional 'meta-policies' are the focus of considerable attention as European public employment services (PES) are currently undergoing profound changes (see Chapter 7).

The German public employment service has been less affected by these reform trends than the PES in other European countries – partly because of the impact of German reunification. However, the *Bundesanstalt für Arbeit* (BA, the German PES) itself has initiated a major process of internal reform, '*Arbeitsamt 2000*' which is currently being implemented.[2] Moreover, in January 1998, a substantial revision of the existing law governing labour market policy came into effect. This reform introduced, among other things, a far-reaching decentralization of responsibility for active labour market policy to the PES district office level. These reforms are the culmination of a decade of debates and a series of more piecemeal reforms.

Parallel to these changes within the PES, the delivery system for active policies has been transformed by a remarkable growth in the importance of local labour market policies under the auspices of local authorities. This development is largely the result of the secular increase in unemployment (especially long-term unemployment), the increasing percentage of the unemployed not eligible for regular unemployment benefit administered by the PES, and the primary responsibility of the local authorities for a rapidly expanding clientèle of social assistance recipients as a result of unemployment.

This chapter addresses two principal and interrelated issues with regard to the functioning of the institutional system of German active labour market policy (ALMP):

1. decentralization and the responsiveness of ALMP to local labour market needs, especially long-term unemployment;
2. co-operation between the PES and local ALMP initiatives, especially for the long-term unemployed and social assistance recipients.

It is based on two complementary types of analysis: a quantitative analysis of policy profiles for 142 western German PES districts and qualitative case studies in three 'best practice' PES districts. The quantitative analysis of PES performance at the PES district (AA) level analyses the effects of two different dimensions of the implementation process on policy profiles:

1. PES resource allocation from the national to the regional levels;
2. PES district influence on resource allocation and policy discretion (policy mix and targeting of participants).

The three 'best practice' PES districts for the qualitative case studies were selected on the basis of their performance profiles in the level and targeting of ALMP. Although the cases selected do not constitute a representative sample, they can be used to examine a number of implementation issues for which no quantitative indicators are available, for example, the importance of co-operative relationships with local authorities. Moreover, like all case studies, they provide a better understanding of the functioning of the PES delivery system. The names of the PES districts studied have been changed to protect the anonymity of our sources.

The remainder of the chapter is organized as follows: section 2 provides an overview of the German PES with particular attention to trends in decentralization, while section 3 presents an overview of the complex relationship between the PES and local ALMP for social assistance recipients in Germany. Section 4 summarizes the results of a regression analysis of regional policy profiles based on PES administrative data. Finally, section 5 reports the results of the three case studies, which give particular attention to co-operation between the PES and local authorities in providing ALMP services to social assistance recipients. Some conclusions are drawn in section 6. For a full list of the abbreviations used in this chapter see p. 214.

2 BUREAUCRATIC ADMINISTRATION IN TRANSITION

The German employment service (Bundesanstalt für Arbeit, BA) is a self-governing body incorporated under public law.[3] It is responsible for both active programmes and for the administration of unemployment benefits. Its self-governing organs have a tripartite structure with equal representation of employees, employers and public bodies (federal, state, and local governments).

The PES is organized into 10 regional employment offices (*Landesarbeitsämter*, LAÄ) and 181 PES district offices (*Arbeitsämter*, AÄ). While the actual importance of the LAÄ regional offices appear to vary, they are generally administrative bodies which exercise legal supervision rather than intervening directly in policy-making for PES districts. The district offices function largely autonomously within the budgetary and legal framework established by the national PES and the labour promotion act – and, since 1998, the corresponding provisions of the new social security law (SGBIII).

2.1 Scope and Limits of Local PES Autonomy

In general it is fair to say that, until recently, the German PES has been one of the most traditional employment services organizations in Europe; with a high degree of reliance on hierarchical co-ordination through line-item budgets, detailed procedural regulations and individual entitlements (*Rechtsansprüche*). Whereas decentralization strategies have been implemented in a number of countries in recent years (for example, USA, UK, the Netherlands), there was little change in Germany until the 1998 reforms. Decentralized implementation of labour market policies can be analysed in terms of programme design, budgeting and control over personnel policy (Mosley and Degen, 1994). In the remainder of this section we focus on the budgeting process, which we regard as the key dimension of the PES management system.

2.2 The PES Regions in the pre-1998 Budgeting Process

The scope and limits of local PES office autonomy in policy-making can be illustrated with reference to the budgeting process. From the point of view of decentralized autonomy there are three principal questions:

1. To what extent can the local PES office influence the level and structure (that is, policy mix) of the ALMP resources allocated to it in the annual budget process?
2. To what extent can budgeted expenditures be reallocated between budget

items during the course of the year in response to changes in the labour market situation or better reflect local priorities?
3. To what extent can local PES offices augment their PES budgets through supplemental funding from other sources (for example, co-financing from municipal, state, or EU sources)?

In this section, we first discuss the old centralized budgeting process as it existed prior to 1998; and then we outline the new, more decentralized procedure in the section that follows.

Formerly, the regional labour offices were allocated budget ceilings by the PES for active programmes which were supposed to be negotiated but were frequently merely handed down by the national PES office (which withheld an intervention reserve). The national office would reallocate funding if it became clear that available funds would not be exhausted. Special procedures laid down by the job-creation (ABM) committee of the PES's council were followed for the allocation of funds for job-creation programmes. Each year, a formula was established for the allocation of available funds. This formula was based on the amount of funding for job-creation measures requested by PES regional offices (LAÄ), the regional unemployment rate and the state's share of problem groups among the unemployed. The PES regional offices steered local PES district expenditure via ceilings or continuous control of expenditure, with the possibility of budget caps if expenditure threatened to exceed available funding. There was little rivalry between regions over the distribution of the expenditure for discretionary programmes owing to the passive, legalistic behaviour of the local PES offices and their limited capacity for implementing (additional) programmes because of chronic personnel shortages (Bruche and Reissert, 1985).

Once annual budgets had been fixed, flexibility depended largely on the extent to which individual budget items had been declared to be fungible (*gegenseitig deckungsfähig*) – which in the past was very limited (Bruche and Reissert, 1985, pp. 73ff). In recent years, greater flexibility has been introduced at the local level: PES district offices were being permitted to shift up to 20 per cent of their funds from job-creation to training measures (and *vice versa*) at their own discretion. Evidence from earlier interviews suggests that, since the national budget allocation process is essentially outside their own control, local PES officials regard this element of flexibility as their primary room for manoeuvring in setting local policy priorities.

2.3 The 1998 Reforms: Towards Decentralization

Since January 1998 local PES district offices have considerably more freedom in implementing ALMP. The most important change was the merger of most discretionary active measures into a single budget; the so-called 'reintegration budget' (§3 SGBIII).[4] While the local PES districts are still obliged to offer all types of measures (§ 71b,3 SGBIV), the local PES is now free to determine the mixture of the measures. The local tripartite administrative committees are formally responsible for ratifying the PES budget (§378,3 SGBIII). Moreover, up to 10 per cent of the reintegration budget can now be allocated to innovative measures (§10 SGBIII); that is, measures not defined in the standard portfolio. The budget allocation from the federal to the state level follows strictly a newly defined allocation formula.[5] The LAÄ are also obliged to use this formula for allocation to the local level, but are permitted to modify the national indicator in response to regional labour market conditions. The LAÄ may withhold a 5 per cent reserve of reintegration budget for 'fine tuning'.

The reforms appear to be a considerable step forward in terms of decentralization, although it is not yet entirely clear what this will mean in practice. Thus the new reintegration balance sheets now required of all local PES offices also represents a possible instrument of enhanced central steering: it includes performance statistics that relate expenditure to ALMP outputs and labour market outcomes by programme type. Details of the operationalization and the weightings of indicators, as well as the use of the balance by the BA's central office, are still unknown. The interpretation and use of this monitoring instrument and the performance indicators ultimately defined will be crucial in defining the scope and limits of the decentralization of the German PES.

3 THE PES AND LOCAL ALMP FOR SOCIAL ASSISTANCE RECIPIENTS

In Germany – as in many other European countries – the delivery system for ALMP is divided into a nationally financed and administered PES system on the one hand, and labour market policies financed and administered by local authorities for social assistance recipients and other problem groups on the other. In the following section, we look at the most important features of German local ALMP and its interplay with the PES.

3.1 The Legal Framework

Social assistance in Germany is financed and administered by the counties and the municipalities in larger (*kreisfreie*) cities. On average, about 80 per cent of the total social assistance costs are borne by the municipal level, while the remaining 20 per cent are financed by the states (*Bundesländer*). Both the financing and administration of social assistance is thus organizationally separate from the PES.

The framework of local ALMP is established by the German social assistance act, which obliges recipients capable of working to accept all employment opportunities that are reasonable (*zumutbar*) and paid at least at a minimum level. Specific policy options for employment opportunities of two major types are provided (BSHG §19,2):

1. Regular employment in a job-creation measure (that is, with a 'real' employment contract) with social security benefits and paid at a rate appropriate to the job. The work must be additional and of benefit to the community.[6]
2. Work for social assistance recipients without an employment contract ('workfare'), which is compensated only in the form of a small supplement to social assistance to cover additional expenses (approximately 2 or 3 DM per hour).

3.2 Implementation Structures for Local ALMP

There is a high degree of institutional diversity in the implementation of local ALMP. The most developed models resemble integrated, 'holistic' approaches (see among others GIB, 1998; Schulze-Böing, 1997). The 'state of the art' in local ALMP is reflected in the ongoing debate on the scope and design of municipal policies. The issues under discussion include the linkage of local ALMP with economic development and structural policies (see, for example, Freidinger, 1995 and Schulze-Böing, 1997), the 'municipalization' and decentralization of labour market policies (Heidinger, 1997), or the modelling of optimal counselling and placement strategies for the (very) hard-to-place (Schulze-Böing and Simon, 1998).

An enormous range of programmes and implementation structures now exists, including intermediary and 'third sector' organizations. The most widespread forms are:[7]

- various types of 'employment and training companies' (*Beschäftigungs- und Qualifizierungsgesellschaften*) (cf. Lindner, 1994);
- special offices or departments for local LMP as a separate tier of the local administration;
- regional co-ordination and co-operation networks and institutions; and
- the 'contracting out' to specialized agencies of counselling and placement activities for the hard-to-place unemployed.

3.3 Clientèle Characteristics

On the basis of the 'tool kit' of instruments outlined above, local ALMP has reached a considerable quantitative level (cf. Fuchs, 1994, 1997). In the

1990s, an estimated 30 per cent of all social assistance recipients of working age received benefits due to unemployment (Breuer and Engels, 1997; Wirtschaft und Statistik, 10/1997). In 1996, around 200 000 persons – that is, about 30 per cent of all employable social assistance recipients – had been employed on the basis of articles 19 and 20 of the social assistance act (most of them in the social welfare and environment fields). This represents an increase of 60 per cent over 1993. On average, 53 per cent of these work opportunities can be defined as a regular employment relationship with social security coverage; while 47 per cent provide no wage, but merely a small supplement to the benefits (under §19,2(2) and §20 BSHG) described above. The former is more common in large cities.

The increasing financial burden of ('passive') social assistance on local authorities is probably the main impetus for the steady growth of local labour market policies from the 'bottom-up' since about the early 1980s.[8] This financial pressure is, moreover, unevenly distributed since the burden of social assistance payments is disproportionately high in larger cities.

3.3 Co-operation between the PES and the Local Authorities

Co-operation between the PES and the municipalities is hardly new. On the contrary: within the framework of the 'traditional' PES active measures under the German labour promotion act (AFG), cities and municipalities have long been quantitatively the most important sponsors and co-financiers of subsidized public jobs (ABM).

Beyond this traditional domain, what interests us in particular is the interplay of the 'primary' PES ALMP and 'subsidiary' local ALMP based on the instruments described above. This question is not easy to answer because there is a low level of formal institutionalization of PES co-operation with local labour market policy for social assistance recipients. Throughout the 1980s, these systems existed and evolved separately. Legislation introduced in the early 1990s obliged the PES and social assistance providers to co-operate in reintegrating social assistance recipients.[9] There is, however, no systematic evidence on the actual impact of these regulations.

The most recent reform of German labour promotion laws introduced in 1998 (SGBIII) reshuffled the cards by removing many of these legal obligations to co-operate and restricting access to PES programmes. Social assistance recipients are, for example, no longer eligible to participate in PES job-creation programmes – eligibility is now restricted to long-term unemployed PES beneficiaries.[10] Moreover, several other ALMP measures are now reserved for PES unemployment benefit recipients.[11] At the same time, however, new guidelines for closer co-operation in bundling resources and sharing responsibilities were issued in the spring of 1998 (IBV, 1998). In addition to the development of joint measures, the establishment of co-ordinating institutions and the integration of 'third' agencies (for example, *Maatwerk*) for placement are highly recommended. The 'guidelines' are, it should be noted, merely non-binding recommendations.

4 REGIONAL ALMP POLICY PROFILES

This section presents the results of an empirical analysis of PES decentralization and policy responsiveness at the regional (AA) level. It investigates in particular the extent to which local ALMP policy profiles vary in uptake, programme mix and targeting, controlling for labour market and clientèle characteristics, and the responsiveness of PES implementation structures to local labour market needs, especially long-term unemployment.[12]

Our empirical model of the determinants of regional level ALMP policy patterns can be summarized as follows:

$$ALMP_{Regio} = \mathrm{f}(\boldsymbol{S}, \boldsymbol{D}, \boldsymbol{I})$$

where $ALMP_{Regio}$ is the regional ALMP level or policy mix, $\boldsymbol{S}$ is a vector of supply-side variables, including the PES case load (unemployment) and the case mix (structure of unemployment); $\boldsymbol{D}$ is a vector of demand-side variables for the employment structure and labour market conditions; and $\boldsymbol{I}$ is a vector of implementation variables related to local PES strategies or characteristics of the local policy arena. The variables actually used in the regression analysis are summarized in Table 8.1. The model is estimated for five different dependent variables: 1) all ALMP programme entrants (ALMP entrants); 2) entrants to training; 3) job creation; 4) wage subsidy measures separately; and 5) targeting on the long-term unemployed, that is, the percentage of long-term unemployed ALMP programme entrants. Participation levels are defined in flow terms (entrants) expressed as a percentage of the civilian labour force in the PES district. The data on ALMP programme participation and targeting analysed are administrative data from the federal employment service at the PES office (*AA-Bezirke*) level for 142 western German PES offices during 1995–7.

4.1 Descriptive Findings

ALMP participation levels

The level of ALMP uptake as a percentage of the labour force varies greatly among PES districts, ranging from a low of 0.91 per cent to a high of 4.07 per cent over the 1995–7 period. For the main components of ALMP, training and

Table 8.1 Table of variables

Variable	Name	Description
Level of unemployment		
Unemployment rate	*ALQ_D*	Registered unemployed as percentage of labour force
Adjusted unemployment rate	*UE_EQ*	Adjusted unemployment (registered unemployed + average annual stock of ALMP participants) as percentage of adjusted labour force (labour force + flow of training participants)
Long-term unemployment rate	*LULF3_*	Long-term unemployed for 12 months or more as a percentage of the labour force
Adjusted long-term unemployment share	*LTU_EQ*	Registered long-term unemployed + unemployed (flow) in ALMP as a percentage of adjusted unemployed, that is, registered unemployed + ALMP participants (stock)
Structure unemployment[13]		
Long-term unemployment share	*LUQ3_*	Long-term unemployed for 12 months or more as a percentage of all unemployed
Youth	*AA_K1T*	Percentage registered unemployed under 20 years of age
Older	*AA_K5T*	Percentage registered unemployed over 50 years of age
Female	*FA_ALO*	Women as percentage of registered unemployed
Labour demand		
Industry	*SHIN*	Employment in industry as percentage of all insured employment, that is, excluding the self-employed, civil servants, and part-time workers under the threshold for social insurance coverage (<15 hours)
Part time	*TZQ*	Part-time workers as a percentage of all insured employment
Trend employment	*DEL_EM*	Percentage change in employment over the period of the last 12 months

Table 8.1 continued

Variable	Name	Description
V/U ratio	*UV_RAT*	Vacancies per 100 registered unemployed
Local implementation		
ALMP entrants	*ALMPF_Q*	All entrants into active measures (training, job creation and wage subsidies) as a percentage of the civilian labour force[14]
Training (rate)	*E_FU_TQ*	All entrants into training (FuU) as a percentage of the total labour force
Training (share)	*E_FU_UE*	All entrants into training (FuU) as a percentage of the registered unemployed
Job creation (rate)	*VABT_Q*	All entrants into job creation measures (*Arbeitsbeschaffungs-maßnahmen*) as a percentage of the civilian labour force
Job creation (share)	*VABT_UE*	All entrants into job creation measures (*Arbeitsbeschaffungs-maßnahmen*) as a percentage of the registered unemployed
Wage subsidies	*F_LKZ_Q*	All entrants into four wage subsidy programmes (Lohnkosten-zuschüsse) as a percentage of the total labour force
Targeting	*TALMPF*	Percentage of long-term unemployed (>12 months) among all ALMP entrants. Based in part on estimates[15]
Targeting index	*TARGET*	Index: percentage of long-term unemployed (>12 months) among all ALMP entrants (TALMPF) divided by their percentage share in all registered unemployed (LUQ3_)
Duration	*ALMP_D*	Annual flow into ALMP measures divided by annual average stock as indicator for average duration of measures

Table 8.2 Descriptive statistics, average 1995–7

Variable	Cases	Minimum	Maximum	Average	Standard Deviation
ALQ_D	142	4.97	16.67	9.92	2.53
UE_EQ	142	5.49	18.87	11.14	2.84
*LULF3_*	142	0.82	7.89	3.18	1.40
LTU_EQ	141	19.6	49.76	32.98	5.77
*LUQ3_*	142	18.10	49.21	31.77	5.99
AA_K1T	142	1.84	5.91	3.49	0.84
AA_K5T	142	17.16	41.75	28.35	4.21
FA_ALO	142	36.08	55.09	45.35	4.09
SHIN	142	16.99	57.64	36.97	8.73
TZQ	142	9.76	18.91	13.43	1.78
DEL_EM	142	–3.52	3.18	–0.82	0.88
UV_RAT	141	0.03	0.35	0.10	0.05
ALMPF_Q	142	0.91	4.08	1.83	0.60
E_FUTQ	142	0.77	2.75	1.35	0.37
E_FU_UE	142	6.72	28.99	14.26	3.77
VABT_Q	142	0.04	1.09	0.30	0.25
VABT_UE	142	0.51	8.03	2.74	1.65
F_LKZ_Q	142	0.05	0.48	0.19	0.07
TALMPF	141	14.55	52.83	34.28	7.56
TARGET	141	0.64	1.63	1.08	0.17
ALMP_D	142	0.88	1.64	1.18	0.14
VALID N	141				

Note: N=141 for some variables due to missing data for West Berlin in 1997.

Source: WZB Regional Data Bank.

job-creation programmes, the uptake ranged from 0.77 per cent to 2.75 per cent, and from 0.04 per cent to 1.09 per cent, respectively (see Table 8.2). This regional diversity in ALMP levels is not surprising: there is a wide diversity in the regional incidence of unemployment, which is reflected both in PES resource allocation to the regions and in local policy response and uptake.

A simple bivariate graph of the relationship between the level of ALMP and the unemployment rate in German PES regions shows that the average incidence of active measures is more responsive to the unemployment rate than reported in earlier research. There is, nevertheless, a great deal of unexplained variation in the incidence of ALMP measures even at similar rates of unemployment, and the variation in ALMP policy response is greater at higher levels of unemployment. Obviously, local PES policy responses and other factors, including policy choices, play a strong role. The incidence of job-creation measures is most strongly related to the unemployment rate, whereas training measures have a weaker relationship to this labour market indicator (Figure 8.1).

Targeting of ALMP on the long-term unemployed

Targeting, that is, operative priorities in the selection of individuals for referral to measures, is a central performance characteristic of PES implementation structures. Our focus here is on the extent to which the long-term unemployed gain access to PES active programmes. Since national eligibility conditions and other guidelines are identical for all PES offices, we assume that – controlling for differences in labour market conditions – variation in targeting is primarily a reflection of local PES policies.

In assessing targeting by the PES, it is important not only to observe the share of long-term unemployed persons among entrants (*TARGETING*), but also to relate this figure to the share of the long-term unemployed among all unemployed in the district (*TARGETING INDEX*).[16] The latter index variable is a measure of whether the long-term unemployed are proportionately represented in ALMP programmes. An index value less than '1' indicates that they are under-represented and a value above '1' indicates that they are over-represented.

The mean value for *TARGETING* is 34 per cent for western German PES districts 1995–7; there is a large variation from a minimum of 15 per cent to a maximum of 53 per cent (see Table 8.2). This variation in PES district office targeting is explicable only in part by local variation in the structure of unemployment: there is a broad spectrum in the targeting index among PES districts, which ranges from a high of 1.6 to a low of 0.6. The mean value of 1.09 for all PES districts indicates that there is no strong targeting of ALMP measures on the long-term unemployed, although they are on average slightly over-represented among all ALMP entrants (see Table 8.2).

Figure 8.2 shows the relationship between targeting defined as the share of the long-term unemployed (more than 1 year) among ALMP entrants and the level and structure of long-term unemployment. Noteworthy in Figure 8.2(a) is the great variation in targeting the long-term unemployed among the PES districts with a similar percentage of long-term unemployed, which suggests that local PES districts are little constrained by national PES policy guidelines on targeting of the long-term unemployed. In all PES districts to the right of the line through the origin, the long-term unemployed are under-represented even in comparison with their share in total unemployment. Figure 8.2(b) shows that the targeting of ALMP on the long-term unemployed is less responsive to this problem group with increasing levels of

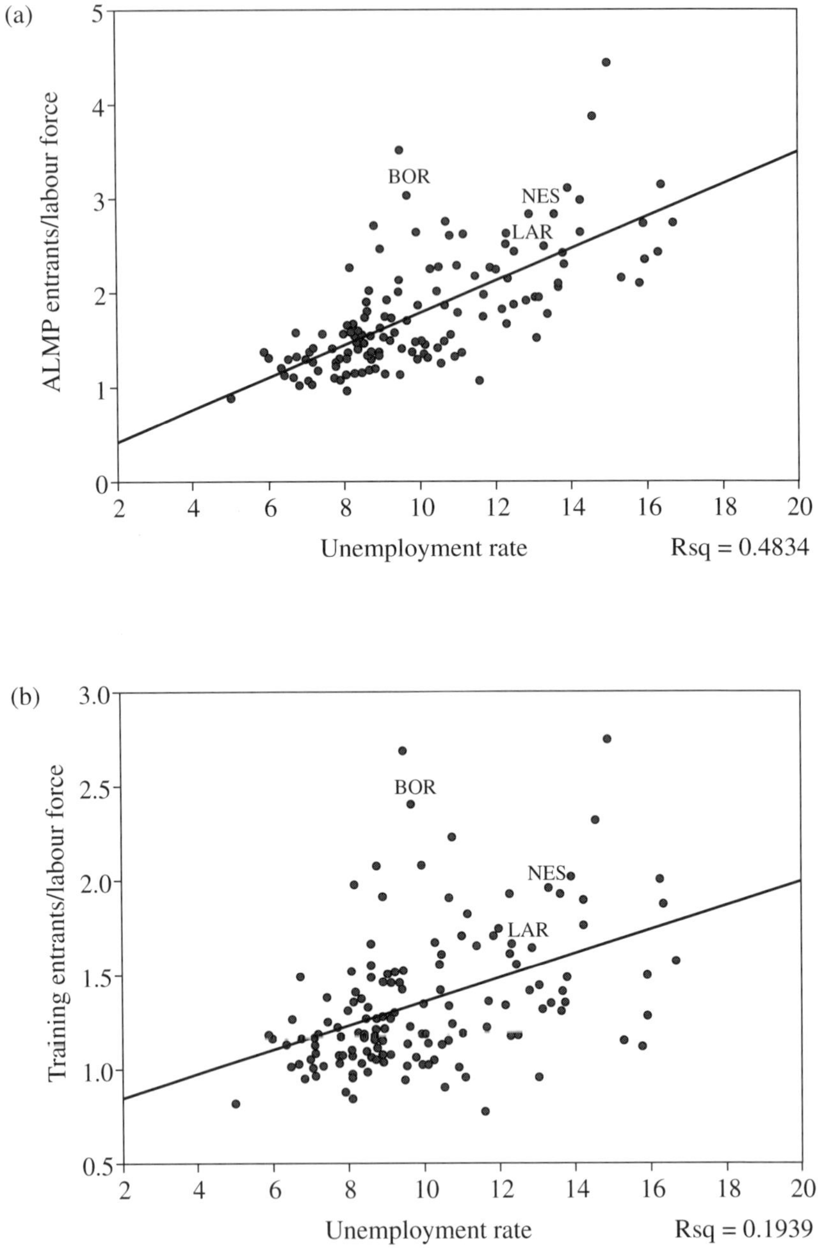

Figure 8.1 *Uptake of ALMP and regional unemployment rates, all ALMP, training and job creation, average 1995–7 (%)*

(c)
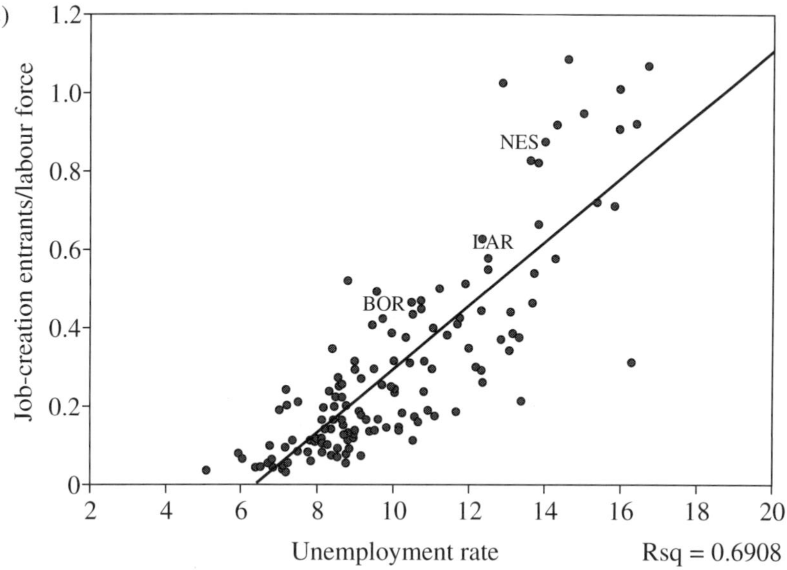

Note: BOR, LAR and NES indicate 'best practice' PES districts; see section 5.

Source: WZB Regional Data Bank.

Figure 8.1 continued

long-term unemployment as a percentage of the labour force. Finally, Figure 8.2(c) shows the values of the Targeting Index, that is, targeting standardized in terms of the share of long-term unemployment. It shows clearly the large variation in local PES policy response to long-term unemployment as well as the decline in responsiveness at a higher level of long-term unemployment. It is unclear whether the latter phenomenon is primarily due to resource constraints or to limited capacity to implement programmes. Both are plausible on the assumption that programmes for the long-term unemployed and other target groups are both relatively more costly and more personnel-intensive.

4.2 Regression Results

ALMP participation

The multivariate regression analysis of the determinants' regional variation in the levels of ALMP suggests a relatively strong national pattern of ALMP resource allocation based on regional labour market conditions. The overall explanatory power of the model is high (R^2 = 0.71, 0.76, 0.82) and strongly

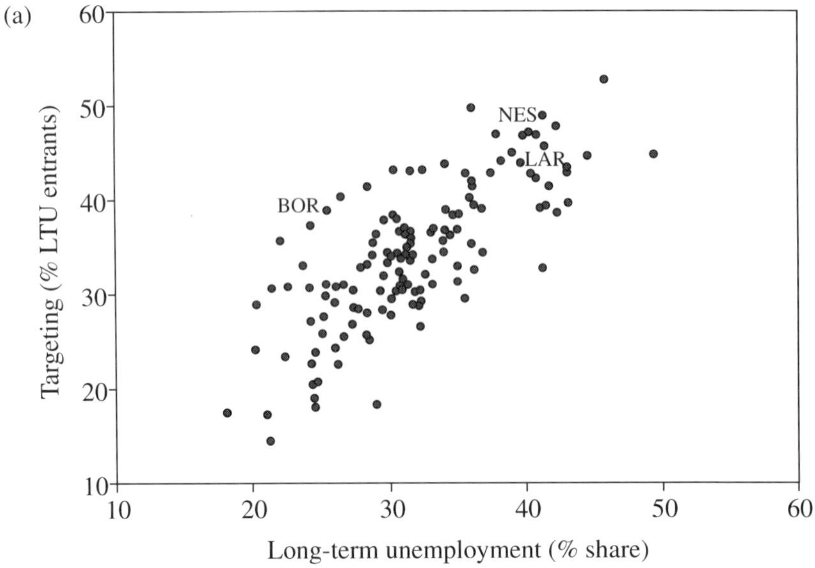

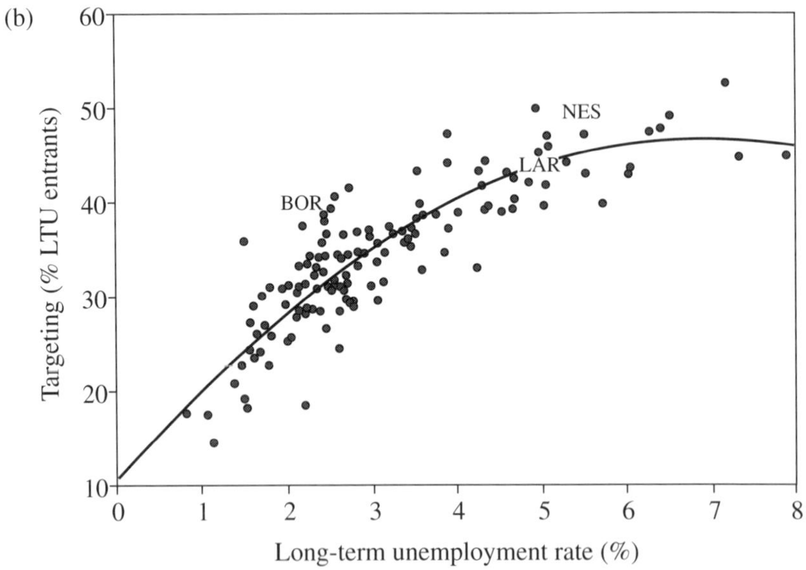

Figure 8.2 ALMP targeting and long-term unemployment, average 1995–7 (%)

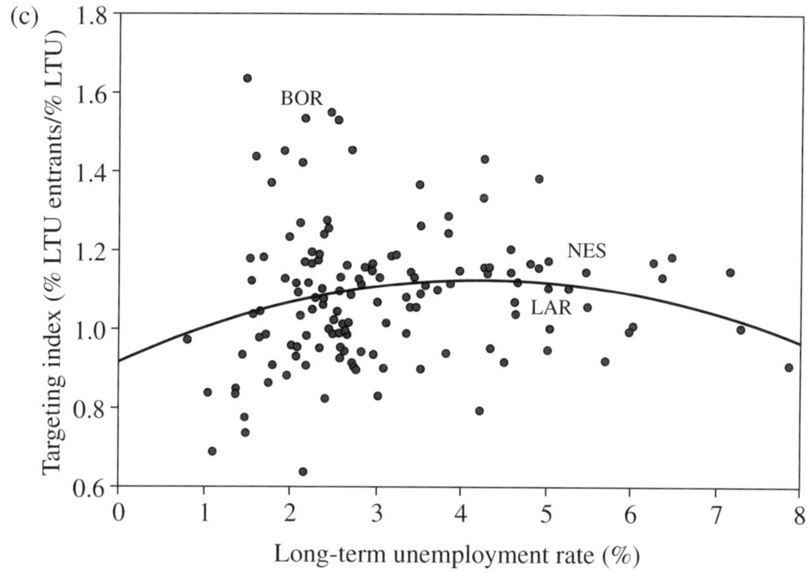

Note: BOR, LAR and NES indicate 'best practice' PES districts.

Source: WZB Regional Data Bank.

Figure 8.2 continued

significant (F sig. = 0.000) for all years in the 1995–7 cross-section results (Table 8.3). Nevertheless, a large percentage of the variation in ALMP uptake (20 to 30 per cent) remains unexplained and can be attributed to local implementation regimes. Two variables, the unemployment rate and the share of long-term unemployment (more than 12 months) account for the bulk of regional variation in overall ALMP participation rates. While the unemployment rate is strongly positively associated with the regional ALMP participation rate as anticipated, the coefficient for long-term unemployment is strongly negative in all three years; that is, among PES districts with a similar unemployment rate, a higher level of long-term unemployment (more than 12 months) is associated with a lower level of ALMP. One possible explanation for this pattern is that the national PES system, administered by the social partners, is demand- and client-oriented and thus gives lower priority to the long-term unemployed, who are hard to place and more likely to be ineligible for unemployment benefit. Another possible explanation is a programme effect: regions with higher levels of ALMP uptake in the cross-section data have, *ceteris paribus*, lower levels of unemployment and long-term unem-

Table 8.3 Determinants of ALMP participation (entrants), western Germany, 1995, 1996, 1997

Dependent variable: log *(ALMPQ2)*	1995			1996			1997		
independent variables	B (t)	Std. error	Beta	B	Std. error	Beta	B	Std. error	Beta
Constant	–0.138	0.154		–0.170	0.135		–0.537***	0.129	
	(–0.894)			(–1.260)		1.231	(–4.155)		
ALQ_D	0.071***	0.006	1.273	0.066***	0.005		0.063***	0.004	1.159
	(12.641)			(13.300)		–0.565	(14.440)		
LUQ3	–0.013***	0.002	–0.634	–0.012***	0.002		–0.011***	0.002	–0.420
	(–5.367)			(–5.259)		0.053	(–5.037)		
AA_K1T	0.019	0.010	0.133	0.009	0.010		0.004	0.009	0.021
	(1.901)			(0.820)		–0.011	(0.398)		
AA_K5T	–0.000	0.002	–0.013	–0.000	0.002		–0.002	0.002	–0.056
	(–0.210)			(–0.202)		–0.098	(–1.168)		
FA_ALO	–0.001	0.002	–0.041	–0.003	0.002		–0.001	0.002	–0.016
	(–0.553)			(–1.503)		0.055	(–0.260)		

DEL_EM	0.014**	0.005	0.144	0.008	0.007		0.009	0.005	0.078
	(2.628)			(1.042)		0.116	(1.832)		
SHIN	0.001	0.001	0.076	0.002	0.001		0.003*	0.001	0.169
	(0.968)			(1.618)		–0.043	(2.588)		
TZQ	–0.004	0.005	–0.052	–0.003	0.004		–0.000	0.004	–0.002
	(–0.911)			(–0.802)		0.012	(–0.034)		
UV_RAT	–0.154	0.159	–0.070	0.035	0.163		0.006	0.133	0.002
	(–0.973)			(0.214)		0.298	(0.047)		
ALMP_D2	0.173***	0.045	0.211	0.222***	0.038		0.334***	0.037	0.377
	(3.877)			(5.861)			(8.912)		
R Square		0.705			0.761			0.817	
Std. error		0.077			0.068			0.063	
F		31.241			41.746			58.222	
Sig.		0.000			0.000			0.000	
N		142			142			141	

Note: N=141 due to missing data for West Berlin in 1997. Significance level of coefficients: * 0.05 ** 0.01 *** 0.001.

Source: WZB Regional Data Bank.

Table 8.4 Determinants of ALMP programme uptake (entrants) and targeting, western Germany, 1997

Dependent variable log	Training (*E_FU_TQ*)			Job creation (*VABT_Q*)			Wage subsidy (*F_LKZ_Q2*)			Targeting (*talmpf2*)		
Independent variables	B (t)	Std. error	Beta	B	Std. error	Beta	B	Std. error	Beta	B	Std. error	Beta
Constant	–0.575*** (–4.111)	0.140		–1.969*** (–4.721)	0.417		–1.429*** (–5.393)	0.265		1.434*** (12.30)	0.117	
ALQ_D	0.047*** (9.873)	0.005	1.024	0.124*** (8.777)	0.014	0.831	0.057*** (6.370)	0.009	0.766	0.01462*** (3.691)	0.004	0.339
LUQ3	–0.012*** (–5.188)	0.002	–0.559	0.001 (0.092)	0.007	0.009	–0.002 (–0.412)	0.004	–0.052	0.009*** (4.639)	0.002	0.443
AA_K1T	0.002 (0.156)	0.010	0.011	0.069* (2.318)	0.030	0.147	–0.003 (–0.158	0.019	–0.013	–0.008 (–0.947)	0.008	–0.058
AA_K5T	–0.000 (–0.429)	0.002	–0.027	–0.011* (–2.053)	0.005	–0.116	–0.009** (–2.600)	0.003	–0.186	–0.009*** (–6.04)	0.001	–0.331
FA_ALO	–0.000 (–0.114)	0.002	–0.009	0.000 (0.010)	0.007	0.001	0.005 (1.200)	0.004	0.109	0.001 (0.457)	0.002	0.032

DEL_EM	0.008	0.006	0.079	0.009	0.017	0.027	0.006	0.010	0.031	0.002	0.005	–0.018
	(1.443)			(0.530)			(0.574)			(–0.374)		
SHIN	0.003*	0.001	0.218	–0.004	0.003	–0.098	0.004	0.002	0.162	–0.000	0.001	–0.034
	(2.593)			(–1.276)			(1.658)			(–0.453)		
TZQ	0.000	0.004	0.000	–0.013	0.011	–0.064	0.003	0.007	0.034	0.000	0.003	0.007
	(0.008)			(–1.182)			(0.487)			(–0.141)		
UV_RAT	0.059	0.144	0.027	–0.217	0.429	–0.030	–0.356	0.272	–0.099	–0.149	0.120	–0.072
	(0.413)			(–0.507)			(–1.308)			(–1.241)		
ALMP_D2	0.378***	0.041	0.510	0.289*	0.121	0.119	0.034	0.077	0.028	–0.0669*	0.034	–0.096
	(9.342)			(2.390)			(0.450)			(–1.981)		
R Square		0.695			0.746			0.590			0.761	
Std. error		0.068			0.2022			0.1285			0.0565	
F		29.624			38.196			18.683			41.359	
Sig.		0.000			0.000			0.000			0.000	
N		141			141			141			141	

Note: N=141 due to missing data for West Berlin in 1997. Significance level of coefficients: * 0.05 ** 0.01 *** 0.001.

Source: WZB Regional Data Bank.

ployment because programme participation reduces unemployment and interrupts the duration of unemployment spells. The multivariate analysis examined this possibility by using adjusted definitions of regional unemployment and long-term unemployment that take programme effects into account and by using a lagged dependent variable. Since these alternative models had little impact on the results, the initial results are apparently robust.

The determinants of regional uptake of ALMP are very similar in all three years for which the regression model was estimated, although the negative relationship of ALMP to long-term unemployment declines somewhat over the 1995–7 period (Table 8.3).

Targeting

The clientèle and labour market variables included in the model explain about two-thirds of the variation in regional targeting of ALMP (TARGETING) on long-term unemployed ALMP programme entrants ($R^2 = 0.76$; see Table 8.4) which means that about one-quarter of the variation may be attributable to endogenous factors at the PES district level. In contrast to ALMP uptake, the percentage share of the long-term unemployed in total unemployment is strongly positively related to targeting on this group. Moreover, targeting is significantly related to the general unemployment rate and is lower in PES districts with a larger share of older unemployed. The later finding suggests that direct and indirect (that is, special unemployment benefits regulation for older workers) forms of early retirement are an alternative to active programmes.

We conclude that – controlling for local labour market conditions – there is a great deal of variation in ALMP uptake and in targeting on the long-term unemployed in PES district offices. This is indicative, on the one hand, of relatively loose central steering, only moderate responsiveness to local labour market conditions, and weak targeting of ALMP resources on the long-term unemployed by the national PES organization and, on the other hand, a remarkable variety of regional policy profiles in individual PES offices. This degree of decentralization in policy patterns is surprising in light of the centralized and rule-oriented formal structure of the German PES as it existed prior to the 1998 administrative reforms. Moreover, the cumulative effect of these two dimensions, that is, the relatively loose relationship between the incidence of ALMP and labour market needs and the loose targeting of ALMP at the PES district office level, implies a relatively weak responsiveness of the PES delivery system to the labour market needs of the long-term unemployed.

5 REGIONAL LEVEL IMPLEMENTATION CASE STUDIES

The quantitative analysis of regional level PES performance was supplemented with three qualitative case studies. In addition to the issues of decentralization and targeting discussed above, the case studies give particular attention to co-operation between the PES and the local authorities in the implementation of local ALMP for social assistance recipients in the case study regions.

5.1 The 'Best Practice' PES Districts

The selection of 'best practice' cases for intensive field studies is based on two criteria: ALMP participation levels and targeting on the long-term unemployed. The ranking of participation levels is not based on simple ALMP participation rates; instead, we used the model of national patterns of ALMP participation discussed above to identify PES offices that performed markedly above or markedly below the national pattern specified in the model, that is, controlling for clientèle characteristics and local labour market conditions. The rank order of targeting is based on the index of targeting on the long-term employed described in section 4.

Two 'best practice' cases (BOR and LAR) were selected on the basis of very high levels of ALMP (controlling for labour market and other factors). These two cases exhibit, however, somewhat different patterns with respect to targeting: while both have an equally high percentage of the long-term unemployed among ALMP entrants (1997 = 44 per cent), this level of targeting is disproportionately high in relation to the share of long-term unemployed in BOR (Targeting Index 1997 = 1.6) but only average in LAR (1.0). Since most top performers on these two dimensions are smaller PES districts with a relatively low degree of urbanization,[17] we selected NES, one of the largest cities in Germany, for the third case study. NES ranks high in both level and targeting of ALMP in comparison with other larger urban PES districts (see Table 8.5).

While the BOR and LAR districts are smaller in population with a small-town and semi-rural composition, NES is one of the largest cities in the industrial heartland of Germany. Although the PES districts examined differ in many respects, all three have marked structural handicaps.

The BOR district is an economically peripheral region with few industries, a weak transportation infrastructure, and no major urban centre. Nevertheless, the development of employment in BOR was markedly favourable until 1996, when the labour market situation deteriorated dramatically. The severity of the crisis was mainly due to the drastic decline in the use of the large

Table 8.5 Regional PES policy responses

Variable	Year	BOR (rank)	LAR (rank)	Average all PES	NES (rank)	Average large PES districts (> 200 000)
ALMP entrants	1995	3.89	2.96	2.04	3.20	1.83
(% labour force)		(4)	(16)		(10)	
	1996	3.03	2.18	1.89	3.32	1.78
		(9)	(39)		(5)	
	1997	2.55	2.09	1.53	2.39	1.44
		(12)	(20)		(11)	
Training entrants	1995	3.07	1.88	1.54	2.05	1.32
(% labour force)		(2)	(39)		(19)	
	1996	2.35	1.38	1.44	2.21	1.28
		(6)	(71)		(11)	
	1997	1.76	1.38	1.06	1.48	0.92
		(6)	(18)		(14)	
Job creation	1995	0.50	0.71	0.31	0.92	0.33
(% labour force)		(24)	(14)		(8)	
	1996	0.39	0.56	0.31	0.92	0.35
		(43)	(22)		(6)	
	1997	0.39	0.48	0.26	0.66	0.30
		(29)	(20)		(12)	
Targeting LTU	1995	33.2	40.8	33.4	45.3	36.8
(% entrants >12m)		(71)	(23)		(8)	
	1996	35.5	40.7	31.7	45.7	35.7
		(43)	(22)		(5)	
	1997	43.7	43.8	38.2	0.50	0.41
		(38)	(36)		(14)	
Targeting Index	1995	1.5	0.9	1.1	1.1	1.1
(targeting/% LTU)		(6)	(122)		(62)	
	1996	1.5	1.0	1.1	1.1	1.0
		(4)	(79)		(40)	
	1997	1.6	1.0	1.1	1.2	1.1
		(1)	(93)		(39)	

Source: WZB Regional Data Bank.

health and convalescence facilities in the region after cutbacks in the health insurance system.

LAR, a border region, is geographically peripheral but, in contrast to BOR, has a very good transportation infrastructure. It is an old industrial region (coal mining, steel, ceramics) undergoing restructuring. After heavy employment losses in traditional sectors in the 1980s unemployment has increased continuously since 1991.

NES, like LAR, suffered large employment losses throughout the 1970s and 1980s as a result of structural change in this old industrial region. NES also has, in common with LAR, a high share of long-term unemployed (about 40 per cent) in recent years. Compared with LAR, however, NES has already undergone a transformation to a service-based economy. It has a high level of service employment and is home to the headquarters of 11 of the largest business companies in Germany. A major labour market imbalance is the mismatch between the skills of many redundant workers and the qualification required in the service sector. Moreover, youth unemployment, particularly among 20–24-year-olds, is fairly high.

5.2 The PES District Office as Policy Actor

The PES districts examined are in a transitional state between more traditional rule-oriented bureaucratic administration and a more decentralized system that has not yet taken definitive shape. In principle, the new budgeting system outlined above (see section 2) gives the local PES leadership, in cooperation with the tripartite administrative committees, near complete discretion in allocating ALMP resources and setting local priorities.

In 1998, when the case studies were conducted, PES offices received their ALMP funding for the 'reintegration budgets' for the first time in the form of block grants. The actual allocation of resources between different types of ALMP programmes appears, however, to have differed little from that in the past in all three PES districts examined. This is attributable to the novelty of the process and to initial uncertainty about the actual degree of discretion permitted. The decentralization of decision-making on ALMP was also coupled with a potentially important institutional change: namely, that local budgets had to be formally approved by the tripartite administrative committees, which before had merely an advisory role. In practice, the initial budget planning is still done by the PES, which is then communicated to the administrative committee. The latter then either agrees to this plan or proposes changes, which are discussed until a consensus is reached.

Although a great deal of monitoring information on local PES performance is collected, there was no systematic use of these data to control or sanction local PES district performance, except for the careful monitoring of the flow of expenditure. The PES districts and their directors are thus relatively free to set local priorities and respond to local conditions in interpreting the very broad policy guidelines articulated by higher organizational levels and in statutory recommendations. The many new performance-oriented indicators introduced in 1998 have not yet changed this situation because, owing to their sheer numbers and the uncertainty about how they are to be interpreted, they fail to provide a clear and binding definition of organizational goals and priorities for PES districts.

The role of the PES director

The policy role played by the local PES depends in particular on the PES's director, who can actively shape local priorities and corporate culture, and hence the style and practice of ALMP in the PES. In all three case study districts, the directors are energetic leaders who are strongly committed to ALMP and actively involved in developing ALMP projects or measures.

In BOR, the PES director considers his role to be more political than administrative. He is proud of his PES achievements in the region, especially its success in mobilizing additional ALMP funds, and of the extent to which ALMP measures are targeted on the long-term unemployed. In his view, he has a great deal of discretion in setting local PES priorities within the general goals set by national PES policy and on the basis of (flexible) interpretation of national regulations. In LAR, too, the PES director displays an active and assertive leadership style with minimal intervention by the national or regional PES offices. He attributes the high degree of policy discretion he enjoys to good relationships with both the PES regional (LAÄ) office and with the main office in Nürnberg. By contrast, the PES director of NES places less emphasis on his relationship with the PES hierarchy; instead he stresses the achievements of the local network approach, which he has worked hard to develop in the course of his long career.

Role of the PES in local ALMP actor networks

The PES is a dominant actor in the ALMP network in both BOR and LAR. In both regions, the PES's central role is based not only on the financial resources it provides in relatively small and semi-rural regions, but also on the active leadership style of the PES and its director in local policy networks. The prominent position of the PES in BOR is apparently also related to the low involvement of other ALMP actors.[18] In NES, by contrast, no single actor plays a similar dominant role. Labour market policy is based on a network involving at least five or six core actors.[19] A project-oriented approach to labour market policy has evolved that attempts to link economic development policies with target-group-oriented labour market measures. In summary, the observed differences in the role of the PES in local actor constellations appear to be primarily a consequence of the personality of the PES's director and the level of involvement of other major actors.

Level of ALMP

How can the high participation levels in ALMP measures (Table 8.5) in the three best practice cases be explained?[20] In general, additional resources for programmes can be obtained either within the PES budgeting system or through co-financing schemes with other actors.

One of the main explanations for the high ALMP participation levels observed appears to be successful competition for funds that become available at the regional (LAÄ) level. This sometimes occurs because other PES offices were less interested in certain types of programmes. For example, LAR, an experienced job-creation programme specialist, was able to acquire funds for this purpose in which other PES offices in the region were less interested. In other cases, the LAÄ may reallocate previously assigned funds from one PES district to another if it becomes apparent in the course of the fiscal year that they will not be used in a timely manner. Both situations arose frequently in the previous era of line-item budgets, but may occur less often in the future. Finally, special programmes or increases in funding on short notice, such as the 1998 'election year bonus' for ALMP, are also partly allocated in an *ad hoc* fashion. PES districts with a demonstrated ability to spend approved funding and with a reputation for useful projects have a competitive advantage in the (re)allocation process at the LAÄ level. Parenthetically, it should be noted that the ability of the PES to absorb available funds and to respond quickly to funding opportunities that become available also depends, to a large extent, on the existence of a well-developed network of programme sponsors. Although all three of our best practice cases possess these qualities that can be expected to result in acquiring higher levels of funding in competition with other district offices within a regional office, we found strong support for this explanation only in BOR and LAR. There was, however, little evidence that this was an important explanation for higher levels of ALMP in NES.

Co-financing of PES ALMP through local ALMP actors (state, county, municipalities and – indirectly – the EU) proved to be less important than expected as an explanation of differences in the level of ALMP in the PES regions – although the limited data available makes it difficult to draw any firm conclusions.[21] In BOR and LAR, the selective evidence available indicates that competitive acquisition of resources within the PES budget is the main explanation for their higher levels of ALMP and that co-financing through local ALMP actors played only a limited role. By contrast, in NES complex co-financing schemes are prevalent in a wide range of projects and are an important explanation for the higher level of ALMP uptake.

Targeting

The PES has, as a rule, a strong orientation towards its own core clientèle of unemployment benefit recipients. Referrals to job-creation measures are now restricted largely to benefit recipients, although these programmes entail a strong element of local co-financing. While social assistance recipients may, in principle, be referred to PES training programmes, only unemployment benefit recipients are ordinarily eligible for training stipends. Beyond such regulatory barriers, the long-term unemployed and social assistance recipients frequently have labour market handicaps that make them difficult to place and less promising candidates for labour market training.

No systematic monitoring data are available on placement of social assistance recipients in PES programmes, nor are any data available on the percentage of entrants who are not unemployment benefit recipients.[22] PES officials in both BOR and LAR reject the assertion that social assistance recipients are excluded *per se*, but they appear to be at least strongly underrepresented. There are, moreover, no binding national PES performance goals for the inclusion of the long-term unemployed or social assistance recipients among ALMP programme participants.[23] The lack of monitoring data or performance goals in this area suggests that the relationship to local ALMP and its clientèle is not a major priority for the PES.

Although all three case-study PES districts ranked high in the level of ALMP, there are clear differences in the degree of targeting of measures on the long-term unemployed. NES and LAR have, on average, the largest percentage of long-term unemployed among programme entrants in 1995–7 (47 per cent and 42 per cent, respectively; Table 8.5), whereas the corresponding rate in BOR is somewhat lower (37 per cent). By contrast, the targeting index shows that BOR is one of the highest ranking PES districts with regard to the representation of the long-term unemployed among programme entrants (1.5 on average), whereas NES (1.15) and especially LAR (1.0) rank markedly lower on this criterion.

In the absence of clear national guidelines, these differences appear largely to reflect differences in local PES policies, as well as the level of long-term unemployment in the region. In BOR, the director strongly supports this policy and has committed the tripartite administrative board to the principle of proportional representation of the long-term unemployed. In NES the participation of social assistance recipients has been mostly based on the long-standing co-operative relationship between the PES and local ALMP actors.

5.3 Local ALMP for Social Assistance Recipients

The three cases examined represent three very different stages of institutionalization and levels of professionalism in the organization of local ALMP for problem groups. The best performers in terms of professionalism[24] are clearly NES and LAR. NES has a long tradition of local ALMP (since 1984) with a highly institutionalized and professional system of implementing local measures aimed at social assistance recipients. The management of local measures is located in the city's social office, in the autonomous 'help-to-work' department. This department's activities cover the whole range of counselling and placement services for social assistance recipients, including referral to measures as well as direct placement in regular employment. For the latter task, two placement counsellors are assigned to the acquisition of vacancies, even beyond the city's limits. In 1998, 45 persons were employed in the department, of whom 26 worked outside the central office in the 15 city districts. The medium-term goal is full decentralization of the placement activities. To this end, a controlling system and a participants' database, which can be accessed from various locations, are currently being developed.

The PES district of LAR represents an intermediate case in which responsibility for local ALMP is divided between LAR and MAR, two counties with very different levels of development. LAR exhibits a high degree of professionalism. The county labour market agency, which was established in 1990/91, in practice operates as the regional management and co-ordination agency for local ALMP. With responsibilities for design, financing, and implementation of programmes, the agency is regarded as an optimal implementation tool for providing local labour market policy with a strategic orientation. It is, for example, currently developing a systematic database on persons suitable for local ALMP measures. The exceptionally high standard of the monitoring system and control of local ALMP in LAR is a result of the institutionalization of responsibility for local ALMP at the county level and county's energetic and capable project manager, who also enjoys strong political support from the *Landrat*, the county chief executive. This approach, which has been successfully implemented only in LAR, is advocated by the state ministry for employment, which has supported the establishment of such general agencies to implement local ALMP for social assistance recipients since 1991.

By contrast, in the neighbouring county of MAR, there are capable providers running successful measures in the same PES district, but the overall situation is characterized by institutional and policy fragmentation. After an effort to set up an agency like that in LAR, the county decided to establish an employment company in MAR in 1994. This organization, which provides labour market services to a specialized segment of social assistance recipients, has had considerable success by focusing its activities on measures for the most employable among the social assistance clientèle. There is, however, in contrast to LAR, no general agency with a specialist staff that systematically records and screens the potential of social assistance benefit recipients in the county. Such activities are carried out, if at all, by overworked municipal officials with other primary responsibilities. For example, the town social worker in MAR is also expected to give initial advice and information and to refer suitable candidates to providers of local ALMP measures. Thus, there are calls in the county for a 'clearing agency' responsible for co-ordination and counselling.

Finally, the BOR region has the least developed implementation structure for local ALMP. There is no county manager or specialist staff for local ALMP, and, until recently, it was simply deemed impossible to devote attention to statistics because of the high workload in the county social office. Thus, from the county's point of view, the recent appointment of an additional employee exclusively responsible for administration and management of local measures for social assistance recipients was a considerable step forward.

The level of professionalism in local labour market policy implementation in the three settings coincides very clearly with the time of its initial establishment. Local programmes were introduced when the number of social assistance recipients had risen to such an extent that politicians began to take notice and placed pressure on employment services, which occurred first in the urban setting of NES, followed by LAR and, most recently, in the BOR region.

The quantitative importance of local ALMP for social assistance recipients in the case-study PES districts is difficult to assess given the shortcomings in available data. In general, the data available at the local level is itself a reflection of the level of organization of this policy area. Thus NES, which has a specialist agency devoted to this policy area, also has the most systematic monitoring data on these programmes, followed by the county of LAR. In the counties of MAR and BOR no systematic information is available. A principal problem is that the municipalities are not even obliged to report participants in local ALMP to the counties. The counties, which have a strong interest in monitoring and controlling participants and costs since they are primarily responsible for financing and administering social assistance, have thus to develop their own methods and strategies for data collection.

Although they should be interpreted with caution, the data available for the PES districts of LAR and NES indicate that participation in these programmes is quantitatively significant even in comparison with the more established and better-funded PES system of ALMP (Table 8.6). The number of local ALMP entrants amounts to about 50 per cent and 26 per cent of the number of PES ALMP entrants in LAR and NES, respectively. It should, of course, be noted that the quality of the measures may differ significantly. For example, PES job-creation programmes typically offer six months to one year of full-time employment; whereas 'workfare', under the extra compensation variant of ALMP for social assistance recipients, may, in many cases, represent little more than casual labour. If we compare PES job-creation measures with local

Table 8.6 Social assistance recipients and local ALMP measures in BOR, LAR and NES, 1997–8

	PES district BOR	PES district LAR		PES district NES
	County BURG	County LAR	County MAR	
Social assistance (HLU)				
(1) total recipients (all ages)	6000	8500	1700	22000
(2) of which number capable of work	n.a.	2000	n.a.	7300
(3) receipt (1) due to unemployment	n.a.	n.a.	n.a.	9700
Local labour market policy (HzA/AsS)				
(4) total participants	n.a.	1000	325	1400
(5) of which (4) employment variant	n.a.	250	165	1100
(6) of which (4) workfare variant	n.a.	750	160	300
(7) placement into regular employment	n.a.	n.a.	n.a.	110
(8) local ALMP participants as % of labour force	n.a.	1.1		0.6
(9) local ALMP (4) as % of PES active measures	n.a.	52.1		23.6
(10) local ALMP employment variant (5) as % of job creation entrants	n.a.	71.4		67.3

Notes: All data for BOR and LAR are estimates based on interview statements. NES data from social office/HzA agency.

ALMP employment covered by social security, the ratio of local to PES measures is very high (LAR = 71 per cent and NES = 67 per cent; see Table 8.6) even in comparison with similar activities of the PES for this clientèle.

5.4 Co-operation between Local Authorities and the PES

We first consider the incentives for co-operation from the point of view of the PES and the local authorities and the actual types of co-operation that have emerged. We then look at how the co-operation partners have dealt with potential conflicts of interest and co-operation gains as perceived by the participants.

Incentives for co-operation

Although the desirability of improved PES co-operation in providing services to unemployed social assistance recipients has been recognized and recent guidelines encourage its further development, co-operation with the ALMP of the local authorities remains purely voluntary for the local PES.

There are, moreover, no national performance indicators that sanction placement of social assistance recipients or monitor their participation in PES programmes.

Although the PES has no strong institutional interest in serving their clientèle, the PES none the less has a strong interest in maintaining good relations with the municipalities. The municipalities have traditionally been important providers and co-financers of PES active measures, especially job-creation programmes. Since there is no guarantee of finding alternative providers to implement the funds available for such active measures, the PES is dependent on continued willingness of municipalities to co-operate. The municipalities, in turn, profit from implementing PES job-creation measures that improve the public infrastructure. This nexus between the municipal level and the PES can thus be regarded in all three cases as one of mutual dependence, and is very important in structuring their overall relationship.

Local authorities appear to have even stronger incentives for seeking co-operation than the PES: as relatively new ALMP actors local authorities have an interest in profiting from the expertise and infrastructure of the PES, especially during the establishment of a municipal ALMP infrastructure. Moreover, the local authorities, like the PES itself, have an interest in avoiding conflict with the PES because of their strong interest in the PES financing of municipal job-creation programmes.

Given the lack of strong central direction, the interest of local PES offices in the clientèle of social assistance recipients appears to be generally low and very uneven. In none of the local PES 'policy guidelines' in the case-study regions was the inclusion of social assistance recipients in PES measures an official goal. In both LAR and BOR, their inclusion appeared to happen rather by chance and was a concern of only minor importance. In both cases, the PES and the local authorities tended to concentrate on 'their own' clientèle – that is, the (PES-registered) unemployed in the case of the PES, and (employable) social assistance recipients in the case of the municipalities. (According to one official interviewed, the agencies operate on the principle of 'your people, my people'.)

Only in NES, where the relationship between the PES and the social office has been very strong for years, has there been an explicit effort to include social assistance recipients in PES programmes. This type of co-operation has always been self-evident for the PES (according to a central manager of the social office). In past years, an estimated 20 per cent of participants in PES ALMP measures have been social assistance recipients ineligible for unemployment benefit. However, the 1998 national reforms in the labour promotion act had an immediate negative impact on this form of co-operation in NES, especially in job-creation measures (ABM). This illustrates the contradictions in national PES policy, which encourages co-operation with social assistance carriers on the one hand but, on the other, restricts participation by their clientèle in PES programmes largely for fiscal reasons.

Generally speaking, the institutional division of labour between PES and local authorities with their separate implementation structures offering specialized services to their respective client groups was accepted as a fact of life by ALMP actors at the local level, while selective co-operation was seen as yielding important benefits.

Patterns of co-operation

The patterns of co-operation observed between the PES and local ALMP are varied. In the PES districts of LAR and BOR, co-operation has been relatively underdeveloped in both scope and degree of institutionalization, although co-operation appears to have increased recently. BOR, for example, plans to establish a new consolidated 'employment company' in which the activities of two existing major ALMP providers are to be merged. This employment company will serve as a specialist agency for developing and implementing a broad spectrum of ALMP programmes. Although the PES participates only informally and indirectly in the governance of this new service organization it represents, in practice, a joint venture with the county, which is primarily responsible for ALMP for social assistance recipients. Since the employment company will implement both PES measures and those of the local authorities for social assistance recipients, it will constitute an important link between the PES and local activities for labour market problem groups.

In LAR there have also been a number of initiatives designed to give a more formal structure to the informal and *ad hoc* co-operation of the past. In spring 1998, co-operation contracts were signed between the PES and the two counties in the district. These contracts call for co-operation in tackling youth unemployment and activation of social assistance. The PES and social offices are now obliged to co-operate in the areas of counselling, individual action plans and placement. They are also in the process of instituting a systematic data comparison of the (separate) databases for unemployment and social assistance beneficiaries. Finally, the co-operation contract calls for the establishment of a 'joint institution for the institutionalization of co-operation between county and PES'. This institution, along with a co-ordination body in charge of counselling and drawing up individual action plans for the target group, will be set up in the near future.

In NES, where the inclusion of social assistance recipients in PES programmes is the primary focus of co-operation, a high level of participation has been attained through intensive, day-to-day contacts between counsellors in the social office and PES placement officials. The designated contact persons represent well-defined channels of communication between the two organizations, but no more formal linkages have been established (for example, staff sharing, co-location). There is an agreed division of labour in placement since the PES regards the direct placement activities of the social office not as unwelcome competition, but as complementing its own activities. A contract which formalizes these well-established co-operation activities was concluded in September 1998. It also provides for an intensification of data exchange between the PES and the social office, and the organization of a semi-annual joint staff conference. In sum, there is an ascending order in the scope of co-operation activities from BOR to LAR to NES, corresponding to the degree of institutionalization of local ALMP. Co-operation is (still) *ad hoc* and informal in BOR and LAR, although in the latter case there are more examples of labour market projects serving both clientèles. In the NES case, co-operation is primarily built on institutionalized communication between the PES and the local social assistance agencies as well as on ambitious co-operative goals. There is no reason to assume that organizational integration (for example, a 'one-stop shop' for both clientèles) would bring about better results. Our small set of cases does not, of course, reflect the full range of organizational forms of co-operation in Germany. However, practical forms of co-operation adapted to the local situation seem to be preferable to forced integration (see Chapter 9).

Conflicts

The PES's relationship to local ALMP is complicated by potential conflicts of interest. The regulation of these conflicts will be decisive for the development of co-operation between the PES and the local authorities in providing services for social assistance recipients. To a certain extent, a competitive relationship exists between PES and local ALMP regarding the services of providers; especially for the participation of the municipalities themselves as sponsors and co-financiers of PES job-creation programmes. Moreover, there is a tendency to use local ALMP as a vehicle for re-qualifying participants for PES benefits and thus shift costs back on to the PES budget.

This conflict potential was evident in the PES districts studied. Thus, from the perspective of the PES, the new 'employment company' in the BOR district represents an improvement over the existing infrastructure of providers. Because of the anticipated efficiency gains and broader 'synergetic effects' for ALMP in the region, the PES has strongly supported this reorganization. From the point of view of the county, however, the new employment company appears to represent a major step towards institutionalization of the county responsibility for local ALMP. The county also considers the company to be the proper instrument for the planned expansion of work opportunities for social assistance recipients which, for reasons discussed above, may compete with PES programmes.

In BOR as well as in LAR, recent anecdotal evidence indicates that the further development of co-operation may have been stalled by implementation deadlocks. In NES, by contrast, the existence of a higher level of trust based on a long-standing relationship between the major local actors has been a critical resource for successful co-operation.[25]

Competition between the PES and local authorities for scarce provider resources may increase because recent legislative changes (SGBIII) may lead some providers to withdraw from the implementation of PES measures. PES job-creation measures must, for example, now be competitively tendered, and the providers are required to write detailed applications with descriptions of the proposed measures in addition to bearing an increased share of co-financing. By contrast, application to sponsor measures for social assistance recipients is less complicated, and the financial risk is sometimes borne by the county and not the programme sponsor. This is the case in LAR, where the county pays the providers in advance the gross costs of measures and bears the risk if, for example, third-party funding is not forthcoming (for whatever reason) or if planned slots cannot be filled. Although this conflict may become more acute, it is not yet a major co-operation problem in the cases studied – largely because the provider networks for the PES and local ALMP overlap only partially.

Finally, in all three cases, the 'revolving door effect', that is, use of job programmes by social agencies to requalify social assistance beneficiaries for PES unemployment benefit, was not a source of conflict between the PES and the social authorities. On the contrary, it was perceived as a normal corollary of the given institutional framework.

Co-operation gains

Finally, we must ask whether there are potential co-operation gains that have not been fully realized owing to the current relatively low development of co-operation between the PES and the social assistance providers. The answer is a qualified 'yes'. The following co-operation gains are probably most important.

- *Economies of scale*. These are called for where there are otherwise too few participants for cost-efficient programmes (for example, specialized training programmes). Efficiency gains may also result from joint use of infrastructure (training rooms and workshops, tools and equipment, data exchange, one-stop shops for initial interviews and counselling).
- *Economies of scope*. These allow for the development of 'tailor-made' reintegration chains, which require a greater variety of measures and the 'right' mix of participants (for example, homogeneity of skills). Since the local 'innovative measures' authorized by the 1998 reform are now explicitly targeted on those eligible for both unemployment

benefit and social assistance, potential co-operation gains may be enhanced.

- *Political gains*. The reputation of the PES and the local authorities (counties and municipal administrations) may be enhanced by practical and visible ALMP co-operation in terms of participants and joint projects. Moreover, ALMP provides not only individual assistance but is often used as a vehicle for local economic development.

It should be emphasized, however, that substantial co-operation benefits will only be realized if serving a common clientèle has been defined as a local policy goal by both the PES and local authorities. As long as the PES and the local authorities continue to define their clientèles largely in terms of institutional categories (that is, PES unemployment benefit and social assistance recipients) instead of labour market problem groups, both the incentives for co-operation, as well as the potential benefits, remain limited.

The NES case shows the possible benefits of such co-operation: economies of scale and scope have been achieved by including unemployed persons from both PES and social office registers in active measures; they have been also attained through labour market projects managed by an extensive network including representatives of chambers of commerce and crafts associations, trade unions, private firms, and the city's administration. Finally, successful co-operative labour market projects have enhanced the reputation of the organizations and persons involved and the network approach to local labour market policy has become a 'trademark' for the city of NES.

6 CONCLUSIONS

In this chapter we have addressed a number of interrelated issues. First, the variation in levels of ALMP and the responsiveness of PES ALMP resource allocation to local labour market needs, especially long-term unemployment, was examined against the background of central PES steering and local PES autonomy in the implementation process. Second, the relationship between ALMP of the PES and local ALMP initiatives was investigated in three case studies. Despite the centralized and hierarchical structures of the German PES, ALMP implementation exhibits a remarkable diversity in levels of uptake, policy mix and styles at the operational level of PES district offices, even controlling for labour market and clientèle characteristics. The unemployment rate alone explains only about 40 per cent of the regional variation in the incidence of ALMP. Moreover, we find a surprisingly strong and negative relationship between the share of long-term unemployment and the incidence of active measures at the regional level. This finding implies that regions in which long-term unemployment is higher (more than 12 months) were relatively disadvantaged in the pre-1998 PES resource allocation process.

Yet another noteworthy empirical result is the lack of preferential targeting of ALMP programmes on the long-term unemployed who are, on average, at least proportionately represented in PES programmes. Even more remarkable in this respect is the extremely varied pattern of targeting among the German regions, whose policies are clearly not strongly constrained by national PES programme eligibility requirements or performance indicators.

Measured by this single standard, German PES implementation structures still perform poorly, despite movement towards improved targeting in recent years. This is, of course, not the only standard for assessing performance. The PES is an organization with multiple goals in ALMP; for example, integration of youth or women in the labour market or assistance to enterprises undergoing restructuring. Nevertheless, our analysis raises serious doubts about whether the PES is adequately addressing the concerns of problem groups at the margins of the labour market, especially the long-term unemployed, and other persons at risk of social exclusion.

Any assessment of the role of the PES *vis-à-vis* labour market problem groups and social exclusion cannot be based on a study of the PES alone. In Germany, as in many other industrial countries, there is an increasing bifurcation of the ALMP implementation structure between the PES and local authorities responsible for social assistance. Dependence on social assistance is due to many causes besides unemployment, but a large and growing number of recipients – estimated to be about one-third in Germany – now receive social assistance for reasons of unemployment. We have investigated in particular how local ALMP for social assistance recipients is organized and its relationship to the PES in three 'best practice' districts. Although there is a great deal of local variation, the institutionalization of professional local ALMP systems has become fairly widespread in large cities and urban settings.

This institutional division of labour is not detrimental *per se*. There is a certain justification in separate implementation structures offering specialized services to their respective client groups. This does not preclude co-operation, but a forced integration of these separate systems is neither realistic nor useful in light of the very different legal framework and, last but not least, the capabilities of many professionalized local structures (for example, in NES and LAR). We conclude, therefore, that what is needed is not the abolition of this division of labour but an institutional reform which leads to an improved correspondence between the labour market policy responsibilities of the local authorities and the financial and institutional resources available to them.

The necessary institutional reform might take the form of the 'restoration' of the original division of labour between 'primary' (PES) and 'subsidiary' (municipal) systems, but this option appears to be both unrealistic and undesirable in light of the capable and professional labour market policy implementation structures that have evolved in many localities. Another option is a 'real municipalization' of ALMP for special target groups, the financing of which would have to be largely borne by the national government. Whatever reform model is chosen, its success depends on a reform of the financing system for labour market policy and, in particular, easing the excessive burden of the cost of social assistance for the German local authorities.

Pending more comprehensive reforms, co-operation between PES and local authorities within the existing institutional remains a 'second-best' alternative. One can, however, question whether the existing pattern of voluntary and *ad hoc* co-operation is sufficient. PES monitoring systems, which are currently too narrowly focused on the PES's own programmes, should include information about social assistance beneficiaries in PES's own 'core' clientèle of unemployment benefit recipients. There is, moreover, an urgent need for more information about forms of co-operation between the PES and other local ALMP actors since, in an era of co-operative labour market policy, the PES is increasingly judged by its capacity to act as a facilitator in regional ALMP policy networks. An initial step in this direction should be the collection of systematic information about patterns of co-financing in ALMP programmes. Finally, since meaningful co-operation in local ALMP depends ultimately on the existence of shared goals, PES performance indicators must give greater priority to serving the long-term unemployed – and, in particular, social assistance recipients – than has been the case in the past.

LIST OF ABBREVIATIONS

AA/AÄ	*Arbeitsamt/-ämter* (PES district officc/s)
ABM	*Arbeitsbeschaffungsmaßnahmen* (job creation measures)
AFG	*Arbeitsförderungsgesetz* (labour promotion law)
AFRG	*Arbeitsförderungsreformgesetz* (labour promotion reform law)
AIA	Aggregate Impact Analysis
ALMP	Active Labour Market Policy
AsS	*Arbeit statt Sozialhilfe* ('work instead of social assistance') (see Table 8.6)
BA	*Bundesanstalt für Arbeit* (German PES)
BSHG	*Bundessozialhilfegesetz* (German law on social assistance)

DGB	*Deutscher Gewerkschaftsbund* (German Union Confederation)
ESF	European Social Fund
FuU	*Fortbildung und Umschulung* (further training and retraining)
HLU	*Hilfe zum Lebensunterhalt* ('help to subsistence')
HzA	*Hilfe zur Arbeit* ('help to employment')
KJHG	*Kinder- und Jugendhilfegesetz* (children and youth assistance act)
LAA/LAÄ	*Landesarbeitsamt/-ämter* (PES office/s on federal state level)
LMP	Labour market policy
LTU	Long-term unemployed resp. unemployment
PES	Public employment service
SGB	*Sozialgesetzbuch* ('act on social law')

NOTES

1. The authors are grateful to Antje Mayer and Christopher Engelmann for indispensable research assistance and to Robyn Wiesener for secretarial support. Special thanks are due to the PES district office directors, their staff, service providers, and local officials, who kindly gave their time for interviews and provided background information. The authors alone are responsible for the contents.
2. This internal reform process is guided by four principles: customer orientation of services, effectiveness of services, efficiency of services, personnel satisfaction. The reform includes the successive introduction of a new organizational model in all German PES offices.
3. Until 31 March 1997 the old Labour Promotion Act (AFG) provided the legal framework for the PES and active policies in Germany. In April 1997 the AFG was amended (AFRG) and finally replaced as of January 1998 by the new Tittle III of the law on social security (SGBIII). The institutional structures of the PES described below remained, however, substantially unchanged.
4. 'Discretionary' includes most labour market training, job-creation programmes and wage subsidies. There are still a number of mandatory active measures – that is, programmes based on individual entitlements – for example, short-time work allowances and winter allowance for construction workers. Moreover, not all discretionary measures are included in the integration title. The main exceptions are money allowance for persons setting up their own business and 'structural adjustment measures' (formerly known as 'productive wage subsidies').
5. Through a weighting procedure, this formula takes fairly strong account of regional labour market conditions. See also Blien (1998) for a more detailed discussion of the new formula.
6. Furthermore, a separate provision provides for work opportunities particularly for young persons, who are not subject to this restriction (BSHG §19, Para 1).
7. See Trube (1997, p. 77) for a useful overview.
8. In western Germany, between 1981 and 1993, the average annual growth rate of social assistance ('*Hilfe zum Lebensunterhalt*') expenditure was 11 per cent; between 1989 and 1993 expenditure increased by 40 per cent.
9. For example, §12b AFG committed employment offices to include recipients of social assistance in further training measures or in public job-creation schemes (ABM).
10. A maximum of 5 per cent of slots in measures are open to other persons.

11. For instance, structural wage subsidies, 'bridging allowance' for self-employment, or 'recruitment subsidies' for new businesses.
12. Western Berlin is treated as a single observation, although it actually comprises several PES district offices.
13. Data on structure of unemployment are for September.
14. Training = '*Fortbildung und Umschulung*'; job creation = '*Arbeitsbeschaffungsmaßnahmen*'; wage subsidies = '*Lohnkostenzuschüsse*'.
15. Precise data at PES district level were available for long-term unemployed entrants into training programmes. Since no data were available at PES district level for job-creation programmes, the percentage share of long-term unemployed in stock of participants in western Germany was applied to all PES districts (1995 = 63.9%, 1966 = 68.4%, 1997 = 74.6%; see ANBA Arbeitsmarkt 1997 Table 3, p. 80). For wage subsidy programmes the following factors were used to classify ALMP entrants: *Eingliederungsbeihilfen* = §54 AFG = actual percentage of long-term unemployed based on PES administrative data ('*Bewilligungen*'); for two other wage subsidy programmes ('Employment Aids for the Long-term Unemployed' and 'Wage Subsidies for the Older Unemployed' (§97 AFG)) all participants were classified as long-term unemployed based on programme eligibility requirements; in the case of another wage subsidy programme (§242s AFG) based on national data available only for 1997, it was estimated that two-thirds of participants were long-term unemployed (ANBA, Arbeitsmarkt 1997).
16. Both variables are based in part on estimates since precise data on the percentage of long-term unemployed entrants were not available for all ALMP programmes. See explanatory note in Table 8.1 for details.
17. This might be interpreted as a higher capacity of smaller districts to influence level and targeting of ALMP, in contrast to larger urban regions.
18. The trade union confederation (DGB) and individual unions are fairly weak in the region, the county government until recently appears to have been content to play a relatively passive role in local ALMP, there was until recently no chamber of commerce office in the county, and any other relevant economic development initiatives or co-ordinating institutions do not exist.
19. The most important actors are the PES, the city administration for urban planning and development, the chamber of commerce, the local crafts association, the DGB, the economic development corporation, and the centre for vocational promotion; in each case represented by directors or central managers of the respective organizations.
20. 'High' here means even after controlling for population size and the local labour market conditions as reflected in national allocation patterns.
21. The lack of systematic monitoring data is itself a symptom of the neglect of co-operative forms of ALMP in PES monitoring systems.
22. It should be noted that the two clientèles (social assistance and unemployment benefit recipients) are not clearly distinct. Many unemployment benefit recipients with a low benefit level may also be eligible for social assistance.
23. As of 1998, the new German labour promotion act does include a non-binding recommendation that problem groups be included proportionally to their share of the unemployed.
24. Measured in terms of actors' expertise and organizational structures.
25. For example, in NES, although the social department might have a theoretical interest in pushing the most difficult-to-place social assistance recipients through the 'revolving door' on to PES unemployment benefits, it would not do so because of the expected disapproving reaction of the PES.

BIBLIOGRAPHY

Amtliche Nachlichten der Bundesanstalt für Arbeit (ANBA) (1998), 'Arbeitsmarkt 1997', Sondernummer, Nürnberg, June.

Blien, U. (1998), 'Die regionale Mittelverteilung für die aktive Arbeitsmarktpolitik: Politikberatung des IAB für Zwecke der Maßnahmesteuerung', *MittAB 4*, pp. 674–789.

Breuer, W. and D. Engels (1997), 'Grundinformation und Daten zur Sozialhilfe. Im Auftrag des Bundesministeriums für Gesundheit', Otto-Blume-Institut für Sozialforschung und Gesellschaftspolitik e.V.

Bruche, G. and B. Reissert (1985), *Die Finanzierung der Arbeitsmarktpolitik. System, Effektivität, Reformansätze*, Frankfurt: Campus.

Freidinger, G. (1995), 'Arbeitsmarktpolitik und Wirtschaftsförderung – zwei sich ergänzende Handlungsfelder', in G. Freidinger and M. Schulze-Böing (eds), *Handbuch der kommunalen Arbeitsmarktpolitik*, 2nd edition, Marburg: Metropolis, pp. 89–109.

Fuchs, L. (1994), 'Kommunale Beschäftigungsförderung. Ergebnisse einer Umfrage über Hilfen zur Arbeit nach BSHG und Arbeitsbeschaffungsmaßnahmen nach AFG', Köln: *Deutscher Städtetag*, 2nd edition.

Fuchs, L. (1997), 'Kommunale Beschäftigungsförderung. Ergebnisse einer Umfrage von 1997 über Hilfen zur Arbeit nach BSHG und Arbeitsbeschaffungsmaßnahmen nach AFG', Köln: *Deutscher Städtetag*.

GIB (1998), 'Aktivitäten der Kommunen in Nordrhein-Westfalen zur Arbeitsmarktintegration von Sozialhilfebeziehern. Ein aktualisierter Überblick der G.I.B.', *Gesellschaft für innovative Beschäftigungsförderung*, Bottrop.

Heidinger, M. (1997), 'Konzertiert, konzentriert und kommunalisiert – Die Dezentralisierung moderner Arbeitsmarktpolitik', in Friedrich-Ebert-Stiftung (eds), *Bündnis für Arbeit in der Kommune: Chance oder Utopie?* Gesprächskreis Arbeit und Soziales, no. 73, pp. 23–30.

IBV 14/98, 'Zusammenarbeit von Arbeits- und Sozialämtern: Gemeinsame Wege zur beruflichen Eingliederung Arbeitsloser', *Informationen für die Beratungs- und Vermittlungsdienste der Bundesanstalt*, Nürnberg.

Lindner, H. (1994), 'Beschäftigung von Sozialhilfeempfängern in Beschäftigungsgesellschaften', in M. Schulze-Böing and H. Johrendt (eds), *Wirkungen kommunaler Beschäftigungsprogramme*, Basel/Boston/Berlin: Birkhäuser, pp. 189–213.

Mosley, H. and C. Degen (1994), *Reorganisation of Labour Market Policy. Further Training for the Unemployed in the United Kingdom*, WZB Discussion Paper FS I, 94–205, Berlin: WZB.

Peters, A. and G. Schmid (1982), 'Aggregierte Wirkungsanalyse des arbeitsmarktpolitischen Programms der Bundesregierung für Regionen mit besonderen Beschäftigungsproblemen', *Zwischenbericht IIM, 82–1*, Berlin: WZB.

Schmid, G. (1996), 'Process Evaluation: Policy Formation and Implementation' in G. Schmid, J. O'Reilly and K. Schömann (eds), *International Handbook of Labour Market Policy and Evaluation*, Cheltenham: Edward Elgar, pp. 198–231.

Schulze-Böing, M. (1994), 'Einleitung: Evaluation der kommunalen Arbeitsmarktpolitik – zur absehbaren Karriere eines Themas', in M. Schulze-Böing and H. Johrendt (eds), *Wirkungen kommunaler Beschäftigungsprogramme*, Basel/Boston/Berlin: Birkhäuser, pp.11–28.

Schulze-Böing, M. (1997), 'Integrierte Arbeitsmarktpolitik auf kommunaler Ebene, in *Innovation, Beschäftigung, Wachstum und Wettbewerb. Strategien zur Halbierung der Arbeitslosigkeit*, Reader zum Fachkongreß am 28/29 April in Berlin (Schriftenreihe der Senatsverwaltung für Arbeit, Berufliche Bildung und Frauen, Band 28), pp. 148–58.

Schulze-Böing, M. and H. Simon (1998), 'Arbeitsvermittlung als soziale Wertschöpfung.

Elemente eines integrierten Beratungs- und Vermittlungskonzepts', Offenbach: *Materialien zur Arbeitsförderung* 1/98.

Trube, A. (1997), *Zur Theorie und Empirie des zweiten Arbeitsmarktes. Exemplarische Untersuchungen und praktische Versuche zur sozioökonomischen Bewertung lokaler Beschäftigungsförderung*, Münster: LIT.

Wirtschaft und Statistik (1997), Sozialhilfeempfänger und Empfänger von Leistungen nach dem Asylbewerberleistungsgesetz, *WiSta No. 10*, pp. 720–26.

9. Activation through co-operation: a case study of the implementation of active measures in the Netherlands

Martijn van Velzen[1]

1 INTRODUCTION

In the concept of 'transitional labour markets', co-operation is regarded as one of the four success criteria (Schmid, 1998, p. 10). More specifically: according to this view, networks should be established at the local level between actors involved in the implementation of active labour market policy (ALMP) in order to facilitate transitions from unemployment to work. Implementation of ALMP should not be left solely to the traditional local public employment service (PES). Instead, partnerships are to be realized including both public and private local actors.

With respect to the co-operation criterion, the development of ALMP implementation in the Netherlands during the 1990s may serve as an interesting example. In the course of the 1990s, at least two remarkable developments have taken place in the field of labour market policy, which can be best characterized as 'co-operation' and 'decentralization'. First, the implementation of ALMP measures, such as job creation and work experience schemes, has increasingly become a shared responsibility of municipalities, municipally linked organizations and the local PES; and, to a lesser extent, administration bodies for employee benefits and temporary employment agencies. Second, aside from being charged with a responsibility for reintegrating the hard-to-place unemployed, municipalities increasingly have a financial interest in placing long-term unemployed persons receiving social assistance.[2]

1.1 Institutional Setting of Dutch ALMP

Traditionally the implementation of active labour market policy in the Netherlands has been organizationally separated from passive labour market measures. The mainly publicly funded[3] tripartite PES, through its 18 regional boards and approximately 220 local employment agencies, carries out active policy such as the implementation of job-creation and work-experience measures and the registration of job seekers, as well as counselling, guidance and placement services. Before 1990, the PES was an integrated part of the Ministry of Social Affairs and Employment. Since 1990, it has become more loosely connected to this ministry, though ALMP formation remains the province of the Ministry of Social Affairs and Employment.

The implementation of passive labour market policy – that is, compensation for income loss as a result of unemployment – is the responsibility of two distinct groups of actors. In the first place, municipalities, by means of their social service departments, are concerned with the administration of the social assistance benefit (SAB). The SAB is a means-tested benefit and is provided to, among others, unemployed job seekers who are not (any longer) entitled to the unemployment benefit (UB). Municipalities are compensated by the central government up to 90 per cent of the benefit amount; the cost of SAB administration falls entirely on the municipal budget.

Since 1996 the administration of the UB has been carried out by the national institute for social security (*Landelijk instituut sociale verzekeringen*, Lisv). The UB is financed by employers' and employees' contributions and amounts to 70 per cent of the daily pay last earned.[4] The actual task of benefit administration is contracted out by the institute to private administration bodies known as 'Uvis' (*Uitvoeringsinstellingen*).[5] Originally these private bodies stemmed from industrial insurance associations managed by employers' and employees' representatives. Until the mid-1990s, these sector-based associations were responsible for the administration of employee benefits such as the UB and the disability benefit. The associations were supervised by the tripartite social insurance council (*Sociale Verzekeringsraad*, SVr), which was dominated by the social partners. In practice, the bipartite boards of the industrial insurance associations were thus monitored by themselves. This questionable situation was denounced in a 1993 parliamentary investigation into the administration of the Dutch social insurance system.[6] Evidence from this investigation suggested that the bipartite boards were responsible for mismanagement resulting in a dramatic increase in the number of people receiving unemployment or disability benefits. The investigative committee recommended cutting the social partners' links to the administrative organization. As a consequence, the bipartite industrial insurance associations were transformed into private administrative bodies. Furthermore, the social insurance council was dissolved and replaced by the independent social security supervision board (*College van toezicht sociale verzekeringen*, Ctsv).

1.2 Towards a Decentralized, Activating Welfare State

In the past, the main function of the Dutch social security system was to compensate people for income loss by providing replacement income. However, after the 1993 parliamentary investigation committee concluded that labour market participation had dramatically decreased, there was widespread awareness that the extent of Dutch social security expenditure had reached its limits.[7] This situation called for a policy shift: actors involved in passive policy implementation – municipalities and the organizations responsible for UB provision – were explicitly charged with the task of reintegrating social assistance recipients and recipients of unemployment benefits.[8]

It also became clear that more structural co-operation at the decentralized level between the PES, the municipalities and the Uvis was necessary.[9] Subsequent modifications in social security legislation included an obligation for actors to co-operate. In addition, the Dutch parliament passed legislation that required the introduction of a single front office for benefit provision and placement activities, the so-called centre for work and income (CWI). Through the CWIs, a 'one-stop shop' approach will be applied towards clients. Within the CWIs, the municipal social service, Uvis and the PES will be located. Initially the co-operation is aimed at working procedures in the front office, such as client intake and identification of the client needs, referral to additional training, guidance or placement. Before CWIs could be nationally established, regional and local experiments took place in order to determine the optimal co-operation structure in terms of the number and type of actors involved, the processes and clients to which co-operation should be directed, and so on. The approximately 200 locally based CWIs should be fully operational before the end of the year 2000.

Following the 1993 social security investigation, an evaluation of the PES operations was carried out in 1995.[10] The 1995 evaluation concluded that the PES lacked appropriate incentives in carrying out its operations. The use of lump-sum funding based on policy outcomes – merely defined in terms of placements – had rewarded 'indicator behaviour'; that is, the PES placed a higher priority on achieving quantitative placement targets than on the quality and duration of the job in which clients were placed. The results of the evaluation study underlined the need for an improved co-ordination of counselling and placement activities.[11] Legislative reform of the PES was recommended. With the introduction of the employment service act in 1996, part of the PES budget was shifted to 19 major cities and to the Uvis. Until the end of 2000, municipalities and Uvis are obliged to spend these earmarked funds on the purchase of PES services, such as intensified counselling, training and placement.[12] Thus municipalities are receiving resources to finance their new task of reintegrating social assistance benefit recipients. Moreover, the purpose of the changes in the budget allocation is to increase the financial stake of the PES in its reintegrating activities.

As a result of the legal reforms in the field of both active and passive labour market policy, the increased importance of local and regional actors in policy implementation, as well as the necessity for co-operation at the local level, have become unambiguously clear.[13] Bottlenecks relating to the simultaneous introduction of CWIs and the competition among Uvis in order to obtain contracts for the administration of employee benefits have, however, been identified. Whereas the CWIs require actors to co-operate, the competition for purchase contracts will induce a more businesslike approach. A situation in which actors co-operate in the front office and compete in the back office is likely to occur.

1.3 Research Aim and Design

This chapter reports on a research project dealing with co-operation structures for ALMP implementation in the Netherlands. The principal aim of the study was twofold. First, dominant structures for ALMP implementation were identified in a selection of Dutch municipalities. The characterization of these structures was based on the extent to which implementing organizations act together at the local level. Second, more detailed information was collected on the process of ALMP implementation, often thought of as a 'black box'. In addition, the performance of implementing structures was assessed. Here policy uptake (in terms of utilization of ALMP measures) was identified as the relevant performance indicator.[14]

The first part of the study was based on a survey of 19 major cities. In these municipalities the implementation structures of ALMP prevailing in the 1990s were identified. The period studied was 1990–97 since, as described above, remarkable changes were made in the fields of both active and passive labour market policy during these years.

The 19 municipalities dealt with in this study were all included in the so-called 'major cities policy' (*Grotestedenbeleid*).[15] This policy focuses on typical metropolitan problems such as long-term unemployment and social exclusion. Within the framework of the major cities policy, initiatives that began as experiments were launched in social and economic areas, and were later introduced nationwide. Initiatives aimed at combating long-term unemployment, as well as innovations within already existing ALMP measures, have spread throughout the rest of the Netherlands. As a consequence of this policy focus (and hence intensified funding) we expected to find a substantial number of initiatives in the field of ALMP within these 19 major cities – the principal reason for including these municipalities in this research.

The local structures studied were all established with the goal of implementing four national schemes. These measures, introduced in the course of the 1990s, were targeted at the long-term unemployed and unemployed youth. Implementation of each of the four schemes required and/or enabled involvement of local and regional actors. Depending on the type of measure, organizations at the decentralized level were either obliged to co-operate or were free to choose their partners in the implementation network. The extent to which the actors were permitted to exercise discretion in shaping the implementation process varied depending on the measures. Legislation on each of the schemes stipulated more or less basic implementation constellations. In section 2.2 more detailed information on each of the four measures will be presented. As can be seen from the description of the four measures, co-operation in implementation processes is, to some extent, enabled or required. Based on our survey of the 19 municipalities, local variation was assessed with respect to the extent to which actors co-operated in the implementation process during the period 1990–97. The observed municipalities were subsequently categorized based on co-operation characteristics such as the nature and number of actors involved, the design of the mutual relationships, and the working procedures involving co-operation. As a result, four types of co-operation in ALMP implementation have been distinguished (section 2.3).

To obtain a closer insight into implementation practices, more detailed case studies were carried out in four municipalities, each representing a single co-operation type. In section 3 case-study results will be presented. Furthermore, performance indicators have been defined and assessed for each of the four cases in this study, facilitating benchmarking on co-operation types (section 4). These outcomes serve to indicate to what extent various types of co-operation in the implementation of the ALMP measures facilitate the reintegration of the long-term unemployed.

2 CO-OPERATION IN ALMP IMPLEMENTATION

2.1 Some Thoughts on Co-operation

It was made clear in the previous section that co-operation is usually thought of as something desirable. The emphasis on co-operation in the concept of transitional labour markets is broadly shared in the literature on inter-organizational co-operation and co-ordination.[16] Typically the concepts of co-operation and co-ordination in an organizational context are often used interchangeably. 'Co-operation' is generally regarded as a collaborative interaction at the operational level between organizations. When interaction takes place at higher levels of organizations, it is often referred to as 'co-ordination'. In this chapter, the term 'co-operation' will also be applied to interaction involving higher-ranking members of organizations.

The general assumption is that concerted decision-making and co-operative programme implementation lead to more successful outcomes than the independent actions of organizations. This is especially the case for organizations that share a preference for the same outcome.[17] Often inter-organizational co-operation is expected to produce economies of scale, thereby enhancing organizational efficiency. Co-operation may furthermore facilitate quality improvements in service delivery. By cutting overlap, working procedures may be shortened, and thus client data may become more reliable owing to a reduction of data transfer between organizations. As mentioned in the introduction, the principal reason why the Dutch government seeks to promote co-operation among local actors involved in ALMP implementation is to streamline operations in order to serve clients better and to economize on labour market policy budgets. Empirical support for the assumption that co-operation between PES and other organizations may contribute to a better performance (in terms of higher placement results) can, for example, be found in de Koning and van Nes (1991) – although co-operation in this study was only one of the ingredients in a more successful policy mix.[18]

Does co-operation always facilitate successful activation? Does the marginal utility of co-operation decline? If inter-organizational relations in implementation structures are considered 'super-organizations',[19] then we may apply principles of organizational theory suitable to a single organizational unit. Since we can expect the need for more agreement and formal organization to increase with group size, one assumption might be that situations occur where the 'co-operation density' (in terms of the number of actors working together, or the number of processes in which parties act together) or 'co-operation complexity' (expressed as the nature of actors working together or the nature of the processes in which parties act together) produce inefficient or ineffective outcomes as a result of rising organizational costs. Here these costs can be defined as in the words of Olsen (1965): costs of communication among group members, the costs of any bargaining among them, and the costs of creating, staffing and maintaining any formal group organization.[20]

Another factor that may influence the success of co-operation is the way in which co-operation has evolved. Co-operation strongly depends on the willingness of players at the decentralized level. If co-operation is mandated by central actors, local actors may regard it as an undesirable intervention since this has ramifications for their authority and autonomy.[21] Thus legally enforced co-operation structures may not necessarily produce fruitful interaction between local organizations.

2.2 ALMP Measures Included in This Study

In this study, implementation structures and the degree to which implementing actors mutually co-operate have been assessed on the basis of four ALMP measures: the labour pool scheme (*Rijksbijdrageregeling Banenpool*), the guaranteed youth employment act (*Jeugdwerkgarantiewet*, JWG), the measure on extra employment for long-term unemployed (*Extra werkgelegenheid langdurig werklozen* EWLW) and the experiments activation through benefit application (*Subsidieregeling Experimenten Activering Uitkeringsgelden* EAU). The latter two schemes are better known as the Melkert 1 and the Melkert 2 measures, respectively.[22] All measures were introduced in the course of the 1990s and implementation is the responsibility of local and regional actors. The amount of discretion given to local actors in implementing these schemes varied.

Launched in 1990, the labour pool programme targeted the very long-term unemployed, that is, those who had been out of work for more than three years (see Tables 9.1 and 9.2). Programme eligibility was restricted to those unemployed whose chances of getting a regular job were considered non-existent. Municipalities were required to submit annually a plan outlining the estimated number of participants in the labour pool scheme and the costs involved. Implementation of the measure was handled by the municipalities, which, in turn, concluded co-operation agreements with the regional PES boards. Principally these agreements governed the division of labour in the implementation of the measure. The actual implementation at the local level was carried out by a special municipal foundation, the so-called labour pool organization. After screening by the local PES and subsequent referral to the labour pool organization, long-term unemployed people were offered a permanent labour contract by the labour pool organization. Labour pool participants received the statutory minimum wage. Once employed by the labour pool organization, participants were subsequently seconded to public sector firms. The most important restriction here was that the places offered by these firms should not replace existing jobs within the organizations. The 'additionality' of a labour pool job was to be tested by special committees in which municipalities and the PES were represented. Initially participants were placed in the labour pool to gain work experience and eventually to flow into a regular job. Yet it became increasingly clear that flows out of the measure into unsubsidized labour was very rare.[23]

Evaluation of the labour pool scheme showed that large regional variations existed with respect to the implementation design. Problems between part-

Table 9.1 ALMP measures included in the Dutch study

Measure	Target group	Implementing actors	Contents	Funding
Labour pool – *Rijksbijdrageregeling Banenpool* (1990)	Those unemployed for three years or more identified by PES as very hard-to-place.	Labour pool foundation supervised by municipality.	Placement of very hard-to-place unemployed in additional jobs in public and private sector. Participants are employees of the labour pool foundation and seconded to other organizations.	Savings on benefit expenditures in the amount of NLG 20 000. Furthermore, fiscal incentives as well as a national subsidy provided by the Ministry of Social Affairs and Employment. PES also subsidizes part of the costs of the measure. Organizations that hire labour pool participants pay a remuneration.
Guaranteed youth employment act – *Jeugdwerkgarantiewet* (1991)	Young people until 21 years and unemployed between 6 and 12 months, and school leavers < 27 years and unemployed 6 to 12 months.	GYEA foundation supervised by municipality.	Aim of the measure is to prevent young people from becoming long-term unemployed. Participants are employed by the GYEA foundation and seconded to an organization providing the 'guaranteed employment'.	National government contributes NLG 16 800 for each participant. Furthermore a national subsidy is provided in order to cover (part of) the implementation costs. Organizations that hire participants receive fiscal incentives.

Measure for extra employment for long-term unemployed – *Melkert 1* (1995)	People unemployed for more than 1 year and receiving social assistance, or participants in labour pool measure.	Jobs in the health sector via umbrella organizations, supervised by the Ministry of Public Health, and in public sector jobs at the municipal level.	Creation of 20 000 extra jobs in the public sector in 48 municipalities on areas of safety, surveillance and supervision, day nursery and education. Another 20 000 jobs are to be realized in the health-care sector.	National government provides a subsidy of NLG 34 500 as well as additional fiscal incentives for employers.
Measure for experiments on activation with benefits – *Melkert 2* (1995)	Those unemployed for more than 1 year and receiving social assistance.	Experiments are carried out by a variety of actors such as municipalities, temporary employment agencies, trade unions, employers' associations and regional PES boards.	The measure intends to test 63 innovative and promising experiments aimed at the long-term unemployed. No common denominator in the type of work.	Assistance benefit funds are applied in order to finance the measure budgetary neutral. National government provides a wage cost subsidy of NLG 18 000 and additional fiscal incentives for employers.

Table 9.2 *Total volume of the measures in million Dutch guilders and in number of participants*

	1991	1992	1993	1994	1995	1996	1997	1998*
Labour pool								
NLG	123	378	454	415	420	987**	1 087**	1 742***
participants	6000	16 000	16 000	20 000	22 000	23 000	24 000	53 000**
GYEA								
NLG	127	228	322	464				
participants	6000	12 000	16 000	22 000	25 000	23 000		
Melkert 1								
NLG					–	–	–	1600
participants					2572	9 575	17 327	20 000
Melkert 2								
NLG					720****	88	140	
participants					1 625	9 693	21 002	

Notes: * Estimated; ** including GYEA; *** including GYEA and Melkert 2; **** budgeted for overall period until date of measure expiry 1 January 1999.

Source: Ministry of Social Affairs and Employment.

ners in the implementation network occurred in the initial stage after its introduction. Typically those problems were caused by differing views on the application and goal of the labour pool. Furthermore, in some implementation structures, actors found it hard to agree on the competence for measure implementation.[24]

The guaranteed youth employment act (GYEA, 1991) was designed to prevent long-term unemployment among young people by offering them work experience places (see Tables 9.1 and 9.2). The aim was for participants to flow out of the measure into training or regular jobs. The group targeted by this measure were persons under 21 years of age who had been unemployed for over six months, and school leavers between 21 and 27 years of age who had been unemployed for over six months.[25] It should be noted that all members of the target group were covered by the measure, and that, in principle, no limits existed on the uptake of this scheme.

Implementation was principally carried out by a special municipal body, the GYEA organization. In practice, municipalities opted to have both labour pool and GYEA implemented by one and the same municipal body: the combined labour pool/GYEA organization. Each municipal GYEA organization had to employ participants by offering them a labour contract. GYEA participants were paid the statutory minimum wage. In order to place participants into work-experience places, GYEA organizations were responsible for the acquisition of a sufficient number of work experience places to cover all target group members within the municipality. Finally the organization had the task of promoting the outflow from participants into regular employment. The work-experience places were initially provided by organizations in the public sector. In a latter stage, GYEA organizations could also place participants in private sector firms.

Legislation establishing the scheme stipulated co-operation between the GYEA organization and the PES. Co-operation was regarded as essential for the inflow of target group members into the measure, as well as for the flow of participants from work experience places into a regular job or training. Co-operation was supposed to take place during the screening and referral of target group members. The main task of the local PES was to place young unemployed into a regular job within six months. After an unemployment duration of more than half a year, youngsters became eligible for GYEA, and the PES then had the task of adequately informing the GYEA organization on participant flows. In addition, the two organizations were required to co-operate in placing participants into the work-experience scheme; and, at a latter stage, in placing them in a regular job or a training course. National evaluation on GYEA implementation showed that one of every ten GYEA organizations judged the co-operation with the PES to be 'inadequate'.[26]

Introduced in 1995, the Melkert 1 measure was expected to create 40 000 regular jobs in the public sector (see Tables 9.1 and 9.2). The target groups for Melkert 1 jobs were unemployed persons who had been registered job seekers or had received social assistance for more than one year. In addition, participants of the labour pool measure could also be placed into a Melkert 1 job.

Half of the Melkert 1 jobs were to be established in the municipal sector; the other 20 000 jobs were allocated to the health-care sector. Implementation of the Melkert 1 measure in the health-care sector was co-ordinated by central bodies linked to this sector. Melkert 1 jobs in the health-care sector were funded by the Ministry of Health. Melkert 1 health-care jobs have been excluded from this study because, owing to their distinct implementation and funding structure, it is difficult to regard these jobs as an integral part of the decentralized labour market policy.[27]

The Melkert 1 jobs in the municipal sector were allocated by the central government to the 19 major cities included in this study. Municipalities received a lump sum of NLG 40 000 from the central government for every Melkert 1 job created. Jobs could be created within municipal departments as well as at municipally linked organizations. Most jobs were created in the field of supervision and security. Of the 20 000 municipal jobs, a maximum of 70 per cent was allocated to the four largest cities (Amsterdam, Rotterdam, The Hague and Utrecht). The remaining Melkert 1 jobs were distributed over the 15 other major cities.

The aim of the Melkert 2 measure (1995) was to facilitate the creation of experimental local and regional employment initiatives through the use of social assistance funds (see Tables 9.1 and 9.2). This measure was targeted at people who had been unemployed for over one year and were receiving social assistance. The aim of the measure was to create a total of 20 000 jobs in the public and private sectors. By the end of 1998, more than 21 000 people had been placed in the measure. A variety of organizations – ranging from municipalities, public and private employment services, training providers and trade unions – submitted proposals. Approximately 60 projects were approved and subsequently funded by the government. Funding of the scheme entailed no additional expenditure. For each job that was created, the central government provided a subsidy corresponding to the social assistance benefit saved. People who were placed in a Melkert 2 job received 120 per cent of the statutory minimum wage.

In early 1998, the labour pool and the guaranteed youth employment act ceased to exist as distinct measures. Under the act on the deployment of job seekers (WIW) – introduced to streamline reintegration policy – labour pool and GYEA have been renamed and have now become part of a wide range of strategies designed to provide the long-term unemployed with work experience.[28] These legislative changes do not, however, affect the present study: the measures included in this research merely serve as the vehicle by which local co-operation is mapped out and analysed.

2.3 Local Implementation Structures: Towards a Typology of Co-operation

Between November 1997 and January 1998, telephone interviews were conducted with PES representatives, staff from municipal social services and managers of municipal foundations in order to assess the local implementation structure for the above-mentioned four schemes. The implementation structures are described on the basis of dominant features in the studied period. The description of local implementation structures reveals the extent to which co-operation had been initiated between key actors in municipal ALMP.

In this case, co-operation is categorized in terms of the following features: the way in which (client) information was exchanged between implementing actors (*ad hoc* or regularly; informally or formally); the degree to which actors were jointly involved in placing clients in a measure (client intake and referral, counselling, guidance, training); co-operation in acquiring vacancies among employers; and combined efforts in placement of participants out of the measure into regular jobs. It should be stressed here that primary attention is paid to the degree and design of co-operation between the local PES and the municipality or the municipal organizations responsible for implementation of local labour market policies.

In nearly all municipalities, some degree of co-operation in the implementation of GYEA and labour pool has been found, which may be explained by the legislative framework on co-operation. After the measures were introduced in the early 1990s, the PES and the municipality concluded agreements to co-operate, generally by means of a covenant or a more binding contract. In nearly all municipalities, the municipal organization responsible for the labour pool was also responsible for implementation of the GYEA. Representatives of the municipality are, in most cases, on the board of this municipal foundation. In some cases, the municipal labour pool/GYEA foundation was a unit of the municipal social service agency.

A remarkable set of implementation constellations can be observed for Melkert measures. In a number of cases, temporary employment agencies co-operated with the PES in a project organization responsible for implementing the Melkert 2 measure.[29] As a rule, the Melkert schemes were co-ordinated by the municipality since they controlled the budgets and had a clear interest in the placement of municipal social service clients. Not only did the major cities policy provide municipalities with funding for local and regional employment policies, the financial flows from the national government to the

PES were partly mediated by the municipalities. As earmarked funding enabled municipalities to purchase PES services, municipalities frequently felt under obligation to buy PES training and placement services. Contracts for the purchase of services is an important feature in the area of Melkert 1 and 2. Although, in most cases, contracts were between the municipality and the PES, some municipalities established contractual relations with temporary employment agencies.

There was considerable local variation in the way and the extent to which co-operation developed in the 1990s, as well as in the dominant forms of co-operation that emerged at the municipal level. In this study, four types of co-operation have been identified (see Figure 9.1). First there are municipalities in which the co-operation between the parties involved does not exceed – or even meet – the standards as set by legislation for GYEA and labour pool, and in which co-operation in the Melkert 1 and Melkert 2 schemes has hardly evolved. This type A co-operation (basic co-operation) is characterized by little formal or institutionalized consultation and feedback on clients and client flows, as well as by the absence of formalized joint working procedures. Type B co-operation (co-operation through joint staff) involves

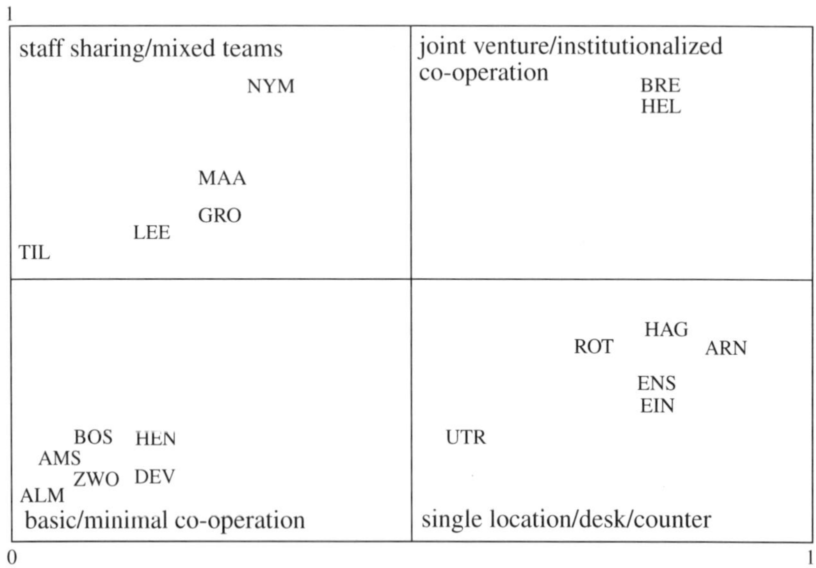

Note: X-axis represents physical co-operation indicators such as joint location; Y-axis represents human-resources co-operation indicators such as joint staff. See note 15 for the full names of the 19 municipalities.

Figure 9.1 Four co-operation types in 19 major municipalities

co-operation that exceeds legislative standards, and which, in many cases, can show evidence of successful attempts at integrating procedures. Other features of co-operation of this type are personnel exchange or joint staff training designed to enable employees coming from different organizations to execute similar tasks.

In the third type of co-operation, type C (co-operation through co-location), actors combine efforts in one counter or at one location. These joint activities are generally aimed at a part of the implementation process (for example, client intake) or focus on specific client groups (for example, Melkert candidates or young unemployed).

Finally type D co-operation (co-operation in a joint venture) represents the most far-reaching form of co-operation. In type D, distinct organizations previously involved in the implementation of ALMP measures are merged into one executing body. Distinct procedures previously carried out by these various organizations are handled by a single organization jointly staffed by personnel stemming from different actors.

3 CASE-STUDY RESULTS

Intensive case studies were carried out in four municipalities, each representing one of the four types of co-operation between the municipality and the PES outlined above: basic co-operation, co-operation in human resources, co-operation by co-location and co-operation through a joint venture. The four cases will be described in terms of the type of actors involved in local implementation, the mutual relationships between the actors, and the processes and clients on which co-operation is focused.

3.1 Case A: Basic Co-operation

In municipality 'A', co-operation in the implementation of all four schemes has been confined to the interaction between two actors: the municipality via the municipal social service, and the municipal foundation established for implementation of the labour pool and GYEA measures. The staff of the municipal foundation was drawn in part from a temporary employment agency, and in part from the municipality. Inter-organizational ties between the two actors were very strong both at the managerial and the implementation level.

Co-operation failure between PES and municipality

Typically in this municipality, ties between the PES and the two other key players – the municipality and the municipal foundation – have hardly developed in the course of the 1990s. The role of the local PES in implementation of the four measures can be best described as being almost negligible. Following the introduction of the labour pool in the municipality, an agreement was reached between the municipality and the PES governing the implementation of the scheme. Occasional consultation took place among the PES, the municipal foundation and the municipality. Information exchange occurred only at the implementation level; never at the managerial level.

There was a serious failure in referral of labour pool candidates by the PES to the municipal foundation during the initial stage of the measure, resulting in too few candidates. The municipality accused the PES of deliberately obstructing labour pool implementation. The PES acknowledged its failure to refer a sufficient number of suitable candidates, but stated that the municipal foundation demanded skilled long-term unemployed candidates, who were usually not available. The municipality ceased co-operation with the PES and decided to refer candidates itself. Potential participants were selected from the long-term unemployed receiving social benefit assistance. Labour pool implementation thus became an entirely municipal province. The municipality referred clients to the municipal foundation, which then placed candidates in the measure.

There were also similar problems concerning the implementation of the GYEA scheme. Both the PES and the municipality acknowledged that insufficient attention was given by the PES to unemployed youth, and that agreements concluded with respect to their division of labour in implementing the scheme were not adhered to. Thus the PES failed in its task of adequately referring youth for the GYEA schemes.

Moreover, although an agreement had been drawn up stipulating the shared responsibility of the PES and the municipal foundation in placing GYEA participants in regular jobs; in practice the PES was not involved in these activities. This was due, on the one hand, to the low priority the PES gave to unemployed youth as a target group, and, on the other, to the fact that GYEA participants succeeded to a considerable extent in finding regular jobs without the help of a mediating organization. When necessary, the municipal foundation itself – through its relations with employers – proved able to place participants into regular jobs. The fact that the municipal foundation originally had ties with a temporary employment agency contributed significantly to successful placements. The PES reported that it was seldom informed on the status of individual clients participating in the GYEA, and that the municipal foundation only transferred client information in the case of a successful placement out of the measure and into a regular job. In 1995, an attempt was made by the municipal foundation to establish a 'youth counter' within the local PES office. This scheme failed, however, due to strategic reasons (in the view of the municipal foundation). Since 1996, the PES and the municipality have regularly, but informally, consulted each other on GYEA candidates. This consultation has taken place at the implementation level.

The municipal foundation was primarily responsible for the implementation of Melkert 1 municipal jobs. The foundation made use of participants in its other ALMP measures and of municipal social service clients. The joint activities of the municipality and the municipal foundation included informing candidates and employers. The Melkert 1 jobs in the health sector were solely implemented by the local PES. The municipal foundation intended to join the PES in this field, but attempts to establish co-operation have so far failed.

Several organizations in the region, such as municipal foundations, were involved in the implementation of Melkert 2 projects. Within municipality 'A', Melkert 2 vacancies were presented by the municipal foundation in the local PES office. Most of the participants in this measure were, however, referred to the foundation by the municipal social service. The acquisition of Melkert 2 jobs among employers was wholly the task of the municipal foundation.

Municipal foundation as key player in ALMP

In time, the PES came to regard the municipal foundation with suspicion as a rival employment service. The municipal foundation had indeed become a significant player in the personnel allocation market, and had been given the responsibility by the municipality of carrying out a substantial part of local labour market policy. For example, the municipal foundation began placing young benefit recipients into regular jobs, sometimes even before they were eligible for the GYEA – a task that was originally handled by the PES. The municipality saw the efforts of the municipal foundation as being in its interest because they helped reduce claims for social benefit assistance and local unemployment.

In the course of the 1990s, several attempts were made to improve the relationships between the PES on the one hand, and the municipality and the municipal foundation on the other. The fact that most of these attempts failed appears to be due to unwillingness at the managerial level of the organizations involved. Some respondents interviewed indicated that organizational strategies merely aimed at surviving through organizational expansion, rather than at serving the interests of target groups. Until the late 1990s, the local situation clearly showed the absence of a climate for co-operation between key actors in the field of reintegrating long-term unemployed. Mutual confidence among the PES, the municipality and the municipal foundation gradually increased under national pressure for co-ordinated local labour market policy, resulting in more or less structured co-ordination among the three actors. However, as one of the respondents in this municipality stated: 'Co-operation can be enforced neither through legislation nor regulation; the organizations involved should acknowledge each other's capabilities.' At the time this research was carried out it was obvious that the municipal foundation, in particular, was very much intent on maintaining its position as the key player in the local labour market.

3.2 Case B: Co-operation through Joint Staff

Case B represents a local implementation structure in which the municipality and the PES co-operated by jointly allocating staff to teams. This type of co-operation originated in the early 1990s and was contractually fixed. One of the reasons for the municipality's willingness to co-operate with the PES was the increased awareness of the need for an intensification of efforts aimed at reintegrating the long-term unemployed. Because of the local PES's expertise in the area of reintegration strategies, the municipality considered it to be the most suitable partner in this undertaking. Small teams consisting of both municipality and PES staff were responsible for offering intensive training and guidance to the hard-to-place unemployed. This form of co-operation was not aimed exclusively at the implementation of the schemes included in this study, but placement of clients into such schemes as the labour pool and the GYEA was nevertheless an essential part of the teams' activities.

Municipal unit including PES staff

The actual implementation of the labour pool and the GYEA schemes was the responsibility of a municipal foundation consisting of personnel from various departments of the municipal social service office. The strong municipal influence is furthermore illustrated by the fact that the municipal foundation was located within the municipal social service. The municipal foundation was staffed by the above-mentioned mixed teams of PES and municipal personnel. This entire cluster of units concerned with reintegrating long-term unemployed constituted the municipal 'outflow section'.[30] With respect to the implementation of the labour pool, the PES carried out its task of client referral as defined in legislation. Since the labour pool was used as the last resort for the hard-to-place, no activities were undertaken to place participants leaving the measure into regular work. In the view of the municipal social service, the PES was hardly involved in the reintegration of GYEA participants for reasons of 'creaming'. Typically the PES reported a lack of information on client flows that were temporarily the responsibility of the municipal foundation, and hence felt that participants in the labour pool and GYEA lacked proper guidance or advice.

Following a two-year period during which organizational interaction was reduced for strategic reasons, co-operation between the PES and the municipality was renewed in 1994. The municipality and the PES began exchanging personnel in order to gain better insight into the working procedures of their respective organizations. In a latter stage, personnel from the two organizations were jointly allocated to business units carrying out intake, guidance and placement of clients. Staff from both the municipality and the PES were trained to carry out similar activities. In 1997 this type of co-operation between the PES and the municipality ceased to exist. On the one hand, this was caused by organizational reforms within the PES; on the other, the introduction of purchase contracts (see section 1) hindered fruitful co-operation since it changed the mutual ties into a more businesslike client–purchaser relationship. Typically co-operation between the two organizations was reinstated in the same year by the introduction of a team consisting of a PES employee and a member of the municipal social service. The main goal in establishing this team was to improve information exchange on client flows. In the second half of 1997, a co-ordination unit was established which incorporated a representative of the PES and of the municipal social service. Within this team, information on individual clients was exchanged and co-ordination of further client-oriented actions took place. This team was also responsible for the flow of GYEA and labour pool participants into regular jobs.

The implementation of the Melkert 1 scheme was the main responsibility of a distinct Melkert 1 organization, which was added to the above-mentioned municipal outflow section. The relationship between the Melkert 1 organization and the PES was mediated by this section. Relationships with other actors in this field, such as temporary employment agencies, were relatively loose and informal. The Melkert 2 scheme was implemented by the municipality in co-operation with both the PES and private employment services. Following the introduction of the measure, the municipality was able to compare the cost-effectiveness of measure implementation by these organizations. In the view of the municipality, private employment agencies proved to be less familiar with the typical client group of hard-to-place unemployed. The local PES was, therefore, the preferred implementation partner; with temporary employment agencies operating in a supporting role.

Notwithstanding the breaks in the shared history of co-operation, confidence evolved between the municipality and the PES. This proved to be an important determinant of the climate for organizational interaction between the two implementing actors, resulting in the establishment of mixed co-ordination teams and business units. Although the PES did not initially condone the fact that local labour market policy – in terms of the implementation of the four schemes – was strongly influenced by the municipality, the parties seem to have developed a mode for joint measure implementation.

3.3 Case C: Co-operation through Co-location

In municipality 'C', an implementation structure was developed in which the key actors in active labour market policy were co-located. In addition to the PES, the municipal social service and the municipal foundation for the implementation of the labour pool and the GYEA, five private employment services and one Uvi were included.

Co-location in job centre with mixed teams

The co-location of key actors in ALMP, which took place in 1995, was preceded by the establishment of a co-ordination team in 1994. The teams were housed in various PES offices within the municipality and were each composed of representatives from the municipal social service, the local PES office and the single municipal foundation for labour pool and GYEA implementation. The main goal of these teams was to co-ordinate flows of mutual clients and client-directed activities better, and to enable constant feedback on individual clients under the direction of the PES representative. Perhaps even more important than the co-ordination of client flows was the fact that organizations were given a means of communicating directly with each other, and thus gained insight into the respective policy views of their co-operation partners. In addition to the co-ordination teams that dealt with, among others, labour pool and GYEA clients, co-operation occurred through monthly consultations in what was called a 'GYEA platform', which was mainly concerned with practical matters of GYEA implementation.

In the view of the PES, the municipal labour pool/GYEA foundation had played a key role in the realization of co-location. The PES and the municipality had traditionally had conflicting strategic interests. The municipal foundation was regarded by both the PES and the municipality as a neutral partner; notwithstanding the fact that the foundation originally had strong municipal ties. In bilateral meetings, the foundation succeeded in reducing resistance to co-operation from the PES and the municipality. The foundation had a considerable stake in establishing co-operation in order to improve its own placement results for the long-term unemployed. In particular, the know-how of the local PES was regarded as crucial to successful placement activities. The foundation also depended largely on the local PES and the municipal social service for the recruitment of potential participants in the measures.

The Melkert 1 measure was carried out by the municipal labour pool/GYEA foundation, which received clients from the municipal social service. The PES was consulted about additional activities, such as training. Co-operation with private employment services generally occurred on an *ad hoc* basis, and had an informal character.

Distinct municipal actor competing with PES

The co-ordinating actor in the implementation of Melkert 2 was an independent foundation which had originally been a part of the municipal labour pool/GYEA foundation. Initially the implementation of the Melkert 2 scheme had been contracted out by the municipality to a commercial organization in co-operation with the PES. After implementation halted in 1996, the municipality decided to have the Melkert 2 measure carried out by a section of the municipal foundation. Formal organizational ties were then loosened between this section and the municipality, with the newly established Melkert 2 foundation being directed from a distance by the municipality and the municipal foundation. The Melkert 2 foundation, led by a manager assigned by the municipality, recruited its staff from the commercial organization initially responsible for the measure. Inter-organizational co-operation between the Melkert 2 foundation and the labour pool/GYEA foundation pertained to client referral and vacancy consultation. With other actors in the area of Melkert 2 (for example, project organizations and private employment services), the foundation concluded agreements on procedures regarding client referral and vacancy submission. Typically the PES acted as a second principal player in this area – and thus competed with the Melkert 2 foundation – by jointly implementing the Melkert 2 scheme with a temporary employment agency.

Co-location facilitates mutual communication

Co-operation in terms of consultation and information exchange between the various actors took place at distinct levels. The job centre was managed by a steering group consisting of the directors of each organization participating in the centre. Steering group meetings took place every two months. Line managers of the participating organizations made up the management team responsible for the implementation of working procedures. The management team gathered once every four to six weeks. At the implementation level, parties met two to three times a week in order to discuss vacancies. Furthermore, at this level, employees from the distinct organizations established cross-organizational one-on-one relations in order to solve practical problems or to discuss implementation procedures. The very existence of these so-called 'short lines of communication' was regarded as one of the strengths of the job centre. Co-operation between private employment services scarcely occurred, which may have been be due to a lack of trust.

3.4 Case D: Co-operation in a Joint Venture

In case D all organizations involved in reintegrating the hard-to-place were incorporated into a single body responsible for the local implementation of the reintegration measures. This organization was a joint venture of the municipality and the regional PES established in the first half of the 1990s. At that time, both the PES and the municipality were convinced that they had a mutual purpose in fighting long-term unemployment, and thus in reintegrating the hard-to-place. Moreover, both parties agreed that the responsibility for the implementation of active measures should be assigned to the local authorities, although the regional PES board retained the supervision and co-ordination of active labour market policy in the region. This was an exception to the general view that the PES should be primarily responsible for the implementation of programmes for the reintegration of the hard-to-place unemployed. The decision to shift implementation responsibility to the municipalities in this particular region was set down in a framework agreement. Furthermore, the municipal government wished to streamline reintegration activities that were then carried out in the municipality by about two dozen public and private organizations. These considerations resulted in the establishment of a joint implemention body incorporating all former organizations, including part of their staff. The PES equipped the joint venture with personnel by seconding placement officers. The above-mentioned framework agreement foresaw quantitative goals set annually by the PES, defined in terms of placements or pre-placement routes.

Both the PES and the municipality were represented in the board of the joint venture. A municipal representative directed the organization and handled the day-to-day responsibilities, thus underlining the influence of the municipality on the implementing body. In the initial financing structure, a fixed amount was allotted to the joint venture by the PES for each client placement. This system prevailed in the period 1993–6. Thereafter the joint venture began operating as a subcontractor of the PES on a portion of the activities aimed at the reintegration of the hard-to-place. With respect to the labour pool, the GYEA and the Melkert schemes, however, the joint venture, as the 'preferred implementing body', had the exclusive right to conclude contracts with the municipality.

Willingness to co-operate evolved at the local level

Although legislation on the labour pool and the GYEA stipulated the interaction between the PES and the municipality, the central government's insistence upon co-operation hardly played a role in the establishment of the joint venture. As one respondent put it: 'Centrally imposed co-ordination structures cannot be successful. Only spontaneous co-operation which arises from the willingness of decentralized actors to interact may be fruitful. Furthermore, successful locally based co-operation depends on the establishment of ties between decentralized government and local business for the supervision of labour market policy.' Another respondent stated that the development of local level co-operation relied heavily on the intentions of key persons in the regional PES board and the municipal government. It may indeed be the case that inter-organizational ties were important facilitators in establishing mutual understanding and ongoing willingness to participate.

Clients who could not be placed in vacancies immediately were referred by the local PES office to the joint venture. Three teams of the joint venture were responsible for client screening or profiling. One team, half of which consisted of PES staff, handled clients who had been directly referred by the PES. This team was located within the joint venture's office. A second team made up of personnel stemming wholly from the municipal social service was responsible for screening or profiling clients receiving social assistance. Screening methods tended to differ between the municipal intake team and the PES team, although there was no evidence that this led to significantly different outcomes with respect to placement into measures. The third team, spread over decentralized locations, focused on persons who were identified as currently having little chance of finding paid employment. After identifying the need for additional skills, all three teams established individual action plans for their respective clients in which they specified the necessary activities to be initiated. Training and education activities were partly carried out by the joint venture, while services were also being purchased from the PES and other specialized agencies.

In implementing the Melkert 1 measure, the joint venture placed people into jobs allocated by central authorities. The central government was responsible for the provision of municipal jobs and the health-care sector bodies for health-care jobs. In 1996 all allocated Melkert 1 places were filled. In implementing the Melkert 2 scheme, the joint venture maintained (more or less close) relations with private employment agencies, although these ties were not contractually fixed.

Integrating back office and front office activities

Inspired by the successful implementation of the joint venture, the municipality, the PES and one of the organizations responsible for carrying out the system of unemployment benefits decided in 1996 to broaden the existing implementation network. Plans were made to co-locate the joint venture with the centre for work and income in the course of 1998. In practical terms, this means that the office where unemployed job seekers flow in, as well as the office responsible for their outflow into regular jobs, are now located under one roof, thus establishing a full integration of all activities aimed at the reintegration of unemployed.

3.5 Conclusion

One of the key findings which can be derived from the case studies is the relevance of informal contacts, communication and subsequent co-operation. This generally seems to occur at the implementation level, even if managers from respective organizations are not on speaking terms. This does not necessarily hinder fruitful implementation. Several times respondents stated that centrally enforced or mandated co-operation could hardly be successful without the willingness of local implementing actors to interact. This is best illustrated by the implementation structure described in case A. Furthermore, in case A, the fact that actors at the management level lacked mutual trust significantly complicated implementation of the labour pool and the GYEA, although no evidence exists that this was at the cost of target group members.[31]

It should be noted that the attitude of the implementing actors towards mutual co-operation in local labour market policy not only differs among the municipalities, but also varies over time. This may be partly explained by the changing strategy of the national PES in the course of the 1990s. The Dutch PES is frequently criticized and regarded with scepticism.[32] In order to legitimate its role in labour market policy, the PES seeks to obtain a significant market share. Local PES offices have therefore been directed to focus their activities on job seekers whose prospects are favourable. In a number of cases, this has meant a reduced PES involvement in schemes for the long-term unemployed and other target groups. However, recent governments have urged the PES to stick to its core task; namely, reintegrating members of target groups, such as women, youth, long-term unemployed and ethnic minorities. Case B represents a situation in which the PES varied its involvement in activities aimed at the hard-to-place in the course of the 1990s.

Case C exemplifies the development of an implementation structure towards co-location via mixed teams of ALMP actors. According to respondents, the absence of physical barriers proved to be an essential facilitator for (informal) communication, resulting in an improved fine-tuning of client-directed activities.

From case D we may learn that a strong consensus on the issue at stake (namely reintegrating the hard-to-place) can bring implementing actors closer together. Obviously the awareness of the parties involved has helped them to cope with possible conflicting organizational and strategic interests, thus enabling physical and organizational integration of tasks and working procedures.

In the following section, we will compare the various co-operation types and attempt to determine the impact of co-operation on the performances of implementation structures.

4 COMPARING CO-OPERATION STRUCTURES

4.1 Measuring and Scaling Co-operation

On the basis of the case-study results, a stylized overview can be given of the extent to which features of co-operation are present within the implementation structure of active labour market policy.

Table 9.3 shows that cases A and D constitute the two ends of a co-operation continuum from low to intense co-operation, while cases B and C lie in between these two extremes. In order to establish an ordinal scale – and thus determine whether we are dealing with an ascending order of co-operation in this case study – we must attribute values to the different co-operation indicators. Here we assume that co-operation has been maximized when it has been physically institutionalized by means of a joint venture or a single organization. We therefore consider physical-organisational features as the most significant indicators of co-operation, followed by co-operation in the field of human resources and, finally, joint consultation and information exchange. The presence of physical-organizational characteristics in a particular implementation structure does not necessarily imply that human resource features can also be observed in this local network. In case C, for instance, no formal joint training or staff exchange was determined, although implementing actors are co-located. In this case, co-location typically enabled a high number of informal brief transfers of staff, as well as joint on-the-job training through *ad hoc* instructions. When applying the ascending order of co-operation as presented in Table 9.3, we should be aware that, in some cases, co-operation indicators may have a highly informal and latent

Table 9.3 Characteristics of co-operation found in the cases

Co-operation indicators		Case A	Case B	Case C	Case D
Physical-organizational	co-location	–	–/+	+	+
	shared desk/counter	–	–	–/+	–/+
	single organization/joint venture	–	–	–	+
Human resources	joint training	–	+	–/+	+
	staff exchange	–	+	–/+	+
	joint personnel allocation	–	–/+	–/+	+
Technical–communicative	irregular/*ad hoc* consultation	+	+	+	++
	regular/structural consultation	–/+	+	++	++
	shared client info-system	–	–/+	+	+

Note: – : absent within the implementation structure; –/+ : partly present within the structure;[33] + : applies to the structure as a whole; ++ : strongly applies to the structure as a whole.

character, but are nevertheless present, thus facilitating co-operation between implementing actors.

4.2 Performance Comparison of Co-operation Structures

There are a variety of concepts of 'performance'.[34] In this study we are interested in the outcomes of implementation structures. In order to assess the impact of distinct co-operation types, we will use three performance indicators: coverage, positive outcomes, and duration. Coverage or 'policy uptake' is defined as the extent of target group coverage, that is, the number of participants flowing into a measure during a year divided by the total size of the target group in the labour force. This coverage indicator provides us with information on the ability of implementing actors to actually reach the target group: the higher the share of target group members reached or covered the 'better' an implementation structure is operating.

In addition to coverage we also examine the positive outflow rate, that is, the number of participants leaving a measure and flowing into either a regular job, another ALMP measure, or a training course expressed as a percentage of all participants in the measure at the end of the previous year. A high 'positive outflow rate' is regarded as being an indicator for the success of the ALMP implementation regime in facilitating positive transitions. Finally, duration is the average time participants spend in the measure. Since all measures have initially been set up to reintegrate people into regular employment, one can argue that the quicker an unemployed person leaves a measure the more successful such 'reintegration tools' function. 'Duration' is defined as the number of persons flowing into the measure as a share of the stock at the end of the year; higher values on this indicator mean a shorter average duration of time spent in a measure.

In order to obtain a composite indicator for the performance of the municipal implementation regimes we calculate an overall 'effectiveness' indicator based on the multiple of the three component indicators. 'Coverage' represents the degree to which actors manage to succeed in the first goal of the measure, helping people to leave long-term unemployment through participation in ALMP schemes; 'duration' and 'positive outflow' indicators together show the extent to which actors meet the second goal of the measure, successful transitions out of the programme. We weigh both goals equally by including coverage twice in the formula for calculating the composite indicator. In the resulting indicator high values for 'effectiveness', resulting from high coverage rates and short duration, in combination with high positive outflow rates represent successful implementation.[35]

Some indicators reported represent approximations owing to limitations in municipal statistics. Thus, although the target group for the labour pool are persons unemployed for over three years, coverage is defined here as a percentage of those unemployed more than one year. The GYEA data are based in part on estimates due to differences in the definitions of age cohorts in municipal statistics.[36]

The labour pool and GYEA measures offer the best monitoring data on the base of which performance indicators might be derived. Table 9.4 shows annual average coverage, duration, and positive outflow indicators for the labour pool and GYEA programmes.[37] In the case-study municipalities we find no clear relationship between the development of co-operation in implementation regimes and the performance indicators examined. While co-operation increases from case A to case D this is reflected only in part in higher levels of performance. Thus the performance indicators for the labour pool are lowest in all three instances for case D, where co-operation is highest (joint venture), whereas case C is the top performer on the coverage and positive outflow indicators and time in the measure is shortest in case B. The composite 'effectiveness' indicator for labour pool shows that overall performance in case D is even lower than in case A where co-operation is least developed.

We conclude that C and (to a lesser extent) A and B perform best, while the municipality with the highest degree of co-operation is the worst performer. One possible explanation for the relatively low labour pool performances in case D might be that the maximum co-operation type (joint venture) entails a complex decision-making process that impedes the capacity of the implementation structure to respond to labour market developments. Thus case D can be interpreted as evidence for a situation in which there are declining returns to co-operation.

In contrast to the labour pool for the long-term unemployed, the overall 'effectiveness' indicator for the GYEA youth programme's implementation regime shows the expected increase in performance as co-operation increases. There are, however, sometimes inconsistencies in individual performance dimensions, for example, case C and not case D shows the best performance with respect to coverage. Although a high level of co-operation does not necessarily entail high performance, the case A in which co-operation is least developed performs worst in terms of overall 'effectiveness' for both programmes owing to relatively poor results on duration and positive outflows.

This simple juxtaposition of types of co-operation and performance cannot, of course, control for the impact of other factors affecting performance such as clientèle characteristics (for example, presence of ethnic minorities) and labour market conditions (for example, unemployment rate), although the observed differences in the case-study municipalities do not appear to be large enough to 'explain' the lack of a consistent relationship between co-operation and performance. Such an analysis is possible but would require

Table 9.4 Performance indicators by municipality and ALMP programme, 1991–7

	Case A (basic co-operation)	Case B (joint staff)	Case C (co-location)	Case D (joint-venture)	National
Labour pool target group[a]					
Average 1991–7	0.024	0.039	0.068	0.011	n.a.
Labour pool duration[b]					
Average 1991–7	0.31	0.38	0.31	0.18	n.a.
Labour pool positive outflow rate[c]					
Average 1991–7	0.09	0.04	0.09	0.09	n.a.
Labour pool effectiveness					
coverage * duration * positive outflow	0.007	0.006	0.019	0.002	n.a.
GYEA target group coverage[d]					
Average 1992–7	0.093	0.058	0.139	0.128	0.102
GYEA duration[b]					
Average 1992–7	0.42	0.75	0.85	0.86	0.80
GYEA positive outflow rate[c]					
Average 1992–7	0.20	0.46	0.34	0.49	n.a.
GYEA effectiveness					
coverage * duration * positive outflow	0.0078	0.0200	0.0402	0.0539	n.a.
Melkert 1					
Target group coverage entrants 1995–7[b]	0.0213	0.0187	0.0238	0.0155	0.0246
Melkert 2					
Target group coverage entrants 1995–7[b]	0.0095	n.a.	0.0143	0.0109	0.0300

Notes:

[a] Number of programme participants at t flowing into the measure as a share of target group at t–1. Due to differences in municipal data, target group set at registered unemployed > 1 year.

[b] Number of people flowing out of the measure as a share of total number in that measure at t.

[c] Number of people at t flowing out of the measure into regular job, training place or other ALMP measure as a share of the total participants in the measure at end of t–1.

[d] Number of programme participants at t flowing into the measure as a share of target group at t–1. Target group set at registered unemployed aged < 27 years. Group size estimated for three cases due to differences in municipal data.

Source: Local data from municipalities, national data from Ministry of Social Affairs and Employment.

more systematic data for additional control variables for all municipalities and for a number of years, which are not available.

Based on the limited data available for 19 municipalities, we analysed performance data for the labour pool and GYEA programmes. Table 9.5 reports the cross correlations between performance indicators and labour market and clientèle characteristics using a pooled data set for the years 1996 and 1997. The results show that municipal implementation structures that have higher positive programme outcome rates for the labour pool measure for the long-term unemployed also tend to do well on the same indicator for the GYEA scheme for unemployed youth (+0.566). The reasons for relative success on this important indicator are not entirely clear. Interestingly, labour market variables such as the rates for general unemployment and very long-term unemployment (more than three years) seem not to be related to this (or other) performance indicators. A partial explanation may be found in the choice of ALMP strategies. In the case of the GYEA scheme, coverage rate and positive outflow are inversely related: implementation structures with higher positive outflows tend to have lower coverage rates (–0.618). A similar pattern is observed for the labour pool scheme, although the results are here not statistically significant. A possible interpretation is that creaming is more prevalent in programmes with low coverage.

The high correlations between the incidence of social assistance recipients and long-term unemployment (+0.797) at the municipal level clearly reflect the special labour market constellation that is the reason for recent efforts to strengthen co-operation between the PES and municipal social assistance carriers. The aggregate data examined do not, however, show any relationship between these clientèle characteristics and programme performance.

Finally, the relationship between co-operation and ALMP programme performance was examined. Based on the ranking of co-operation forms reported in Figure 9.1, the relationship between two dimensions of co-operation, human resources co-operation and physical co-operation and ALMP performance was examined. The rank order correlation results for 19 municipalities in the 1996–7 period provide little evidence for a co-operation effect on the performance indicators examined. The only significant relationship observed is that between physical co-operation (for example, co-location, joint venture) and positive outflows in the GYEA youth programme (+0.494; Table 9.6). The data also show the same strong inverse relationship between coverage and positive ouflows for the GYEA scheme noted above (–0.642).

5 CONCLUSIONS

In this chapter we have examined the forms of co-operation that have evolved in the course of the 1990s in Dutch municipalities with respect to the implementation of four job-creation schemes. Rules and legislation either

Table 9.5 Correlation matrix for labour market variables and performance indicators, 1996–7

		LP positive outflows	LP coverage	GYEA coverage	GYEA positive outflows	Unemployment	Social assistance	Minorities	Long-term unemployment
LP positive outflows	Pearson coefficient	1	–0.207	0.379	0.566*	–0.051	0.188	–0.097	0.181
	sign. (two-tailed)	–	0.343	0.062	0.028	0.809	0.379	0.643	0.386
	N	25	23	25	15	25	24	25	25
LP coverage	Pearson coefficient	–0.207	1	0.372*	–0.489*	–0.162	–0.062	0.053	–0.127
	sign. (two-tailed)	0.343	–	0.039	0.046	0.383	0.754	0.778	0.505
	N	23	31	31	17	31	28	31	30
GYEA coverage	Pearson coefficient	0.379	0.372*	1	–0.618**	0.016	–0.056	–0.219	0.195
	sign. (two-tailed)	0.062	0.039	–	0.008	0.926	0.759	0.205	0.269
	N	25	31	35	17	35	32	35	34
GYEA positive outflows	Pearson coefficient	0.566*	–0.489*	–0.618**	1	–0.178	0.068	–0.067	–0.167
	sign. (two-tailed)	0.028	0.046	0.008	–	0.494	0.804	0.798	0.521
	N	15	17	17	17	17	16	17	17
Unemployment	Pearson coefficient	–0.051	–0.162	0.016	–0.178	1	0.657**	0.183	0.772**
	sign. (two-tailed)	0.809	0.383	0.926	0.494	–	0.000	0.271	0.000
	N	25	31	35	17	38	35	38	37
Social assistance	Pearson coefficient	0.188	–0.062	–0.056	0.068	0.657*	1	0.585**	0.797**
	sign. (two-tailed)	0.379	0.754	0.759	0.804	0.000	–	0.000	0.000
	N	24	28	32	16	35	35	35	35
Minorities	Pearson coefficient	–0.097	0.053	–0.219	–0.067	0.183	0.585**	1	0.434**
	sign. (two-tailed)	0.643	0.778	0.205	0.798	0.271	0.000	–	0.007
	N	25	31	35	17	38	35	38	37
Long-term unemployment	Pearson coefficient	0.181	–0.127	0.195	–0.167	0.772**	0.797**	0.434**	1
	sign. (two-tailed)	0.386	0.505	0.269	0.521	0.000	0.000	0.007	–
	N	25	30	34	17	37	35	37	37

Notes: *Significant on 0.05 level (two-tailed); **significant at 0.01 level; positive outflow rate = participants leaving measure for regular job, another measure or training; coverage = stock of programme participants at year's end as percentage of target group in labour force; minorities = ethnic minorities as percentage of population 15–64 years as of 1 January 1997; social assistance = social assistance recipients as percentage of population 15–64 years as of 1 January 1997; unemployment = average unemployment rate 1992–4; long-term unemployment = long-term unemployment rate (> 3 years) 1995–6.

Table 9.6 Rank order–correlation of co-operation and ALMP performance indicators, 1996–7

		PHYSCOOP	HUMACOOP	RLPSC	RPOSOUTR	RGYSC	RGYPOSR
PHYSCOOP	Pearson coefficient	1	0.497**	0.227	0.042	–0.248	0.494*
	sign. (two-tailed)	–	0.001	0.220	0.842	0.150	0.044
	N	38	38	31	25	35	17
HUMACOOP	Pearson coefficient	0.497**	1	0.126	–0.046	–0.224	0.252
	sign. (two-tailed)	0.001	–	0.498	0.826	0.196	0.328
	N	38	38	31	25	35	17
RLPSC	Pearson coefficient	0.227	0.126	1	–0.089	0.362*	–0.404
	sign. (two-tailed)	0.220	0.498	–	0.687	0.045	0.107
	N	31	31	31	23	31	17
RPOSOUTR	Pearson coefficient	0.042	–0.046	–0.089	1	0.378	0.396
	sign. (two-tailed)	0.842	0.826	0.687	–	0.063	0.413
	N	25	25	23	25	25	15
RGYSC	Pearson coefficient	–0.248	–0.224	0.362*	0.378	1	–0.642**
	sign. (two-tailed)	0.150	0.196	0.045	0.063	–	0.005
	N	35	35	31	25	35	17
RGYPOSR	Pearson coefficient	0.494*	0.252	–0.404	0.396	–0.642**	1
	sign. (two-tailed)	0.044	0.328	0.107	0.413	0.005	–
	N	17	17	17	15	17	17

Notes: * Significant on 0.05 level (two-tailed); ** significant on 0.01 level (two-tailed); PHYSCOOP = physical co-operation features; HUMACOOP = human resources co-operation features; RLPSC = labour pool target group coverage; RPOSOUTR = positive outflow labour pool; RGYSC = GYEA target group coverage; RGYPOSR = positive outflow GYEA.

enforced (GYEA and labour pool) or enabled (Melkert 1 and Melkert 2) co-operation at the municipal level. Within this framework, a variety of co-operation forms in the implementation of ALMP measures for the long-term unemployed have been identified for the period up to 1997. The types of co-operation ranged from minimal co-operation between key actors (type A co-operation), to highly institutionalized co-operation in the form of a joint venture (type D co-operation). In between these extremes, two types of co-operation have been identified; one in which implementing bodies acted together by exchanging staff (type B co-operation), and another in which actors responsible for scheme implementation were physically co-located (type C co-operation). To gain better insight into local level implementation, four municipalities were selected for more intensive case studies; each representing one of the four co-operation types. We then examined the impact of co-operation forms on performance indicators for these schemes.

What have we learned about local level co-operation as a facilitator of transitions from unemployment to work? This study shows that co-operation characterized by close physical proximity of the implementing actors and short horizontal, inter-organizational ties enhances implementation as measured by uptake of target group members into the measure. Co-operation which has been further developed in terms of the organizational integration of actors and working procedures does not necessarily lead to better policy outcomes, as illustrated by case D with respect to implementation of the labour pool. One explanation might be that decision-making in such an implementation structure involves consensus-building and negotiations among all organizations participating in the joint venture. These time-consuming processes possibly hinder timely and effective policy implementation.

These outcomes and explanations strongly depend, of course, on the indicators applied. What we set out to do in the present study was to determine the impact of co-operation on policy outcomes of policies produced by co-operating actors. Although we have attempted to open the black box of the policy implementation process, the assessment of co-operation effects remains a very difficult task, and our analysis merely provides indirect evidence for the impact of the interaction of implementing actors.

More importantly, the study has provided us with evidence on preconditions for co-operation. Centrally imposed co-operation structures seem to work – that is, co-operation between actors actually occurs – only if local key players are willing to interact. If implementing actors are not willing to co-operate – for example, due to a lack of confidence, fear of loss of autonomy or dissatisfaction with the co-operation partner's performance – the chances that co-operation will occur appear to be very small. This, however, does not necessarily imply that the implementation of measures cannot be successful. Where co-operation does not develop satisfactorily, key actors individually seek ways to promote efficient and effective implementation. The absence in these cases of a local climate for co-operation should not be regarded as something 'bad'. Actors seek and find, within the constraints imposed by local circumstances, the optimal structure for implementing measures. Enforcing co-operation for the sake of co-operation may only intervene in the process of creating an optimal local constellation for the implementation of ALMP. It therefore seems wise to regard co-operation as one possible means for the implementation of ALMP but not as a goal in itself.

LIST OF ABBREVIATIONS AND DUTCH NAMES

Abw (Algemene bijstandswet): national assistance act
ALMP: active labour market policy
Arbeidsvoorzieningswet: employment service act
Ctsv (College van toezicht sociale verzekeringen): social security supervision board
CWI (Centrum voor Werk en Inkomen): centre for work and income
EAU (Subsidieregeling experimenten activering uitkeringsgelden): experiments on activation through benefit application
EWLW (Extra werkgelegenheid langdurig werklozen): measure on extra employment for the long-term unemployed
GSB (Grotestedenbeleid): major cities policy
GYEA: see JWG
JWG (Jeugdwerkgarantiewet): guaranteed youth employment act
Lisv (Landelijk instituut sociale verzkeringen): national institute for social security
Melkert 1: see EWLW
Melkert 2: see EAU
Osv (Organisatiewet sociale verzekeringen): act on the organization of social insurances
PES: public employment service
Rijksbijdrageregeling Banenpool: labour pool scheme
SAB: social assistance benefit
SVr (Sociale Verzekeringsraad): social insurance council
UB: unemployment benefit
Uvis (Uitvoeringsinstellingen): private administration bodies
WW (Werkloosheidswet): unemployment benefit act
Wiw (Wet inschakeling werkzoekenden): act on the deployment of unemployed job seekers
WAO (Wet op de arbeidsongeschiktheid): disability benefit act

NOTES

1. Hugo Sinzheimer Institute, University of Amsterdam (velzen@jur.uva.nl). Many thanks go to Stefan Speckesser for his tremendous work in the data analysis and for constructive discussion on the content of this chapter. The author is also grateful to Hugh Mosley and Ton Wilthagen for their helpful comments on earlier versions of this study. Adriaan van Liempt and Antje Mayer have been of invaluable research assistance. The empirical work would not have been possible without the co-operation of PES representatives, managers of municipal social services, and directors of municipal foundations in the municipalities studied.
2. See OECD (1998, pp. 63ff).
3. PES budgets have to be approved by the parliament. In 1997 the Ministry of Social Affairs and Employment allocated approximately NLG 1 billion to the PES (1996: 1.5 billion), constituting over 60 per cent of the total PES budget. Complementary to this PES receives financial resources from, among others, the European Social Fund.
4. Contribution rates for employers and employees amounted to 5.55 per cent and 2.70 per cent, respectively, of an employee's salary (rates as of January 1997). Entitlement to unemployment benefit depends on the length of the period a person has worked – and thus made contributions – prior to his unemployment.
5. After the year 2000 Uvis have to mutually compete in order to obtain administration contracts. Contracts may then be concluded between individual firms and a Uvi or between an industrial sector and a Uvi.
6. See Buurmeijer Commission (1993) for further reading on this.
7. The volume of people receiving disablement benefits (WAO) increased from 463 000 in 1980 to 569 000 in 1993 (1997: 510 000). The number of people receiving unemployment benefit (WW) grew from 69 000 in 1980 to 370 000 in 1996 (1997: 288 000). Finally the so-called inactive/active rate (the number of benefit recipients divided by the number of people having a paid job) developed from 65.7 (1980) to 83.2 (1985), 82.1 (1990) and 82.4 (1995) respectively. The increasing rate indicates a decrease of the financial support for the social security system. The rate for 1997 amounts to 77.6, showing the results of the policy in revitalizing the social security system. (Data derived from Ministry of Social Affairs and Employment.) See also OECD (1993, pp. 17ff).
8. The introduction of a more active labour market policy was already suggested by the Dutch Scientific Council in 1987. This advisory body to the cabinet identified the loose organizational ties between social security and public employment service as a possible cause for the relatively weak efforts that could be made to reintegrate the long-term unemployed (WRR, 1987). More recent and internationally directed recommendations with respect to an institutional integration of passive and active labour market policies can be found in OECD (1997).
9. Co-operation – albeit not always structured and on a regular basis – in the field of ALMP and benefit provision structures at the decentralized level has, to some extent, been present in the past two decades or so. A detailed report on regional co-operation structures at the beginning of the 1990s can be found in Esser *et al.* (1994).
10. See Van Dijk *et al.* (1995).
11. Van Dijk *et al.* (1995, p. 71).
12. See paragraph 144 of the National Assistance Act 1996 (*Abw 1996*) and the 1997 Decree on the Purchase of PES Services by Municipalities (*Besluit inkoop dienstverlening Arbeidsvoorziening door gemeenten 1997*). PES services purchased by municipalities amounted to NLG 35 million in 1996 and NLG 49 million in 1997. Uvis spent NLG 21 million in 1997 on PES services. After expiry of this 'truck system' in 2001 municipalities and Uvis are free to spend their budgets. The PES will then have to compete with commercial providers of guidance, training and placement services.
13. See paragraph 72 of Unemployment Benefits Act (*Werkloosheidswet*, WW), paragraph 111 of the National Assistance Act (*Algemene bijstandswet* ABW), paragraph 45 of Act on the Organization of Social Insurances 1997 (*Organisatiewet sociale verzekeringen*, Osv)

and paragraph 6 of Employment Service Act 1996 (*Arbeidsvoorzieningswet*). The emphasis that is laid on co-operation at local level implementation of labour market policy is particularly clear in the Act on the Deployment of Job Seekers (*Wet inschakeling werkzoekenden* wiw), which was enforced on 1 January 1998. In this Act municipalities not only carry the main responsibility for the reintegration of the long-term unemployed and other target groups (paragraph 2 wiw), it is also stipulated that co-operation should be realized between municipality, the public employment service and Uvis (paragraph 7 wiw). Furthermore, training providers and temporary employment agencies are likely to become partners of the local network for the implementation of labour market policy.

14. Cf. Schmid (1996), pp. 223ff.
15. The 19 cities that have been included in the major cities policy are: Almelo, Amsterdam, Arnhem, Breda, Den Bosch, Deventer, Enschede, Eindhoven, Groningen, Den Haag, Helmond, Hengelo, Leeuwarden, Maastricht, Nijmegen, Rotterdam, Tilburg, Utrecht, Zwolle.
16. See for an extensive overview: Rogers and Whetten (eds) (1982).
17. See for example: Laumann and Knoke (1987).
18. Other elements found to be relevant for improving placement results were: allocation of more personnel resources to target groups, conducting regular interviews with long-term unemployed, visiting potential employers, and finding vacancies corresponding to the capabilities of target group members.
19. Cf. Collins (1988, pp. 484ff).
20. Olsen (1965, p. 47). See also: Blau and Schoenherr (1971).
21. Halpert (1982, p. 68).
22. Named after Mr A.P.W. Melkert, Minister of Social Affairs and Employment, 1994–8.
23. Van Opstal *et al.* (1998).
24. Van der Aalst *et al.* (1993, pp. 15ff).
25. The definition of the GYEA target group has been modified in the course of time, initially comprising unemployed aged under 18 and unemployed school leavers up to 21 years.
26. This figure pertains to a 1996 evaluation. A 1994 study showed that over 30 per cent of the GYEA organizations was not satisfied with the co-operation with the PES (Olieman *et al.*, 1996).
27. In addition, placement results of people in health-care jobs lagged considerably owing to mismatches in required and offered skills. In the year 2000 responsibility for the implementation of Melkert 1 health-care jobs will be shifted to the municipalities.
28. Depending on evaluation outcomes the Melkert 2 measure might also be included in the new act.
29. This project organization was called 'Premie Pool' which was set up as a joint venture between the PES and Start temporary employment agency. Furthermore, projects were initiated at the national level by the temporary employment agencies Randstad and Vedior, respectively. However, the projects were not carried out in every municipality included in this study.
30. Here 'outflow' refers to the flow out of unemployment into paid labour.
31. Complications particularly with respect to the implementation of the labour pool scheme were – nationwide – caused by differing organizational interests leading to different attitudes towards the client groups and subsequently diverging interpretations of the measure. During the 1990s the PES obviously struggled with its responsibility as a public body to focus on the hard-to-place unemployed. PES policy-makers at the national level emphasized the need to gain a substantial share in the market for employment services, something that would not be possible by focusing only on long-term unemployed. In a substantial number of cases this led to negligence by the PES of target group members, particularly of labour pool clients. This caused irritation among other implementing actors such as municipalities and municipal foundations, notably in case A of this study.
32. Cf. Van Bekkum (1996).
33. For instance, physical-organizational characteristics, like co-location and desk-sharing, may only apply to a subset of the local implementing actors.
34. See also Speckesser *et al.* (1998) on performance measurement in the public sector.

35. As with many ALMP measures 'creaming' takes place. Even where measures are aimed at the very hard-to-place unemployed job seekers implementing actors may seek for relatively easy-to-place clients. We have no evidence about the extent to which creaming occurs in the cases examined.
36. Here GYEA data includes all unemployed people aged under 27, possibly including young unemployed who do not belong to the target group. For example, young unemployed not labelled as 'school leaver' or persons who are between 21 and 27 years but unemployed for less than six months.
37. No comparable data on outflows and duration was available for Melkert 1 and Melkert 2.

REFERENCES

Blau, P.M. and R.A. Schoenherr (1971), *The Structure of Organizations*, New York, US and London, UK: Basic Books.

Buurmeijer Commission (1993), *Enquête naar het functíoneren van de organen belast met de uitvoering van de sociale-verzekeringswetten* (*Investigation into the Functioning of the Bodies Concerned with the Implementation of Social Insurance Legislation*) (in Dutch only), The Hague: SDU.

Collins, R. (1988), *Theoretical Sociology*, San Diego, CA: Harcourt Brace Jovanovich.

Esser, R., H. Dekkers and A. Vissers (1994), *Samenwerking in beweging* (*Co-operation in Transition*), Rijswijk: Landelijk Bureau Arbeidsvoorziening.

Halpert, B.P. (1982), 'Antecedents', in D. Rogers and D. Whetten (eds), *Interorganizational Co-ordination*, Ames: Iowa State University Press, pp. 54–72.

Koning, J. de and P.J. van Nes (1991), 'A Quantitative Approach to Process Evaluation: the Case of the Vermeend–Moor Act', *Government and Policy*, 9, pp. 111–18.

Laumann, E.O. and D. Knoke (1987), *The Organizational State: Social Choice in National Policy Domains*, Madison, WI and London, UK: University of Wisconsin Press.

OECD (1993), *The Labour Market in the Netherlands*, Paris: OECD.

OECD (1997), *Labour Market Policies: New Challenges – Enhancing the Effectiveness of Active Labour Market Policies: a streamlined public employment service*, Paris: OECD.

OECD (1998), *The battle against social exclusion: volume 2 – Social assistance in Belgium, the Czech Republic, the Netherlands and Norway*, Paris: OECD.

Olieman, R., J.H. Gravesteijn-Ligthelm, I. van der Weijde, A. Verkaik, P.F.H. Nijhuis and J. de Koning (1996), *Evaluatie Jeugdwerkgarantiewet* (*Evaluation Guaranteed Youth Employment Act*) (in Dutch only), The Hague: VUGA.

Olsen, M. (1965), *The Logic of Collective Action: Public Goods and the Theory of Groups*, Cambridge, MA: Harvard University Press.

Rogers, D. and D. Whetten (eds) (1982), *Interorganizational Co-ordination*, Ames: Iowa State University Press, pp. 9–31.

Schmid, G. (1996), 'Process Evaluation: Policy Formation and Implementation', in G. Schmid, J. O'Reilly and K. Schömann (eds), *International Handbook of Labour Market Policy and Evaluation*, Cheltenham, UK and Brookfield, US: Edward Elgar, pp. 198–231.

Schmid, G. (1998), *Transitional Labour Markets: A New European Employment Strategy*, Berlin: WBZ.

Speckesser, S., H. Schütz and G. Schmid (1998), 'The development of benchmarking in the private and public sector', in L. Tronti (ed.), *Benchmarking Employment*

Performance and Labour Market Policies, Berlin: Institute for Applied Socio-Economics, pp. 51–75.

Van der Aalst, M., S. Bavinck, D. Grijpstra and C. van der Werf (1993), *Landelijke evaluatie banenpool – eindrapport* (*National Evaluation Labour Pool – Final Report*) (in Dutch only), Rijswijk: Landelijk Bureau Arbeidsvoorziening.

Van Bekkum, R. (1996), *Tussen vraag en aanbod: op zoek naar de identiteit van de arbeidsvoorzieningsorganisatie* (*Between Demand and Supply: In Search of the Identity of the Public Employment Service*) (in Dutch only), The Hague: Sdu.

Van Dijk, C.P., M.W.M. Vos-van Gortel, W.J. Dercksen, S.W. Douma and M. Scheltema (1995), *Arbeidsvoorziening in perspectief: Evaluatie Arbeidsvoorzieningswet 1991–1994* (*The Public Employment Service in Perspective: Evaluation of the 1991 Reform*) (in Dutch only), The Hague: VUGA.

Van Opstal, R., H. Roodenburg and R. Welters (1998), 'Low skilled jobs through job creation and wage cost subsidy', *CPB Report*, 2, pp. 32–36.

WRR (Scientific Council for Government Policy) (1987), *Activerend arbeidsmarktbeleid* (*Activating Labour Market Policy*) (in Dutch only), The Hague: SDU.

10. Towards intensified local level co-operation in the design and implementation of labour market policies: an evaluation of some Swedish experiments and reforms[1]

Lars Behrenz, Lennart Delander and Harald Niklasson

In May 1996 the Swedish parliament voted to initiate a series of pilot projects aimed at strengthening and improving co-operation at local level among the various agencies and organizations working to reduce high unemployment and assist the unemployed. Since July 1996 these pilot projects have been initiated in 27 municipalities on the basis of contracts between each of these municipalities and the government.

At the same time, the parliament also voted to carry out an institutional reform aimed at strengthening the role of local actors in the design and implementation of labour market policy (LMP) measures, including activities financed by means of funds specifically earmarked for such purposes by the government. As a consequence of this reform, local LMP in all Swedish municipalities (not just, as was originally conceived, in the 27 'experimental municipalities') is now led and co-ordinated by a local committee in which the chairman and the majority of the members are appointed by the municipality. The remaining differences between the 'experimental municipalities' and other municipalities are that the former (1) have signed contracts with the government obliging them to implement a specified set of pilot projects; and (2) have committed themselves to contributing a minimum of 25 per cent of the total cost of these projects.

These pilot projects are designed to support the development of new methods or models for co-operation among the various local labour market actors, as well as to encourage a more efficient and innovative use of public funds. The institutional reform has a similar aim: to promote closer co-operation among the various actors involved in the selection and implementation of LMP measures. As a result of this reform, all municipalities are finding it easier to initiate and implement new LMP activities similar to the pilot projects being tested in the 'experimental municipalities'.

Both the institutional reform and the pilot projects are expected to contribute to a renewal of Swedish labour market policies. The major shifts which have taken place on the Swedish labour market over the last several years – including a dramatic increase in unemployment and a significant decrease in labour market participation – may render traditional means and methods obsolete or inappropriate.

The broad outline of this chapter is as follows. In section 1 we describe the main characteristics of the institutional framework for labour market policies in Sweden. We also attempt to explain why recent developments in the economy and on the labour market may have rendered traditional LMP means and institutional arrangements obsolete and inefficient. In section 2 we begin by discussing the meaning of 'local level co-operation' in the design and implementation of labour market policies. The subsequent critical analysis of the implemented policies examines the expectation that intensified local level co-operation will result in a more efficient use of public funds, as well as the fear that the changes actually brought about – including an increase in municipal influence – may conflict with national interests and thus be misdirected. Several empirical studies are presented in section 3. We concentrate on a comparison between experimental municipalities and a matched control group with regard to the development of target variables. In section 4 we conclude with some remarks on the results of the empirical studies in relation to the descriptions and analysis in sections 1 and 2.

1 BACKGROUND

The institutional reform described above has strengthened – at least formally – the role of the municipal decision-makers in the design and implementation of LMP measures. This may come into conflict with the Swedish tradition in which the LMP is regarded as a national and integrated part of the government's economic policy as a whole (see for example Johannesson and Wadensjö, 1995).

It may be argued that it is difficult to reconcile this traditional view of LMP as a national concern with a high degree of decentralization of LMP decision-making to the local level. Prior to the most recent reforms, especially in the 1980s, the quest for decentralization was manifested by the attempt to establish and refine a 'management by objectives system' (MOS) within the public employment service governmental organization (Niklasson and Tomsmark, 1997). The object of this system was to give employment service offices at the local level a large degree of freedom in considering local or regional conditions when choosing among the various means of meeting the main objectives and guidelines set by the government.

The corresponding institutional arrangements and the LMP means and methods applied by the governmental agencies were perhaps appropriate and functioned fairly well under the conditions of the 1980s. They may, however, be less suited to handling the problems of the late 1990s, that is, the consequences of the deep and lingering crisis that hit the Swedish economy at the beginning of the 1990s. Institutional innovations and new means and methods may well be needed.

A critical analysis of the government's efforts to accomplish a renewal of the Swedish LMP by means of facilitating and stimulating the co-operation among various actors at the local level must consider certain aspects. In this section we will establish some points of departure for such a critical analysis. We begin by presenting some fundamental features of the institutional framework for the LMP decision-making and implementation processes in Sweden. We will then give a very short review of the developments in the Swedish economy in the 1990s, especially those affecting the labour market and labour market policies.

1.1 The Institutional Framework

As a background to the Swedish projects and reforms analysed in this chapter, this section briefly outlines the national Labour Market Administration and the system of means-tested social assistance and social insurance in Sweden.

The Labour Market Administration

Overall responsibility for Swedish labour market policy rests with the Riksdag (the Swedish parliament) and the government (the cabinet). Within the cabinet the responsibility for labour market policy is entrusted to the Ministry of Labour. Under the Ministry of Labour is the Labour Market Administration (AMV)[2] which implements labour market policy on behalf of the cabinet.

General guidelines for AMV's activities are laid down in the Labour Market Policy Activities Ordinance. AMV is, for example, required to ensure that job seekers quickly obtain work and that job vacancies are quickly filled, condition labour demand through job promotion measures, promote the entitlement of women and men to work on equal terms and pay special attention to measures for promoting the recruitment of workers with reduced working capacity. Overriding annual targets for the labour market policy are established in Riksdag resolutions on the government's budget bill. More specific objectives or quantifiable operational targets of AMV are given in the government's appropriation warrant and in other directives.

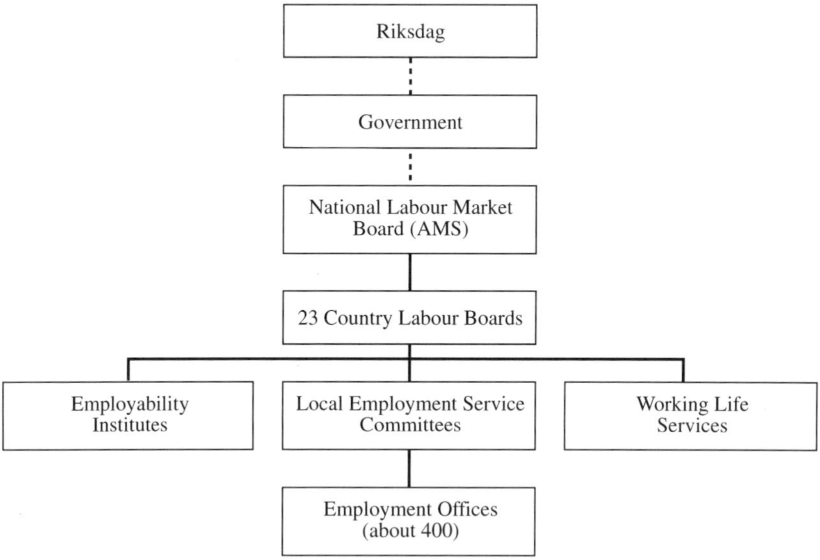

Figure 10.1 Organization of the Swedish Labour Market Administration (AMV)

AMV includes the National Labour Market Board (AMS)[3] and the county labour boards. There are 23 county labour boards which operate the public employment offices (which together make up the public employment service), the employability institutes, and the working life services.

Figure 10.1 summarizes the organization of the Labour Market Administration. AMS is the central administrative agency – the head office of AMV – which superintends the county labour boards. It is responsible for managing, co-ordinating and developing Swedish labour market policy to comply with the guidelines set by the Riksdag and the cabinet; for establishing goals and guidelines for the county employment boards; and for following up and evaluating the results of their activities.

According to the Labour Market Policy Activities Ordinance instructions for the Labour Market Administration, the principal responsibilities of county employment boards are to manage, co-ordinate and develop labour market activities in the counties.

In each municipality, the county labour boards have organized a local employment service committee, a joint body charged with shaping labour market policy to suit local conditions. The members of the committee represent the county labour board, the employment service, the municipality, local employee organizations and the local business community. The chairman and a majority of the committee's members are appointed upon the recommendations of the municipal government, which thus enjoys a decision-making majority. The work in the committees is guided by the targets and objectives of national labour market policy and by the powers with which the committees are vested by the county employment boards.

The publicly run employment service is represented in nearly all municipalities by employment offices which are responsible for providing hands-on assistance to job seekers and employers.[4] In many of the larger towns and cities there are specialized offices catering to specified occupational categories. Employment offices are engaged in providing information about job openings, placement services for job seekers and employers, and employment counselling services. Most labour market policy resources are delegated to the employment offices. Thus the instruments of labour market policy are in the hands of the employment offices, and most of the decisions regarding the use of various measures are made by employment service officers in their dealings with job seekers and employers. The great majority of Swedish job seekers register with the public employment service since this is a prerequisite for obtaining unemployment benefits. Yet although employers are required by law to notify officials of job opportunities in their companies, only some 40 per cent of all job vacancies in Sweden are reported to the employment service.

The employment service has a control function where unemployment compensation is concerned. The employment service must insist that a recipient of unemployment compensation seek work and be prepared to accept a suitable job offer or to take part in a labour market policy programme. Otherwise the unemployed person can be denied benefits for a period of time.

After its budget bill has passed the Riksdag, the government allocates funding for the AMV and for labour market policy programmes and states the goals for their utilization. In 1997–8 the government even defined quantitative targets for labour market programmes. This means that the government stipulated for each year a minimum number of participants in counter-cyclical programmes and in special programmes for occupationally handicapped job seekers.

Following a discussion on operational planning throughout the AMV, the National Labour Market Board (AMS) defines the county operational targets and the allocation of funding to the county labour boards. The requirement concerning the number of persons taking part in labour market programmes is distributed by AMS according to the allocation of funding. The county labour boards, in turn, distribute funding within their counties to employability institutes and employment offices (via local employment service committees). A system of management by objectives allows local freedom but at the same time controls fulfilment of targets through monitoring and evaluation. After each quarter, the county labour boards report to AMS on the outcomes with respect to operational targets. These reports are used as input documentation for AMS quarterly reports to the government.

Social assistance and social insurance

As people exhaust their unemployment benefits, municipalities are legally responsible for disbursing social assistance to ensure that these people still maintain an acceptable standard of living. Means-tested social assistance in Sweden is based on and regulated by the Social Services Act. It provides general guidelines for authorities at the municipal level who deal with matters concerning cash assistance for the fulfilment of basic needs. Households are entitled to social assistance if their disposable income adjusted for housing costs falls short of the so-called ‘social assistance norm’.

There can be little doubt that the recession of the 1990s in Sweden has increased the incidence of poverty. Workers who earn low wages may be especially vulnerable to the effects of unemployment. The growth of transfers has not succeeded in providing a completely effective income guarantee for those without incomes from work. This incomplete coverage is due to inadequate benefit levels for certain workers, for example, for persons with poor employment records who may only be entitled to the basic unemployment insurance which covers those who are not members of an unemployment insurance fund.

Between the end of the 1980s and the middle of the 1990s, the number of households receiving social assistance increased by more than 40 per cent. This figure suggests that the strong growth of unemployment has placed a heavy financial burden on local governments and illustrates the need for increased co-operation between the municipalities and the AMV. As a response to this crisis, local authorities and employment offices have, in many localities, developed joint projects of a more or less permanent nature to support the transition of unemployed recipients of means-tested social assistance into regular employment.

In many cases a third party, the local social insurance office, is also engaged in such co-operative efforts. With the exception of unemployment compensation, social insurance benefits in Sweden (for example, cash benefits during illness and rehabilitation benefits) are administered at the local level by these offices, which are supervised by the National Social Insurance Board. Close co-operation between the social insurance office and the employment office is increasingly being used to enhance the employment opportunities of people who have had prolonged periods of illness or who are undergoing rehabilitation.

1.2 The Crisis of the 1990s

In the late 1980s, the rate of unemployment in Sweden was well below 2 per cent. The rate of participation in ALMP (active LMP) measures was at about the same level. At that point in time Sweden could look back on more than three decades of very low unemployment. It was widely believed that ALMP could not effectively fulfil its role as an integrated part of the government's economic policy if the rate of ALMP participation and the rate of unemployment were much above 3 per cent, that is, if the 'total unemployment' was above 6 per cent.

In the early 1990s, unemployment levels in Sweden soared. By 1993 'total unemployment' approached 14 per cent, meaning a rate of unemployment higher than 8 per cent and an ALMP participation rate at around 6 per cent. The rate of labour market participation had fallen from around 84 per cent to about 79 per cent. (For further details, see Ministry of Finance, 1995.) The general picture has not changed very much since then despite very significant improvements in a number of other economic indicators (for example, elimination of the public budget deficit, lower interest rates, and recovery in manufacturing).

The increase in the unemployment has of course led to major changes in the use of different kinds of ALMP instruments. There have also been some changes in the ALMP objectives stipulated by the government and imposed on the local decision-makers. These objectives have tended to become more detailed than they were before, thus rendering the decentralization developed within the framework of the MOS in the 1980s less meaningful.

As long as the main ALMP objectives stated by the government were expressed in terms of labour market conditions and developments and not tied to the ALMP activities *per se*, local officials enjoyed real freedom to choose among different kinds and combinations of programmes. In such a management system it is for example possible for local decision-makers to defend and carry out expensive training programmes or other kinds of measures that entail disadvantages (costs) in the short run, including an increase in current unemployment; but which also entail advantages (benefits) in the longer run, including a decrease in the future unemployment. If, however, many of the 'objectives' imposed on local authorities affect ALMP activities *per se*, then local policy discretion has become more limited. This has, to some extent, happened in Sweden in the 1990s. The means, that is, programme participation, have tended to become the objectives. As a consequence of the high unemployment the government has tried to regulate the use of different ALMP means so that the number of ALMP participants is high and current unemployment lower.[5]

High unemployment levels have led to a very large increase in the expenditures of other public authorities, including the social insurance offices.

The size of their expenditures is, however, very much dependent on the policies chosen by the labour market authorities. High unemployment has made the borderline between the aims and means of the ALMP and the aims and means of the 'social policy' less distinct. As a consequence of the existence of such interdependencies, a well-considered co-ordination of the activities pursued by different authorities may become necessary for an efficient use of public funds. To a very large degree, that co-ordination has to take place at the local level, where the individuals meet the public agencies in charge of their cases.

The unemployment benefits paid out are often too small to make it possible for the unemployed individuals to sustain acceptable standards of living for themselves and their dependants. Furthermore, not all the unemployed are entitled to such benefits. The increase in unemployment since the beginning of the 1990s, as well as many policy measures aimed at decreasing the public budget deficit, have contributed to a significant increase in the number of Swedish individuals and families who are dependent on municipal social assistance based on means tests. The municipalities' expenditures for such grants have become very substantial.

Thus the municipalities have considerable incentive to carry out 'labour market policies' and 'industrial policies' of their own, and to find ways to utilize governmental funds to finance such activities or to support the unemployed. As a consequence, the need for co-ordination between the activities of the municipalities and the activities of other public agencies involved (mainly the labour market and the social insurance authorities) has greatly increased. The absence of co-ordination may lead to considerable inefficiency in the use of public funds – the taxpayers' money.

2 A CRITICAL DISCUSSION

For a prescription to be effective, it should be based on a correct diagnosis of the disease. It should also be remembered that few medicines or treatments are free of costs. Even if the prescription 'intensified co-operation' can be expected to have some positive effects, it should not be taken for granted that these effects are large enough to justify the corresponding co-operation costs. Furthermore, it must not be forgotten that most medicines have secondary effects. 'Intensified local level co-operation' may cause some distortions in the national economic system, for example, as a result of rent-seeking behaviour on the part of different local actors participating in the co-operation or the occurrence of local or municipal 'protectionism'.

In this section, we will look at the possible existence of adverse secondary effects and address the need for correct diagnoses of the causes behind the observed crisis symptoms. We will start, however, with a short discussion of the concepts 'co-operation' and 'co-ordination' .

2.1 Why Co-operation? Or Why Not?

When we talk about co-operation between two (or more) parties, we mean joint activities with the goal of finding and exploiting existing possibilities of obtaining net gains for both (or all) parties by means of co-ordinated decision-making and implementation.

'Co-operation' and 'co-ordination' are generally viewed as positive and desirable terms. Co-operative activities are not, however, free of costs. This is why the firms in industries characterized by a high degree of competition and the absence of significant technological external effects do not co-operate in the sense indicated above. Of course the firms may be involved in business transactions with each other (buying and selling) but they do not try to co-ordinate their production processes because it is not profitable for them to do so. Co-operative activities entail additional costs but no additional revenues. Instead, each firm chooses its own course of action (its production) within a set of feasible alternatives. This set of possibilities is often conceptualized as a 'production function'. The absence of technological external effects means that the production function of each firm is independent of the choices made by other firms.

In contrast to these companies, firms in industries characterized by oligopoly very often attempt to co-ordinate decision-making. This is not primarily a result of external technological factors, but rather due to the existence of opportunities for these firms to reach mutually profitable agreements on prices and production volumes (see for example Schotter, 1997, pp. 359–94). It is well known that this kind of co-ordination may be contrary to economic efficiency. 'Intensified co-operation' can be socially harmful even if it is gainful for the parties involved. In the interests of social welfare, governments should, in some cases, obstruct rather than stimulate co-operation between actors.

Our discussion has so far focused on co-operation and co-ordination among commercial firms. But what about co-operation between public agencies, or between such agencies and private actors? In the following discussion, we assume that each public agency has been given the task of maximizing an 'outcome function' (corresponding to the profit of a private firm), meaning that it is expected to apply some well-defined appraisal criteria. The agency is subject to a number of constraints; including a production function, input and financial constraints, and certain rules and regulations that must be respected. We also assume that each public agency is motivated to try to successfully complete its tasks. When discussing governmental agencies, including the ones operating at the local level, we assume that their outcome functions (that is, the appraisal criteria applied) as well as the input and financial constraints and the rules and regulations applying to them are determined by the government, which in turn is obliged to pursue national interests, that is, the interests of the citizens of the country as a whole. Municipalities (that is, all municipal agencies) are likewise subject to certain rules and regulations imposed by the national government or a superior municipal agency. They are expected to pursue the interests of the inhabitants in the municipality. This is reflected in the appraisal criteria – the outcome functions – applied. Other actors (for example, individuals, firms, organizations) are, of course, equally subject to rules and regulations, some of which are determined by the government and others by the municipalities. When talking about rules and regulations, we include the duties and rights determined by the tax and transfer system.

Given this structure, co-operation between a local governmental agency such as an employment office and a municipal agency should be expected to emerge where possibilities exist for a mutually gainful co-ordination of the two agencies' decision-making and implementation processes. Co-operation that does not promise to be gainful and feasible for both agencies will not occur.

If the government wants the existing local public agencies to intensify their co-operation, then it must change the constraints (mainly the rules and regulations) imposed upon local agencies and/or change the appraisal criteria (the outcome functions) that the governmental agencies are instructed to apply.[6]

2.2 Too Little Co-operation? Or Too Much?

In some cases, a municipal agency may seek to initiate a specific co-operative activity which is regarded by the local PES as undesirable or not feasible. This means that the form of co-operation proposed would violate either the appraisal criteria or the constraints imposed on the PES by the government. The fact that the proposal is rejected by the PES may therefore be seen as suggesting that it is contrary to national interests. If such an interpretation is correct, then the absence of the form of co-operation in question would be compatible with national efficiency or distribution goals. If, however, this is not correct, then the government has failed to furnish its own agencies with either the incentives, the instructions or the resources necessary to develop decision-making processes which efficiently promote the government's interests and intentions.

There are many reasons why co-operation between municipal (or private) actors and governmental agencies may give rise to adverse secondary effects. Some co-operative activities put forward by municipal agencies may involve, more or less directly, subsidies for firms operating in the municipality; or the creation of extraordinary job opportunities for the local unemployed in the production of local public services. The adverse secondary effects of such policies may not be easily perceptible at the local level (that is, for the inhabitants of the municipality) but they may be quite significant from a national point of view. If the co-operative activities suggested are rejected by the PES, then this may be – in accordance with the interpretation mentioned above – because the appraisal criteria and the constraints imposed on the PES by the government are designed to guard against the use of means and methods that will imply secondary effects not compatible with national interests.

The subsidizing of firms may lead to distortion of competition between the subsidized companies and other firms, including firms in other parts of the country. If the use of such means is permitted – or not strictly regulated – then municipalities may become involved in a 'prisoners' dilemma game' entailing long-run losses for all, or most, municipalities rather than an efficiency-enhancing institutional competition. Furthermore, the kind of employment-creating measures described above may mean, more or less directly, that extraordinary jobs financed by means of governmental funds are substituted for regular jobs financed by the municipality.

It is also possible that some co-operative projects which are proposed by municipalities (perhaps because they include governmental contributions to the financing) and which aim at the creation of job and/or training opportunities will counteract labour mobility between different parts of the country or other kinds of desirable adjustment processes. Most kinds of LMP measures mean changes in the possibilities – the sets of possible choices – available to job seekers and employers (private firms as well as public agencies). As a consequence, they may influence the nature and outcome of the contract formation processes (that is, the adjustments) constantly in progress on the labour market. In a worst-case scenario, they may prevent or delay desirable changes in the behaviour of different actors (for example, their propensity to offer or accept various alternatives in terms of wages, working conditions or geographical localization) that may be needed to alleviate structural imbalances, or mismatch prevailing, on the national labour market.

It is also possible, of course, that co-operative activities proposed by the governmental agencies will be resisted by their municipal counterparts. Perhaps some of the costs of the measures or projects proposed by the PES will burden the local economy, while some of the benefits will accrue to other municipalities. If the interpretation outlined above is applied consistently, then the fact that the measures or projects are put forward by the PES would indicate that their national net benefits are positive; that is, that the municipality's refusal to co-operate is contrary to national interests. The 'intensified local co-operation' needed for the elimination of this national inefficiency can be brought about by a revision of the rules and regulations imposed on the municipal agencies and/or the PES by the government.

Governmental interventions may reward the municipality for co-operating, and/or they may punish the municipality for refusing to co-operate; that is, the government may alter the rules and regulations determining the distribution of costs and benefits associated with various feasible alternatives. One possibility is to allow the PES to offer better conditions for the municipality, meaning that the constraints imposed on the PES are made less rigid than before. Another alternative may involve legislative reforms providing for changes in the municipality's set of feasible (allowed) courses of action, so that the alternative to co-operation becomes the best of the remaining feasible alternatives. In an extreme case, the reforms may make it impossible (not allowed) for the municipality to refuse to participate in the activities proposed by the PES. In such a case, however, it is meaningless to talk about 'co-operation' – the co-ordination of different means and methods aimed at is accomplished by transferring the policy-making authority from municipal to governmental agencies.

It is interesting to observe that an institutional reform recently carried out in Sweden (see above) represents a strengthening rather than a reduction of the role and influence of municipal actors in local LMP decision-making. This was accomplished by requiring that the chairman and the majority of the members in the local employment service committees be appointed by the municipalities. Thus the representatives of the municipality have – at least formally – the ability to apply municipal appraisal criteria when choosing among feasible LMP alternatives. It may be argued that this will weaken the governmental agencies' ability to guard against the use of means and methods that are contrary to national interests. Provided the government recognizes the existence of conflicts between local and national interests, a consequence may be an increase in the need for detailed rules and regulations determined by the government and delimiting the local agencies' freedom of action. Thus the reform may counteract a development in the opposite direction sometimes described as desirable: that is, a decrease in the use of specified rules and regulations combined with decentralized decision-making based on adequate appraisal criteria.

2.3 Management by Directives or by Objectives?

According to the results of the questionnaire sent to PES managers and to municipal politicians and civil servants, there has been a very rapid development of the local level LMP co-operation between municipal agencies and the PES in most Swedish municipalities in recent years. In addition to intensified discussions and exchanges of information, as well as the establishment of new committees, consultation groups or similar institutions, the intensified co-operation has involved the initiation and carrying-out of co-operative activities, often referred to as 'projects' or 'models'. Thus many opportunities for co-operation have been identified and deemed desirable and feasible by both parties. They have come about without any interventions (measures to stimulate local level co-operation) on the part of the government.

In their answers to the questionnaire, however, most local actors claimed that many LMP activities judged as appropriate and desirable by the actors themselves are hindered by the rules and regulations imposed on the PES by the government (or the national labour market board).[7] Thus the LMP renewal sought by the government, including the introduction of 'non-traditional' means and methods, seems to be hampered by governmental rules and regulations.

Some of the stipulations (for example, regarding the means and measures permitted or eligibility criteria for participation) are general in the sense that they are mandatory for all employment offices. Under some circumstances, these stipulations are perhaps appropriate: they prevent the use of means and methods causing unwanted secondary effects. But neither these circumstances nor the negative secondary effects are present in all cases. Thus these general stipulations may turn out to be very indiscriminate and rough policy instruments. Sometimes – perhaps often – they prevent the use of means and methods that would promote national as well as municipal (or other) interests.

The use of more selective stipulations, in which different employment offices receive different directives, presupposes a very detailed knowledge on the part of the government or the central governmental authorities about the current problems and conditions on different local labour markets. The local actors may regard this management by selective and detailed directives as being based on misconceptions about local conditions, problems and possibilities. They might feel incapacitated by the government (or other central authorities). Many of the answers to the questionnaire mentioned above express such perceptions and reactions.

It should also be observed, however, that some of the answers from PES managers reflect apprehensions regarding the consequences of the strengthening of the power and influence of the municipal agencies or their representatives on the local LMP decision-making level. They express concern about the municipal representatives' lack of knowledge and understanding of the aims and functioning of LMP measures. Sometimes they also mention the danger of 'local protectionism' and municipal rent-seeking in the local LMP. The municipal representatives themselves tend to stress that the social policy, the industrial policy and the labour market policy pursued at the local level should be co-ordinated and integrated, not viewed as separate policy areas; and that this presupposes a strengthening of the role and influence of municipal agencies as well as the abolition of governmental directives, rules and regulations.

If there were no significant conflicts between local and national interests, then a very far-reaching decentralization of the corresponding decision-making and implementation processes to municipal agencies may be justified. However, as has been indicated above, it would be somewhat naive to assume that no such conflicts of interests exist. Thus, an increase in the municipal agencies' decision-making authority (that is, in their authority to determine the choice between available policy alternatives) may curtail the government's propensity towards administrative deregulation if government wishes to guard against local policies counteracting national interests. The set of policy alternatives available to the municipal agencies must be regulated.

If, on the other hand, the government wants to decrease the use of directives, rules and regulations in order to widen the set of policy alternatives available to the local decision-makers, then it has to ensure that the choices made by the local actors are based on appraisal criteria that support national interests. Especially when it comes to means and activities involving the use of governmental resources, it is reasonable to maintain that they should be approved by a governmental agency attempting to apply such criteria. The task of carrying out the required examinations may be delegated to a local agency accountable to a superior governmental authority; ultimately to the national government. However, ideas and proposals for new LMP means and methods originating from different local actors (including municipal agencies), and perhaps demanding co-operative activities, should not be ruled out from the beginning because they do not fit into an existing set of detailed and complicated directives, rules and regulations. They should be subjected to unprejudiced appraisals. The reasons for approval or rejection should be clearly stated in terms of pros and cons. Of course, the issue of accountability becomes very important. The activities of the local agency in charge of the examinations should be subjected to evaluations carried out on behalf of superior agencies.

To some extent, the pilot projects carried out in a number of Swedish municipalities can be regarded as an attempt to initiate a development in the direction now indicated. The projects are based on contracts between each 'experimental municipality' and the government. They have been initiated and are implemented in co-operation with various local actors, especially municipal agencies and the local PES. They use municipal as well as governmental resources. The municipalities have agreed to contribute to the financing. In spite of this, the projects have been judged as promoting municipal interests. Although the projects involve some deviations from governmental rules and regulations normally applied, the fact that the government has co-signed the contracts indicates that the projects have been judged to be compatible with national interests. Our interpretation is that some kinds of relatively unprejudiced considerations, or appraisal criteria, have been substituted for the use of very rigid rules and regulations.

However, the authority to represent the government in the contract formation processes has not been delegated to the local governmental agencies, at least not when it comes to the final appraisal and decision-making. The step towards carrying out such a more far-reaching decentralization within the governmental organization – to empower the local agencies – would perhaps trigger the emergence at the local level of much more inventive and dynamic development and contract formation processes than the ones hitherto observed, including the flowering of a diverse set of deliberate co-operation activities between different local actors representing different interests.

Deregulation combined with a very high degree of decentralization presupposes, of course, that the local governmental agencies are given the instructions, as well as the capabilities and incentives, needed for appropriate appraisals to be carried out at the local level. Such appraisals – in practice, perhaps, relatively pragmatic considerations and criteria promoting national interests and guarding against the use of means and methods that are contrary to the government's intentions – must be substituted if the rules and regulations are to be abolished or loosened.

In the 1980s, the Swedish efforts to create a very decentralized and smoothly functioning management by objectives system (MOS) within the governmental LMP organization seemed to point in the direction now indicated. However, the very deep crisis in the Swedish economy in the 1990s caused somewhat of a return to the use of management by directives. This is reflected in many of the answers to our questionnaire (sent out at the beginning of 1998). Many local actors are very irritated by the large number of directives, rules and regulations which they are obliged to follow. Some of them are, in fact, very angry; and feel not only restricted, but also bullied from above.

2.4 The Need for Directives, Rules and Regulations?

The results of the questionnaire completed by Swedish local actors suggests that the emergence of an institutional structure and a rich and varied flowering of co-operation activities based on agreements (more or less formal contracts) between different actors has been very much hampered by the detailed directives, rules and regulations imposed on the local employment offices by the government or the central governmental authorities. Despite the general movement towards intensified local level co-operation, many means, methods and activities regarded as potentially feasible and fruitful by the local actors have yet to be exploited. The hypothesis that a deregulation combined with a far-reaching decentralization would trigger a much more inventive and dynamic renewal of the Swedish ALMP – including the creation of new institutional arrangements corresponding to the concept of transitional labour markets – seems to be supported by many municipal politicians and civil servants as well as by many PES managers. This being the case, a very important question arises: why do all these directives, rules and regulations exist?

As discussed above, LMP measures may have unwanted secondary effects; such as the distortion of competition between different producers, the locking-up of employees in low-productivity jobs, the displacement of regular employment and the deterioration or slowing-up of the labour market adjustments needed for the alleviation of existing mismatch phenomena. The directives, rules and regulations (in what follows we use, for simplicity, only the word regulations) established by the government are designed to guard against the implementation of LMP measures that will have significant adverse effects. The idea of a decentralized and deregulated LMP decision-making process suggests that at least some – perhaps rather many – of the regulations should be abolished or made less rigid or detailed; and that there should also be appraisals which take into account significant impacts, including secondary ones.

The task of carrying out such appraisals is not an easy one! In order to illustrate this, let us consider a project proposal in which a number of long-term unemployed people are given extraordinary jobs in the municipal social welfare department with the goal of improving the quality of life of elderly people. The proposal presupposes that the project is co-financed by the municipality, the government via the local employment office and the unemployment insurance funds. The project is regarded as desirable by the municipality but, according to existing regulations, it is not feasible for the PES. So for the local employment office, reaching a decision is very simple.

Following deregulation, however, it becomes possible for the employment office to participate in the project. Again, at first glance the decision-making process may appear to be very simple. If the project is carried out, a number of unemployed people belonging to the target group will be given the opportunity to produce something of value – something for which a significant willingness to pay does exist – instead of producing nothing. Unemployment will decrease and the quality of life for some elderly people and their close relatives will be improved. This should be in accordance with the interests the PES is supposed to pursue.

However, the PES is obliged to consider other issues such as the net impact of the project on public budget balances. In principle, it must apply a shadow price larger than one on public revenues and expenditures. The larger the need for a reduction of the public debt (or the public budget deficit or the taxes) is judged to be, the larger the appropriate shadow price of public funds becomes. If the increase in net public expenditures incurred by the project burdens mainly the municipal budget, then this shadow pricing will be handled by the municipal decision-makers. It is quite possible, however, that the project has been constructed in such a way that it will heavily burden governmental budgets (perhaps also through the budgets of the social insurance funds). In that case, the appropriate shadow pricing must be handled by governmental agencies.

The PES also has to consider the possibility that the project will imply some substitution of extraordinary jobs for regular employment. It is possible, for example, that some employees in private firms or public agencies providing services for elderly people will become unemployed as a consequence of the project. If such displacement effects are judged to exist and to be significant, then the corresponding real costs have to be brought into the project appraisal.

In an economy with high tax rates and generous transfer systems, the displacement of regular employment will cause very significant real costs, not only because of the direct loss of production, but also due to very large decreases in public revenues (direct and indirect taxes, including social security taxes) and increases in public expenditures (transfers to the displaced individuals).[8] If labour productivity is considered to be lower in extraordinary employment than in regular employment, then rather limited displacement effects may be sufficient for the project to be judged as contrary to economic efficiency. On the other hand, if the productivity difference is small, then the displacement effect may easily become rather large. This dilemma explains the existence of some of the regulations criticized by many of the local actors.

Roles and responsibilities

The secondary effects on regular employment can be quite varied in kind. It is, for example, possible that the municipality – more or less deliberately – will substitute extraordinary jobs for regular jobs in the production of municipal services; but also that municipal provision becomes substituted for private provision of similar services (close substitutes). Furthermore, individuals in the target group may become deterred from searching for and/or accepting regular job openings existing or coming into being on the labour market, perhaps in other municipalities; or from reducing their 'reservation wages' in order to get more job offers. Indeed, even if the project *per se* is very simple and well defined, it is not very easy to estimate its net impacts on the size and structure of regular employment, including the impacts arising as a result of the project's repercussions on the contract formation constantly in progress on the labour market.

The existence of a large number of regulations restricting the local actors' freedom of action in terms of local LMP (in a broad sense) may be seen as a lack of trust on the part of the central governmental authorities in the local actors' capabilities and/or incentives to carry out and apply adequate appraisals. Considering the difficulties pointed out above, this mistrust may appear to be justified. However, the local actors' scepticism about the central authorities' wisdom and capabilities may be equally justified. The idea that very much of the knowledge and many of the skills missing at the local level are to be found at the central level must be questioned. Even when it is possible to identify the motivations behind centrally established regulations, the corresponding notions about the direct and indirect impacts of different kinds of LMP interventions are almost always debatable, especially when superimposed on the specific conditions of a specific local labour market in a specific period of time. This explains, at least to some extent, why very detailed and rigid regulations cause so much distress and irritation among local actors.

The reform proposal described above can be summarized as a move towards deregulation combined with a decentralization of governmental decision-making processes and the corresponding appraisal activities to local agencies accountable to superior governmental authorities. Such a reform does not, of course, mean that the motivations behind the abandonment of the regulations can be forgotten. The corresponding aspects have to be considered in the appraisals, but the ways in which this is done may differ from case to case or from one local market to the other depending on differences in relevant preconditions. The aspects that must be considered and the ways of thinking that should be applied may be brought into operation by means of guidelines and recommendations (rather than rigid regulations) laid down by the central authorities and conveyed to the local agencies. These agencies know that their activities will be evaluated by superior authorities and that apparent deviations from the guidelines and recommendations will come to light.

Recurrent discussions with superior authorities will be normal elements in these decision-making processes. Local initiatives, that is, the introduction of new means and methods, can be brought into these dialogues. These initiatives may include proposals originating from actors other than the PES, such as municipal agencies. They will be discussed and assessed on the basis of their own merits and demerits, not rejected simply because they do not comply with a set of rigid regulations. The soil for the development of new co-operation activities, including the creation of new transitional labour markets, will thus become less stony.

3 ESTIMATES OF EFFECTS OF INTENSIFIED LOCAL CO-OPERATION

This section presents estimates of effects on target variables of (a) the pilot projects based on contracts between the municipalities involved ('experimental municipalities') and the government (subsection 3.1) as well as of (b) the intensified local co-operation that has developed as a consequence of the institutional reform which gave a decision-making majority in local employment service committees to all Swedish municipalities – a development that may be regarded as a natural experiment (subsection 3.2).

3.1 Estimated Effects in Experimental Municipalities

Estimates of effects of the pilot projects (the experiments that have been pursued in a number of municipalities) are based on comparisons of the outcome of target variables in experimental and comparison municipalities, respectively. The municipalities in the comparison, or control, group were selected on the basis of a division of Sweden into local labour market areas (LMAs) and employment zones laid out in a joint work of Statistics Sweden and the Expert Group on Regional and Urban Studies (Carlsson *et al.*, 1993).

Briefly, LMAs can be described as functional labour market areas consisting of integrated housing and working areas within which commuting is common and natural. The 284 municipalities of Sweden have been grouped into 111 LMAs. Next, clustering techniques were used to develop groups of LMAs with the goal of creating a manageable number of zones – employment zones – with similar properties regarding variables of importance for the functioning of the labour market. Each of the 10 employment zones contains LMAs which share similar characteristics and problems more or less independently of their geographic location in the country. Thus, each of the employment zones is homogeneous in terms of the character of regional economy and structure of the labour market. These clusters are more relevant for regional analysis in terms of the stability and vulnerability of demand for and supply of labour than either the municipalities or the counties.

Each experimental municipality has been matched with a comparison municipality in the same employment zone. If the experimental municipality is a dominant municipality in its LMA, it has been paired together with a comparison community with the same position in its local area.

Since the evaluators had no way of influencing the choice of experimental municipalities, selection bias might be a problem. However, results from regressions reported in Tables 10.2 and 10.3 do not suggest large differences in unobservable characteristics between experimental municipalities and their corresponding controls. This is indicated by the fact that in almost all the regressions, the coefficient of the dummy variable representing experiment and control group, respectively, is not significant in regressions based on observations from the period before the experiments had started.

Estimates of effects have been based on data collected from an events database, called Händel, kept by the National Labour Market Board. Everything happening to job seekers and job vacancies registered with the public employment service is saved daily in that database, which also contains background data about job seekers and vacancies. The 'events' can be status changes for job seekers, such as 'obtained work' or 'commenced employment training'. Using Händel, one can follow the progress of individual job seekers or groups of job seekers during a particular period regarding offers of employment, unemployment compensation received, participation in employment programmes, and so on. Thus, through operational monitoring systems, it is possible to gauge the efficacy of different labour market policy instruments. The time series of Händel begins in August 1991 and contains data on nearly two million persons and 1.6 million registered job vacancies. Altogether, more than 90 million events have been entered.[9]

Currently, evaluation estimates of effects are based on comparisons of 25 experimental and 25 comparison municipalities regarding the development of target variables from a period before to a period after the start of the pilot projects and the intensified local co-operation. The period before is 15 January 1995–15 February 1996 and the period after is 15 January 1997–15 February 1998. For the estimates of effects of pilot projects, information was collected from Händel about all job seekers who were found in the registers of the employment service in the experimental and comparison municipalities (93 645 persons in the period before and 89 150 persons in the period after).

For the evaluation of the institutional reform, which will be presented in section 3.2 below, information was also collected from samples of 10 per cent of registered job seekers in those municipalities which do not belong either to the experimental or the comparison groups (33 727 in the period before and 32 164 persons in the period after).

In the light of the development of 'co-operative labour market policy' and the limited knowledge that we have about the impact of labour market policy interventions, there is a great need for tests and evaluations. Although it would be presumptuous to allege that the results of the present study are unambiguous indicators of the success or failure of the pilot projects and/or the institutional reform, we advocate a more frequent use of experiments to evaluate the effects of new policies or of changes in policy or in its institutional framework. The basic evaluation problem is how the impact of what is being tested compares with what had been achieved if an alternative course of action had been chosen – a problem of obtaining data on both actual and counterfactual outcome. The account in this section of the chapter should be seen both as a presentation of evaluation results *per se* and as a description of a design which we think is also potentially useful for evaluation of other labour market policy interventions.

Observed differences between pairs of municipalities in the development of target variables

An effect evaluation implies a comparison between different courses of events which are associated with alternative modes of action. One alternative in the present evaluation is, of course, represented by the pilot projects contracted for in the experimental municipalities, which have resulted in a certain course of events in the labour market. If the pilot projects had not been implemented, another course of events would have been expected. From an evaluation point of view, effects must be defined as differences between these alternative courses of events. These differences can be interpreted as net outcomes, that is, outcomes which can reasonably be attributed to the intervention and are free of changes among targets due to influences from other causal processes that may also have occurred (Rossi and Freeman, 1985, p. 190).

The first type of effect estimates to be reported here are based upon comparisons in pairs between changes from the period before to the period after in experimental municipalities and corresponding changes in their matched controls in terms of the following target variables:

- Mean duration of unemployment[10] where it has been postulated that the pilot projects will produce a decrease.
- Proportion of job seekers who were cancelled from the registers but who returned to the employment service during the observation period (considered as a proxy for quality of placements). For this variable, as well, a decrease has been postulated.
- Utilization of labour market policy programmes measured by the number of days in such programmes per job seeker. With regard to the quantitative target for participation in labour market policy measures stipulated by the government, an increase was postulated.

The 'experiment effect' was calculated as follows:

$$e = \left(\frac{Ca / Cb}{Ea / Eb} \right) - 1 \qquad (10.1)$$

Where *Ea* and *Eb* represent the after and before figures, respectively, in an experimental municipality and *Ca* and *Cb* represent the comparison municipality, after and before. This methodology excludes as far as possible external processes that might affect target variables.

A positive outcome to equation (10.1) indicates a reduction due to the intervention in form of pilot projects in an experimental municipality relative to the change observed at the control. The number $e \times 100$ will indicate the estimated effect in per cent. Results of effect estimates, expressed in per cent, are presented in Table 10.1.

Table 10.1 Summary of effect estimates

Pairs of experiment and comparison municipalities	Reduction of mean duration of unemployment	Reduction of the proportion of job seekers re-entered into the registers of the employment service	Increase of utilization of labour market policy programmes
Ale/Mark	–	6%	–
Borlänge/Sandviken	–	59%	8%
Falkenberg/Karlskrona	–	–	–
Falun/Gävle	10%	–	15%
Gullspång/Götene	–	–	–
Huddinge/Botkyrka	4%	3%	–
Höganäs/Laholm	–	26%	3%
Lindesberg/Arvika	20%	10%	–
Malmö/Stockholm	–	–	–
Norrköping/Jönköping	5%	7%	–
Nybro/Alvesta	3%	–	9%
Nyköping/Eskilstuna	6%	35%	12%
Skellefteå/Härnösand	14%	35%	–
Skövde/Växjö	–	–	9%
Sundbyberg/Solna	–	40%	–
Södertälje/Haninge	–	–	1%
Trelleborg/Ystad	–	46%	11%
Tyresö/Vaxholm	9%	–	–
Vara/Tibro	20%	45%	15%
Varberg/Västervik	1%	–	8%
Vetlanda/Hultsfred	–	–	–
Värmdö/Ekerö	–	19%	–
Åre/Berg	–	26%	16%
Älmhult/Tranås	–	59%	–
Älvdalen/Tanum	4%	–	6%

In only 11 of 25 experimental municipalities could an effect be observed in the form of shorter mean duration of unemployment in the after period than could have been expected without the pilot projects. A close look at the questionnaire used as a data source in the evaluation scarcely revealed any systematic differences between these 11 and the 14 other municipalities in answers to questions regarding the progress of local co-operation in labour market policy matters. The only divergence that could be observed was that a larger proportion of the local politicians and the local government employees among the respondents in the group of 11 (where a postulated effect was perceived) held the view that there had been an increase in actual, not just perfunctory, co-operation between local actors in the design and implementation of labour market policy.

For the other two target variables, reduction in job seekers re-entering unemployment and increased programme utilization, the evaluation also shows no clear-cut picture with regard to the results of the pilot projects. Postulated effects were observed only in approximately half of the experimental municipalities. The results in Table 10.1 do, however, provide some support to the hypothesis that there were pilot projects which provided more permanent placements for job seekers. In 11 municipalities, there was a reduction of no less than between 10 per cent and 59 per cent in the proportion of job seekers who were re-entered into the registers of employment offices during the observation period. It would therefore appear that in a number of experimental municipalities many job seekers were sufficiently satisfied with the jobs found to keep them longer, on average, than employed clients in the control municipalities kept theirs.

In some municipalities, the contracts with the government stipulated that additional efforts should be made for particular groups of job seekers, such as the long-term unemployed and/or young job seekers. This was, for example, the case in six of the 14 municipalities where no effect on the mean duration unemployment was detected in estimates based upon observations for all job seekers. The question then arises as to whether this focus of programmes would make co-operation impact more likely among specific target groups. In order to find out if this had been the case, measurements were made of changes in these municipalities of unemployment duration solely in target groups specified in the contracts relative to corresponding changes in their respective controls. These estimates did not, however, indicate expected effects on the length of unemployment for job seekers belonging to the target groups.

Answers to the questionnaire distributed to selected policy-makers and administrators in all Swedish municipalities indicate that in the control group changes from the before to the after period regarding local co-operation in labour market policy matters have been very similar to the changes in the group of experimental municipalities. In such circumstances, it is not very surprising that the attempts at evaluating the pilot projects that have been presented here have not given an unambiguous and easily understood picture of effects of the schemes contracted for in the experimental municipalities.

Effect estimates based on multivariate analyses of differences between experimental and comparison municipalities

The results obtained from the direct comparison of programme and comparison municipalities are, as we have seen, somewhat mixed. Further insight might be gained from using regression analysis to assess the impact, if any, of intensified local co-operation on the exit rates from unemployment. This will make it possible to 'hold constant' other variables (for example, individual characteristics of job seekers) which influence exit rates. In the data that form the basis of this study, there exists censoring in the sense that a number of job seekers were still unemployed when the data collection was finished. This means that we do not have information about, for example, the lengths of their completed unemployment spells. This might give rise to a certain bias in regression coefficients estimated by OLS.

A possible approach is then to use the Cox regression model in a competing risk context. In our analysis we have used a proportional model. There is no particular reason to assume that the probability of getting a job should be influenced to the same extent by explanatory variables as the probability of being placed in a labour market policy programme. Therefore, in the analyses reported below, a so-called competing risk approach has been used. This means that we have studied the determinants of the probability that a job seeker will exit unemployment to four different destinations: 'regular employment', 'temporary employment' which also includes jobs with wage subsidies and sheltered work, 'labour market measures' and 'unknown' (other reason or lost contact).

The Cox proportional hazard model has the following form:

$$h(z,t) = e^{\beta Z} h_0(t),$$

where $h_0(t)$ is the baseline hazard at time t which is independent of individual characteristics. The conditional probability that individual i 'exits' at time t_i, given that some individuals (the risk set = R_i) could exit at time t_i is:

$$e^{\beta z_i} h_0(t_i) / \sum_{i \in Rti} e^{\beta z_i} h_0(t_i) = e^{\beta z_i} / \sum_{i \in Rti} e^{\beta z_i}$$

Thus, the duration dependence (included in for example the Weibull model) is eliminated and the model is allowed to be completely unspecified (see Kalbfleisch and Prentice, 1980). The results of regressions based on our data are presented in Tables 10.2 and 10.3. A positive regression coefficient indicates that the variable has a positive effect on the probability of having left unemployment at point of time t. We will begin with comments on the results of the estimations regarding flows into temporary employment and regular employment.

Table 10.2 Results of the Cox semi-parametric model for transitions from unemployment to temporary and regular employment

	Temporary employment				Regular employment			
Explanatory variables	1995		1997		1995		1997	
Age	–0.01**	0.001	–0.01**	0.001	–0.02**	0.001	–0.03**	0.001
Number of former jobs	0.15**	0.01	0.13**	0.005	0.14**	0.01	0.13**	0.004
Number of former unemployment spells	–0.05**	0.01	–0.04**	0.004	–0.04**	0.01	–0.06**	0.004
Immigrant 1	–0.20**	0.06	–0.11**	0.05	–0.47**	0.05	–0.41**	0.05
Immigrant 2	–0.16**	0.09	–0.07	0.06	–0.40**	0.07	–0.12**	0.05
Part time	0.02	0.05	–0.06	0.05	–0.14**	0.05	–0.35**	0.06
Secondary school 1	0.13**	0.03	0.12**	0.03	0.21**	0.02	0.16**	0.02
Secondary school 2	0.07*	0.04	0.09**	0.03	0.26**	0.03	0.24**	0.03
University	0.21**	0.05	0.16**	0.05	0.48**	0.03	0.42**	0.04
Interregional job seeking	0.06**	0.03	0.01	0.03	0.05**	0.02	0.11**	0.02

Good experience	0.25**	0.04	0.19**	0.03	0.26**	0.03	0.18**	0.03
Some experience	0.18**	0.04	0.19**	0.03	0.01	0.03	0.02	0.03
Occupation 1	0.35**	0.05	0.78**	0.11	–0.35**	0.03	0.84**	0.11
Occupation 2	0.50**	0.05	0.86**	0.11	–0.50**	0.03	0.60**	0.10
Occupation 3	0.10**	0.05	0.53**	0.11	–0.15**	0.02	0.99**	0.10
Occupation 4	0.40**	0.06	0.72**	0.11	–0.69**	0.04	0.42**	0.11
Handicapped	0.37**	0.04	0.38**	0.03	–0.99**	0.05	–0.89**	0.06
Municipality	0.02	0.02	0.09**	0.02	0.004	0.02	–0.02	0.02
u/v-quota	0.12**	0.01	0.07**	0.008	–0.03**	0.01	–0.04**	0.006
Gender, female	0.38**	0.03	0.44**	0.03	–0.40**	0.02	–0.32**	0.02
–2 Log L.	156 685.9		195 656.73		314 937.3		276 477.58	

Notes:
The first column under each year gives regression coefficients corresponding to each variable; the second column gives standard errors of the regression coefficients.
** denotes significantly different from zero at the 5 per cent level; * at the 10 per cent level.
Immigrant 1 = immigrants from Africa, Asia and Latin America; immigrant 2 = immigrants from Eastern Europe.
Secondary school 1 = two years secondary school; secondary school 2 = three years secondary school. The reference for the education variables is compulsory school as highest education.
Occupation 1 = white-collar jobs with high demands on education and experience; occupation 2 = the service sector; occupation 3 = the manufacturing sector; occupation 4 = no special demand for education. The reference for: occupation 1–occupation 4 is that the job seeker searches no specific occupation.
Municipality = 1 for experimental municipalities and 0 for comparison municipalities.
u/v-quota = number of registered job seekers/number of registered vacancies in the actual local county.

Table 10.3 Results of the Cox semi-parametric model for transitions from unemployment to destinations 'unknown' and labour market policy programme

	Unknown				Labour market programmes			
Explanatory variables	1995		1997		1995		1997	
Age	–0.01**	0.001	0.002**	0.001	–0.01**	0.001	–0.001**	0.001
Number of former jobs	–0.05**	0.01	–0.04**	0.01	–0.05**	0.01	–0.05**	0.004
Number of former unemployment spells	–0.008	0.01	–0.01**	0.005	0.05**	0.005	0.05**	0.003
Immigrant 1	0.06	0.04	0.05	0.04	0.31**	0.03	0.17**	0.03
Immigrant 2	22 –0.05	0.06	–0.10*	0.05	0.49**	0.04	0.18**	0.03
Part time	0.15**	0.04	0.23**	0.03	–0.32**	0.04	–0.21**	0.03
Secondary school 1	–0.19**	0.02	–0.20**	0.02	0.14**	0.02	0.14**	0.02
Secondary school 2	–0.18**	0.03	–0.12**	0.03	0.22**	0.02	0.11**	0.02
University	–0.23**	0.04	–0.29**	0.04	0.01	0.03	–0.04	0.03
Interregional job seeking	–0.11**	0.03	–0.05**	0.03	0.10**	0.02	0.03	0.02

Good experience	–0.14**	0.03	–0.22**	0.03	–0.22**	0.02	–0.02	0.02
Some experience	–0.02	0.03	–0.07**	0.03	–0.04*	0.02	0.01	0.02
Occupation 1	–0.33**	0.03	–0.13**	0.06	0.48**	0.03	–0.05	0.05
Occupation 2	–0.29**	0.03	–0.02	0.06	0.51**	0.03	0.04	0.04
Occupation 3	–0.47**	0.03	–0.25**	0.06	0.37**	0.03	–0.18**	0.04
Occupation 4	–0.26**	0.04	0.03	0.06	0.40**	0.03	–0.10**	0.05
Handicapped	–0.11**	0.04	–0.20**	0.04	0.36**	0.02	0.33**	0.02
Municipality	–0.03	0.02	–0.02	0.02	0.03**	0.01	0.005	0.01
u/v-quota	–0.13**	0.01	–0.05	0.006	0.11**	0.01	0.09**	0.005
Gender, female	0.23**	0.02	0.17**	0.02	0.17**	0.02	0.24**	0.02
–2 Log L.	238 007.72		246 875.76		404 699.23		455 859.50	

Notes:
The first column under each year gives regression coefficients corresponding to each variable; the second column gives standard errors of the regression coefficients.
** denotes significantly different from zero at the 5 per cent level; * at the 10 per cent level.
Immigrant 1 = immigrants from Africa, Asia and Latin America; immigrant 2 = immigrants from Eastern Europe.
Secondary school 1 = two years secondary school; secondary school 2 = three years secondary school. The reference for the education variables is compulsory school as highest education.
Occupation 1 = white-collar jobs with high demands on education and experience; occupation 2 = the service sector; occupation 3 = the manufacturing sector; occupation 4 = no special demand for education. The reference for: occupation 1–occupation 4 is that the job seeker searches no specific occupation.
Municipality = 1 for experimental municipalities and 0 for comparison municipalities.
u/v-quota = number of registered job seekers/number of registered vacancies in the actual local county.

During the period prior to the programme (1995), we found significantly negative effects on transitions from unemployment to temporary employment for the following characteristics: higher age, several unemployment spells and immigrants. Significant positive effects were found for the following characteristics: number of former jobs, education higher than compulsory school, interregional job seeking, some or quality experience in the sought-after occupation, the desire for a specific kind of work, handicapped, higher u/v-quota and for women.

Turning to the period after the programme (1997), we found negative effects for the following characteristics: higher age; several unemployment spells; immigrants from Asia, Africa or Latin America and being registered at an employment office in an experimental municipality. We found positive effects for the following characteristics: number of former jobs, education higher than compulsory school, some or quality experience in the sought-after occupation, the desire for a specific kind of work, handicapped, higher u/v-quota, gender (female) and being a job seeker in an experimental municipality. The analysis thus indicated a positive impact of intensified local level co-operation on transitions from unemployment to temporary employment.

During the period prior to the programme we found negative effects on transitions from unemployment to regular employment for the following characteristics: higher age, several unemployment spells, immigrants, the desire for part-time work, the desire for a specific kind of work, handicapped, higher u/v-quota and for women. A positive effect was found for the following characteristics: number of former jobs, education higher than compulsory school, inter-regional job seeking and experience in the sought-after occupation.

Again, turning to the period after the programme, we found negative effects for the following characteristics: higher age, several unemployment spells, immigrants, the desire for part-time work, handicapped, higher u/v-quota and for women. A negative but not significant effect on the exit rate to regular employment was found for local co-operation. A positive effect on the exit rate to regular employment was found for the following characteristics: number of former jobs and education higher than compulsory school, interregional job seeking, experience in the sought-after occupation and the desire for a specific kind of work. According to the results of the regressions, there was no impact of local cooperation on the transition from unemployment to regular employment.

Table 10.3 presents the results of regressions regarding destinations 'labour market policy programme' and 'unknown'. We found negative effects on the transition from unemployment to labour market policy programmes for the following characteristics during the period before the programme: higher age, number of former jobs, the desire for part-time work and some or quality experience in the sought-after occupation. On the other hand, we found positive effects for the following characteristics: former unemployment spells, immigrants, high school as highest education, interregional job seeking, the desire for a specific kind of work, handicapped, higher u/v-quota and for women. There was a positive and statistically significant effect of being registered at an employment office in a municipality belonging to the experimental group.

For the period after the programme, statistically significant negative effects were found for the following characteristics: higher age, number of former jobs, the desire for part-time work and the desire for a specific type of work (with the exception of jobs in the service sector). Positive effects were found for the following characteristics: former unemployment spells, immigrants, high school as highest education, handicapped, higher u/v-quota and for women.

The regressions indicate that the intensified level of co-operation had a negative effect on transitions from unemployment to labour market policy programmes since the coefficient for 'municipality' was not significant in the period after the programme but significant and positive in the period before.

The estimates for the destination 'unknown' (other reason or lost contact) indicate a negative effect during the period before the programme for the following characteristics: higher age, number of former jobs, secondary school or university as highest education, interregional job seeking, quality experience in the sought-after occupation, the desire for a specific type of work, handicapped and higher u/v-quota. For the following characteristics we found a positive effect: the desire for part-time work and being female.

After the programme, the results indicate negative effects for the following characteristics: number of former jobs, former unemployment spells, immigrant from eastern Europe, secondary school or university as highest education, interregional job seeking, some or quality experience in the sought-after occupation, the desire for a white-collar job with high demands on education and experience, the desire for a job in the manufacturing industry, and handicapped. We found a positive effect for the following characteristics: higher age, searching for a part-time job and being female. We found no statistically significant impact on transitions from unemployment to some unknown destination for job seekers in the experimental municipalities.

In the regressions we have analysed, the effects on exit rates from unemployment of individual characteristics of job seekers, their domicile (experimental or non-experimental municipality) and labour demand (u/v-quota). As regards the dummy for being registered at an employment office in an experimental municipality, we found a change from an insignificant effect in the period before the start of the experiment to a significant positive effect in the period after for transitions from unemployment to temporary employment. This may be an effect of some importance considering that, for many job seekers, a temporary job is the first step in the process of being integrated into the mainstream of the labour market. The regressions for the other destinations, however, do not indicate positive effects of the pilot projects carried on in municipalities in the experiment group. In some of these, the projects contracted for with the government included a number of participants that was rather small in relation to the size of the local labour market. It is possible, therefore, that projects simply were not large enough to have an observable impact on overall labour market performance as measured in the regressions. Another conceivable explanation for the absence of measured effects is a possible impact of an increase in local co-operation in municipalities outside the experimental group as a response to the deteriorated situation on the Swedish labour market in the 1990s. It may also be that the time allocated for the evaluation was too short for target-related effects that may occur to work themselves out.

3.2 A Natural Experiment

In the literature on evaluation research, we find descriptions of how controlled experiments solve certain kinds of evaluation problems, but also of the problems associated with such experiments. There is a tendency to regard evaluations based on 'natural experiments', which in this case would mean 'spontaneous' changes in methods of implementing labour market policy in different parts of the country, as a means of circumventing the problems and limitations related to controlled experiments. But analyses of effects of such changes will demand relatively detailed data to control for various kinds of differences between regions. In this study, we have used the possibility to design a natural experiment. One question in our questionnaire was: 'To what extent has the development in the municipality during the last two years brought about an increased real (that is, not just formal) co-operation between the municipal and other organizations on the one hand; and, on the other hand, employment offices and other government agencies and institutions?' We selected nine municipalities among those in which the representatives of the municipalities and the local employment offices have responded that there had been a significant or very significant increase in real co-operation at the local level in labour market policy matters. For each of these nine municipalities, a comparison municipality was selected in which municipal officials and politicians have responded that the increase in co-operation had been 'scarcely significant' or 'nearly non-existent'. The municipalities were also chosen in such a way that the municipalities in each pair were located in the same employment zone, ensuring greater comparability.

We have analysed the effects on the exit rate to regular employment and temporary employment of an intensified local level co-operation in this 'natural experiment context'. From Cox estimations, we found that the following characteristics increase the chances of obtaining regular employment: having had many previous jobs, having at least three years secondary school as highest education, having quality experience in the sought-after occupation and being an interregional job seeker. Unemployed job seekers with many previous unemployment spells, women, older people, those living in an area with high u/v-quota and the handicapped find it more difficult to find a permanent job. The effect of local co-operation on the chance to rapidly find a permanent job seems to be non-existent. During both the before and the after period, the probability of rapidly getting regular employment was lower for job seekers living in municipalities where the local officials and the heads of the employment offices have responded in the questionnaire that local co-operation had been significant than it was for job seekers in other municipalities.

Estimations regarding temporary jobs indicate that unemployed job seekers who had had several previous jobs, had some or quality experience in sought-after occupation, were searching for a specific job, were living in an area with a high u/v-quota, had high school as highest education and women have greater chances than other seekers to rapidly get a temporary job; while older job seekers and unemployed with many previous periods of unemployment have a smaller chance. During the period before, the chance of getting a temporary job was less for the unemployed living in municipalities where the officials declared that there had been a high degree of co-operation. During the period after, the probability of rapidly getting a temporary job was higher for the unemployed living in these municipalities. These results indicate that there was a positive effect of a high degree of local co-operation on the probability of rapidly getting a temporary job.

In this section, we have described the results of an analysis based on comparisons between municipalities where, according to the results of the questionnaire, there had been a significant increase in local co-operation during the last two years and municipalities where no large increase was reported. The analysis indicates that an increase in co-operation had a positive effect only on the chance of rapidly getting a temporary job. No effect could be observed in terms of placements in permanent jobs.

4 CONCLUDING REMARKS

According to our study, intensified local level LMP co-operation achieved by means of contracts between the national government and the municipalities does not generate the hoped for noticeable target-related impacts. It is possible, however, that some such impacts need some time to work themselves out and become strong enough to be observed. Since most of the pilot projects have been prolonged, this hypothesis will be examined by means of repeated impact evaluations.

Regrettably we do not expect the repeated evaluations to reveal the existence of very significant impacts. We believe that the differences between the 'experimental' and the 'control' municipalities in the policies pursued will remain too small for observable differences in the development of target variables to occur. Nor do we have any strong confidence that repeated evaluations based on the 'natural experiment' approach will give reliable impact estimates. While large differences between municipalities in terms of the local LMP pursued may occur spontaneously (without governmental interventions), to a significant degree these differences are also likely to reflect differences in the problems and preconditions that the local decision-makers have to face.

However, for reasons discussed in section 2 above, we do think that there is a need for unprejudiced reconsideration and renewals of Swedish LMP; and believe that the emergence of intensified local co-operation based on interests and incentives between different local actors should be facilitated. Our main recommendation is that the government should initiate much more radical experiments than the ones so far attempted. In a number of experimental municipalities, a very far-reaching deregulation and decentralization of the LMP decision-making and implementation processes should be carried out. In these municipalities, the use of centrally stipulated directives, rules and regulations should, to a very large extent, be abandoned and substituted by the use of recommendations, guidelines, dialogues and systematic evaluation. The experiments thus initiated should be subjected to impact evaluations methodically similar to the ones presented in section 3 above.

It should be added, however, that we do believe that for such a radical deregulation and decentralization to the local level of LMP decision-making to be successful, it has to be based on very clear distinctions between the governmental and the municipal agencies and between their respective roles and responsibilities.

NOTES

1. This chapter is based on research carried out at the request of the Swedish Ministry of Labour by the Centre for Labour Market Policy Research (CAFO) at Växjö University. It presents the principal results of an impact evaluation of the pilot projects ('experiments') initiated by the government as well as a more general analysis of the nature and consequences of the current development towards an intensified local level co-operation in the design and implementation of Swedish labour market policies (Behrenz *et al.*, 1998).

2. The name of the department in Swedish is *Arbetsmarknadsverket*.
3. *Arbetsmarknadsstyrelsen* in Swedish.
4. The employment service of the Labour Market Administration once enjoyed a monopoly on job placement, but since 1993 private employment offices have been allowed in Sweden.
5. For descriptions and analyses of the crisis of the 1990s in the Swedish economy see, for example, Gylfasson (1997). Somewhat different interpretations are found in Korpi (1996).
6. This way of looking at decision-making processes, including the role of project appraisals, inherent in our discussion are closely related to the analyses in Sugden and Williams (1978, pp. 3–9 and 229–41), and Williams (1993).
7. About 4–5 per cent of the municipal politicians and civil servants but about 25 per cent of the PES managers claim that the rules and regulations mentioned do *not* represent significant obstacles to desirable LMP activities. About 67 per cent of all respondents (79 per cent of the politicians and 42 per cent of the managers) characterize the obstacles as very significant.
8. As regards Swedish conditions see Behrenz and Delander (1998).
9. Transfer to Händel is entirely automatic via the computerized placement system of the Labour Market Administration used by employment office staff in their dealings with job seekers and employers; there is no manual reporting by individual placement officers.
10. Calculated from job seekers' lengths of stay as unemployed in the active files of the employment service.

REFERENCES

Behrenz, L. and L. Delander (1998), *The Total Fiscal Costs of Unemployment: An Estimation for Sweden*, Växjö: CAFO, Växjö University. (Report to the European Commission.)

Behrenz, L., L. Delander, H. Niklasson and E. Nyberg (1998), *Utvärdering av lokal samverkan mot arbetslöshet*, Växjö: CAFO, Växjö University.

Carlsson, F., M. Johansson, L.-O. Persson and B. Tegsjö (1993), *Creating Labour Market Areas and Employment Zones*, Umeå: CERUM, Umeå University.

Gylfason, T. (ed.) (1997), *The Swedish Model under Stress: A View from the Stands*, Stockholm: SNS.

Johannesson, J. and E. Wadensjö (eds) (1997), *Labour Market Policy at the Crossroads*, Stockholm: EFA, Ministry of Labour.

Kalbfleisch, J.D. and R.L. Prentice (1980), *The Statistical Analysis of Failure Time Data*, New York: John Wiley and Sons.

Korpi, W. (1996), 'Eurosclerosis and the Sclerosis of Objectivity: On the Role of Values among Economic Policy Experts', *Economic Journal*, 106 (November), 1727–46.

Layard, R., S. Nickell and R. Jackman (1991), *Unemployment: Macroeconomic Performance and the Labour Market*, Oxford: Oxford University Press.

Ministry of Finance (1995), *The Medium Term Survey of the Swedish Economy*, Stockholm: Fritzes.

Niklasson, H. and L. Tomsmark (1997), 'Zielsteuerung der Arbeidsmarktpolitik in Finland, Norwegen und Schweden', in C. Riegler and F. Naschold (eds), *Reformen des öffentlichen Sektors in Skandinavien*, Baden-Baden: Nomos Verlagsgesellschaft, pp. 197–248.

Rossi, P.H. and H.E. Freeman (1985), *Evaluation: A Systematic Approach*, Beverly Hills, CA: Sage Publications.

Schmid, G. and B. Reissert (1996), 'Unemployment Compensation and Labour Market Transition', in G. Schmid, J. O'Reilly and K. Schömann (eds), *International Handbook of Labour Market Policy and Evaluation*, Cheltenham: Edward Elgar, pp. 235–76.

Schotter, A. (1997), *Microeconomics: A Modern Approach*, New York: Addison-Wesley.

Sugden, R. and A. Williams (1978), *The Principles of Practical Cost–Benefit Analysis*, Oxford: Oxford University Press.

Williams, A. (1993), 'Cost–Benefit Analysis: Applied Welfare Economics or General Decision Aid?', in A. Williams and E. Giardina (eds), *Efficiency in the Public Sector*, Aldershot: Edward Elgar, pp. 65–79.

PART III

Conclusions

11. Conclusions

Jaap de Koning and Hugh Mosley

The principal conclusions of our research on active labour market policy (ALMP) and employment transitions can be summarized and discussed under three main headings:

1. the aggregate impact of ALMP on unemployment and particularly on long-term unemployment;
2. variation in ALMP implementation and its impact on programme performance;
3. active policies and employment transitions: an agenda for research and policy.

1 THE AGGREGATE IMPACT OF ALMP

Aggregate impact analyses were carried out for five countries: France, Germany, the Netherlands, Spain and Sweden. All the studies are based on an agreed framework, although there are a number of differences in the approaches followed by the various national research teams. The main features of the data and models used are summarized in Table 11.1. All contributions examine the impact of active labour market policies on transitions from unemployment using aggregate data at the regional level. Moreover, all use simple log-linear and/or linear models in which the fixed effects method is used as the estimation technique in order to cope with the endogeneity problem: in regions experiencing high unemployment more is spent on ALMP than in low-unemployment areas. If the impact of ALMP on unemployment is relatively small, we may observe a positive correlation between the two, rather than a negative one.

The overall conclusion of the aggregate impact analysis of ALMP based on the evidence for the five countries is that there is some empirical support for the claim that ALMP helps to reduce total unemployment and long-term unemployment. However, the results are partly conflicting and not always easy to interpret. Only in the German case was some evidence found for an impact of ALMP on the level of long-term unemployment. Given the data limitations and the confidence intervals of the estimators the results do not exclude that ALMP reduces total unemployment and long-term unemployment, but we can fairly say that the overall impacts are relatively small in any case. These findings are consistent with the results of evaluation studies based on micro-data.

Before discussing the results it is important to note the differences in approach since only the French and Swedish analyses, which were treated in the same study, are identical. Thus ALMP is measured differently in the Dutch case (ALMP expenditure instead of participants) and not only active programmes but also expenditure for placement services is included (see Table 11.1). Moreover, in the Dutch case it was not possible to analyse all types of ALMP activity separately. The periods covered by the four contributions differ somewhat, although the 1994–5 period is common to all four. An important limitation of the French/Swedish contribution is that – unlike the other studies – only hirings from unemployment are used as the dependent variable: it contains no separate analyses for the impact of ALMP on unemployment or long-term unemployment. However, since it is the only study based on monthly rather than annual data, its results would appear to be the most reliable. The German contribution is the only one in which implementation indicators are included in the analysis.[1]

Table 11.2 summarizes the main conclusions for the various countries. The most convincing results are obtained in the French/Swedish contribution. According to these results ALMP measures have a significant upward effect on the outflow from unemployment to employment, albeit with relatively small impact. On the basis of the elasticities computed, the conclusion is that an enormous increase in ALMP is needed to realize a moderate effect on hirings from unemployment.

A significant but again relatively small impact of ALMP on hirings from unemployment was also found in the Dutch aggregate impact analysis. Remarkably, in this contribution there was no significant impact on the (change in the) level of unemployment. A possible explanation of this finding is that ALMP increases participants' chances of finding employment but at the cost of reducing the chances of other job seekers. As a result, increasing hirings from unemployment can go hand-in-hand with increasing inflows into unemployment, leaving the level of unemployment unaffected. However, in the Spanish case a significant impact was found on the level of total unemployment, but not on the flow from unemployment to employment. One possible explanation of this result is that participation in an ALMP measure reduces the probability of becoming unemployed in the future again, but does not have a significant effect on the transition probability from unemployment to employment in the current unemployment spell.

Table 11.1 Main features of the aggregate impact analyses for the five countries

	France/Sweden	Germany	Netherlands	Spain
Estimation period	1991–5	1994–7	1991–5	1987–95
Type of data	Monthly, regional cross-section	Yearly, regional cross-section	Yearly, regional cross-section	Yearly, regional cross-section
Measurement of ALMP	Number of participants	Number of participants	Expenditure	Number of participants
ALMP measures include job placement activities	No	No	Yes	No
ALMP is broken down by type of measure	Yes	Yes	Expenditure data can be attributed to specific measures only to a limited extent	Yes
Dependent variables used	Hirings from unemployment	Outflow from unemployment Change in the level of unemployment Structure of unemployment	Hirings from unemployment Change in the level of unemployment Change in the number of unemployed beneficiaries	Hirings from unemployment Level of unemployment
Separate analyses long-term unemployment	No	Only analyses with respect to long-term unemployment	Yes	Yes
Implementation indicators included as explanatory variables	No	To a limited extent	No	No
Mathematical form model	Loglinear	Both linear and loglinear	Both linear and loglinear	Both linear and loglinear
Fixed effects method used in estimation	Yes	Yes[a]	Yes	Yes

Note: a. With the exception of the outflow analysis, for which only cross-sectional data for one year was available.

Table 11.2 Summary of the estimation results for the five countries

	France/Sweden	Germany	Netherlands	Spain
Impact on:				
The flow from total unemployment to employment	Significantly positive	n.a.	Significantly positive	Positive, but not significant
The flow from long-term unemployment to employment	n.a.	Not significant or significant with the wrong sign[a]	Positive, but not significant	Positive, but not significant
The level of total unemployment	n.a.	n.a.	n.a.	Significantly negative
The change in the level of total unemployment	n.a.	n.a.	Negative but not significant	n.a.
The level of long-term unemployment	n.a.	Negative, partly significant	n.a.	Significantly negative
The change in the level of long-term unemployment	n.a.	Mostly not significant	n.a.	n.a.
The share of long-term unemployment in total unemployment	n.a.	Mostly negative, partly significant	n.a.	n.a.

Note: a. Based on information for only one year.

In neither the Dutch nor in the Spanish cases do the results point to a particularly strong impact of ALMP on long-term unemployment. In the Dutch case the effect on hirings from long-term unemployment was not even significant. In the German case, too, no effect on the outflow from long-term unemployment was found, although the lack of significant results may be due to data limitations: only data on the total outflow from unemployment was available, which also includes the outflow from unemployment to other forms of inactivity, and the analysis was based on data for only one year. In the German contribution, analyses of both the level of and the change in long-term unemployment rate as well as the share of long-term unemployment in total unemployment yielded mixed results: sometimes a significant negative impact on long-term unemployment was found, but in other models the effect is not significant. As noted above, the French/Swedish contribution does not contain separate analyses for long-term unemployment.

There are several possible explanations for these surprisingly weak findings. One is of a technical nature, the so-called endogeneity problem. In cases where a positive impact of ALMP on unemployment was found the explanation could be that the government tends to raise ALMP expenditure in response to increasing unemployment. When the impact of ALMP is relatively small, we may still observe increases in both unemployment and ALMP expenditure, suggesting that ALMP is ineffective. We tried to deal with the problem by applying the fixed effects technique on pooled regional data for a number of years, but perhaps this approach did not solve the problem entirely. In none of the contributions was an attempt made to estimate a policy response function, which is difficult since the policy response function is different for each type of measure.

Another possible explanation for the apparently low effectiveness of ALMP in the results of these aggregate impact analyses may have to do with deficiencies in implementation. Impact evaluations tend to assume a simplified input–output model in which the implementation process is automatic, underestimating the importance of programme variation, for example, in policy mix, targeting, and in the delivery system. Labour market training, job creation, or wage subsidy programmes provide complex services that are in practice very heterogeneous. Programme 'treatments' are seldom so standardized as the (misleading) analogy to medical research suggests.

In principle, this shortcoming can be remedied by giving more consideration to the role of implementation in modelling the impact of ALMP measures and by collecting appropriate data. In practice, this is difficult and due in particular to the general scarcity of good data on the implementation process. Thus data limitations made it impossible to give more systematic attention to implementation variables in the aggregate impact analyses in this volume, which would have required a comprehensive survey of regional level variation in implementation.

It is difficult to draw any general conclusion about the relative effectiveness of the various types of measures. Even for the same country different results were found with respect to the effectiveness of the various measures depending on the specification used. As far as a conclusion can be drawn one could say that training is probably more effective than are job-creation measures. It partly depends on the purpose of the 'treatment'. There is evidence that job-creation measures are effective when targeted to people with very few prospects to a job in the sense that they put people to work who would have remained unemployed otherwise. But at the same time there is hardly any evidence that this helps them to find a 'normal' job eventually. The information about placement subsidies is too scanty to draw any conclusion. The same is true for job brokering which was dealt with only in the Dutch study, in which it was the most effective measure.

An important limitation of the analyses is that the ALMP data could not be broken down according to characteristics of the participants. It would be particularly important to have a breakdown with respect to unemployment duration. Evaluation studies based on micro-data suggest that the effectiveness of measures may differ strongly between the short- and the long-term unemployed. It could be that often the wrong 'treatment' is offered to the various groups among the unemployed. In the Dutch contribution reference is made to an analysis based on national time series data. On national level both unemployment (in this analysis measured as the number of people with an unemployment benefit) and ALMP participants can be broken down according to unemployment duration, making it possible to estimate the model for different duration classes. The results indicate that in the Netherlands the activities of the Public Employment Service (placement services and training) have had mainly an impact on short-term unemployment. Furthermore, this effect is relatively small. Job-creation measures, on the other hand, helped to reduce, in the first place, long-term unemployment. However, the latter impact is to a large degree artificial, because most of the people involved do not move to regular (non-subsidized) jobs.

As mentioned above, only the German contribution made an attempt to incorporate the quality of ALMP measures into the model analysis. According to the results the duration of a 'treatment' may influence the effectiveness. However, the outcomes are ambivalent and cannot act as a guide for policy recommendations at this stage.

Shortcomings in the delivery system may also account for the relatively low effectiveness of ALMP. In the period under consideration the implementation of active policies was still the responsibility of government or employment service organizations, which behaved in a bureaucratic way. In this type of organization the incentives to increase quality and efficiency are often weak. Recently, this has changed. Increasingly, management principles are borrowed from the market sector according to which quantitative targets are formulated and funding is made dependent on the results obtained. Furthermore, there is a tendency to give more room to private employment services and to involve private agencies in the implementation of active policies. Whether these changes have helped to reduce unemployment and to improve the quality of active policies is as yet unknown. The next section discusses findings from the implementation studies and their implications.

2 PROCESS EVALUATIONS: THE ORGANIZATION AND IMPLEMENTATION OF ALMP

The three implementation studies reported in Part II of this volume address a number of issues related to the ALMP implementation process and its impact on ALMP outcomes at the regional level in Germany, the Netherlands, and Sweden (see Table 11.3). All three address issues related to co-operation in the implementation process, especially between the PES and municipal authorities responsible for social assistance. Moreover, the German and Swedish studies both examine the issue of decentralization in implementation.

The Dutch study examines the forms of co-operation that have developed between the PES and municipal social assistance agencies and investigates whether co-operation in the implementation process has had an impact on the performance of four ALMP programmes for the long-term unemployed. The evaluation of government-sponsored pilot projects to promote co-operation between the PES and municipalities is the focus of the Swedish study which investigates, in particular, whether enhanced co-operation in the experimental municipalities result in higher transition rates out of unemployment. The German implementation study investigates the responsiveness of the PES to long-term unemployment and its interaction with local ALMP for social assistance recipients. Whereas the former two studies attempt to assess the impact of co-operation on programme and labour market outcomes, the focus of the latter is on explaining patterns of co-operation in terms of the incentives provided by the institutional framework of labour market policy and potential co-operation gains. Moreover the German study and, from a theoretical perspective, the Swedish study also examine the issue of decentralization in the PES, that is, the extent to which local PES offices are allowed to develop independent policy profiles and strategies in implementing ALMP.

Although methodologically more heterogeneous than the aggregate impact analyses, the implementation studies share a number of common features: all three are based on a regional level analysis of the ALMP implementation

Table 11.3 Research design and principal findings of the implementation studies

	Netherlands	Germany	Sweden
Principal themes	Co-operation	Decentralization, co-operation	Co-operation, decentralization
Period	1991–7	1995–7	1994–7
Research questions	What forms of co-operation have developed between the PES and municipal social assistance agencies? Does co-operation in implementation have an impact on programme performance in four programmes for the long-term unemployed?	Do local PES districts develop decentralized ALMP policy profiles? Is PES resource allocation responsive to local labour market needs, especially long-term unemployment? Do the PES and local authorities responsible for social assistance recipients co-operate? Why or why not?	Evaluation of impact of pilot projects to promote co-operation between PES and municipalities: does enhanced co-operation between PES and municipalities result in higher transition rates out of unemployment?
Methodology	Telephone survey on forms of co-operation in 19 Dutch municipalities; regression analysis of impact of forms of co-operation between PES and municipalities on programme uptake, outflows, positive outflows; in-depth case studies in four municipalities representing principal types of co-operation.	Regression analysis of ALMP resource allocation and targeting in PES delivery system based on aggregate data on ALMP entrants in 142 western German PES districts; case studies of co-operation between PES and local authorities in three western German PES districts.	Matched comparison of outflows from unemployment in 25 experimental and 25 control municipalities at two points in time based on individual data from unemployment records. A supplementary 'natural experiment' comparing probability of transition to employment in 18 matched municipalities with and without significant real increase in local co-operation.

Principal results	1) In the case-study municipalities there is no consistent relationship between the development of co-operation in implementation regimes and the performance indicators examined. 2) Analysis of a pooled data set for 19 municipalities in 1996 and 1997 provides little evidence for a co-operation effect in local ALMP. Moreover, the municipal implementation regimes show no consistent pattern of 'good practice' across different programmes or even different indicators for the same programme.	1) Despite the centralized and hierarchical structures of the PES, there is a remarkable diversity in uptake, policy mix and styles at the operational level of PES district offices. 2) The allocation of ALMP resources to PES districts is not highly responsive to local labour market conditions. Moreover, targeting of ALMP on the long-term unemployed is weak with great variation among PES offices. 3) Although co-operation is very uneven, the institutional division of labour between PES and local authorities is not *per se* detrimental. What is needed is an improved correspondence between the new ALMP tasks of the local authorities and their financial resources.	1) The pilot programme to promote intensified local level co-operation has not generated the anticipated positive impact on labour market outcomes for the unemployed. Although a significant positive impact on transitions from unemployment to temporary employment was found, there was no impact on exit rates to regular employment. 2) In the 'natural experiment' an increase in co-operation had a positive effect only on the chance of rapidly getting a temporary job, but no effect could be observed in terms of placements in permanent jobs.

process either at the municipal level (Sweden, Netherlands) or at the PES district level (Germany). Moreover, all combine qualitative and quantitative methods of analysis, although with important differences in emphasis and approaches. While the Dutch and German implementation studies are based on a regression analysis of aggregate data at the local (municipal or PES district) combined with selective case studies, the Swedish study, which evaluates a pilot programme, is based on a logistic regression analysis of the probability of transitions out of unemployment in a matched comparison of experimental and control municipalities. On both the Dutch and the Swedish studies it was possible to gather qualitative information on types or levels of co-operation for a large sample of municipalities based on a telephone survey and a written questionnaire.

The co-operation problem addressed by all three studies has its roots in trends affecting most European countries. The stylized facts can be summarized as follows: a secular increase in unemployment and long-term unemployment has led to a tightening of eligibility conditions for unemployment benefit, resulting in the exclusion of more and more unemployed individuals from the PES's core clientèle of unemployment benefit recipients. Parallel to this trend has been a remarkable growth in the importance of local labour market policies for the long-term unemployed and other marginal groups dependent on social assistance. As a consequence of these trends, there is an increasing fragmentation in the delivery systems for ALMP with the PES and the local authorities each primarily responsible for their separate clientèles. This results in specific co-ordination problems. More importantly, this unfavourable division of labour permits the public employment service to shift responsibility for problem groups in the labour market on to the local authorities, whose ALMP activities are often less professionalized and less well endowed with resources than are those of the PES.

Both the Dutch and the Swedish studies attempted to assess the impact of co-operation between the PES and local authorities on programme performance indicators and on individual transitions to employment, respectively. In both cases only weak evidence is found for a positive 'co-operation effect'.

In the Netherlands both the regression analysis and the more in-depth case studies showed no consistent relationship between forms of co-operation in implementation regimes and programme performance indicators. For the 19 municipalities examined a statistically significant relationship was found only between physical co-operation (for example, co-location, joint venture) and positive outflows in a programme for long-term unemployed youth, one of three programme indicators for one of two programmes examined. Moreover, the analysis of 19 municipal implementation regimes showed no clear pattern of good practice across different performance indicators and programmes. Different performance indicators for the same programme are either not highly correlated or show the wrong sign and only positive programme outcome rates were significantly correlated for both schemes. This study suggests that more intense forms of co-operation such as a joint venture or joint staffing do not necessarily lead to better policy outcomes and that best practice in implementation has to be tailor-made to fit local circumstances and even specific programmes.

The Swedish pilot projects to promote intensified local level co-operation between the PES and the local authorities do not generate the anticipated positive impact on labour market outcomes for the unemployed. While the regression results do show a significant positive impact on transitions from unemployment to temporary employment, there was no impact on exit rates to regular employment. Moreover, the programme appears to have had a negative effect on transitions from unemployment to labour market policy programmes. These weak findings in support of a co-operation effect may be due in part to methodological problems, for example, the time-frame of the evaluation may have been too short for the effects that may occur to work themselves out.

The analysis of the institutional bifurcation in ALMP implementation between the PES and local ALMP for social assistance recipients in Germany showed a great deal of local variation in the degree of institutionalization of professional local ALMP delivery systems, which have become fairly widespread in urban areas. The institutional division of labour between PES and local authorities is not *per se* detrimental: there is a certain justification in separate implementation structures offering specialized services to their respective client groups. This does not preclude co-operation, but a forced integration of these separate systems is neither realistic nor useful in light of the very different legal framework and the capabilities of many professionalized local structures. What is needed is an institutional reform which leads to an improved correspondence between the labour market policy responsibilities of the local authorities and the financial and institutional resources available to them. Moreover, the problem of providing labour market services to the socially excluded, here social assistance recipients, cannot be regarded in isolation from reform of the PES itself. While improved co-operation might mitigate shortcomings in the implementation structure the PES currently lacks strong institutional incentives to co-operate with local authorities in serving the social assistance clientèle of the local authorities. Indeed the empirical findings on ALMP resource allocation and targeting appear to reflect a pattern of institutional creaming that raises serious doubts about whether the PES is adequately addressing the concerns of problem groups at the margins of the labour market, especially the long-term unemployed.

3 AGENDA FOR RESEARCH AND POLICY

The need for active policies still exists and may even be increasing. More flexible labour markets mean more transitions between employment and unemployment, enhancing the risk that people may become unemployed and, particularly in recession periods, long-term unemployed. Furthermore, unemployment levels remain high. Even in countries that have experienced a relatively favourable labour market development, such as the Netherlands, the unemployment rate still reaches levels of 8 per cent or more when hidden unemployment is taken into account. Full employment is a distant goal that is most likely unattainable. Wage moderation, stimulation of education and training, industrial policy and other policies all help to improve the economy and the labour market, but will not solve the unemployment problem. Therefore, the government, in co-operation with the social partners, has to look for ways to deal with the unemployment problem in a socially acceptable way, and there are few alternatives to ALMP. In principle, ALMP may have an impact on overall unemployment and can at least help reduce long-term unemployment by providing job search assistance and training and by offering subsidized employment for those still unable to find a regular job. In this way active policies can play an important role in combating social exclusion.

However, on the basis of the results of aggregate impact analyses for five countries we cannot be too optimistic about the effectiveness of ALMP in practice. The results confirm earlier results from micro-evaluation studies, namely that the overall impact of ALMP on total unemployment and on long-term unemployment is relatively small. Does that mean that we have to conclude that, in practice, ALMP is not much help in dealing with the unemployment problem? Maybe in the end we will be forced to draw this conclusion, but it is still possible that the relatively small impact of ALMP has to do with shortcomings in the organization of ALMP and suboptimal implementation:

- the inadequate targeting of ALMP measures;
- a suboptimal product mix;
- shortcomings in programme management;
- insufficient incentives.

Because implementation seems to be an extremely important factor for the quality and the effectiveness of ALMP it was given equal treatment with aggregate impact analysis in this book. However, on the basis of the contributions in this book dealing with implementation, improving the labour market impact of active policies through changes in organization and implementation is a difficult and challenging task. However, the alternative would be to acquiesce in current levels of unemployment, which is not acceptable.

Further research on the aggregate impact of ALMP should, in our opinion, concentrate on the description and analysis of the organization and implementation of active policies, on the development of implementation indicators, and on relating these indicators to policy outcomes. The analysis should be both cross-regional and cross-national in character. The cross-regional element takes into account the fact that regional authorities can to a large degree make their own decisions, which results in considerable variation in product mix and in targeting. By comparing countries the role of institutions in ALMP could be studied more closely. It seems that countries are moving in different directions. In some, perhaps most countries, public employment service organizations will continue to play the dominant role in the implementation of active policies, while in other countries policy implementation is increasingly outsourced to private agencies. It would be extremely interesting to see what works better: a government-oriented system adopting new management principles or a market-oriented system relying more and more on private employment services.

The Dutch, German, and Swedish implementation studies clearly identify common European problems with respect to the implementation of active measures for the long-term unemployed and social assistance recipients: 1) the co-operation problem between the PES and local authorities responsible for social assistance; 2) the related issues of the allocation of ALMP resources and targeting: either the PES has to give greater priority to the long-term unemployed and social assistance recipients or ALMP resources have to be reallocated to enable the local authorities to better serve their clientèle; 3) the need to find the right balance between central steering and decentralized implementation in the PES delivery system in order to enhance efficiency, adaptation to local labour market conditions, and the PES's capacity to interact with other ALMP actors at the local level.

There is strong reason to believe that many other European countries have similar structural problems because the distinction between insurance-based and means-tested benefits is widespread, and they are usually implemented by different national and local agencies. Even where this is not the case (for example, France), the trend towards the 'activation' of benefits has led to a proliferation of institutional actors involved in the implementation of ALMP – with corresponding co-ordination problems between these respective systems.

The national institutional contexts are so diverse that there are no standard solutions, although the structural problems of ALMP implementation are similar. Our principal recommendations, therefore, are primarily directed at improved knowledge of the policy problem and policy options at the European level. There is a need, first of all, for information at the European level about the targeting of PES programmes on the long-term unemployed and social assistance recipients. There is, moreover, an urgent need for more information about local ALMP and its interaction with the PES. In most countries we know a great deal about PES programmes and activities, but there is little or no systematic information available about ALMP activities of the local authorities and their interaction with the PES.

Comparative studies can serve to clarify policy options. The German case in which the policy response has been merely to encourage voluntary co-operation is interesting primarily as an example of policy failure. The local case studies carried out in Germany illustrate different *ad hoc* coping strategies. By contrast, in the Netherlands these issues have been addressed in a frank and lively policy debate on the appropriate priorities in targeting PES resources, which has resulted *inter alia* in a contracting model in which PES resources have been partially reallocated to the municipalities to purchase ALMP programmes for social assistance recipients. In Sweden the governance of local PES offices has been restructured by replacing the previous tripartite boards with governing bodies in which the municipalities nominate a majority of the members. Finally, in the USA and the UK restrictive programme eligibility requirements are used to target ALMP programmes on those deemed most in need.

Reform of PES management systems based on 'new public management' needs to give explicit consideration to equity as well as efficiency. The PES should not be primarily guided by criteria of organizational efficiency (market share, programme placement rates, costs per placement, and so on), which are likely to result in 'creaming', that is, serving those who can be placed with the least effort and investment, but the labour market impact and hence real efficiency of PES programmes will be enhanced by focusing on relatively disadvantaged labour market participants, who would be unlikely to find employment in the absence of PES intervention. On the other hand, the same theoretical considerations that lead us to reject creaming do not imply that the most severe labour market problem groups should be the primary target of PES programmes. Labour market programmes are a specific type of policy intervention and are not appropriate for every clientèle, for example, for persons with problems related to drug abuse, and physical or mental handicaps. There must be some prospect of successful integration based on the policy instruments available in the form of labour market programmes. Although mass unemployment has blurred the borderline between labour market and social policy, ALMP programmes are not a substitute for tailor-made social programmes that address the needs of special groups.

Prevention is the new magic word in active labour market policy. It is sometimes presented in a rather naive way: provide assistance to unemployed people in a very early phase of their unemployment so that they do not become long-term unemployed. In reality, the matter is much more complicated. Prevention presupposes first of all that it is possible to predict whether individuals will become long-term unemployed or not with reasonable precision. In the second place it assumes that 'treatment' in the early stage of an unemployment spell is effective. On the basis of existing research both assumptions are debatable. Perhaps preventive measures only make sense for specific groups among the unemployed with very low job chances right from the start. In our view more needs to be known about the following questions:

1. What type of instrument works best for which group of unemployed?
2. What is the best moment during the unemployment period to apply a given measure?

Giving 'treatment' at a very early stage of unemployment may lead to high deadweight loss, and waiting too long may imply that job chances decrease rapidly, making reintegration in the labour market increasingly difficult. The optimal moment of intervention will be somewhere in between.

Preventing people from becoming unemployed in the first place would be even better than prevention of long-term unemployment for those who become unemployed. However, this is feasible only under relatively favourable labour market conditions in countries with rapidly declining unemployment rates such as Denmark and the Netherlands. In these countries unemployment is still a severe problem under specific groups, that is, young people from ethnic minorities and older people. It should be recalled, however, that the traditional repertoire of labour market policy also includes preventive measures such as short-time work, retraining, outplacement, and early retirement designed to assist firms undergoing restructuring.

Active policies for the employed may also become more important. For example, activity rates among older people of 50–65 years of age tend to be low. Given the ageing of the population, continued low participation rates for older people will lead to a reduction in the size of the labour force. For countries with current high unemployment levels this may seem a blessing but, in fact, it is not. The long-term effects of a reduced labour force on employment and prosperity will be negative. Moreover, some countries are already experiencing bottlenecks on the labour market which will tend to increase further in the coming decade. Therefore, a shift may be needed in active policies from assistance to the unemployed to specific groups among the employed, for example, older workers and women. Although individuals, firms and the social partners all have responsibilities in achieving this goal, government also has a role to play.

Active policies also need to be regarded more and more in conjunction with incentives in the social security system. There is a trend towards changing incentives in unemployment and disability insurance schemes to discourage their use and to encourage transitions to employment. This can be a powerful tool in preventing unemployment. If employers face a financial penalty in case of above average flows from their workforce into unemployment and disability, this will provide an incentive for alternative adjustment mechanisms such as assisting workers to find a new job, improving working conditions, and so on. At the same time individuals can be stimulated to accept job offers by providing rewards for finding employment and penalties for passive job-search behaviour.

Labour markets will be increasingly characterized by job mobility and changes in job contents. On the one hand this development will entail a higher risk that workers become unemployed and remain in unemployment for a long period. However, increased mobility can also enhance employability by forcing people to continue learning and to gain new experience. Public policy will have an important task in helping individuals, firms and sectors to cope with these changes. Active policies in conjunction with appropriate incentive structures in social security can play an important role. This may lead to a gradual change in active policies from reactive measures for the long-term unemployed, to preventive measures for the unemployed, and finally to measures preventing people from becoming unemployed in the first place. An economic policy aiming at increased labour demand and a flexible labour market would be a necessary complement.

A shift in the focus of active policies away from the unemployed would also have consequences for the delivery system. The role of the public employment service in active policies will be less central than in the past. Since unemployment will never be completely eliminated, traditional types of active labour market policy will remain necessary, if on a reduced scale.

The result of this scenario might be labour markets characterized by increased mobility between jobs and between occupations, and between employment and other types of socially useful activity with lower unemployment. However, we still know too little about the potential scope and effectiveness of such 'proactive' transitional labour markets in the future of the labour market.

NOTE

1. The duration of participation in a measure, which is regarded as an indicator for the quality of the measure.

Index